T0310843

Affordability Issues Surrounding the Use of ICT for Development and Poverty Reduction

Sam Takavarasha Jr.
University of Fort Hare, South Africa & University of Zimbabwe, Zimbabwe

Carl Adams
University of Portsmouth, UK

A volume in the Advances in
Wireless Technologies and
Telecommunication (AWTT) Book
Series

Published in the United States of America by
    IGI Global
    Information Science Reference (an imprint of IGI Global)
    701 E. Chocolate Avenue
    Hershey PA, USA 17033
    Tel: 717-533-8845
    Fax: 717-533-8661
    E-mail: cust@igi-global.com
    Web site: http://www.igi-global.com

Library of Congress Cataloging-in-Publication Data

Names: Takavarasha, Sam, Jr., 1965- editor. | Adams, Carl, 1958- editor.
Title: Affordability issues surrounding the use of ICT for development and
    poverty reduction / [edited by] Sam Takavarasha Jr. and Carl Adams,
    editors.
Description: Hershey, PA : Information Science Reference, [2018]
Identifiers: LCCN 2017016111| ISBN 9781522531791 (hardcover) | ISBN
    9781522531807 (ebook)
Subjects: LCSH: Digital divide--Developing countries. | Information
    technology--Economic aspects--Developing countries. | Economic
    development--Developing countries.
Classification: LCC HN981.I56 A44 2018 | DDC 303.48/33091724--dc23 LC record available at
https://lccn.loc.gov/2017016111

This book is published in the IGI Global book series Advances in Wireless Technologies and
Telecommunication (AWTT) (ISSN: 2327-3305; eISSN: 2327-3313)

British Cataloguing in Publication Data
A Cataloguing in Publication record for this book is available from the British Library.

All work contributed to this book is new, previously-unpublished material.
The views expressed in this book are those of the authors, but not necessarily of the publisher.

For electronic access to this publication, please contact: eresources@igi-global.com.

Advances in Wireless Technologies and Telecommunication (AWTT) Book Series

ISSN:2327-3305
EISSN:2327-3313

Editor-in-Chief: Xiaoge Xu, Xiamen University Malaysia, Malaysia

MISSION

The wireless computing industry is constantly evolving, redesigning the ways in which individuals share information. Wireless technology and telecommunication remain one of the most important technologies in business organizations. The utilization of these technologies has enhanced business efficiency by enabling dynamic resources in all aspects of society.

The **Advances in Wireless Technologies and Telecommunication Book Series** aims to provide researchers and academic communities with quality research on the concepts and developments in the wireless technology fields. Developers, engineers, students, research strategists, and IT managers will find this series useful to gain insight into next generation wireless technologies and telecommunication.

COVERAGE

- Mobile Communications
- Virtual Network Operations
- Grid Communications
- Radio Communication
- Digital Communication
- Cellular Networks
- Mobile Technology
- Telecommunications
- Mobile Web Services
- Wireless Broadband

IGI Global is currently accepting manuscripts for publication within this series. To submit a proposal for a volume in this series, please contact our Acquisition Editors at Acquisitions@igi-global.com or visit: http://www.igi-global.com/publish/.

Titles in this Series

701 East Chocolate Avenue, Hershey, PA 17033, USA
Tel: 717-533-8845 x100 • Fax: 717-533-8661
E-Mail: cust@igi-global.com • www.igi-global.com

List of Reviewers

Mohammad Alhusban, *Southampton Solent University, UK*
Abraheem Alsaeed, *University of Portsmouth, UK*
Indira Ananth, *Loyola Institute of Business Administration, India*
Willie Chinyamurindi, *University of Fort Hare, South Africa*
Liezel Cilliers, *University of Fort Hare, South Africa*
Kathleen Diga, *University of KwaZulu-Natal, South Africa*
Kamolrat Intaratat, *Durban University of Technology, South Africa*
Ayse Kok, *Google HQ, USA*
Dennis Lupiana, *Institute of Finance Management Dar Es Salaam, Tanzania*
Richard Millham, *Durban University of Technology, South Africa*
Donnar Musiyandaka, *Chinhoi University of Technology, Zimbabwe*
Juliao Mussa, *Universidade Pedagógica de Moçambique – Delegação de Nampula, Mozambique*
Karna Naidoo, *University of Kwa Zulu Natal, South Africa*
Madhava Priya, *Loyola Institute of Business Administration, India*
Taurai Rupere, *University of Zimbabwe, Zimbabwe*
Ambika Samarthya-Howard, *Praekelt.org, USA*
Bill Tucker, *University of the Western Cape, South Africa*
Abraham van der Vyver, *Monash University, South Africa*
João Varajão, *Universidade de Minho, Portugal*
John Walubengo, *Multimedia University of Kenya, Kenya*
Husam Yassen, *University of Portsmouth, UK*
Muhammad Yusuf, *University of Portsmouth, UK*
Ngonidzashe Zanamwe, *University of Zimbabwe, Zimbabwe*

Table of Contents

Section 1
Key Methods of Fostering Affordable Access

Chapter 1

Sam Takavarasha Jr., University of Fort Hare, South Africa
Carl Adams, University of Portsmouth, UK
Liezel Cilliers, University of Fort Hare, South Africa

Chapter 2

Liezel Cilliers, University of Fort Hare, South Africa
Ambika Samarthya-Howard, Praekelt.org, USA

Chapter 3

Benny Nyambo, University of Zimbabwe, Zimbabwe
Benard Mapako, University of Zimbabwe, Zimbabwe
Michael Munyaradzi, University of Zimbabwe, Zimbabwe

Section 2
Applications and Case Examples

Chapter 10

Detailed Table of Contents

Section 1
Key Methods of Fostering Affordable Access

Section 1 of this book presents some key methods that the contributors found useful for fostering affordable ICT access. While some of them provide case examples about how these approaches may be deployed, the goal of this section is to elaborate on the usefulness of these methods.

Chapter 1

     Sam Takavarasha Jr., University of Fort Hare, South Africa
     Carl Adams, University of Portsmouth, UK
     Liezel Cilliers, University of Fort Hare, South Africa

Mobile ICTs have addressed the digital divides between the global south and the global north. While a phenomenal mobile penetration in developing countries has enabled ICT4D innovations by connecting previously unconnected people, several communities suffer adverse inclusion or lack access altogether. Such digital divides within countries have been attributed to technical, social, and economic issues. As a result, many approaches to bridging the digital divides have been used by both academics and practitioners. This chapter, therefore, discusses the potential use of community networks for providing sustainable and affordable access to rural communities in developing countries. In addition to the advantages of community networks, the chapter presents the challenges thereof, and it contributes to the vexed question about how to harness ICTs to empower the disadvantaged communities in developing countries. A case study of Zenzeleni Makhosi community network in South Africa's Eastern Cape province is presented and analysed using Sen's capability approach.

Chapter 2

Liezel Cilliers, University of Fort Hare, South Africa
Ambika Samarthya-Howard, Praekelt.org, USA

Information and communication for development thinkers has come up with many plausible interventions that promise to improve the lives of underprivileged people in developing countries. The people that these interventions are meant for have not always benefited from these initiatives because they have limited ICT access due to its cost. There is therefore a need to improve universal access by enabling affordable access by the poor. This chapter, therefore, discusses free basics and how they can be used to improve affordable ICT access in order to facilitate ICT4D interventions in African countries. Since the use of free basics is not without controversy, a balanced analysis and an overview of the advantages and disadvantages of this initiative are provided. Social capital is used as the theoretical lens for evaluating the use of free basics for improving ICT access for those who cannot afford it. The chapter makes a case for the viability of using free basics through a discussion of case studies on how free basics have been used to empower underprivileged people, especially girls in Africa.

Chapter 3

Benny Nyambo, University of Zimbabwe, Zimbabwe
Benard Mapako, University of Zimbabwe, Zimbabwe
Michael Munyaradzi, University of Zimbabwe, Zimbabwe

The people living in remote parts of the underdeveloped world usually do not have access to affordable internet, either because it is too expensive to lay fibre to these areas or mobile data is just too expensive to use every day. There has always been a need to find a way to bring fast, cheap, and reliable internet access to these people. This is where the TV white spaces (TVWS) or unused TV band spectrum comes in. TVWS refers to the gaps found between TV channels. It can be used to provide cheaper and reliable broadband to remote areas. Wi-Fi typically covers short distances and has trouble passing through obstacles. TVWS, on the other hand, can travel long distances and can penetrate obstacles. This makes TVWS suitable for long distance internet provision in remote areas. This chapter explores the possibilities and advantages of delivering broadband to remote areas of underdeveloped nations using TVWS with the intention of poverty reduction. The concept of TV channels digitalization also frees the whole analogue TV spectrum and allows it to be used in TVWS technology.

Chapter 4

Ngonidzashe Zanamwe, University of Zimbabwe, Zimbabwe
Benard Mapako, University of Zimbabwe, Zimbabwe
Taurai Rupere, University of Zimbabwe, Zimbabwe
Benny M. Nyambo, University of Zimbabwe, Zimbabwe

Infrastructure sharing has been viewed as a plausible route to affordable ICT access in the wake of duplication of ICT infrastructure in developing countries. In spite of this belief in its effectiveness, getting ICT operators to share infrastructure can be inhibited by several challenges relating to regulatory approach, competition between players, and lack of consensus between regulators and business. This chapter uses evidence from Zimbabwe to assess how infrastructure sharing can be implemented in developing countries where coverage competition is yet to give way to service provision-based competition in the wake of disproportionate investment by network operators. It suggests that instead of push factors alone, infrastructure can best be shared when business' commercial interests and regulators' quest for affordable universal services coincide to form a win-win situation built on both push and pull factors.

Jay Pancham, Durban University of Technology, South Africa
Richard Millham, Durban University of Technology, South Africa

Telecentres were conceived and designed in order to provide internet access to designated disadvantaged groups that could not otherwise afford this access. In this chapter, the concept of telecentres, with its goal of affordable internet access for the community, is introduced. A few of the common challenges faced by telecentres and their evolving business models are discussed. The problem of monitoring, with its related aspect of affordability is discussed. In order to provide uniform data on usage and user profiles, a common set of data attributes for telecentre operational monitoring is obtained through a literature review of telecentre data collection projects and through interviews with local telecentre managers. Traditional monitoring methods for telecentres, such as through questionnaires, are evaluated as to the timeliness of their data and their associated cost which impact telecentre affordability. The common set of attributes form the basis of an electronic monitoring system with its advantages of continuous data collection and lower costs.

Section 2 presents case examples about how affordable access has been achieved using some of the methods discussed in this book. In addition to case examples, some domain-specific issues that call for improved access as a route to a more inclusive world are presented. For example, in Chapter 7, Indira Ananth discusses the use of mobile phones by street vendors, and in Chapter 8, Alsaeed and Boakes highlight the need for access to e-services by displaced communities.

In 2000 the General Assembly of the United Nations accepted their Millennium Declaration. Two of their main foci are the eradication of poverty and the economic upliftment of disadvantaged societies. In Thailand, three initiatives contributed to the eradication of poverty. The "One Tambon, One Product" (OTOP) that was launched in 2001 has as its mission to stimulate the economy by creating small economic hubs in each subdistrict (Tambon). The OTOP initiative grew exponentially and a total of 85,173 products have been registered by 2010. The growing network of telecentres helped to close the digital divide. It also anchored many of the OTOP projects. In the third instance, the social networks redefined the business environment and created new communication platforms to promote entrepreneurial hubs. The researcher combined field studies with content analysis of the social media in order to establish to what extent these drivers of poverty eradication have been integrated.

The mobile phone has come to be recognized as one of the key instruments of ICT. Its easy acceptance as a communication device enhances its usage. India is one of the fastest growing markets for the government has been keenly promoting a digital India programme with a vision to transform India into a digitally empowered society and knowledge economy. There has been much focus on mobile phones and their applications in the light of delegalisation of notes in India. It has gained attention in the scenario of moving to a cashless economy. It has brought into focus more sharply the need for mobile phone literacy. This chapter discusses the use of mobile phones among street vendors in Chennai, a capital city and the fourth largest urban agglomeration in India. The study found that most owned a basic mobile phone. The vending business continued to be practiced in old ways with no new management skills. The business was run and was highly dependent on cash payments. The respondents did not consider the mobile phone as an important tool for daily business.

Chapter 8

Abraheem Alsaeed, University of Portsmouth, UK
Rich Boakes, University of Portsmouth, UK

Refugees and displaced people who have been affected by disaster or political instability (uprooted from their homes in search of safety) are an interesting group of citizens when we consider e-government services since they face extra challenges of access to such government services. The chapter explores challenges faced by e-service delivery to refugee and displaced people which are often characteristic of unstable societies. This chapter reports on a study of Syrian refugees and displaced people using a survey exploring the use of e-services for citizens inside and outside of Syria. The authors apply institutional theory as a theoretical lens using the dimensions of economic, political, technical, and social to understand the context and issues of providing e-government services within this very challenging domain. The results indicate six themes influencing sustainable and effective support for e-services for such groups of people, namely importance of e-services, connectivity, awareness, e-service availability, financial constraints, and digital literacy.

Chapter 9

Ambika Samarthya-Howard, Praekelt.org, USA
Debbie Rogers, Praekelt.org, South Africa

This chapter explores three existing financial approaches to scaling mobile technologies in low- and middle-income countries: user-paid services, reverse billing, and zero-rated platforms. As affordability is an impediment to internet access, key strategies focusing around the involvement of mobile network operators and governments are investigated in relation to sustainability, scale, reach, and impact for mobile technology projects in the world. Various examples under each type are explored as a starting point for understanding the risks and benefits of each approach. The chapter also discusses the importance of mobile initiatives in tackling social issues today.

Chapter 10
Carl Adams, University of Portsmouth, UK
Sam Takavarasha Jr., University of Fort Hare, South Africa

This chapter explores the impact of a disaster on communities from a development perspective and the corresponding importance of access to ICT. Poorer communities are often most vulnerable to disasters, a situation that can affect the economic development of such communities for decades. The chapter uses the UN's Sendai framework to emphasize the role of ICT in supporting communities throughout the different stages of disaster situations, towards long-term recovery and development. Some key themes emerge in the chapter, notably access to technology is a key support mechanism; a longer-term temporal perspective of such disasters indicates there are likely to be different waves of "disaster" refugees; the initial ones being classed as humanitarian migrants with all the humanitarian supports that they attract; whereas longer term any resulting "refugees" would more likely be classed as economic migrants. The chapter also explores longer term support mechanisms such as the role of remittances.

Foreword

The field of Information and Communication Technologies for Development (ICT4D) is two decades old, and it started with interventions set up to facilitate access to digital technologies for people living in contexts in which the "one household – one computer" model was not affordable. The underpinning idea, moving international organisations, governments and non-for-profit entities, was that this kind of interventions offering public places to access ICT would allow poor communities to take part in the information society, with the ultimate goal of contributing to their socio-economic development.

In the last two decades, ICT4D has grown into an interdisciplinary field of research, and academics have focused on application domains in which digital technologies could make a difference for the lives of disadvantaged people around the world, such as education, agriculture, finance, and health. In the meantime, also digital technologies evolved: social media and mobile devices opened up new strands of research and revolutionised the concept of access. Nonetheless; the issue of affordability is still a key concern, preventing most of the world population to benefit from accessing the internet, with communities around the world still having unaffordable access while others having none at all.

This book has the great merit to bring the topic of affordability at the forefront of the academic discourse, rightly claiming that affordable access is an entry point factor that promotes or inhibits ICT adoption and, therefore, a sustainable use of ICT for development. It does not ride the wave of trendy and easy-publishing research topics but goes back to the root of the problem: how can we make any kind of ICT4D intervention affordable and therefore relevant for underprivileged communities? How can the potential of digital technologies become impact in the life of the most neglected? The book does so by exploring a variety of methods to make digital technologies affordable to the poor of the poorest and by presenting several case studies to exemplify geographical and topical contexts of application.

The field of ICT4D will continue to grow, hopefully maintaining its interdisciplinary, and pushing for a real integration of perspectives, disciplines, and voices from academics working from all over the world. In the meantime, technologies will evolve, and new opportunities to tackle development issues and poverty will emerge. Nevertheless, we need, as a community of researchers, practitioners and policy makers, to work on innovative ways to address the affordability issue, if we want our interventions to be truly designed to contribute to poverty reduction.

Isabella Rega
Bournemouth University, UK

Isabella Rega *is Senior Lecturer in Digital Literacies and Education at CEMP – Centre of Excellence in Media Practice and member of the Civic Media Hub at Bournemouth University. She has been working in the field of Information and Communication Technologies for Development (ICT4D) as researcher and practitioner for almost 20 years, working in international projects in Jamaica, Brazil, Mexico, South Africa, Kenya, Mozambique, and Malaysia. She co-founded Associazione seed, a non-profit organisation promoting the use of educational technologies in the non-profit sector.*

Preface

INTRODUCTION

This book enters the scene to promote affordable access at a time when information systems (IS) scholars are embarking on the endeavor to use ICTs for creating a better world (Walsham, 2012; Qureshi, 2015; Sahay, 2016). At the same time, development thinkers like Armtya Sen and Mahbub ul Haq have successfully introduced ethical thinking as the teleological end of development economics. This progressive movement has ushered concepts like human development, (Stanton, 2007) as well as goals to end extreme poverty in all its forms and reduce inequalities within and between countries by 2030 (UNDP, 2015). Standing on the shoulders of the visionary social thinkers of this epoch, the authors of this book endeavor to improve the world we live in, by using affordable access for rescuing the marginalized people of the developing world. The book adds its voice to the ongoing IS' quest to harness ICTs for fighting poverty and fostering development.

The use of Information and Communication Technologies (ICTs) for poverty reduction and development is widely believed to be a viable route for developing countries that seek to escape poverty and foster development. This can be seen through the efforts of both academics and practitioners that are championing ICT for Development (ICT4D) projects as well as presenting ICT as a useful tool for development. Several applications of ICTs to agriculture, small scale mining, education and health have been implemented with a view to improve livelihoods, improve knowledge and reduce mortality among other things. There are about 38 ICT4D journals (IPID, nd) and approximately 24 conferences (ICTWorks, 2017) at a time when international bodies are promoting access. Notably, UNESCO has declared September 28 as the International Day for Universal Access to Information, and the Sustainable development goals SDG 16.10 aims to ensure public access to information. In spite of this extensive academic activity and confidence in the usefulness of ICTs in fostering development, there is a weak understanding of how to harness ICT for poverty reduction and development in different contexts. While there are some success stories, there has been some evidence that shows that over 85% of ICT for development projects have been failing (Dada, 2006; Heeks, 2003).

There are several factors that affect the viability of ICT4D projects, but this book focuses on the affordability of ICT access because it also affects the possibility of ICT interventions in developing countries. This concern is motivated by the apparent lack of affordable access in developing countries where there is a need to harness ICTs for poverty reduction and development. Evidence shows that less developed regions of the world offer less affordable internet access than more developed countries. The data from the Association for Affordable Internet (A4AI) shows that the cost of 1GB of a prepaid mobile broadband package as a percentage of the gross national income (GNI) per capita ranked in descending order of affordability is; North America, Europe, Latin America, Pacific, Asia and lastly Africa (A4AI, 2017).

Just as the development thinkers adopted human development index (HDI) as a yard stick for measuring human development, universal access scholars have devised several indices for evaluating ICT access. These includes, digital access index, ICT development index, bundled value index and value for money index discussed below. While these axiomatic tools are commensurable, there are several post positivist frameworks and models that are built on qualitative methodologies and are amenable to case studies conducted on an interpretivist epistemological front.

The authors acknowledge the burgeoning literature that advocates for a look beyond access by analyzing other critical factors that reveal the relevance of ICTs for their intended purposes (Gilwald, 2017). Without attempting to downplay the importance of the call for this critical transition, this book looks at affordable access as gate keeper factor that inhibits ICT adoption. Furthermore, it is also an enduring impediment that inhibits the continuous use of ICTs by people of low income and those of erratic and seasonal incomes.

By use of selected case examples and conceptual discourses, the chapters of this book propose a few ways of achieving affordable access in developing countries. This book's focus on the affordability of ICT access is predicated on the idea that the tool for poverty reduction must be affordable to poor people for them to be able to use it. This calls for a deeper understanding of poverty and poor people in particular. Firstly, because the socio-technical information systems domain calls for an understanding of both technical and social imperatives and also because the usage of ICTs for development is dependent on the target population's ability to access and effectively use ICTs as articulated by Bednar and Welch (2017). The various research projects we have conducted in our scholarly and consultancy work show that people cannot use ICTs for any purpose unless they have adequate access to it. We, therefore, posit that the cost of ICT access is more critical in ICT4D interventions where poor people endeavor to use ICTs as tools for poverty reduction and development.

·   The co-existence of poverty and digital exclusion must disturb both ICT4D practitioners and academics. This is because while poverty affects about three-quarters of a billion people worldwide, about 50% of them (living below 1.90 USD per day) reside in Sub Saharan Africa, a region with the least affordable access. World Bank (2016) estimates that 6 billion people are excluded from the digital economy and ITU (2017) shows that the majority of these are in developing countries. This should compel IS scholars analyze whether the digital divides are the cause or effect of poverty or whether both of them are due to other exogenous factors. While there are many factors that cause this exclusion from information society, the International Telecommunications Union (ITU) focuses their gaze on affordability, infrastructure, knowledge, and quality of access. They employ these as parameters for calculating the digital access index (ITU, 2003).

This book will focus on the affordability of access because it is an addressable factor that discernably affects access, quality, infrastructure, and to a lesser extent knowledge. People will not access what they cannot afford just as quality and infrastructure will not be deployed to those that do not afford them. Furthermore, knowledge has a chicken and egg relationship because it restricts access yet affording constant access may also foster the increase of knowledge. As a result of the central role of affordable access, the contributors are confident that addressing it, will unlock several constraints and open many windows that will stimulate increased usage by the people in developing countries.

Internet access is increasingly being viewed as a human right because too many livelihoods and pleasurable opportunities that are available on the internet are not as ubiquitously accessible elsewhere at such speed and with such efficiency elsewhere. This, therefore, calls for the promotion of universal access in order to avail this human right to all. The recurrent theme in this book is that poverty affects the ability of people to access the internet and other ICT enabled platforms because it is priced above their income. Before we highlight that point, we must emphasize that the digital divide is also exacerbating the economic divides that ICT4D practitioners seek to fight with ICTs. This chicken and egg relationship between digital divides and economic divides makes it imperative to attack this two-headed monster from many fronts as we attempt to do with this book project.

The importance of affordable access puts the ball in the court of various stakeholders who will be challenged by this book to address digital inequality through the affordability lens among other fronts. Policy makers will be challenged to make pro-poor ICT policies. Development agencies will be challenged to introduce and implement ICT4D initiatives that are relevant to the poor and under-privileged they seek to rescue from under development and poverty. Technologists are challenged to invent and mainstream innovations that make access possible to those that are being left out because of the affordability factor.

We must hasten to acknowledge that over the last two decades, the advances in technology have continuously introduced cheaper ways of communication. In spite of the reduction in the cost of hardware, infrastructure, and mobile devices, some communities in developing countries continue to have unaffordable access while others have none at all. This suggests that the question of access cost or affordability of ICT access is a context-specific issue that continues to rear its ugly head in spite advances in technologies. It, therefore, calls for the use of pro-poor policies as well as pro-poor technological and process innovations to address affordability challenge. There are demographic, economic, and other structural imperatives that affect the ability of MNOs to provide affordable access to communities of poor people in remote parts of the developing world. These are usually context-specific challenges that make it difficult to reuse methods that have been found to be useful in other jurisdictions. This, therefore, re-emphasises the crying call for the use of socially embedded approaches for designing IS interventions in developing countries as articulated by Avgerou (2010) and Hayes and Westrup (2012).

To set the scene for this book, this introduction will present the problem that articulates the importance of making ICTs affordable to the poor. Towards that end, the rest of this preface will highlight the problem at stake, suggest a multi-pronged approach to solving it and then summarize some of the key solutions proposed by the authors in subsequent sections of this book.

Promoting ICT Access for Poverty Reduction and Development

This book presents ICT enabled poverty reduction and development on the understanding that ICTs can address the communication and the information components of development initiatives. This challenges the authors of this book to find ways of availing ICTs to poor people.

The teleological end of ICT4D studies has been to lift the underprivileged people from deprivation. This endeavor to improve the livelihoods of the bottom billion compelled the authors of this book to propose ways of fostering digital inclusion and digital equality through ICT access that is affordable to the people that would benefit from ICT4D initiatives that are documented in several ICT4D studies.

This book, therefore, presents affordable access as a means to ICT enabled poverty reduction and development not as an end in itself. Such an endeavor compels the authors to aim for particular configurations of affordable access. We have already pointed out that our fundamental concern is the plight of the poor people that live in remote parts of the developing world where communication infrastructure is either unavailable or inadequate because of the unattractiveness of these areas to Mobile Network Operators (MNOs).

They yield the low return on investment in these areas because of the low population density and poor incomes of the people that live there. The subsistent farming communities in rural areas of developing countries often have seasonal incomes that are not in line with ICT tariffs that operate in monthly cycles of salaried economies. As a result, they depend on prepaid tariffs which are generally higher than contract lines. While rural populations are of concern to this book it also addresses some key segments of populations in urban areas that do not afford ICT access because it is too expensive for them. These people are victims of poverty and un-development and targets of ICT4D interventions as proposed here and in other works that seek to improve people's livelihoods through ICTs.

The main concern of this book is people's inability to access the ICTs that are supposed to provide access to ICT4D initiatives that are meant for them. Several studies have articulated the validity of ICT to development and poverty reduction endeavors. These have not been adequately complemented by affordable access. They have presented poverty reduction and development as an end and here we present ICT access as a means to achieving that end. This book focuses on accessing the various ways that ICT enabled development can be accessible to poor people.

WHAT IS INFORMATION COMMUNICATION TECHNOLOGIES FOR DEVELOPMENT?

Information Communication Technologies for development (ICT4D) refers to the use of ICT for supporting developmental interventions. It endeavors to use ICTs for fostering development and for fighting poverty in developing countries (Avgerou, 2010). It uses theories adopted and adapted from development studies and social theories (Walsham, 2012). These include Giddens's (1984) Structuration theory, and Pettigrew (1995)'s Contextualisation theory and Latour's (2007) Actor-Network Theory and lately Activity theory (Karanasios, 2014).

This book will mainly focus on the livelihoods of people that live in rural areas of the developing world because they are left out both in terms of ICT access and developmental benefits that their counterparts in the cities are enjoying. While literature has often addressed digital divides between the developing world and the developing world, there are serious in-countries divides both on the digital and economic front. These require attention because developing countries have inequalities that emanate from the dual economies that combine a subsistence rural economy and an industrialized urban economy which is driven by different economic factors. The dual economy is also responsible for the digital inequalities that compel us to act and simultaneously discourages others from attempting to address such a mammoth task. This also presents a challenge for innovators that view economies as monolithic entities that can be analyzed using indices that are developed by experts from the Western world. This book will also discuss challenges to do with reaching people that live in places that are not attractive to Mobile Network Operators (MNOs) either because of their geographical location or their low or seasonal income.

Why Do Poor People Need ICTs?

The usefulness of ICTs to poor people has been questioned by people who could not perceive how people living below one dollar a day could afford ICT access (Ojo, 2005). Instead of questioning whether poor people need ICTs, this book challenges the access costs that are unaffordable to the poor. It invokes the rhetorical question of whether we should cut the people to fit the garments or vice versa? The contributing authors are largely suggesting that when it comes to the use of ICT4D, poor people are facing challenges due to their failure to afford access cost. As a result, they are proposing more inclusive and affordable cost models that promote universal access and harness ICTs for making a better world. To make this possible, our scientific reasoning must critically analyze the dynamics between the causes and its effect in order for us to produce models that relate proposed solutions to the needs of the targeted populations.

Against this background, we strenuously assert that as long as the livelihoods endeavors of poor people have information and communication components, the ICTs can address them (McNamara, 2003). In other words, if the poverty reduction and development models we propose for poor people include some storage, processing, and communication of information, there is no better tool for such an endeavor that ICTs. So if we agree that poor need markets for their surplus produce then we must admit that ICTs have a role in providing market information for them. Furthermore, if we accept that poor people need agricultural extension services to help them to adopt new farming methods and enhance their agricultural produce, then we must accept that ICTs have a role in enhancing their well-beings. And if we believe that poor people need employment from companies and from their better-off neighbors, then we must accept that ICTs can be harnessed to inform them about job opportunities on offer. Lastly, if we admit that poor people need to send and receive remittances with speed and reliability, we must also admit that mobile money transfer is ideal for them.

Our experience from academic work and consultancy projects suggests that disadvantaged people need ICTs but they cannot afford its exorbitant cost. For instance, ICTs can shrink distances and reduce costs between markets and farmers yet farmers in remote areas cannot afford to use it. Their failure to afford access is not because they lack resources but it may be because their income is seasonal yet mobile bills are monthly and more frequent in the case of pay as you go packages.

This book, therefore, aims to cut the affordability and sustainability garments of ICT access to match the poor people instead of cutting the people to match the proverbial garments.

Given the usefulness of ICTs to poor people, this book aims to justify the need for policymakers to navigate the treacherous road to universal access that is a minefield of difficult choices and possible errors. The authors want to mainstream the affordability debate in order for us to overcome the undesirable state of the unequal digital world we live in. Since more and more opportunities are available online, we wish to emphasize that digital access is fast becoming a human right. On that premise alone we propose that all efforts must be made to defend universal access like other inalienable rights. Failure to foster universal access will worsen inequalities and deepen poverty.

The industrialized world has successfully availed Internet access at affordable prices to most of its inhabitants. This is not the case in developing countries where Internet access remains too exorbitant for the low-income inhabitants that constitute the majority of the population. This makes it critical to address the affordability challenge in developing countries given the fact that it is in these places that ICT4D domain endeavors to employ ICTs for poverty reduction and development.

More than academic inquiry, fostering universal access resembles advocacy for the marginalized communities in remote parts of the developing world. These communities' voice is generally muffled by their isolation from the rest of the world due to their lack of access to the wider media platforms. If they chose to protest against exclusion from the digital world, their protests would be out of reach of cable media and hence nonconsequential. To make matters worse, these communities are not going to protest about the absence of a facility they do not know as Sen (1999) states that marginalized people may get so used to their deprivation that they will not seek to question it.

This book also endeavors to highlight the plight of muffled voices of underdeveloped communities that are often trapped in poverty. The mainstream agendas of the 21st century are largely pushed by self-interest and the loudest voices in the digital world tend to set the agenda. These include the business and other interest groups that have the capacity to lobby, pressure and publish their agendas. As a result, the supply side narrative is often heard through the mouthpiece of funded research while the demand side remains muffled. Academia is also motivated to highlight its agendas via academic outlets, opinion pieces and sometimes through funded research.

The Nexus Between Development and Affordable ICT Access

The usefulness of ICTs for poverty reduction is often taken for granted without any meaningful effort to challenge the validity of such a claim. The disadvantage of taking such critical relationships as given is that doubt will always loom in the minds of the key players that influence political will and implementation. They may not find it politically correct to challenge the usefulness of ICTs to poverty reduction and reduction but the lack of evidence may compel them to give it a lower priority.

Takavarasha Jr (2017) attempted to clarify that question by analyzing the relationship between various ICT access indices against HDI. He found that there was a positive correlation between HDI and ICT access through proxies like Digital access index (DAI), ICT Development Index (IDI) and Internet penetration. While this approach can be problematized for not assessing causal relationships between HDI and various indices, the consistent correlation between ICT access and human development need to be taken seriously.

Using 2017 data for African countries alone they found an impressive correlation between DAI and HDI (r= 0.851). It is interesting to note that DAI consists of affordability, quality, knowledge, and infrastructure all of which are critical for this book project. He also found a positive correlation between ICT Development Index (IDI) and HDI (r= 0.889). ITU (2009) describes IDI as a three-stage model that shows a country's progress towards an information society. It consists of ICT readiness, ICT intensity, and ICT impact. They also accessed the relationship between HDI and internet penetration and they found a positive correlation between the indices (r=0,721994). While this is interesting to this study, the use of Internet penetration as a proxy for access has the weakness of assuming that all the people within a networked area have equal capacity to use ICTs.

In addition to the above, Takavarasha Jr (2017) analyzed the relationship between Bundled Value Index and HDI. According to Research ICT Africa (2017), BVI adds the value of voice, SMSa and data and divides it by the price. Takavarasha Jr (2017) found a weak correlation index of r 0.17502 between BVI and HDI. Although the correlation index was rather close to zero it is still a positive correlation which confirms the above trends instead of opposing it. There is, however, a need to conduct causality analysis using time series data instead of a 2017 snapshot, it can be concluded, with analytical humility, that ICT access has an impact on development.

The Challenges That Are Faced by Developing Countries in Using ICT4D

As this book endeavors to addresses affordable access in order to improve the livelihoods of people in developing countries, it is critical to present the challenges that are being faced by the developing world in its attempt to use ICTs for development. There is also a need to develop a deeper understanding of their causes as well as the implications of addressing any of its multifaceted dimensions. These constraints include undeveloped economies, poor ICT and physical infrastructure, low internet penetration and a lack of ICT skills.

Undeveloped Economies

The vast majority of people in Sub Saharan Africa and India are living in countries that have a low human development Index (HDI) (UNDP, 2016). These countries are still struggling to address health education and food security. Against this background, ICT investment is often seen as a luxury of lower priority. That challenge is also faced by inhabitants who often have to choose between ICTs and basics like food and health. Developing countries tend to have a large proportion of their population living in rural areas that have poor ICT and physical infrastructure. The rural people are largely unwaged, they, therefore, have no credit ratings or proof of addresses which are often used by mobile networks for determining whether to issue a contract line to a client or not. Their counterparts who also make the largest proportion of city population also face similar challenges. As a result, the inhabitants of developing countries are mainly using pre-paid mobile packages which are usually more expensive than the contract lines when usage is compared. While their counterparts in the cities may have a better situation, they also face some structural impediments that this book seeks to address.

Low Internet Penetration

According to Internet World Stats (2017) the Sub Saharan African internet penetration stands at 28. 3% while the world average penetration is 49.7%. This only amounts to about 56% of the world average. There has been a lot of progress made in Sub Saharan Africa on the mobile penetration and particularly mobile money. Many unbanked people now have access to mobile money. It is however disturbing to note that the financial inclusion and the ICT access that the mobile users have is less than adequate for several reasons. Firstly, because mobile connectivity is not at par with fixed connectivity. For instance, the United States' Federal Communications Commission (FCC) set the standard for mobile connectivity at 10mbps/1mbs while fixed broadband is 25mbps/3mbps. This puts fixed broadband at two and half times the speed of mobile download while upload is three times faster. So when developing countries chose to be content with mobile broadband they are settling for less than half of what the Western countries are achieving through fixed access. In practice, the African countries that have not installed cutting age technologies like LTE will actually find it difficult to achieve 10mbps/1mbs. We must hasten to state that both 'infrastructure' and 'quality' of connectivity are key parameters of the digital access index (ITU, 2003).

A survey conducted by the Alliance for Affordable Internet Access shows that of 50% of the developing countries in their sample were using a full-cost plan while 21% used public WiFi. Furthermore, 19% of them used service-specific plans (A4AI,2016). The challenge with full-cost services is that it discourages fuller use since the cost rests on the shoulder of the subscriber. On the other hand, those that use public Wifi have limited access because they get disconnected as soon as they leave the Wifi zone. Finally, the service specific plans allow the user to access selected services like Facebook or WhatsApp while the other internet based sites are either completely inaccessible or available at prohibitive cost. Such impediments to the effective use of the internet cannot be underestimated.

Africa has the lowest number of households with Internet access. It has 18% while Arab states have 47.2% and Asian states have 48.1% of households with Internet. This amounts to 42.9% developing countries compared to 84.4% of developed countries (ITU, 2017).

Poor Infrastructure

The low penetration discussed above is also related to the low investment in infrastructure in developing countries particularly Least Developed Countries (LDCs). Infrastructure investment is often driven by the private sector since the government has other priorities to meet basic services like food and healthcare. This is not necessarily bad but the challenge is that the private sector tends to invest in areas where they can acquire a justifiable return on investment. As a result, poor and remote areas of low population density usually attract low or at times no investment simply because they are not commercially viable. MNOs get a justifiable return on investment in areas where they can reach about 3000 subscribers per base station. Such high subscriber numbers are difficult to achieve in remote areas of the developing world where population density is low. Furthermore, these areas often lack electricity and this compels the mobile networks to use expensive sources of electricity like generators.

As Rupere et al. discuss in chapter 5, regulatory authorities can employ universal access funds to introduce connectivity to these remote areas that TELCOS are not interested in making expensive investments. The authors also suggest that such areas often compel TELCOs to share passive infrastructure in order to reduce both capital expenditure (CAPEX) and operating costs (OPEX). These approaches have their own challenges as discussed below.

Low Smartphone penetration: In spite of high mobile penetration, the majority of connected subscribers cannot access the internet because they have no smartphones. Errickson (2016) Africa has (36%) the lowest number of people who use smartphones (Ericsson, 2016). The limited functionality of voice and SMS based communication does not allow its users to search for information on the internet as smartphone users can do. This should be seen as adverse inclusion because while these subscribers are beneficiaries they are left out of the critical benefits of the information age. While cheaper brands of smart phones and replicas of reputable brands are now available at lower prices in developing countries, they are still priced above what the majority can afford.

A similar challenge is also experienced on the financial inclusion front where mobile money is far less than the banking services that brick and mortar banking offers. It is expensive and often restricted to money transfer services instead of interest-earning banking services or access to credit. Without savings and access to credit, the economic benefits associated with brick mortar banking cannot be realized. Against these premises, it must be stated that African countries that are celebrating mobile connectivity as it stands are settling for less than they deserve. The progress from zero connectivity to where we are now is quite impressive but it is just not enough. The developing world requires more effort for them to enjoy the full benefits of the information society or to at least match their counterparts in the industrialized world. At this juncture, however, it is critical for innovators to encourage universal access to the mobile technologies that are appropriate for some ICT enabled development. It is, however, important to emphasize that after achieving universal mobile access African countries need to advance further towards faster broadband access and more holistic models of mobile banking.

Finally, we posit that since the information systems domain is situated between the social and natural sciences (Mingers, 2004), it is positioned to deal with technological and socio-economic imperatives that affect the affordability issues that affect ICT4D. It is, however, critical to know that every step we take to address each problem using any of the solutions discussed in this book may uncover new problems as discussed in the next section.

As a result, we will also emphasize that the approaches recommended in this book need to be deployed with prudence on the part of innovators and regulatory authorities. Since ICT interventions combine the socio-technical and socio-economic imperatives, they may trigger unexpected legal and economic challenges. An in-depth knowledge of the context in which they are implemented is as necessary as an understanding of the implication of the slightest move taken. As Alkire (2010) suggests that, a misconceived development approach can kill, we must posit that an ill thought out interventions can backfire. To overcome such challenges, regulatory authorities often invite submission from stakeholder before they introduce new regulation. This is however not a full proof approach because some policy clashes only surface as a result of implementation. There are also some stakeholders that get left out of policy discussions because they are neither conversant with the policies that affect them nor aware of ongoing discussions yet they will react to negative consequences that affect them.

Without delving into the deeper issues that are only discernible to insightful enquirers, we must take note of some recent examples of mishaps that followed plausible efforts of well-meaning regulators to foster affordable access. For instance, the imposition of mandatory infrastructure sharing and the use of price controls for solving access cost may discourage TELCOs from investing in infrastructure. It may also result in downsizing or labor lay-offs as happened in Zimbabwe when the Post and Telecommunications Regulatory Authority of Zimbabwe (POTRAZ) reduced tariffs based on the LYRIC pricing model. The Independent Communications Authority of South Africa (ICASA) was taken to court by MTN and Vodacom court for termination rate reduction 2014. To avoid such negative consequences, the innovators and policymakers must develop a deeper understanding of the socio-economic implications of the chosen approaches.

The Role of Stakeholders in Fostering ICT for Development

The contributors answer the call to make a better world with ICTs as sustainable goal 17 calls for partnerships in strengthening the means of implementation and revitalization of the SDGs (UNDP, 2015). In line with this call for partnerships, the authors beckon the stakeholders in the ICT ecosystem to assume their complementary roles in fostering affordable access. The importance of a multi-stakeholder approach and how key stakeholders on the eco-system can contribute to universal access is discussed below.

A Multi-Stakeholder Approach to Fostering Universal Access

In developing countries have weak institutions and isolated attempts by different stakeholders to foster universal access through independent silos that are often uncoordinated. These disjointed approaches may conflict with each other if their approaches are not philosophically harmonized. We, therefore, advocate for a meeting of minds and capacities of different stakeholders in order to address a multifaceted problem like providing affordable and universal ICT access in a particular country. The universal access rights groups often dismiss business players as the prime causers of inequalities while business views them as unnecessary spoilers. On the other hand, open internet activists are often unwilling to cooperate with dictatorial political players who often view alternative opinions as opposition to their hegemony. This is a major problem in developing countries and transitional economies where ruling class perceives its policies as infallible.

Against this background, we recommend that all stakeholders must harmonize their approaches with each other since they all have a peculiar contribution to universal access. This will avoid policy conflicts and enable peer review. Our experience with developing countries also shows that interventions that are not in harmony with the development objectives of a country are unlikely to succeed. In view of the foregoing, we propose a symphony of different stockholders that work towards a common goal using different methods as discussed below.

The Role of National Regulatory Authorities

Regulatory bodies can employ many measures for improving affordability and inclusion in order to foster more equal digital access in a country. These among other things include the use of universal access funds (USF), price control, Infrastructure sharing, regulation and, policies that can improve internet governance.

The universal access fund is a pot that is used in most countries for subsidizing ICT infrastructure in areas that are unprofitable for mobile network operators to invest. It may be in the form of a levy on the mobile communications tariffs that are collected by MNOs from digital communications in the country. They can use this fund for building base stations and other infrastructure that will be used by all networks that need to expand their coverage into the areas of low return on investment. In other words, the USF is meant for subsidizing the services that promote universal access by enabling access for poor people. The challenge with USF is that developing countries often abuse it. MNOs complain that it is prone to abuse by governments especially in situations where the state also owns a network that competes with other MNOs. Furthermore, developing countries often face the tough choice between spending the USF on ICT infrastructure or spending it on more pressing needs like food and health.

The use of price controls is a traditional means of protecting subscribers from being charged unjustifiable tariffs. Regulators often use this for enforcing the tariffs that are based on efficient services. This approach has been discredited by the wave of free market-oriented players that seek to encourage investment through market forces. It is therefore critical for regulatory bodies to use their powers for fostering universal service and universal access because it will enable people to benefit from ICT4D interventions.

Role of Non-Governmental Organizations

Non-governmental organizations (NGOs) have the capacity to champion intervention that fosters digital equality. These include community networks and telecentres and various initiatives that enable access to the underprivileged communities and hence improve their well-beings. They may also engage in advocacy work that includes pressuring, publishing and lobbying on behalf of the communities that are excluded from the digital world. It is easy for governments to ignore the plight of the underprivileged while they continuously react to the demands of commercial players that contribute to their tax revenue. Consumer watchdogs and international agencies have the capacity to introduce international best practices that regulatory bodies and the government may be unaware of. They may also help build capacity for pro-poor policymaking in both government and regulatory sector.

Role of Business

Business is increasingly engaging in cooperate social responsibility initiatives. These include models like donations of devices and development infrastructure in underprivileged areas. They also use other models like Zero rating/ free basics, promotions and loyalty bonuses which also benefit the societies as well as their own future business growth. We propose that such packages also need to be customized for the poor who live in remote rural areas. Business actors need to develop packages that can accommodate subsistence farming communities that earn seasonal income. This may include seasonal bundles that last until the next harvest while enhancing the usefulness of ICT4D initiatives to rural communities.

Business and MNOs in particular, often introduce packages that make ICT access affordable these include bundles, service specific plans and public WiFi access. In the case of free basics, international actors like Facebook have teamed up with local MNOs to provide zero-rated content to underprivileged communities as discussed by Cilliers and Samarthya-Howard in this book. The Association for Affordable Internet Access, this model was being used by 4% of people in their sample were using zero-rated plans (A4AI, 2016). This suggests that business actors are engaging in corporate social responsibility endeavors that foster universal access.

Role of Academia

Academic institutions have a key role in formulating approaches to universal affordable access for the sake of enabling ICT4D initiatives. This is an important role which ensures that the approaches taken to complex issues like universal affordable access and ICT4D initiatives can achieve the intended outcomes without contradicting other desirable goals. This is a primary purpose of academic texts like this book project.

The key role of academia is to conduct research and disseminate their findings in ways that inform research-based policies and strategies. This enables policymakers and business to keep abreast with the current state of play in the sector as new technologies continue to open new frontiers of innovation. Given the complex interplay between the factors involved, academia needs to think through the treacherous path between tools like ICTs and outcomes like poverty reduction and development in ways that practitioners would not achieve.

THE THEMES THAT ARE COVERED IN THIS EDITION

Seventeen chapters were submitted by contributors from Africa, Asia, Europe and the United States. After a peer review by a minimum of three experts per chapter, ten chapters were accepted for publication in this book. There were interesting chapters that were excluded because they did not adequately fit into the theme and/or standard of the incumbent book project. The following section presents the themes under two parts i.e. Part One: Methods of fostering affordable access and Part Two: Application and case examples of affordable access

Section 1: The Methods of Fostering Affordable Access

Part one opens with this preface which present the background and introduces the chapters contained in this publication.

The introductory Chapter sets the scene of this study by discussing the background issues surrounding the digital exclusion issues that necessitate the need for affordable access to ICTs. It presents the state of play in academic and ICT4D practice circles with a view to reveal the platforms on which the contributor of this project stand. Through the introduction, the authors present the diverse nature of the digital divides that the authors attempt to solve.

In Chapter 1, Takavarasha, Adams and Cilliers present the use of community networks as an approach for reducing communication costs in rural areas that are inhabited by people that cannot afford the costs of mobile access. Using Sen's Capability approach, they present a case example of Mankosi community network in the Eastern Cape of South Africa for demonstrating how community networks can reduce communication costs and support the use of ICT for poverty reduction and Development. Their analysis interestingly relates the concept of community networks to the information culture and communitarian ethos of people developing countries like Sub Saharan Africa. They emphasize the need to go beyond networks of gadgets to networks of people they also demonstrate

In Chapter 2, Cilliers and Samarthya-Howard discuss Free Basics and how they can be used to improve ICT access in developing countries. Using a few examples on the African continent they also highlight the controversy zero rating and net neutrality. They also propose a balanced overview of the advantages and disadvantages of freebasics. A basic overview of Free Basics is provided including a discussion on net neutrality which free basics are often said to violate. Social capital is used as the lens through which Free Basics can be used to improve ICT4D in Africa through the discussion of case studies where Free Basics had been used to empower especially girls on the continent.

In Chapter 3, Benny Nyambo proposes the use of TV white spaces for providing affordable mobile communication in remote parts of the developing world. The author discusses the technical reasons that make it cheaper for mobile networks in developing countries to make use of the spectra that were originally reserved for analog broadcasting. He makes a compelling argument that the use of TV white spaces will require less expensive equipment because they would reach more people per base station than what GSM and LTE are currently achieving. Based on his argument, the capacity of mobile network operators to reach remote communities that are currently being shunned for their low return on investment will be improved. Ben posits that MNOs will be able to cover wider areas with less CAPEX and OPEX and hence justifying more affordable access.

In Chapter 4, Rupere, Zanamwe, Mapako, and Nyambo, present infrastructure sharing as an approach for reducing the cost of mobile tariffs in developing countries. Their analysis is based on the supply side of the mobile communication ecosystem and they suggest that infrastructure sharing will shift the focus of mobile networks in developing countries from competing on coverage to competing on service differentiation since the infrastructure sharing TELCOs will have the same network coverage. Based on their case example of the Zimbabwean scenario, they present infrastructure sharing as an appropriate cost reduction model which requires careful analysis by regulatory authorities. Based on their case example, they also demonstrate that the regulators need to understand the business environment before deciding how and whether to implement mandatory or voluntary infrastructure sharing model.

In Chapter 5, Pancham and Millham present telecentres as entities designed to provide Internet access to disadvantaged groups. Telecentres challenges such as declining initial client base, are discussed along with subsequent evolving telecentre business models to address the resulting shortfall in projected income. In order to provide a more accurate picture of the evolving client base and usage, telecentre monitoring of user profiles and usage is introduced. Through a literature review and interviews with local telecentre managers, a common set of data attributes for telecentre operational monitoring was obtained in order to provide this uniformity. After evaluating the timeliness and cost of traditional telecentre evaluation methods like questionnaires, they propose an electronic monitoring system given its advantages of reliable and continuous data collection and lower costs.

Section 2: Applications and Case Examples of Affordable Access

In Chapter 6, Abraham Gert van der Vyver, investigates the contribution of the social media to two of Thailand's major development initiatives namely the OTOP program and the establishment of a network of telecentres. He posits that whilst the OTOP model provided a platform for the growth of SMME'S, the telecentre network contributed affordable ICTs thereby overcoming the digital divide. He also argues that while the advent of the social media furnished citizens with an important networking and empowerment tool, there is evidence that the social media is not yet used to its full potential. He concludes that social media platforms hold the key to affordable and efficient community communication.

In Chapter 7, Indira Ananth, addresses the usefulness of mobile phones in small businesses given its high acceptance as a communication device. In the background of India's growing market economy and government's aim to transform India into a digitally empowered society and knowledge economy, the chapter focuses on street vendors in one of the largest urban agglomerations in India. The recent scenario of delegalisation of notes has also brought into focus more sharply the need for mobile phone literacy. The study found that most respondents owned and used a basic model but the instrument was not considered an important tool for daily transactions.

In Chapter 8, Alsaeed, and Boakes introduce the question of armed conflict which is arguably a serious cause of hardships and an impediment of eGovenment for development. They explore the challenges of delivering eService to refugee and displaced people from conflict zones. Their study focuses on Syrian refugees and displaced people. They apply Institutional Theory as a theoretical lens and a survey for exploring the use of eServices for citizens in and outside Syria. Their study analyses Institutional Theory's Economic, Political, Technical and Social dimensions to understand the context and issues of providing eGovernment services in an unstable domain. The results indicate six themes influencing sustainable and effective support for eServices for refugees and displaced people. These are, Importance of eServices, Connectivity, Awareness, eService Availability, Financial constraints, and Digital literacy.

In Chapter 9, Ambika Samarthya-Howard and Debbie Rogers: explore three existing financial approaches to scaling mobile technologies in low and middle-income countries: user-paid services, reverse billing, and zero-rated platforms. As affordability is an impediment to internet access, key strategies focusing on the involvement of mobile network operators and governments were investigated in relation to sustainability, scale, reach, and impact for mobile technology projects. They present various examples under each type with a view to understanding the risks and benefits of each approach. The chapter will also discuss the importance of mobile initiatives in tackling social issues today.

In Chapter 10, Adams and Takavarasha Jr, discuss digital divides from the stand point of non-geographically grouped communities which are displaced from their home countries by wars and are in search of refuge and livelihoods. After defining how armed conflict create poverty and inhibit development, the authors elucidate the critical role of affordable ICT platforms in fighting poverty and uniting the displace communities that suffer deprivation and stigmatization in foreign lands while they still need to maintain cross-diasporic links with family and friends in home countries.

Finally, a conclusion ends this book with a summary of the methods used and gaps identified.

Sam Takavarasha Jr.
University of Fort Hare, South Africa & University of Zimbabwe, Zimbabwe

Carl Adams
University of Portsmouth, UK

REFERENCES

A4AI. (2017). *2017 Affordability Report*. Retrieved from: http://1e8q3q16vyc81 g8l3h3md6q5f5e.wpengine.netdna-cdn.com/wp-content/uploads/2017/02/A4AI-2017-Affordability-Report.pdf

Alkire, S. (2010). Development 'a misconceived theory can kill. In C. Morris (Ed.), *Amartya Sen: Contemporary Philosophy in Focus*. New York: Cambridge University Press.

Avgerou, C. (2008). Information systems in developing countries: A critical research review. *Journal of Information Technology*, *23*(3), 133–146. doi:10.1057/palgrave. jit.2000136

Avgerou, C. (2010). Discourses on ICT and development. *Information Technologies and International Development*, *6*(3), 1–18.

Bednar & Welch. (2017). *The innovation-diffusion cycle: Time for a sociotechnical agenda*. Twenty-Fifth European Conference on Information Systems (ECIS), Guimarães, Portugal.

Dada, D. (2006). The Failure of e-Government in Developing Countries. *The Electronic Journal on Information Systems in Developing Countries*, *26*(1), 1–10.

Giddens, A. (1984). *The Constitution of Society*. Cambridge, UK: Polity Press.

Gilwald, A. (2017). *Beyond access. Addressing digital inequality in Africa*. Paper Series: NO. 48 — March 2017. Retrieved from: https://www.cigionline.org/sites/default/files/documents/GCIG%20no.48_0.pdf

Heeks, R. (2003). *Most e-Government for Development Projects Fail: How can Risks be Reduced?* iGovernment Working Paper Series, Paper no. 14. Retrieved from http://unpan1.un.org/intradoc/groups/public/documents/NISPAcee/UNPAN015488.pdf

ITU. (2003). *World telecommunication development report 2003 Access Indicators for the Information Society Executive summary*. Retrieved from: https://www.itu.int/ITU-D/ict/publications/wtdr_03/material/WTDR2003Sum_e.pdf

Karanasios, S. (2014). Framing ICT4D research using activity theory: A match between the ICT4D field and theory? *Information Technologies and International Development*, *10*(2), 1–17.

Latour, B. (2007). *Re-assembling the social: An introduction to Actor-Network-Theory*. Oxford, UK: Oxford University Press.

Pettigrew, A. M. (1985). Contextualist research and the study of organisational change processes. In E. Mumford, R. Hirschheim, G. Fitzgerald, & A. T. Wood-Harper (Eds.), *Research Methods in Information Systems* (pp. 53–78). Amsterdam: North -Holland.

Qureshi, S. (2015). Are we making a better world with information and communication technology for development (ICT4D) research? Findings from the field and theory building. *Information Technology for Development*, *21*(4), 511–522. doi:10.1080/02681102.2015.1080428

Sahay, S. (2016). Are we building a better world with ICTs? Empirically examining this question in the domain of public health in India. *Information Technology for Development*, *22*(1), 168–176. doi:10.1080/02681102.2014.933522

Stanton, E. A. (2007). *The human development index: A history*. Working Paper Series Number 127. Retrieved From: http://scholarworks.umass.edu/cgi/viewcontent.cgi?article=1101&context=peri_workingpapers

Takavarasha, S., Jr. (2017). *The impact of affordable access on ICT4D initiatives in Africa*. Key note address at The 3rd ICT Summit on ICT for Digital Entrepreneurship and Industrial Revolution Institute of Finance Management, Dar Es Salaam, Tanzania.

UNDP. (2015). *Transforming our world: the 2030 Agenda for Sustainable Development*. Retrieved from: https://sustainabledevelopment.un.org/content/documents/21252030%20Agenda%20for%20Sustainable%20Development%20web.pdf

UNDP. (2016). *Human development for everyone*. Retrieved from: http://hdr.undp.org/sites/default/files/2016_human_development_report.pdf

Walsham, G. (2012). Are we making a better world with ICTs? Reflections on a future agenda for the IS field. *Journal of Information Technology*, 27(2), 87–93. doi:10.1057/jit.2012.4

World Bank. (2016). *World development report 2016: Digital dividends*. Washington, DC: World Bank. Retrieved from: http://documents.worldbank.org/curated/en/896971468194972881/pdf/102725-PUB-Replacement-PUBLIC.pdf

Acknowledgment

The editors would like to acknowledge the help of all the people involved in this project and, more specifically, to the authors and reviewers that took part in the review process. Without their support, this book would not have become a reality.

First, the editors would like to thank each one of the authors for their contributions. Our sincere gratitude goes to the chapter's authors who contributed their time and expertise to this book.

Second, the editors wish to acknowledge the valuable contributions of the reviewers regarding the improvement of quality, coherence, and content presentation of chapters. Most of the authors also served as referees; we highly appreciate their double task.

Introduction

INTRODUCING THE AFFORDABILITY ISSUES SURROUNDING THE USE OF ICT FOR DEVELOPMENT AND POVERTY REDUCTION

As the world gets more and more connected, there is evidence that certain communities in developing countries are being left behind yet others getting more digitally capable. The digital divide is, therefore, widening because, at a time when some communities are building smart cities and intelligent communities, others still lack basic access. Many people cannot afford internet access while some of them do not have the necessary skills and knowledge about how to use it. New technologies and applications are continuously being invented and they are enhancing the capabilities of the privileged communities while others are inadequately connected or totally unconnected altogether. This widens the digital divide as well as the economic divides. These growing divides continue to worsen inequalities at a time when progressive forces in academia and practitioners (business and government) are trying to reduce them.

This world of unequal digital access and unequal ICT enabled opportunities, presents a challenge to ICT4D scholars and Information systems (IS) scholars in general. The ICT4D scholar must realize that the disadvantages of the exclusion of some people from the digital world is that their lack of exposure and lack of access to knowledge and information affects their ability to explore opportunities that determined livelihoods in the information age. They are therefore, investigating the social and technical issues that inform the systems design and adoption oriented causes along with the concomitant investment and deployment challenges that shape ICT4D roll out.

Addressing socio-technical issues like the ICT access and adoption discussed in this book, presents the challenge of handling social problems using continuously evolving technologies that also influence the dynamism of the human actor's communication needs. Against this context, the IS scholars from the hermeneutic tradition of interpretivism have prioritized having to investigate the much more enduring and fundamental 'WHY' question ahead of the ephemeral 'HOW' solutions that change with technological advances and context. However, in this era of the ICT4D discipline, the challenge of deploying ICTs for addressing poverty and development in the wake of unequal access to ICTs is proving to be more of a 'HOW' than 'WHY' question. This is because both academics and practitioners have reached a stage where they generally know more of the reason why inequalities persist than how to address them. We face the need to investigate how ICT access and adoption can be promoted in different jurisdictions with different socio-economic contexts and different kinds of infrastructure. This paradoxically calls for IS theories that are widely applicable (Bolar, 2007) as well as solutions that are context specific (Hayes and Westrup, 2012).

There is a consensus that ICTs can help address the development and poverty reduction conundrum that is affecting billions of people who are left out of digital opportunities including those that are unaware of their exclusion. Academics believe that ICTs are useful for poverty reduction and development as evidenced by the literature and models they develop. On the other hand, practitioners are devoting time and resources to ICT enabled interventions. In spite of this consensus and confidence in the usefulness of ICTs, there is very little literature that guides how to harness ICT4D. There are many trials and pilot studies covered in the literature, but there are very few longitudinal studies that last long enough to track the gradual effect of ICTs on development. This is worsened by the multi-dimensional facets of poverty reduction and development which are also complicated by a multiplicity of exogenous factors that make it difficult to isolate the causal effects of ICT interventions on development. The ICT4D is a complex domain which demands intellectual curiosity and a sense of moral obligation to fight poverty and foster development in the Global South.

Without excusing our failure to produce a full proof solution to the problems we face in the IS domain, we must admit that what we face is a problem that affects similar domains that lie outside the boundaries of natural sciences. It is a problem that Immanuel Kant wrestled with -in his Critique of Practical Reason- until he concluded that the confidence with which we understand the 'starry heavens above' (astronomy/natural science) cannot be achieved in what he called the 'moral law within' (social sciences) (Kant, I. 1956 [1788]). As a discipline that draws from both natural and social sciences, there are disagreements among IS scholars about what epistemological and ontological positions. Scholars are torn between taking a more social or technical approach to their research. Since questioning one's epistemological stance is akin to asking them to question the very lenses which they see the world (Radnitzky, 1973), we will mainly seek to challenge the ICT4D scholars about the usefulness of their proposed interventions to the attempt to fighting poverty and promote development. For that reason, this book has laid aside the cold and erudite theoretical discourses in favor of the practical discussions that practitioners can employ in future interventions.

Against this background it is inevitable for scholars to settle this at the conceptual level by identifying causal relationships between phenomena. In some cases, academics engage in depth discourse about WHY we should harness ICTs for poverty reduction and development. The moralistic answer to this debate is often used for defining HOW ICTs must be harnessed. This definition of the outcome as a HOW, instead of a specification of the methods and procedures, is often presented in the form of models and frameworks for harnessing ICT and for providing universal access for poverty reduction and development. Our willingness to accept such theoretical frameworks instead of practical solutions is responsible for the confusion that bedevils ICT4D practice three-decade after its inception. We argue that there is a crying call for a methodological 'How' (approach), not just the teleological end which simply defines what we must endeavor to achieve. It must not be a How answer which sounds the same as a why answer to the reason or the factors of the desired outcome. This explains why Walsham and Sahay (2005) called for action research oriented towards processes of change, and more generally process-oriented research

This confusion between a definition of the outcome of ICT access and a specification of the method of achieving reveals the disconnect between theory and practice. it shows that there is a narrow conceptual gap between the why and how question of many practice oriented disciplines like ICT4D and information systems in general. This if not properly acknowledge and conceptualised may trivialise the HOW question that often asked after one has understood why it is necessary to bridge digital divides and harness ICTs for poverty reduction and development. This is supported by the statistics of poverty and digital divide studies. We understand that we need to make a more equal world with ICTs because we are disturbed to learn that inequalities are growing instead of decreasing. We also understand from digital divide statistics that we need to include the excluded populations into the digital economy. In addition to the records of the demographics segments that are excluded and we have research based evidence which shows the effect of their exclusion. Against this background, it would be woefully inadequate for us to settle for conceptual frameworks and models for solving digital inequalities by simply enumerating the qualities of the intended outcomes

This book is not immune from these same problem, because it is written by academics (editors and authors) from the same IS tribe and culture as problematized above. It needs to say why poverty reduction and development require the use of

ICTs and it also needs to define how this must be done it falls short in some parts. The contributors were charged to define the appropriate tools for enhancing ICT access and they were also meant to describe the methods that describe how to deploy these tool in order to produce digital equality. They therefore attempted to work from need to solution so as to inform the practitioners and other academics enquirers about how to deploy the universal access enhancing tools described in this publication. In order to achieve the dual role of describing methods and showing how to use them indifferent contexts, this book will devote section 1 to describing the methods that are useful for improving access and for bridging divides. In this section the contributors identify a couple of methods that have worked in other developing countries and they propose these for use in similar situations.

After this, the second section endeavors to discuss how the proposed methods can be deployed in developing countries that endeavor to solve the digital access problem. By so doing the book has attempted to define the methods as well as the approaches to deploying the methods of fostering affordable access with a view to use it for fighting poverty and for fostering development.

Given the multiplicity of the challenges that are faced by the excluded people of this world. The book project will address the different levels at which they occur. International Telecommunications Union's digital divide presents four parameters we will discuss below. These are Infrastructure, Knowledge, Quality and affordability (ITU, 2003). Our experience and previous work suggests that, the digital access inequalities occur firstly occur at the technological level. At this stage we address the lack of infrastructure that is necessary for access. At the next stage next stage of the digital inequalities problem is the lack of knowledge as well as the lack of ICT skills. The proposed beneficiaries of ICT enabled poverty reduction and development are often unaware of the availability and the usefulness of the communication tools. This explains why they may not endeavour to use the tools that may be at their disposal.

There is also a problem to do with the quality of access. Assuming that the user has the infrastructure and the knowledge prerequisites, the quality i.e. slowness and unreliability of the connectivity may also discourage the knowledgeable user from using the technologies that maybe at their disposal. The chapters of this book will include the challenge of unreliable electricity supply. The erratic supply of power is a challenge that affects ICT access in developing countries and often compels MNOs to employ more expensive power sources. This brings our assessment to the affordability factor that this book is mainly centred on. After the infrastructure, knowledge and quality factors, ITU (2003) presents the affordability challenge. The impact of the access cost factor, is what inspires the authors of this book to tackle the affordability divides using the approaches that are mentioned in the chapters of this publication.

DEMOGRAPHICALLY DEFINED CHALLENGES

The affordability challenges that developing countries face are also demographically defined. The opportunity freedoms or the substantive opportunities of people in developing countries have been found to be demographically defined. Sen (1999) defines the freedom to access the livelihood enhancing opportunities as capabilities. These demographic issues speak to the contextual issues that shape the digital divides that we seek to address through publications like this one.

Information systems researchers have shown great interest in understanding the socio-cultural issues that shape opportunities and information cultures of the countries they deploy ICT for poverty reduction and development. This is meant to enable them to design their interventions in ways that allow them to address the targeted challenges in a context specific manner. For that reason, some of the chapters in this book will expressly discuss contextualism while others simply comply with it. Varying degrees of both former and latter will be conspicuously evident in the case studies contained in this book.

The preface of this book discussed a few indices that are being used by practitioners and policy makers for analysing digital access. They are quite useful for assessing the different digital access scenarios that are experienced by different countries. They are however, not designed to assess the socio cultural dynamics that shape the demographic imperatives that determine the contours of digital divides and opportunities in different countries.

The editors of this book are also concerned with gender, income, culture and geographically determined factors that shape access patterns. We suggest that these issues will result in difference in access and affordability of access by different groups between and within different countries. For instance, the geographical divides are being discussed in many chapters of this book. They see the challenges that mobile network operators face in deploying infrastructure in certain parts of the same country. Rural areas in both developing and industrialised countries are poorly connected.

Geographically defined digital divides: ICT connectivity is applauded for its ability to shrink distances. It is often said that an email to a colleague in the next office is not delivered in any faster than the same one copied to a colleague in an overseas office. While this is true, there is a need to acknowledge that such university of delivery speed and access to information is highly dependent on the infrastructure that connects these communicators that a located in offices that geographically remote from each other.

Such realization of the nexus between infrastructural deployment and connectivity will enable us to draw parallels between connectivity and the income, development and poverty of individuals, communities and countries. The infrastructure -geographic spatial nexus is clearly demonstrable in the rural to urban digital divide. This needs attention because it is responsible for digital inequalities within developing and industrialised countries. Understanding the infrastructure -geographic spatial nexus will also enable us to practically assess when, where and how certain interventions will work or fail. This is because geographical spatial factors have economic, class, income and knowledge issue associated with where people live. A deep understanding of peoples and places where they live give us the ability to assess the success and failure factors that should enable innovators to design successful ICT4D interventions.

Some of the chapters of this book will discuss the rural and urban digital divides within countries of the developing world. Their primary concern is with the absence of ICT infrastructure in these places. They will argue that MNOs are not motivated to install infrastructure in places where the subscriber density will be too low for them to make acceptable returns on investment. While this is the case to access oriented digital divide studies, it is rather inadequate for the ICT4D innovators that have deeper concerns with connectivity and it usefulness to development.

While some of these chapters will leave their analysis at the access level it is critical to consider the importance of physical infrastructure which will be critical in meeting the developmental goals of ICT4D. As it is in traditional ecommerce, transactions need both an initiation mechanism and an order fulfilment mechanism. The dot com bubble bust is a clear evidence of the importance of a balance between transaction initiation and transaction fulfilment. The e-fullfiment aspect of ecommerce and hence ICT4D will require physical infrastructure like roads, railways and transportation systems being operated by couriers and freight companies. Without this ecosystem it is not practical to talk about shrinking distances between producers in developing countries and consumers in developed countries.

The absence of a combination of ICT infrastructure and physical infrastructure that support each other will exclude a community from ICT enabled development as well as the benefits of globalisation. This explains the cry call by top ICT4D researcher for us to gaze our research spectacles beyond access as we discuss before (Gilwald, 2017).

NON-GEOGRAPHICAL DIVIDES

After discussing geographically defined communities and the challenges that they face in accessing the internet, this book also devotes two chapters to communities that are scattered across foreign lands by war. Diasporan communities are not new, but they are an under researched group, particularly in the relatively new ICT4D domain. As mentioned in the preface of this book, the disruptive effect of the wars and political persecution exacerbates poverty and inhibits development. It hurts development by discouraging investment and fuelling brain drain as skilled worker and investors migrate to safer places where they hope to find livelihood and refuge. However, their lives in foreign lands are not always rosy although some of them eventually make it. Most of them struggle to get legal status some of them remain in the shadows where they are vulnerable to several forms of exploitation like being underpaid and living in substandard houses. They are also convenient victims of scapegoating by populist political movements that include the far right parties and some marginalised working class people whose jobs migrants compete for.

These diasporan communities are an interesting unit of analysis in our endeavour to fight poverty and foster development using ICTs. A look at their needs can reveal interesting insights for the IS scholar. Firstly, we may need to assess the role of ICTs in addressing their situation in the receiving countries that have become their new home. Secondly, research can consider the role of ICTs in the cross diasporic links that they maintain with their home lands. In their new country of residence, they need to find opportunities as well as services that range from education, health and employment. They also need to share ideas and to associate with fellow country men and women with whom they share cultural rapport. The diasporan communities have therefore used web portals where news from home country and cultural content can be accessed in their native languages. Such portals also advertise services that include remittance sending platforms, e-commerce and hometown associations.

The chapters of this book have also highlighted the perennial concern with their home countries. The contributors have discussed e-government services which they continue to require. It is interesting to note that ICT access plays a key role in maintaining such cross diasporic connections in the information age. The challenge faced by refugees in acquiring access has been found to be higher than that faced by other local communities discussed in this book. For instance, the ability to acquire a mobile SIM card now depends on one 's legal status. This is because one needs to register a card using identification particulars and proof of residence that undocumented immigrants may not have. Some countries have forbidden refugees like the Royingas from acquiring mobile SIM cards. In addition to their challenges with registering mobile phones, the itinerant poor like the Royingas are bound to suffer affordability challenges that stable communities face as discussed in the rest of this book.

INCOME STRATIFIED DIGITAL DIVIDES

Another significant issue of great concern to this book project is the role of income in shaping the ability of individuals and communities to enjoy internet connectivity. Income here covers the amount of money and the rate at which it is received by the receiver. We want to define it this way because we believe that this has an impact on one's ability to remain connected. In the absence of some of the methods that the contributors of this book have proposed for correcting the access challenges that are faced by underprivileged individuals and communities, both the amount of disposable income and the frequency are very important.

This is because the providers of internet connectivity expect their customers to pay them in monthly subscriptions. Even in cases where they sell bundles, there is a periodic cycle that the subscriber needs to comply with. The bundle tends to vary between networks and packages. As a result, the subscribers often need to choose the one that suits their requirements. Some prefer month bundles because they earn their income monthly while others choose daily bundles which either match their daily income as vendors or their inconsistent use of the service on offer.

In developing countries where mobile internet is mainly accessed on a pre-paid service plan, the subscribers have option to use full cost plans or service specific plans. These packages generally determine the level of access that the subscriber achieves. The full service plan is the ideal package because it is comprehensive. On the other hand, the service specific bundles are dedicated to a particular platform like Facebook or WhatsApp. These packages have the advantage of allowing the access that a subscriber can avoid. They however, show the extent to which income can shape the quality of access that the users of each package can acquire. While the full service plan allows comprehensive access, the service specific packages tend to restrict the user to the access they purchased. This kind of connectivity is woefully inadequate for one who aspires to be a full participant of the information age. They cannot access the information they did not anticipate they will require or enjoy the resourcefulness of the open internet.

Two chapters of this book will discuss the situation faced by the users of free basics. In their case studies they will also reveal the disadvantages of restricted access to the free content that is available to them. The advocates of free basics also belief that users of free basics will aspire to upgrade their limited access to full service as they gain more experience (Carew (2015). This shows that the basic access to zero rated content is inadequate for them. Some users of this restricted access have been found to believe that the internet is about the sites that they have access to. This in our view is a misnomer which further perpetuates the digital divides that IS scholars and policy makers are fighting. It also contrary to the endeavour to have free basics users to upgrade their access to the entire internet as articulated by Carew (2015). It is one of the main reasons that the advocates of net neutrality present in favour of the open internet (Walubengo and Takavarasha, 2017). On the opposite side of the debate on Free Basics, some scholars are arguing that some access is better than no access. They suggest that since some people in the lower income brackets are getting left out because of affordability, it is better to grant them some limited access than to sacrifice them on the altar of net neutrality (Carew, 2015; Gilwald, et al., 2016).

Income determined digital divides are a key challenge that will feature in the chapters of this book because of its focus on affordability of access. The reader is also ward that the income divide is also gender stratified. This is particularly the case in developing countries where the gender income gap is more pronounced. By this statement we are in agreement with feminist literature that suggests that the gender income gap is also evident in the industrialised world.

GENDER-BASED DIGITAL DIVIDES

The gender inequality is one of the pernicious issues that affect digital divide and economic divides in the developing world. While other inequalities are reducing, Web foundation (2013) found that the global Internet user gender gap is increasing. It grew from 11% to 12% between 2013 and 2016. It is much larger the world's Least Developed Countries (LDCs) where is stands at 31%. This is obviously due to the patrilineal culture of most parts of the global south. Women and girls have less access to education and some opportunities that are knowledge based. Some families do not allow give as much education to the girl child as their boys who are culturally expected to work while the girls get married and focus on household duties.

These culturally defined gender roles are responsible for a gender education gap that tends to create a gender knowledge and income gap which has an impact on ICT access. The low education that women have in most of the developing countries is also believed to be a cause of the gender stratified poverty which has been found to affect women more than men. Some studies have suggested that women are the drivers of informal production in parts of the developing world. These are mainly places where the informal sector characterised by vending in prevalent. There is evidence that women are over represented in vending than their male counterparts. This may suggest that the gender income gap that affects women at the formal work place may be different at the informal sector level.

There is also some literature which suggests that women are at the fore front of agricultural activity at house hold level.

Their low education will inevitably affect their ability to participate in the knowledge economy. Of particular concern is the effect of such a scenario on their capacity to participate in ICT4D projects that are meant for poverty reduction and development. It is therefore not surprising to not that gender inequality is related to extreme poverty. For instance, USAID's (2015) analysis of gender inequality and extreme poverty shows that the countries that have gender inequalities that are above-average also have higher extreme poverty rates compared to those that have better gender equality.

A COLLECTIVIST FOCUS

The issues affecting unequal access that were discussed above, have proved to be more on a collective than individual front. These include the demographic, gender, income and geographical location. It is clear that all of these factors affect people's digital access collectively because of their sex, level of income or where they stay. This approach is quite significant in collectivist cultures like the ones in developing countries as articulated by Hofstede's (1980) and endorsed (Jones and Alony, 2007) while criticized (Walsham, 2001; Myers and Tan, 2002). The book also draws from Sen's (1999) capability approach which also influences the human development approach which features in this book as a proxy for measuring development. We acknowledge the controversy of using an individualistic approach for conceptualising development in collectivist societies. Since space limitations do not allow a fuller exposition of CA's evaluative capacity, we point the reader to Robeyns' (2008) rebuttal that proponents of group capabilities fail to distinguish between positive individualism and negative individualism and that CA's focus on the individual level of analysis makes it an opportunity based theory instead of an outcome based theory.

The chapters of this book will address the ability of communities to access infrastructure in affordable and sustainable ways. Towards this end the contributors present methods like community networks and community telecentres to enhance access to internet at micro level. Some contributions address issues that address affordable access across the board on a more macro-level these include infrastructure sharing and open access to educational content. There is also a focus on sectoral level issues. Here the authors focus on the use of ICT access by vendors in an urban informal sector situation. The informal sector chapter reveals the effect of the lack of knowledge on part of the vendors. They have access to mobile internet but they either lack the smart phone technologies for accessing the internet or fail to see the usefulness of ICTs to their business. As a result of lack of knowledge they use their access for voice telephony only while lack of affordable access compels them to adopt innovative methods like missed calls for prompting others to call them. This ironically similar to the use of a mobile phone as a beeper.

The collected works in this book will contribute to both theory and debate within the general development domain by highlighting specific challenges of getting affordable access to ICT for the poorer and disadvantaged communities of the developing world. As the chapters demonstrate having affordable access is important to these communities in many ways covering their abilities to have access to and participate in education, health, social and economic activity. This contribution to the growing general development debates addresses a gap in existing works and provides an important lens to more fully understand the complexities of the underlying issues.

Finally, the IS scholar must look at some of the access inhibiting challenges that are discussed in this book. More work needs to be done in order to enhance their usefulness to the people that are excluded and those that are adversely included. Of particular concern are the those that are locked in poverty traps by some inescapable demographic factor like gender. Equally as critical is the need for innovations that will bring affordable connectivity to remote areas.

Sam Takavarasha Jr.
University of Fort Hare, South Africa & University of Zimbabwe, Zimbabwe

Carl Adams
University of Portsmouth, UK

REFERENCES

Baloh, P. (2007). Role of Fit in Knowledge Management Systems: Tentative Proposition of the KMS Design. *Journal of Organizational and End User Computing*, *19*(4), 22–41. doi:10.4018/joeuc.2007100102

Carew, D. (2015). *Zero-rating: Kick-starting Internet ecosystems in developing countries*. Policy Memo. Progressive Policy Institute. Retrieved from: http://www.progressivepolicy.org/wpcontent/uploads/2015/03/2015.03-Carew_ZeroRating_Kick- Starting-Internet-Ecosystems-inDeveloping-Countries.pdf

Gilwald, A. (2017). *Beyond access. Addressing digital inequality in Africa*. Paper Series: NO. 48 — March 2017. Retrieved from: https://www.cigionline.org/sites/default/files/documents/GCIG%20no.48_0.pdf

Gilwald, A., Chair, C., Futter, A., Koroteng, K., Odufuwa, F., & Walubengo, J. (2016). *Much ado about nothing? Zero-rating in the African context*. Academic Press.

Hayes, N., & Westrup, C. (2012). Context and the processes of ICT for development. *Information and Organization*, *22*(1), 23–36. doi:10.1016/j.infoandorg.2011.10.001

Hofstede, G. (2001). *Culture's Consequences: Comparing Values, Behaviors, Institutions and Organizations Across Nations*. Thousand Oaks, CA: Sage.

ITU. (2003). *World telecommunication development report 2003 Access Indicators for the Information Society Executive summary*. Retrieved from: https://www.itu.int/ITU-D/ict/publications/wtdr_03/material/WTDR2003Sum_e.pdf

Jones, M., & Alony, I. (2007). The Cultural Impact of Information Systems – Through the Eyes of Hofstede – A Critical Journey. *Issues in Informing Science and Information Technology*, *4*, 407–419. doi:10.28945/960

Kant, I. (1956). *Critique of practical reason* (L. W. Beck, Trans.). Indianapolis, IN: Bobbs-Merrill. (Original work published 1788)

Myers, M., & And Tan, F. (2002). Beyond models of national culture in information systems research. *Journal of Global Information Management*, *10*(2), 24–32. doi:10.4018/jgim.2002010103

Radnitzky, G. (1973). *Contemporary schools of metascience*. Chicago: Humanities Press / Henry Regnery Company.

Robeynes, I. (2008). Sen's capability approach and feminist concerns. In F. Comim, M. Qizilbash, & S. Alkire (Eds.), *The Capability approach: Concepts, measures and applications*. Cambridge, UK: Cambridge University Press. doi:10.1017/CBO9780511492587.004

Sen, A. (1999). *Development as freedom*. Oxford, UK: Oxford University Press.

USAID. (2015). *Gender and extreme poverty Getting to Zero: A USAID discussion series*. Retrieved from: https://www.usaid.gov/sites/default/files/documents/1870/Gender_Extreme_Poverty_Discussion_Paper.pdf

Walsham, G. (2002). Cross-cultural software production and use: A Structurational analysis. *Management Information Systems Quarterly*, *26*(4), 359–380. doi:10.2307/4132313

Walsham, G., & Sahay, S. (2005). *Research on IS in developing countries: Current landscape and future prospects*. Retrieved from http://www.ifi.uio.no/forskning/grupper/is/wp/022005.pdf

Walubengo, J., & Takavarasha, S. Jr. (2017). The Challenges of using zero-rating (Free Basics) for addressing the affordability of ICT access in developing countries. *International Journal of ICT Research in Africa and the Middle East*, *6*(2), 47–61. doi:10.4018/IJICTRAME.2017070104

Web Foundation. (2016). *Digging into Data on the Gender Digital Divide*. Retrieved from: https://webfoundation.org/2016/10/digging-into-data-on-the-gender-digital-divide/

Section 1
Key Methods of Fostering Affordable Access

Section 1 of this book presents some key methods that the contributors found useful for fostering affordable ICT access. While some of them provide case examples about how these approaches may be deployed, the goal of this section is to elaborate on the usefulness of these methods.

Chapter 1

Community Networks for Addressing Affordability of ICT Access in African Rural Areas:
A Case Study of Zenzeleni, Makhosi

Sam Takavarasha Jr.
University of Fort Hare, South Africa

Carl Adams
University of Portsmouth, UK

Liezel Cilliers
University of Fort Hare, South Africa

ABSTRACT

Mobile ICTs have addressed the digital divides between the global south and the global north. While a phenomenal mobile penetration in developing countries has enabled ICT4D innovations by connecting previously unconnected people, several communities suffer adverse inclusion or lack access altogether. Such digital divides within countries have been attributed to technical, social, and economic issues. As a result, many approaches to bridging the digital divides have been used by both academics and practitioners. This chapter, therefore, discusses the potential use of community networks for providing sustainable and affordable access to rural communities in developing countries. In addition to the advantages of community networks, the chapter presents the challenges thereof, and it contributes to the vexed question about how to harness ICTs to empower the disadvantaged communities in developing countries. A case study of Zenzeleni Makhosi community network in South Africa's Eastern Cape province is presented and analysed using Sen's capability approach.

DOI: 10.4018/978-1-5225-3179-1.ch001

INTRODUCTION

The use of ICTs for development and poverty reduction has been greatly enabled by a phenomenal mobile penetration during the last two decades. The teledensity in many developing countries has increased 74 to 94 subscribers per 100 inhabitants of developing countries. The better-off developing countries and industrialised countries have exceeded 100 subscriptions per 100 inhabitants during the last decade (ITU, 2016). While such figures suggest full access, there are several parts of the developing countries that remain unconnected. World Bank (2016) estimates that about 6 billion people do not have internet access. These are mainly remote rural areas that are inhabited by people that are either too few or too poor to guarantee a return on investment to the mobile network operators (MNOs). It is not viable for MNOs to invest in areas where they reach less than 3000 paying customers per base station (Mishra, Hwang, Filippini, Du, Moazzami and Subramanian, 2005; Balancing Act, 2017).

DIGITAL ACCESS INDEX

Information Systems (IS) scholars have conducted extensive research on how to bridge various causes of digital divides (Fuchs and Horak, 2007; Acilar, 2011, Bornman, 2016). Digital divides refer to unequal patterns of access, usage capabilities and ICT enabled benefits that emanate from demographic and technical stratifications that produce classes of winners and losers of the information society, (Fuchs and Horak, 2007). Digital divide studies have identified impediments that range from demographic imperatives like gender, innumeracy, lack of information literacy and income. They have also identified structural ones like infrastructure, unaffordability of access among other causes (Mansel, 2001; Acilar, 2011). These studies have attributed these structural challenges to the lack of resources to invest in the installation of the required ICT infrastructure. They have however applauded the advent of mobile technologies as a viable solution to connecting previously unconnected parts of the developing world. While the phenomenal mobile penetration in developing countries has diminished researchers' focus on infrastructure oriented digital divide studies in the 90s, the discourse has shifted from mono-topical to multi-dimensional frameworks of digital inequalities. This shift toward users from technology is due to evidence of differential access where parts of the developing world either lacks or has inadequate access to ICTs (Barzilai-Nahon, 2006).

There is undisputable evidence that shows that mobile ICTs have made substantial progress to bridging digital divides in developing countries. In spite of this evidence, there are millions that are excluded from the information era by poor infrastructure and unaffordable cost of access. This emanates from the high cost of mobile infrastructure which translates to high tariffs that low-income users cannot afford. Of particular concern to this chapter are the people in the developing countries that cannot effectively use ICT for Development due to high access cost. Qureshi (2006) posits that people must have access to both information and expertise for them to improve their livelihoods. Other scholars have therefore argued that the perception that mobile will usher universal access to the developing world is a myth given their unaffordability to communities in rural areas (Subramanian, Surana, Petra and Sheth, nd; Gillwald et al., 2016). While this chapter focuses on affordability we must emphasise that connectivity does not correlate with information inequality (Gillwald, 2017).

In 2003 the International Telecommunication union introduced the digital access index (DAI), to track internet usage using a multivariate index that combines both technical and social imperatives (Barzilai-Nahon, 2006). Affordability, infrastructure, knowledge and quality of broadband access are indicators of the DAI. Interestingly, they have a discernible linkage to poverty of both individuals and nations. Poor people who should benefit from the usage of ICT for development and poverty reduction are often left out because of the chicken and egg nexus between poverty and DAI indicators. This suggests that addressing affordability should be a key enabler of ICT4D initiatives. It also corroborates that the communication platforms that enable poverty reduction must be affordable to the poor for them to be able to utilise them fully. To this end, methods like freebasics, Infrastructure sharing and tele-centres were implemented in various countries (Walubengo and Takavarasha Jr, 2017). These for various reasons were often found to be less effective than expected (Oja, 2005; Attwood and Braathen, 2010). This, therefore, calls for the introduction of more sustainable approaches to affordable connectivity in remote.

Against this background community networks like the Makhosi network discussed in this chapter are proposed as a viable approach to both affordability and sustainability of ICT access. This is because they can enable internet access and intranet access while using electric grid or renewable energy sources such as solar power and they manageable on a not for profit model. They can also take advantage of the communitarian culture of people in developing countries like Ubuntu of Sub Saharan Africa. Their use would improve livelihoods of people in these communities by facilitating cheaper communication and fostering development. Especially in models where local networks enable free local communication and facilitate access to local opportunities which are more relevant to locals as discussed latter. This can reduce the cost of internetwork calls to about half of the cost charged by TELCO owned GSM mobile connectivity while facilitating access to distant markets.

In spite of the above advantages, there are challenges that impede the deployment of mesh networks in many parts of the developing world. These include regulations, initial investment outlay cost and local socio-political power and trust issues. It is because of these challenges that we wish to discuss how community networks can be used for poverty reduction in developing countries.

After this introduction, this chapter discusses the technical configuration of community networks followed by capability approach and the Zenzeleni Makhosi case study. The chapter ends with an analysis of the Makhosi case study and the policy implications thereof.

ASSESSING COMMUNITY NETWORKS THROUGH THE CAPABILITY APPROACH

The use of community networks for addressing connectivity issues in rural areas has been applied in industrial countries (Ishmael, Bury, Pezaros and Race, 2008). Western examples include guifi.net and eXO (Spain), Ninux.org (Italy), FDN and Tetaneutral (France) (netCommons, 2017). There are therefore some lessons for developing countries to draw from the international technical community. It is important to highlight that community networks in the developing world are meant to address unaffordable access as well as the absence of connectivity in remote areas. As a result, we urge that developing countries can learn from success stories like W4C (India), Endaga (Indonesia, Philipines, Pakistan, Somalia) and Rhizomatica (Mexico) because these have more in common with them Western applications that to some extent apply on the technical than they are on socio-political and socio-economic front. This, therefore, challenges the technicons in developing countries to adopt social embeddedness approach instead of an a-contextual diffusion and transfer approach that has been criticised in IS literature for technological determinism (Avgerou, 2008:2010; Duesek, 2007).

In this chapter, community networks will be used as an approach to harnessing ICTs for poverty reduction and development. Sen's (1999) CA will be adopted as a tool for conceptualising relevance to ICT4D. The capability approach puts freedom at the centre of human development, and it presents freedoms as the means and end of development. Freedom is, therefore, the absence of constraints (unfreedoms) to pursue valued ends and it is central to CA because it defines one's ability to realise valued opportunities. Since CA puts freedom at the centre of wellbeing, the freedom and unfreedom to pursue opportunities, is used for categorising our empirical evidence as impediments and enablers of ways of life and ICT use.

- **Functionings:** The Aristotelian term "functionings", refers to the "valuable being and doings" which people have achieved. The basic ones include; being nourished, being clothed, being safe and being healthy while complex ones are, the ability to shape society and having self-respect (Robeyns, 2006). The achievements that one has realised or well-being achievement is measured in terms of functionings (Alkire and Deneulin, 2008). While economists have always used functionings as a measure of standard of living, they do not provide a complete picture of what else one could achieve. Functionings measure the current state of life, but they are oblivious of the underlying choices being made (Jasek-Rysdahl, 2001).

- Measuring functionings cannot reveal the difference between one who spends less in order to acquire more tomorrow from one who has no choice e.g. a student living in crowded accommodation while acquiring a degree and a labourer who cannot afford decent accommodation (Robeyns, 2003). Their capabilities, or freedom to pursue other well-being achievements are however different (Sen, 1999). The endeavour to foster poverty reduction and development using ICT must focus on capabilities and evaluate functionings only as a way of improving the current way of life.

- **Capabilities:** The term 'capabilities' refers to sets of functionings that one can achieve if they wanted. They provide a better way of measuring well-being because they indicate the set of vectors of functionings that one can achieve or the substantive freedom to achieve alternative combinations of functionings (Sen, 1999 p. 75). For instance, the capability set of a person who chooses not to use ICTs when they are available is different from the person in an unconnected area although their measurable functionings are similar. They have different well-being freedoms measurable by their capability set.

- **Instrumental and Constitutive Freedoms:** Sen (1999) categorizes freedoms as instrumental and/or constitutive, that is, as means and freedom as an end of development. These are not always mutually exclusive, for example, the freedom to pursue education and avoid premature morbidity is a desirable 'end' (i.e. constitutive features), but it is also 'instrumental' - i.e. a means to the freedom to be gainfully employed - (Sen, 1999). While the adoption of ICT is instrumental in expanding other freedoms to pursue well-beings, it must be viewed as constitutive i.e. an end in itself.

- **Critiques and limitations of CA:** Several scholars have criticized CA for its individualistic evaluative framework (Devereux, 2001; Stewart, 2005; De Herdt and Deneulin 2007) its heterogeneity as well as the incommensurability of capabilities (Crespo, 2008). There is no practical way of measuring a non-homogeneous issue as capabilities on a common scale. It is more challenging to evaluate agency freedoms (Zheng and Stahl, 2011). Sen (1999) admits that '*some capabilities are harder to measure than others*', but he does not consider it entirely necessary or possible. In his own words, Sen posits that '*attempts at putting them (capabilities) on a 'metric' may sometimes hide more than they reveal*' p. 81. Conservative economists also alienate CA from economics for attempting to reunite ethics and economics (Daka, 2006).

While other scholars have criticised CA for not holding people to account for not exploiting opportunities at their disposal, we problematize it for not assessing why some capabilities are not turned into functionings. The concept of freedoms to pursue valued opportunities may mask the causes of non-adoption which would be viewed as a choice not to adopt.

Community Networks and Their Usefulness

Community networks can be described as wireless distribution networks that connect a community to its own inhabitants or to other external networks. They can be developed as mesh topologies or nodes that have directional/sector antennas and point to point links. The former topology is ideal for high user density areas while the latter is for lower user density areas like rural areas. While technologies like wifi, microwave or WiMAX may be used, wifi is recommended for being cheaper and hence more ideal for rural connectivity (Subramanian, Surana, Petra and Sheth, nd).

The user density and user income must determine the design of the topology and the choice of the equipment that will be used. If this is not carefully considered, the affordability and sustainability of the project suffers. While there are other design factors that affect the quality of service and choice of equipment, we will concentrate on the cost and sustainability issues. This is because these have a direct impact on the relevance of the network for ICT4D.

Having discussed the technical aspects, it is important to highlight the way they are applied to meet communication requirements in developing countries. Community networks have been used for both data and voice in intranets and over the Internet. The ones that are dedicated to local content are the cheapest to install and operate. This is because they do not have to meet the cost of Internet connectivity. In Sub-Saharan Africa the cost of connecting to the Internet via VSAT is about USD XXX. As stated earlier, Internet access is expensive for inhabitants of many developing nations. Equally as challenging is the cost of communicating with other telephonic networks.

Connecting to external networks also requires licensing and registration which both access and registration costs. We must, however, hasten to acknowledge that certain countries require all communications to be connected to a monitoring system which may attract infrastructure costs and licensing issues. Other countries have legislation that allows communities to install local networks without any licensing (Rey-Moreno, 2013; Rey-Moreno et al., 2015). A community network may also wish to connect itself to similar networks which maybe proximate to it. Depending on the jurisdiction and its regulations, this may be considered to be an extension of a network that does not require licensing. In the absence of special legislation, this may attract costs which may reach millions for any Internet Access Providing license in countries like Zimbabwe.

In the case of Zenzeleni Networks of Makhosi discussed latter, the network had to be registered as a telecommunications co-operative for it to be able to connect to other mobile networks. In Mexico, the regulator introduced a Social Purpose GSM License which communities can use for licensing community networks (Rey-Moreno, 2013; Rey-Moreno et al., 2015).

HARNESSING AFFORDABLE ICTs FOR POVERTY REDUCTION AND DEVELOPMENT

In this section, we discuss the role of ICTs in fostering affordable access to promote ICT for development and poverty reduction. Having discussed development, we discuss the terms poverty and affordability to clarify how they are used in this chapter

Matching Affordability to the Right Poverty Groups

The cost of ICT access has been considered affordable if the cost of monthly usage is a small percentage of monthly GNI (Dymond et al. 2010) e.g. 2-5%. We suggest that this approach is problematic in countries of high inequalities because it is likely to produce tariffs that are too high for the poor. Since affordability means different things to different income groups, we propose that affordable tariffs for poverty reduction be conceptualised from the stand point of poor people. Equally as problematic is the description of poverty as people who live on less than USD1.90 /day. This approach presupposes measurable and regular income which is not always the case in parts of the developing world. Poverty itself is a contested term whose definition depends on social political, cultural and historical context of a community. Scholars have conceptualised poverty under three categories namely; relative poverty, subjective poverty and absolute poverty (De Vos and Garner 1991).

Sen (1999), posits that poverty or wellbeing dispossession should be understood as the deprivation of capabilities. In this chapter, we are concerned with the people that are currently excluded for ICT enabled development because they cannot afford to pay the current mobile access tariffs. This may be because they have very low income or because their income is irregular because they are not part of the main stream economy which is characterised by wage and salaries that match billing cycles of mobile network operators. Some of the excluded people earn seasonal income after the harvest of their crops and the sale of surplus produce. This group should not really be considered poor because they work and they earn something for their livelihood. The long periods of times they spend before their next harvest may render them income poor. These groups will be unable to foot any recurrent bills for some months before harvest (Zimvac & Fewsnet, 2010).

In spite of their different economy, they people need to use ICTs for them to enhance their incomes. They need to improve their produce for them to achieve higher levels of surplus. This entails access to improved methods of farming through extension services, whether forecast, and access to markets for their surplus. The tariffs that these people will find affordable and the billing cycles they can comply with require a deeper analysis than the current percentage of GNI per month does. We therefore present community networks as a sustainable approach to granting them affordable access in the context of ICT4D.

Using Community Networks for Poverty Reduction and Development

The relevance of ICTs enabled communication to poverty reduction has been extensively discussed in the burgeoning literature (Moradi and Kebryaee, 2010). In this section, we focus on the usefulness of community networks to poverty reduction and developmental endeavour of people in previously unconnected parts of developing world. We discuss the extent to which they provide local connect, e-government, NGO content, markets, whether focus and access to local opportunities.

Local content is often marginalised as digital divide literature focuses on connecting supposedly isolated rural communities to external communities in the context of an increasingly globalised world. Such misreading has caused people to view rural communities as victims of information poverty (Barja and Gigler, nd; Britz, 2007) a Library Information systems term that has been associated with digital divides (Haider and Bawden, 2007; Yu, 2010). Such a characterisation of the plight of communities in developing countries has been problematized for leading to misguided approaches to ICT4D interventions (Wilson, 2002). We critique such models firstly on the role of ICTs in development and poverty reduction and on the type of information that is required by these communities.

First generation studies in ICT4D have conceptualised development in as articulated by the discredited modernisation motif of Daniel Lerner (Lerner, 1958) which equated development to Westernisation (Ojo, 2005; Matunhu, 2011). They suggested that ICT enabled development entails dismantling local culture and bringing certain information to the developing world. Instead, theorists like Armtya Sen view it as enhancing capability freedoms or the capacity to pursue valued opportunities. On this basis, we posit that local opportunities can best be disseminated through local platforms in local languages by local people. While we applaud the viability of enhancing access to opportunities in distant places such as distant markets and job markets, we contend that local content is key for local development.

We will return to this argument latter, for now, let us focus on the role of ICTs in development. This we help us to understand the usefulness of community networks to development. McNamara (2003) suggests that the role of ICTs has been overestimated because ICTs can only address the information and the communication components of development. So the usefulness of ICTs to poverty reduction and development of communities can be a conceptualised is how far ICTs can go in addressing the information and communication component of their livelihoods.

The community networks have the advantage of being lead and championed locally. The content in local intranets and community radio present a rich source of local content that is relevant to local development and poverty reduction. The conviviality of local intranets and VOIP is that it allows each player on the network to generate content and share it with others on the network. This creates Habermas's (1984) Ideal speech situation if other social power dynamics are addressed on *alto ego* basis.

Contextualising Community Networks

The challenge of applying community networks to serve communities must start with an understanding of communities and their socio cultural standing. NetCommons (2017) posits that each community network is different from others. They should, therefore, develop local institutions and organizational structures of divergent complexity as they endeavour to comply with different contexts and divergent needs. Of particular importance to the use of community networks for supporting communication systems that can support development and expansion of people's capabilities in compliance with their information culture. Without this deep understanding of how information is perceived and used in developing countries, many foreign interventions are bound to fail. Before we consider this to be farfetched, we must be reminded of the unsuccessful endeavours to harness ICTs for supporting people in developing countries. This suggests that key lessons may be drawn from telecentres and communication for the development project of the modernisation era (Oja, 2005).

Information systems scholars have acknowledged the importance of information culture as a key requirement for contextualization. This interest was allegedly influenced by cultural sensitivity in organizational and management studies (Li, 2004). The ground breaking work of Hofstede (1980) is considered as highly influential to IS researchers. Follow up empirical studies have concluded that culture shapes the values, perceptions, preferred styles of communication, and cognitive and learning styles (Ardichvili, et. al, 2006 p.94). In this regard, culture has been found to have an impact on design, development, implementation, use and management of information systems (Myers and Tan, 2002, Jones and Alony, 2007). Due to the preceding, we suggest that the usefulness of community networks must be predicated on contextualism.

There are five dimensions of culture that have influenced IS studies. These are individualism/collectivism, uncertainty avoidance, power distance, masculinity/femininity and short-term/long-term orientation. Information systems scholars have disagreed on these Hofstedian dimensions. Jones and Alony, (2007) endorsed them, but other IS scholars problematized them along both rationality and methodological lines (Walsham, 2001; Myers and Tan, 2002). Key issues raised against Hofsted's (1980) cultural studies that require attention are assumption of cultural homogeneity, inadequate attention to cultural dynamism and lack of significant analysis of detailed work patterns (Walsham, 2002).

In spite of the contention in burgeoning literature on intercultural studies, there is a common understanding on the dichotomy between individualist and collectivist cultural divides. These two cultural backgrounds were found to have different ways of processing information and constructing knowledge (Bhagat et al., 2002). These two backgrounds can be mapped to key actors in the community network projects in developing countries. The interventions are mainly being initiated by international development agencies that often define the approaches that they sponsor in rural areas. The beneficiaries are associated with collectivist cultural backgrounds. The Western backed NGOs and development agencies are generally individualist oriented.

ROLE OF GOVERNMENT, REGULATORS, BUSINESS IN FACILITATING COMMUNITY NETWORKS

The implementation of community networks in developing countries calls for the involvement of regulators, business government and above all the communities. The primary role is government policy. This is a role played by the ministry of ICT, and this may be enforced by the telecommunications authority regulator. Different countries may have different systems, but this is usually the case in most countries. In the following section, we discuss how each of these can enable the installation of community networks in developing countries. An appreciation of these roles may help consumer advocacy groups to identify who to lobby in times of need.

- **The Role of Government:** The central government in partnership with parliament is expected to pass legislation that enables community networks. The political will of a government to enable parallel or complementary structures to existing MNOs is dependent on their economic ideologies. Some governments will resist this while pro-poor governments will enable prioritise and seek to enforce this. Supply side oriented policies have not enabled the poor to harness ICT4D, it is necessary to employ price controls (Gliwald, 2017) or policies that allow alternatives like not-for-profit networks in remote areas.

- **Regulators' Role:** The ICT sector regulator may either propose policy to government according to their knowledge of regulatory best practice in other jurisdictions. They may also be instructed by the government about what out comes to achieve. This mandates them to find appropriate ways of achieving these ends without disrupting other stake holders.

- **The Role of Business:** Commercial players are critical in the provision of affordable service. There are few models that can successfully avoid their involvement. These could be intranets that are limited to communities, but when interoperability is to be achieved, they have to be involved. Giving them too much freedom can earn them profits at the expense of the people and constraining them can discourage infrastructure investment. This, therefore, calls for dialogue and cooperation with MNOs.

- **Communities:** Finally, the communities play the most interesting part because they are the end user of the community networks. We will discuss elsewhere in this chapter that unless communities create social networks, the network of devices is of no use. The socio-political and socio-economic imperatives on the end users are critical. These determine the context in which systems operate and the usage that will be achieved. In some instances, any external intervention that excludes local players may fail. The participation of local players is key to sustainability and acceptance.

Sustainability is shaped by the community's ability to protect the project political and technically. On the social front, interventions need the support of local leaders. It also needs the support of residents who will house and protect the technology on their properties. On the technical front, it is essential to have local technicians that can maintain the equipment. Without installation and maintenance, the project is dead no matter how much support it has from local government and NGOs.

From Connected Devices to Connected People

The challenge of connecting devices has been discussed above. It involves the acquisition of capital and the application of technical knowhow. This endeavour can be easily accomplished by donor agencies that seek to help developing countries. We contend that the connectivity of devices does not necessarily lead to the benefit of ICT access. Many projects have suffered underutilisation while the impact of other projects remained minimal. Baron and Gomez (2014) posit that ICT access can improve relationships, enhance learning, and facilitate effective transactions.

Knowledge networking is therefore necessary for enabling people to improve their own livelihoods (Qureshi, 2006). It facilitates collaboration which enhances livelihood if information technologies like mesh networks are applied to development efforts. Schrage (1990) defined collaboration as the shared creation and/or discovery in which two or more individuals with complementary skills interact to create a shared understanding that none had previously possessed or could have come to on their own. The rest of this chapter will highlight the need to connect people to each other by discussing a case study of the Zenzeleni community network that moved beyond access to socio-economic benefits.

THE CASE OF ZENZELENI NETWORKS LTD BUILDING COMMUNITY TELCO

The Zenzeleni Makhosi case study is about how a rural community became a telecommunication operator in order to reduce communication cost for its community with the assistance of University of Western Cape (UWC). While Makhosi is the name of a place, the term 'Zenzeleni' is a Xhosa term which means 'do it for yourself'. This is a call to action for the previously oppressed black communities to shape their own destiny post in the post-Apartheid democratic era.

Mankhosi is situated in the Eastern Cape province of South Africa along the coast of the Indian Ocean. It is a beautiful coastal area that attracts tourists to its shores. It serves twelve villages, 580 households which amounts to about 3500 people. The Makhosi Community network project covers about thirty square kilometres between Coffee Bay and Port St. Johns. The area has one junior secondary school (Sikoma) and one senior school (Ntshilini). Regarding infrastructure, Makhosi area has low access to services. It has dusty or un tarred roads, and only 2.1% of its households are connected to the electricity grid. Like most rural areas in the Eastern Cape, Mankhosi is inhabited by people of low income. Their average income is about R388/month per person which translates to about 30 USD per month. It is regarded as having a low level of education because only about 13% of its inhabitants completed matriculation i.e. high school (Rey-Moreno, Blignaut, May and Tucker, 2016).

Before the intervention, communications in Makhosi has constrained by cost and lack of electricity. While 86.66% of its inhabitants were using mobile phone services on a weekly basis, about 22% of their disposable income (from remittances and social security from Government) was being spent on mobile phone services. This included the cost of charging their mobile phone batteries as well as the cost of calling credit and it suggested that government was subsidising MNOs. It is reported that R5 airtime was being sold for R7 in the area. The local people were making an average of 4 calls a week and the average calling time was found to be 17 minutes. Forty percent of that time was said to be without airtime i.e. receiving calls from better off relatives from outside the community. Regarding data usage, about 8.25% of the population was found to have bought Internet bundles in the month before the survey conducted by UWC. Furthermore, at least 15% of people in Mankhosi reported that they had to sacrifice on basic food in order for them to use mobile phone services (Rey-Moreno et al., 2016).

Zenzeleni Networks: Makhosi

The UWC initiated the Zenzileni community network to overcome the above challenges. They started by building a relationship with the local community, and the local leadership agreed since they saw how it would benefit the people (Rey-Moreno et al., 2016). To meet the technical requirement to install stations 2km apart with visibility to each other, the tribal authorities sat down with the people and selected the houses that would host the stations. In this regard, the tribal authorities were the security for the equipment. They, therefore, selected responsible households that had positive images in the community. After that UWC sat down with the community and designed the network together with them. This participatory approach was behind its success because it produced a locally designed sustainable network. Skilled members of the community were selected, and they worked on the design and installation of the network.

At the beginning, there were 10 mesh potatoes (mesh Wi-Fi devices from Village Telco) and there are now 13:" They can now recharge handsets using solar power more cheaply than their competitors. They have re-charged 5-6,000 phones. The phones can be connected using VoIP". Thus far, 13 nodes in a mesh network have been successfully installed. Internal calls are free, and 'break out' calls are offered for a small fee. It is now connected to the Internet via a 3G gateway, and it serves the community as planned. To make the project sustainable, the mesh nodes double as charging stations for mobile phones. This manages to generate revenue that is used for maintaining and upgrading the current services hence making the project self-sustaining (Balancing Act, 2017: July 28). After Mankosi network proved to be successful in its earlier stages, the users wanted it to be connected to other networks. To make this possible, a non-profit Telecommunications cooperative was registered with the DTI. This ECSN/ECS license was exempted by ICASA i.e. a legal ISP. (Moreno-Rey et al., 2015).

Services Being Provided

The Makhosi community network has benefited the community by providing phone Charging service at half the price they used to pay before its inception. It also provides break out calls from the 12 public phones at half the market price. The network enables Internal calls for free among its public phones. It also allows break-in calls to its 12 public phones from any network. Furthermore, there is IVR based billing system in IsiXhosa (vouchers and prepaid with change).

Talking about the services provided, a local project leader said, 'I am the chairperson of this project, we provide calling and charging services, the phones we use are not different from the usual mobile phones. Our aim when we started this project the first of its kind was to provide mobile phone charging services, sell vouchers and internet. It's the first project because there is no project like this (Mazantsana, nd).'

Building Social Structures

Makhosi community network has facilitated the development of social structures that create empowerment, confidence, spill over into other economic activities. Project facilitator Carlos described a social engagement with community as follows, 'We wanted to put tech in the hands of people and wanted to try this in the rural areas. We started conversations with people in Mankosi in April 2012 and it started as a partnership between the University of the Western Cape and Mankosi. We wanted to see if it was feasible for them to run the project by themselves' (Rey-Moreno as cited in Balancing Act, 2017). He described the challenges they faced with language barrier and rapport building as follows, 'Initially we went through local guys who spoke English, then went through the Tribal Authority, meeting with the head man. We needed to find out what the community was ready to commit to. We wanted to listen to the community and try and understand if they wanted to do something". A project champion,

He added,

They were quite pragmatic and hard-headed about the money side of things. The most important part of this project is that the cooperative members are running the project instead of expatriates. They understand the project and the needs of the community and will always be there to manage the project without any need to call for waiting for outsiders. According to a local champion, they faced some challenges in building the project but they eventually succeeded. He advised that the first challenge was that 'most people take time to under what a project means. In some people's minds, a project is initiated by someone from outside. That is aligned with a top down approach because most people think a project is about employment (Siya, nd).

To maintain a sense of ownership and involvement, the cooperative holds monthly meetings with all its members. Through these meetings, they developed more business ideas that are relevant to the needs of the community.

He also advised that their biggest challenge was skills training to cooperative members. In his words, "My recommendation to whoever wants to start a community project, is that people must sit down and discuss the whole plan and what we want to achieve for their community. If the plan of the project is only known by one project, it becomes a problem. It is vital to inform everyone about the finances and paper work of the project" (Siya, nd). On the operational front, he added, that their 'challenge is transportation problem because the cooperative meets to discuss the project activities monthly. We have to solve problems quickly when technical faults happen on the stations.

He we went further saying,

Consider project as tenders which are about making a profit just for one person who won the tender. It is also important to have detailed work plan so that you can know the time lines and the targets of the project. Communication and consideration are key in carrying out the project as they bring out different views. Continuous training is also very important as this helps people to understand that they are working towards something and who at a certain stage will do a certain task. It was not easy when we started this project, but we are satisfied as Makhosi to have managed to reach this stage, we now have a better way of communicating at reduced cost (Siya, nd).

Using Telecommunication for Human Development

Since people don't have electricity, they decided to charge their mobile phone batteries for R3 instead of R5 being charged elsewhere. Through these monthly meetings, they also came up with an idea to have their phones to call outside the community network i.e. to other providers. To get that license, they needed to register as a nonprofit cooperative. This was successfully done with the assistance of UWC. Their phones now call outside using their own vouchers and prepaid system at 60 cents a minute which is less than USD 5cents.

The local community has realised human developmental and livelihood benefits from Makhosi project. This includes non-Telecommunications facilities like Microcredits. One of its success stories is that it has enabled 12 students to enrol at institutions of Higher Education. According to the chairman, 'The revenue we generate from these services, .. we save it and put it aside so that we can be able to create a better future for the youth in this community, including sending to university those who passed grade 12 to ensure their prosperity (Mazantsana, nd)'

Zenzeleni has had a positive impact on the community. There are a few local students who are now enrolled at universities because of Zenzeleni. One girl child beneficiary said,

My name is A I am 23 years old I am from Mankhosi. I was doing nothing last year, but the project has assisted me to process my application for university and NSFAS. My life is going to change because after completing my studies I will be able to apply for employment and earn money and do everything I want. I am studying Electrical Engineering at Buffalo City College, thanks to Zenzeleni project (Athini, nd).

Another girl child added,

I am PS, I am 22, and I am from Ngqeleni Makhosi. I passed my metric in 2013, and I could not access admission to study further. I was assisted last year by Zenzeleni project to apply. We were trained how to use a computer to apply, and we applied for ourselves. It was easy and better to apply online because you get a prompt response. This year I got admitted at Walter Sisulu University, and I am doing a degree in human resources management (Siya, nd).

After the above success, a project champion advised that the Makhosi project aims for future Steps which include the Internet to school and other anchor tenants. The 'Internet to schools' project started when Zenzeleni was approached by a local school to provide internet to the 33 computers that were donated by government and were not being used. Zenzeleni found this as one of the revenue streams for the community because local schools are struggling to get internet connection. They liked the idea since the revenue would be invested in the community to support community development.

ANALYSING THE ROLE OF MAKHOSI COMMUNITY NETWORK IN LOCAL DEVELOPMENT

Smith, Spence and Rashid (2011) categorise the functionings into three networking dimensions namely; 1) enabling and strengthening social networks, 2) enabling and strengthening economic networks - i.e. connecting citizens to financial institutions, expanding market boundaries and improving supply chains - and 3) enabling and strengthening governance networks i.e. access to government services. In the following section, we discuss Smith et al.'s (2011) first two categories of functionings in the context of Zenzeleni 's Makhosi project.

Enabling and Strengthening Social Networks

The Mankhosi project was designed to be a bottom up project built on a participatory in nature. Unlike most development agencies that champion interventions in developing countries, the University of Western Cape had no intention to have a permanent presence at Makhosi. They, therefore, introduced a more self-sustaining project than most interventions usually endeavour to achieve. In fact, most aid giving countries insist on using expertise and equipment from their countries. Such an approach may ensure technical competence, but they often lack sustainability due to lack of local buy in. This must be applauded as a rare development of social networks that benefited the community. The participatory approach they used from the design to the implementation of the project managed to bring the members of the community together.

The second phenomenon that enhanced social networking is the development of a communication system. Unlike any other communication network, the Makhosi network happens to be free for local people to use for communicating with each other. This enables constant communication and enables deeper collaboration between actor that would otherwise be separated by distance. This phenomenon is similar to the way the information revolution characterised by the Internet automates globalisation. The projects champions of Makhosi may struggle to enumerate subtle benefits that may be intangible and incommensurate like social cohesion. For that reason, we list a few functionings with due cognisance that a comprehensive list cannot be easily produced.

Enabling and Strengthening Economic Networks

As a subsistence farming community are constrained from achieving livelihoods by distance to market, lack of market information, and distance from extension services. Makhosi is described as an area that had low access to services. As a result, ICTs would be useful for expanding opportunity freedoms by shrinking distances as well as market information and extension services information. The previous point still applies in that economic networks are also strengthen economic networks. This is because economic activities have a communication and an information component that ICTs can automate as articulated by McNamara (2003). In the Makhosi project, there are a few examples of the strengthening of economic network. The rural economy should be conceptualised as human development, and the following human development examples are reported to have taken place at as a result of the Makhosi Zenzileni project.

My name is A I am 23 years old I am from Mankhosi. I was doing nothing last year, but the project has assisted me to process my application for university and NSFAS. My life is going to change because after completing my studies I will be able to apply for employment and earn money and do everything I want. I am studying Electrical Engineering at Buffalo City College, thanks to Zenzeleni project (Athini, nd).

Another girl child added,

I am PS, I am 22, and I am from Ngqeleni Makhosi. I passed my metric in 2013 and I could not access admission to study further. I was assisted last year by Zenzeleni project to apply. We were trained how to use a computer to apply, and we applied for ourselves. It was easy and better to apply online because you get a prompt response. This year I got admitted at Walter Sisulu University, and I am doing a degree in human resources management (Siya, nd).

There are also other capability enhancing activities which include the internet for schools and the training programs. According to one of the project champions, 'There has been some training in marketing by the SEDA ICT incubator which is opened to other community members (Rey-Moreno, 2017).

Internet to School and Other Anchor Tenants

After the above success, the project aims for future Steps which include the 'internet for school' project. Zenzeleni was approached by a local school to provide internet to the 33 computers that were donated by government and were not being used. Zenzeleni found this as one of the revenue streams for the community because local schools are struggling to get internet connection. The revenue that will come from the school will be invested in the community to support other endeavours towards community development.

Finally, as a project, Makhosi make some income which is ploughed back into its maintenance as well as the development of the community as stated above. In the words of the the the chairman, 'The revenue we generate from these services, .. we save it and put it aside so that we can be able to create a better future for the youth in this community, including sending to university those who passed grade 12 to ensure their prosperity (Mazantsana, nd).' The vision to help the local primary school graduate to acquire higher education is a key step towards human development as discussed below.

Thapa and Saebo (2014) used CA for developing a framework for assessing ICT4D projects on the parameters that include the objectives of the project, the capabilities provided by the project to the community and the conversion factors that impede the achievement of the functionings. We adopt Thapa and Saebo's (2014) framework for accessing the objective of the Makhosi project, the capabilities provided to the community and the conversion factors.

The aim of Makhosi project is to facilitate affordable ICT access to the local community. According to the chairman of the project who happens to be an inhabitant of the Makhosi, the primary aim was met. They managed to provide free calling within their community, to provide Internet and mobile phone charging facilities for local people. In addition to this, they went on to extend their network to like with other phone networks and thereby becoming the first South African community network to become a TELCO. Since we have already discussed the capabilities in the previous section, we will discuss the conversion factors in the following section.

How the Project Enhanced the Capabilities of the Community

Thapa and Saebo's (2014) framework also includes the assessment of the capabilities provided by the project to the community. Through this lens, we found that the Makhosi project has enhanced the capacity for growth and opportunity for further human development. We have discussed above how it enabled school leavers to find opportunities for further education. This suggests that enhanced communication has also opened doors for other knowledge based opportunities. In a subsistence farming community like Makhosi, there is a need for market information for members of the community to sell their surplus produce. ICTs also present an opportunity for learning new ways of farming. The opportunities may not be exploited, but the freedom to exploit them when necessary has been enhanced.

In the previous section, we discussed Makhosi's emerging partnerships with local schools in the provision of internet. This is going to enhance the schools' capacity to educate thereby solving a key problem that the area faces. The fact only 13% of the community had passed matriculation may suggest that the teaching tools were in adequate. The introduction of schools to internet is a window to other opportunities for human development.

A project champion highlights some opportunities for partnerships as follows; 'there's potential for partnerships with other institutions this emanates from its current infrastructure, network asymmetry, revenue spent on communication (Moreno-Rey, 2017).' Instead of competing with large MNOs that are meant for profit, they see an opportunity for partnership. He added, 'Community networks like Mankhosi ltd presents various opportunities for partnerships with other interested players. This includes R120K revenue that is being spent in airtime every month in communities like Makhosi 'This will improve their capacity to enhance human development (Rey-Moreno, 2017).

Over 90% of the inhabitants use the same MNO (MTN) this presents an opportunity for the dominant MNO to offer loyalty bonuses and cement this customer base. Furthermore, there are some underutilised resources in these areas that include (spectrum, fibre, towers) that could be used for reducing the cost of communications to levels that are below 1/2 for voice, below 1/10 for data (Rey-Moreno, nd).

Conversion Factors

Sen (1999) presents three groups of conversion factors which affect a person's ability to turn opportunities/means into desired outcomes/ ends. These can be categorised as, personal, social, and environmental. Since we are assessing a community project from a collective instead of an individual point of view, we will dwell on social imperatives which affect the entire community. We must, however, acknowledge that while low education can be viewed as a personal attribute, it is also a social impediment that affects most people in the Makhosi community. Only 13% of the community had reached matriculation. This has a negative on human development disused below.

A key challenge that project champions faced in Makhosi was people's perception of what a project should be. According to a project champion, 'most people take time to understand what a project means. In some people's minds, a project is initiated by someone from outside.' This desire to see projects being led by outsiders who must employ them instead of desiring self-determination is a mind-set that the 'Zenzeleni' motif meant to overcome by encouraging a community to do it for themselves. This mentality can be traced back to the impact of Apartheid on the black community. We argue that it may also emanate from the top down approach that NGOs and development agencies have employed. The project provided the opportunity to turn equipment and their own efforts and skills into a capability enhancing endeavour, but they could not easily comprehend it. We expect this phenomenon to be affecting other endeavours to exploit opportunities.

Another critical conversion factor that was identified by the project champions is lack of skill. In the words of one leader, 'The biggest challenge is skills training to cooperative members (Siya, nd).' The fact that the project leaders considered skill to be one of their main challenges confirms Sen's (1999) position that human development is the panacea of development. Sen suggests that capabilities give a person the freedom to make the decisions that help him to achieve the ends that is desirable to them. Skill including the capacity to harness ICTs for expanding one's capabilities is a central aim of the ICT4D project (Oxby, 2009).

CONCLUSION

The critical lesson that comes out of the Makhosi Zenzeleni case study is that community networks are an appropriate way of addressing the affordability of ICT access in developing countries. This case study has shown how affordable access can assist the harnessing of ICT for poverty reduction and development. It has also shown that local communities can improve their livelihoods through affordable communication and raise revenue by managing their own community network. The cost of ICT access was taking 22% of local people's incomes but it has now been reduced to 50% of the cost of external calls and 0% of local calls. Furthermore, reduced costs have improved the scope for effectiveness of business communication like negotiating and bargaining since there's less need to worry about costs. The oral culture of Sub Saharan Africa's people gets affected when access cost compels them to talk briefly. This exacerbates the challenge of using ICT poverty reduction and development. Makhosi case study therefore exemplifies how to harness community networks for tackling the crippling effect of affordability on ICT4D interventions.

Another key lesson that must be learned from Makhosi community network is that The use of community networks for supporting the use of ICTs for enabling poverty reduction and development should happen when technical imperatives coincide with social imperatives (Avgerou, 2001; Hayes and Westrup, 2012). This compels us to transcend beyond bytes to heart beats. The networking of electronic gadgets must not be an end in itself. A socio-technical approach that puts people ahead of technologies will guide us to build social networks parallel to mesh networks. We must think of how to move from physical /technical networks to social networks that aim to fight poverty together for the common good. We must appreciate that most of the communication that takes place on the network will be social interaction. This social interaction must not be mistaken for a misapplication of technologies that meant for development but rather as a cementing of the networks that enable collaboration to happen on the livelihoods front. In Sen's (1999) view of development, the very existence of the opportunity freedom to use the ICTs for the processes they value is what amounts to development. Whenever the community identifies what they endeavour to achieve we should be able to enumerate the functionings that they achieved.

We must also be mindful of the conversion factors that enable or impede the conversion of opportunities to functionings. The Makhosi project saw education and skills training as key impediments, and they introduced training programs for reducing them.

The characterisation of community networks as a technical phenomenon that addresses a social phenomenon like poverty reduction and development is problematic. This is because separating the social and the technical imperatives would result in unintended failure. We posit that it is critical to think of this endeavour as a socio-technical endeavour from the onset. The main stream idea of having technicons doing their job independent of development informatics actors is ill advised. This is because the failure of ICT4D interventions which has been reported to be over 85% (Heeks, 2003; Dada, 2006) has mainly been due to the gap between design and reality.

Policy Implication

Due to the forgoing discussion of the Makhosi case study, it is clear that the use of community networks for affordable access requires the support to policy makers. There is need to create legislative instruments that allow local leaders and development agencies to introduce community networks in areas that established mobile networks are not interested in due to a low return on investment. Such legislature must enable the community networks to mirror the activities of MNOs. They must enforce scalability and interoperability because as is evident from Makhosi, as soon as local connectivity is established interoperability will be required for access to external markets and other frontiers of ICT4D through access to wider networks. Policy makers, however, need to facilitate areas of collaboration and fair completion between the strong MNOs and the emerging community networks.

Summary

This chapter has discussed the role of community networks in fostering affordable ICTs for poverty reduction and development. It has used the Makhosi case study to demonstrate that community networks can go beyond the use of ICT for development to generating income from the provision of communication services. Using Sen 's capability approach we have presented community networks as both instrumental and constitutive freedoms.

ACKNOWLEDGMENT

The authors wish to acknowledge the assistance rendered by Carlos Rey-Moreno and Bill Tucker of the University of Western Cape by providing the information about the Mankosi project. We also wish thank Masbulele Jay Siya and Lwando Mdleleni who provided background information as well as critical information on the impact of the project to Mankosi community.

REFERENCES

Alkire, S., & Deneulin, S. (2008). Introducing the Human Development and Capability Approach. In S. Deneulin (Eds.), *Development and Freedom: An Introduction to the Human Development and Capability Approach, Earthscan*. Retrieved from www. ophi.org.uk

Ardichvili, A., Maurer, M., Li, W., Wentling, T., & Stuedemann, R. (2006). Cultural influences on knowledge sharing through online communities of practice. *Journal of Knowledge Management, 10*(1), 94–107. doi:10.1108/13673270610650139

Attwood, H., & Braathen, E. (2010). *Telecentres and poor communities in South Africa: What have we learnt?* Paper presented at the panel "Comparative Experiences of Chronic Poverty and access to Information and Communication Technologies (ICT)", Manchester, UK.

Avgerou, C. (2001). The Significance of Context in Information Systems and Organisational Change. *Information Systems Journal, 11*(1), 43–63. doi:10.1046/j.1365-2575.2001.00095.x

Avgerou, C. (2008). Information systems in developing countries: A critical research review. *Journal of Information Technology, 23*(3), 133–146. doi:10.1057/palgrave.jit.2000136

Avgerou, C. (2010). Discourses on ICT and development. *Information Technologies and International, 6*(3), 1-18.

Barja, G., & Gigler, B.-S. (n.d.). *The Concept of Information Poverty and How to Measure it in the Latin American Context*. Retrieved from: http://citeseerx.ist.psu.edu/viewdoc/download?doi=10.1.1.571.5933&rep=rep1&type=pdf

Baron, L. F., & Gomez, R. (2013). Relationships and Connectedness: Weak Ties that Help Social Inclusion Through Public Access Computing. *Information Technology for Development, 19*(4), 271–294. doi:10.1080/02681102.2012.755896

Barzilai-Nahon, K. (2006). Gaps and bits: Conceptualizing measurements for digital. *The Information Society*, *22*(5), 269–278. doi:10.1080/01972240600903953

Bhagat, R., Kedia, B., Harveston, P., & Triandis, H. (2002). Cultural variations in the cross-border transfer of organizational knowledge: An integrative framework. *Academy of Management Review*, *2*, 204–221.

Bornman, E. (2016). Information society and digital divide in South Africa: Results of longitudinal surveys. *Information Communication and Society*, *19*(2), 2016. do i:10.1080/1369118X.2015.1065285

Britz, J. J. (2007). *A critical analysis of information poverty from a social justice perspective* (Unpublished D.Phil thesis). University of Pretoria.

Chimuka, T. (2001). Ethics Among the Shona. *Zambezia, 28*(1).

Crespo, R. (2008). *On Sen and Aristotle*. Working paper series IAE Business School – Austral University CONICET. Retrieved www.iae.edu.ar/pi/.../Working%20Papers/DTIAE%2003_2008.pdf

De Herdr, T., & Deneulin, S. (Eds.). (2007). Special Issue: Freedoms as Relational Experiences. *Journal of Human Development*, *8*, 2.

Devereux, S. (2001). Sen's entitlement approach: Critiques and counter critiques. *The Journal of Development Studies*, *29*, 245–263.

Dusek, V. (2007). *Philosophy of Technology: An introduction*. Oxford, UK: Blackwell.

Gillwald, A. (2017). *Beyond access: addressing digital inequality in Africa*. Centre for International Governance Innovation and Chatham House. Retrieved from: https://www.cigionline.org/sites/default/files/documents/GCIG%20no.48_0.pdf

Gillwald, A., Chair, C., Futter, A., Koranteng, K., Odufuwa, F., & Wa lubengo, J. (2016). *Much ado about nothing? Zero-rating in the African context*. Retrieved from: https://www.researchictafrica.net/publications/Other_publications/2016_RIA_Zero-Rating_Policy_Paper_-_Much_ado_about_nothing.pdf

Gurumurthy, A., & Chami, N. (2016). Internet governance as 'ideology in practice' – India's'Free Basics' controversy. *Internet Policy Review*, *5*(3). doi:10.14763/2016.3.431

Habermas, J. (1984). The Theory of Communicative Action.: Vol. 1. *Reason and Rationalization of Society*. Boston, MA: Beacon Press.

Hayes, N., & Westrup, C. (2012). Context and the processes of ICT for development. *Information and Organization*, *22*(1), 23–36. doi:10.1016/j.infoandorg.2011.10.001

Ishmael, J., Bury, S., Pezaros, D., & Race, N. (2008). Deploying Rural Community Wireless Mesh Networks. *IEEE Internet Computing, 12*(4), 22–29. doi:10.1109/MIC.2008.76

ITU. (2016). *Key ICT indicators for developed and developing countries and the world (totals and penetration rates).* Retrieved From: http://www.itu.int/en/ITU-D/Statistics/Pages/stat/default.aspx

Jasek-Rysdal, K. (2001). Applying Sen's capability framework to neighborhoods: Using local asset maps to deepen our understanding of well being. *Review of Social Economy, 59*(3), 313–329. doi:10.1080/00346760110053923

Johnson. (n.d.). *Evaluation of a single radio rural mesh network in South Africa.* Retrieved from: http://www.fmfi.org.za/wiki/images/3/3e/Peebles_mesh_ictd_india.pdf

Jones, M., & Alony, I. (2007). The cultural impact of information systems –through the eyes of hofstede – A critical journey. *Issues in Informing Science and Information Technology, 4,* 407-419. Retrieved January 14 2012 from http://proceedings.informingscience. org/InSITE2007/IISITv4p407-419Jone365.pdf

Lerner, D. (1958). *The Passing of Traditional Society: Modernizing the Middle East.* New York: Free Press.

Matunhu, J. (2011). A critique of modernization and dependency theories in Africa: Critical assessment. *African Journal of History and Culture, 3*(5), 65–72.

Mazantsana, S. (n.d.). *Zenzileni networks Makhosi Ltd, Youtube video.* Retrieved from: https://www.youtube.com/watch?v=YxTPSWMX26M

McNamara, K. S. (2003). *Information and Communication Technologies, Poverty and Development: Learning from Experience Information for Development Program.* A Background Paper for the infoDev Annual Symposium, Geneva, Switzerland. Retrieved from www.infodev.org

Mishra, S. M., Hwang, J., Filippini, D., Du, T., Moazzami, R., & Subramanian, L. (2005) Economic Analysis of Networking Technologies for Rural Developing Regions. *Workshop on Internet and Network Economics.* doi:10.1007/11600930_19

Myers, M., & And Tan, F. (2002). Beyond Models of National Culture in Information Systems Research. *Journal of Global Information Management, 10*(2), 24–32. doi:10.4018/jgim.2002010103

Ojo, T. (2005). Wiring sub-Saharan Africa for development. *International Journal of Education and Development using Information and Communication Technology, 1*(3), 94-107.

Oxoby, R. (2009). Understanding Social Inclusion, Social Cohesion, and Social Capital. *International Journal of Social Economics*, *36*(12), 1133–1152. doi:10.1108/03068290910996963

Qureshi, S. (2006). Collaboration for knowledge networking in development. *Information Technology for Development*, *12*(2), 87–89. doi:10.1002/itdj.20039

Rey-Moreno, C. (2013). *Alternatives for Affordable Communications in rural South Africa Innovative regulatory responses to increase affordable rural access.* Retrieved from: http://www.r2k.org.za/wp-content/uploads/Policy-brief-Cost-to-Communicate_13092016_FOR-SUBMISSION.pdf

Rey-Moreno, C. (2017). *Report on Understanding Community Networks in Africa.* Keynote Presentation at 2nd Summit on Community Networks in Africa Agenda, 2nd Summit on CN's in Africa, Nairobi, Kenya. Retrieved from: https://www.youtube.com/watch?v=uX4TDHWVClo&feature=youtu.be&list=PLi2ljTGe63GIB_WMlbKsz8Rym95uvqbR_

Rey-Moreno, C., Blignaut, R., Tucker, W.D. &May, J. (2016). An in-depth study of the ICT ecosystem in a South African rural community: Unveiling expenditure and communication patterns. *Information Technology for Development, 22*(S1), 101-120. DOI: 10.1080/02681102.2016.1155145

Rey-Moreno, C., Sabiescu, A. G., Siya, M. J., & Tucker, W. D. (2015). Local Ownership, Exercise of Ownership and Moving from Passive to Active Entitlement: A practice-led inquiry on a rural community network. *The Journal of Community Informatics*, *11*(2).

Rey-Moreno, C., Tucker, W. D., Cull, D., & Blom, R. (2015). Making a community network legal within the South African regulatory framework. *Proceedings of the 7th international conference on information and communication technologies and development*, 57. doi:10.1145/2737856.2737867

Robeynes, I. (2003). The Capability Approach in Practice. *Journal of Political Philosophy*, *14*(3), 351–376. doi:10.1111/j.1467-9760.2006.00263.x

Robeynes, I. (2008). Sen's capability approach and feminist concerns. In F. Comim, M. Qizilbash, & S. Alkire (Eds.), *The Capability Approach: Concepts, Measures and Applications*. Cambridge, UK: Cambridge University Press. doi:10.1017/CBO9780511492587.004

Schrage, M. (1990). *Shared minds: The new technologies of collaboration*. New York: Random House.

Sen, A. K. (1999). *Development as Freedom*. Oxford, UK: Oxford University Press.

Siya, M. R. (n.d.). *Zenzileni networks Makhosi Ltd, Youtube video*. Retrieved from: https://www.youtube.com/watch?v=YxTPSWMX26M

Smith, M., Spence, R., & Rashid, A. T. (2011). Mobile Phones and Expanding Human Capabilities. *Information Technologies and International Development, 7*(3), 77–88.

Stewart, F. (2005). Group Capabilities. *Journal of Human Development, 6*(2), 2. doi:10.1080/14649880500120517

Walsham, G. (2002). Cross-Cultural Software Production and Use: A Structurational Analysis. *Management Information Systems Quarterly, 26*(4), 359–380. doi:10.2307/4132313

Walubengo, J., & Takavarasha, S. Jr. (2017). The Challenges of Using Zero-Rating (Free Basics) for Addressing the Affordability of ICT Access in Developing Countries. *International Journal of ICT Research in Africa and the Middle East, 6*(2), 47–61. doi:10.4018/IJICTRAME.2017070104

World Bank. (2016). *World Development Report 2016: Digital Dividends*. Washington, DC: World Bank. Retrieved from http://documents.worldbank.org/curated/en/896971468194972881/pdf/102725-PUB-Replacement-PUBLIC.pdf

Yu, L. (2010). How poor informationally are the information poor? Evidence from an empirical study of daily and regular information practices of individuals. *Journal of Documentation, 66*(6), 906-933. <ALIGNMENT.qj></ALIGNMENT>10.1108/00220411011087869

Zheng, Y., & Stahl, B. C. (2011). Technology, capabilities and critical perspectives: What can critical theory contribute to Sen's capability approach? *Ethics and Information Technology, 13*(2), 69–80. doi:10.1007/s10676-011-9264-8

ZIMVAC & FEWSNET. (2010). *Zimbabwe Livelihoods Zone Profiles*. Accessed 14 May from: http://pdf.usaid.gov/pdf_docs/PNADG540.pdf

Chapter 2
"Everyone Will Be Connected":
Free Basics in Africa to Support ICT4D

Liezel Cilliers
University of Fort Hare, South Africa

Ambika Samarthya-Howard
Praekelt.org, USA

ABSTRACT

Information and communication for development thinkers has come up with many plausible interventions that promise to improve the lives of underprivileged people in developing countries. The people that these interventions are meant for have not always benefited from these initiatives because they have limited ICT access due to its cost. There is therefore a need to improve universal access by enabling affordable access by the poor. This chapter, therefore, discusses free basics and how they can be used to improve affordable ICT access in order to facilitate ICT4D interventions in African countries. Since the use of free basics is not without controversy, a balanced analysis and an overview of the advantages and disadvantages of this initiative are provided. Social capital is used as the theoretical lens for evaluating the use of free basics for improving ICT access for those who cannot afford it. The chapter makes a case for the viability of using free basics through a discussion of case studies on how free basics have been used to empower underprivileged people, especially girls in Africa.

DOI: 10.4018/978-1-5225-3179-1.ch002

INTRODUCTION

Information and Communication Technologies for Development (ICT) can be used to promote access to, and exchange of information, to enable the population to create and enhance social networks. The population is thus able to use the information and technology in a meaningful way to improve the quality of their lives (Yim, Gomez, & Carter, 2017; NDP 2030).

Globally there is a concern that unless high-speed broadband Internet is made available at competitive prices, the technology will never be inclusive (NDP 2030). The International Telecommunication Union (2014) reported that worldwide there are 4.3 billion people who do not have access to the Internet, and of these people 90% live in developing countries. The majority of the online activity in developing countries have been found to be on social media with some reports suggesting that users do not differentiate between the Internet and social media networks (Gebhart, 2016).

In order to increase access to the Internet, Facebook launched Internet.org in 2013, and re-launched as Internet.org in 2015. It allows users to access and use Facebook and other selected websites for free (Sen et al., 2017). The initiative was launched 'in hopes that one day, everyone will be connected' (Kalyani, 2016). Free access is made possible through a partnership between Facebook and local mobile operators in 60 countries across Asia, Africa, South and Central America (Yim, Gomez, & Carter, 2017; Internet.org, 2015). Free Basics started gathering momentum in the past year with 25 new countries joining the programme since May 2016 (Sen et al, 2017).

However, the Free Basics initiative has not been without controversy. Internet activists have raised concerns about a number of issues including the lack of data privacy when users access Free Basics services as Facebook still controls all the proxies through which the web requests and responses are directed (Sen et al, 2017). The second concern is that net neutrality may be compromised. The principle of net neutrality enables and protects free speech on the Internet. This means that the ISP cannot block or discriminate against any application or content. Similarly, the ISP is not allowed to slow down the competitors' content, provide preference to content companies that can afford to pay for better services or block content that it disagrees with. The open Internet thus guarantees that all users receive the same service at the same speed (Kalyani, 2016). These concerns were serious enough to ban this program in India. So while Mark Zuckerberg, the founder of Facebook, maintains that Free Basics is more than just providing access to the mobile Internet, but can also change and save lives, there is much more that needs to be done to understand how this initiative impact on developing communities (Careerride, 2016). The purpose of this chapter is to investigate if Free Basics should be used to affordable access in order to support ICT4D developments in Africa.

Introduction to Free Basics

There were 124.6 million Facebook users in Africa by the end of 2015. One of the most important drivers fueling this growth is the African reliance on mobile Internet access. By 2016 the penetration rate of mobile broadband subscriptions in Africa was almost 30% (Willems, 2016). However, the cost of mobile phones and data remains an obstacle to increasing the mobile Internet uptake. In Africa, Mobile broadband costs are disproportionally high when compared to the rest of the world (Dutta, Geiger, & Lanvin, 2016).

In order to overcome the cost barrier, zero-rating services has been introduced in developing countries. These services were developed to increase the users' awareness and use of the Internet which will prompt them to buy larger data plans as they move onto paid services (Gerbhart, 2016).

Figure 1 depicts the typical Free Basics architecture which consists of three independent service providers. First the network service provider in a specific country agree to carry data for the Free Basics service at no cost to the user (Sen et al., 2017). On the African continent MTN is the most popular service provider of Free Basics, while in South Africa, Cell C is providing specific free website services to their customers. The free content includes the following:

- **Communication:** Cell C; Facebook; Messenger.
- **Education:** Be Smart; D-Sliders; FunDza; LoveWords; Scholars4Dev; Wattpad; Worldreader.
- **Health:** CHAPS; Facts for life; Health 24; HIV360.
- **Finance:** Moneymatters; Smart Business; Your money.
- **Information:** Bing Search; OLX; WikiHow; Wikipedia.
- **Jobs:** Careers 24; Harambee.
- **News:** BBC News; Gumtree; News24.

Figure 1. Free Basics architecture
Sen et al., 2016.

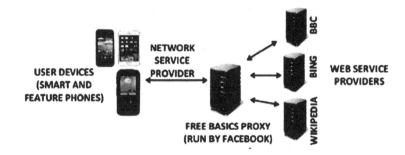

- **Sport:** Supersport.
- **Women:** BabyCenter & Mama; iLearn; Intel ®She Will Connect; Girl Effect.

The second part of the Free Basics architecture is the proxy service provider. Currently all Free Basics traffic is routed through Facebook proxies. The third and final part of the architecture is the web service provider that must re-design their services according to a set of technical requirements (e.g., absence of JavaScript, high resolution images, videos or iFrames) in order to qualify and be accepted onto the Free Basics network (Sen et al., 2017). These restrictions are placed on the content in order to make it accessible on older phones that access the Internet via WAP or similar technologies (Ahmad et al., 2016). In order to assist and help bring social good organisations onto the platform, who may not have the technical expertise or background, Facebook partnered with local South African organisation, Praekelt.org, to incubate 100 NGOs by the end of 2016 to help them transition to the platform. Finally, the user access the Internet via their mobile browser or by installing the Free Basics mobile application (Sen et al., 2017).

HISTORY OF FREE BASICS

The platform helps those who can't afford to pay for data, or who need a little help getting started online. For students who can't afford the internet, Wikipedia is a necessity... (Yim, Gomez, & Carter, 2017, p. 259).

Originally the free Internet service was launched as Internet.org in 2013 by Facebook and other mobile telephony companies such as Samsung, Ericsson and Nokia. The aims were to provide affordable access to selected Internet services to users in developing countries in Africa, South America and Southeast and South Asia (Lele, 2016). The information provided could benefit health care, education, job information and to stay in touch with family and friend (Kalyani, 2016). Initially, Facebook approved free access to 33 websites, but increased this to 80 websites subsequently (Careerride, 2016).

The initiative became known as the 'walled garden' due to Facebooks restrictive guidelines. Facebook was seen as the gatekeeper with too much leverage as they could define what a 'basic' service was (LaFrance, 2016). This was seen as prohibitive for small content providers who were not able to participate in the local content (Yim, Gomez, & Carter, 2017). These issues generate a common concern that providers of ICT may be restricting users' freedom to make their own decisions about information access and usage.

Several web publishers withdrew from the project during this time as there was concern that net neutrality was being compromised (Hempel, 2015). In 2015 Facebook rebranded the initiative to Free Basics. While still in control of the content of Free Basics, Facebook now claimed that the platform was open as anyone could add their website to the Free Basics Platform as long as the website complied to the guidelines for older phones and slower network connections (Internet.org, 2015).

What Is a Zero-Rating?

In order to improve access to users in developing countries, zero-rating was introduced as a new tool in mobile broadband data plans. Users can access specific data and applications free of charge when making use of zero-rated programs. There are 5 different models of zero-rating that can be offered to the user. These are false zero-rating; sponsored data zero-rating, categorical zero-rating, single and multi-site zero rating.

False zero-rating is a simple work-for-content model where end-users earn free data in exchange for watching an advertisement or other content (Shangaza, 2015). This model let users earn free data credits on any content and does not violate net neutrality principles.

Sponsored data zero-rating supplement data plans with some zero-rated content. This model is often used as an incentive for post-paid subscribers that can access free content if they pay their bill etc. However, the model is seen as anti-competitive as sponsored data directly violates net neutrality rules. This is because large Internet Service Providers tend to prioritise their own content or those of their vertically integrated partners.

Categorical zero-rating provides content for entire categories of applications to users e.g. education, social media or health related content. While this model also violates net neutrality rules, it does provide users with a choice over what content they want to access (Keenan-Alspector, 2016).

Single-site or service zero rating offers end users free access to limited content. The most notable single-site zero-rated applications include Wikipedia Zero, Google Free Zone, and Facebook Zero. These sites provide content for free, but vary the amount of free content that is available and in most cases offer a watered down or 'lite' version of the product as can be seen in the table below (Keenan-Alspector, 2016). Single-site zero-rating only offers limited to users' content and therefore violates net-neutrality principles.

Compound zero-rated programs are similar to the single-site service model, but offers a bundle of free content to the user instead of one site. The content is still restricted and can be considered the 'lite' version of the paid content. Free Basics is the best example of this model. There is a debate whether this model violates net

Table 1. Zero-rated single sites

Zero-Rated Single Sites	
Provider	**Free Content**
Wikipedia Zero (Wikimedia Foundation, 2016)	Full free access all the free knowledge on Wikipedia.
Google Free Zone (Mybroadband, 2013)	Free Access to limited suite of Google products including: Google Plus, Gmail, and Google Search. (discontinued)
Facebook Zero (Wikipedia, 2016)	Provides text-only Facebook content, all other media content is subject to data usage.

Keenan-Alspector, 2016.

neutrality: proponents of the model argue that it 'connects the unconnected', while the critics believe that all content is not free and open but subject to paid prioritisation and blocking (Keenan-Alspector, 2016).

Free Basics were launched in Zambia in 2014. It was the first African country where users could make use of the service. Research conducted by Willems (2016) suggest that subsequent to the launch, Free Basics has not become very popular in the country. Users indicated that the app had a stigmatising effect which indicated that 'you were broke' if you had to make use of the platform. Others complained about the usability of the app which does not allow users to purchase data while the restriction on the use of pictures limit the interaction between users. This research is supported by the Alliance of Affordable Internet that published a report which found that less than four percent of respondents in eight countries in Africa, Asian and Latin America were using zero rated services e.g. Free Basic (Willems, 2016).

However, most research that has been conducted in developing countries on zero-rating has focused on net neutrality and not the end user of the technology. After India banned Free Basics, it became the focal point of this research as the center of the net neutrality debate (Gerbhart, 2016). In Africa, the Free Basics debate is considered to be far less controversial, however, in countries that are politically unstable, the government has been known to order mobile operators to block access to social media during periods of elections or protests citing concerns over national security. These countries include Burundi, Chad, Congo, Uganda and Zimbabwe (Willems, 2016).

Free Basics for Social Good

For many organisations working particularly with vulnerable adolescents who may not own their phones, but potentially have access to them, Free Basics allows the organisation to augment impact and outreach. Praekelt.org is an international nonprofit, with headquarters in South Africa, that uses mobile technology to improve the health and wellbeing of people and communities. The *Praekelt.org Incubator for Free Basics is* a tool to support organisations and developers building for the Free Basics Platform. Announced at AfricaCom in November 2015, the partnership between Praekelt.org and Facebook supports developers and social change organisations in their efforts to build accessible online services designed mostly by and for people living in the developing world. The *Praekelt.org Incubator for Free Basics* has received thousands of applications since the Programme was announced, and 100 partners were selected by an external independent international selection panel following a rigorous evaluation process.

The organisations that were accepted cover sectors including health, economic empowerment, youth, gender equity, youth, agriculture, citizen engagement, and education, and are based in different regions of Africa and Asia. Many of these organizations do not have the technical background to take advantage of the Free Basics program. Through Praekelt.org's training, technical tools and support, many smaller as well as local organizations have successfully become part of the Free Basics Platform.

A few of the partners now live on Free Basics through the help of the Incubator include:

- **She Inspires Her:** An organization aimed to inspire aspiring entrepreneurs and promote small but growing women-owned businesses on the African continent.
- **HelpMeSee:** Which eradicates preventable blindness caused by cataracts
- **SEED Madagascar:** Which teaches people in Madagascar better English though their SEED English mobi-site.
- **Edukayson:** A site in the Philippines working towards zero unemployment through helping young people plan their education for careers.
- **Da Subject Matter:** Part of Planned Parenthood and based in Nigeria.
- **African Trust Academy:** Inspires and educates people by providing financial education and fin-ed based credit scoring to increase financial inclusion.
- **WeFarm:** Aims to help farmers to improve their lives with increased access to information from animal husbandry and planting to fertilisation and harvesting crops.
- **doctHERs:** Connects women by aiming to influence health-seeking behaviour and improving their health and ultimately transforming lives.
- **Vahan.co:** Makes education more accessible and effective for low-income populations for the purpose of enhancing their employability.
- **We Dream Africa:** Delivers engaging African-themed entertaining ebooks.

Applicants appreciated and saw value in the training and tool. "Being selected to participate in the Praekelt Incubator has been an incredible opportunity. We're a small social enterprise and have bootstrapped all our initiatives to date so it's been a huge boost to access the platform and receive highly responsive technical support to enable us to get our content into the hands of those who needs it most - entrepreneurial women with little to no internet access who need support in starting and growing businesses." shared Lisa O'Donoghue-Lindy, Founder of She Inspires Her.

Praekelt Group Founder and CEO, Gustav Praekelt said:

Praekelt believes that access to essential information and basic services is a human right. When people have access to the tools and knowledge that the internet and other digital communication technologies provide, they have access to opportunities that will make their lives better. (Praekelt Foundation Blog, 2015).

One example of a platform that is thriving on the platform is Educate a Girl (EAG), a global non-profit charity with a mission to empower a million uneducated women to have a transformational impact on the world. Tara Uzra Dawood, who studied at Cornell, Oxford and Harvard Law School, is the Founder.

EAG teaches skills and has modules in entrepreneurship, leadership, coding, negotiations, communications, grooming, self-confidence, public speaking, etc. They have completed live trainings of 250 girls in Lagos (Nigeria) and Karachi (Pakistan) and are currently educating 1000 girls in Lahore and fundraising for Casablanca (Morocco).

Launched in September 2013, it was uploaded onto Free Basics in May 2017 through the Praekelt.org Incubator for Free Basics. By July 2017, they already had 900 active Free Basics EAG users who were learning from the modules on Free Basics and every day these numbers are increasing. To circumvent law and order situations to enter Turkey and Qatar, they partnered with Facebook for an online version with 1000 online modules created by Harvard Business School alumni, translated by Google translator, with cultural sensitivity checks by 18 year old girls in different cities. Educate a Girl has been recognized by the World Bank as top 2% of women-led initiatives in the MENA region.

In this way the platform allows smaller organisations, non-profits, and other groups to be able to take advantage of a zero rated platform to communicate their message. Particularly for those with limited access to mobile phones and internet, Free Basics can help reach many with important information and services.

Issues, Controversies, Problems

The formal definition of network neutrality reads as follow: "has been used to describe a data network that assigns all transmissions equal priority as they are passed along the network" (OECD, 2006, p. 3).

In the ICT4D context, small business owners, start-ups and entrepreneurs rely on the open Internet to launch their businesses, advertise and distribute products to customers. In many African countries these businesses rely on social media to create a market, and do not have formal websites which are costly to develop and maintain. Net neutrality is used to lower the barriers of entries for these businesses, enabling them to compete with more established companies and create employment in the economy (Kalyani, 2016; Knieps & Zenhäusern, 2007).

The advantages of net neutrality include that it creates an equal playing field where the ISP cannot block access, change services or alter the flow of data to become more competitive. There are controls in place to prevent illegal activities as each ISP is treated as a regulated common carrier.

Innovation is protected as all businesses whether they are big companies or small business owners start on the same footing when the Internet remains neutral. ISP providers are considered to be utility providers that can improve the quality of life as long as the user is able to pay for the service. However, it doesn't matter how much money the user has or what kind of business they run, everyone receives the same service. Lack of censorship of blogs, services and businesses is available to protect freedom of expression as long as the website operates legally. Illegal content is easily identified and can be dealt with by the relevant authorities (Kalyani, 2016).

As with any technology, there are disadvantages that must be considered. Streaming services, such as real-time video calls and Netflix, allows for an enormous amount of data to be consumed without any compensation to the ISP. If users that consume large amounts of bandwidth were asked to pay more for their high usage, the added income can be used by the ISP to upgrade their existing infrastructure. Currently net neutrality prevents charging higher tariffs to high bandwidth user. This means that the opportunity to raise infrastructure investment capital from this revenue is missed. In developing countries that need to extend network coverage it will be a long time before fiber networks may reach under services rural communities.

On the other hand, consumer choice will be limited if network neutrality in violated. An ISP will be able to assign higher speeds to the network or services it owns or those that can pay for this privilege. The user will have to choose a ISP provider based on the services and content they want to access. This will affect the open internet as we currently know it and that is an issue of concern to proponents of net neutrality.

At the moment, the content that is offensive is readily available because of net neutrality. While there are tools available to help the user block this content, ISP's would be able to do this more effectively but they are forbidden by network neutrality constraints.

The digital divide would most likely become worse in developing countries if network neutrality did not exist. ISPs would be able to charge whatever they wanted and there would be no incentive to provide free Internet access to developing communities. It is clear from the discussion that developing countries have the most to lose if network neutrality is not protected. Currently there is no law in place to govern network neutrality, although researchers have argued that more regulation to govern network neutrality will slow down the access to the Internet as more hurdles are put in place for new services to be put in place (Lele, 2016; Gerbhart, 2016).

Free Basics in Low- and Middle-Income Countries

Part of the business strategy of Facebook in recent years has been to expand its reach on the African continent. In August 2016, the founder of Facebook, Mark Zuckerberg visited Nigeria, his first visit to an African country. Two of the strategies that the company has since rolled out include providing Internet access to African users through the solar powered Aquila drone and Facebook's Free Basics app that allows African users in 21 countries to access a text based version of Facebook free of charge (Willems, 2016). Figure 2 below provide some of the statistics that the Free Basics initiative has used to justify the services it provides to African users under the headings of affordability, accessibility, inclusion, readiness and relevance.

Proponents of Free Basics often put forth the 'something is better than nothing' argument to justify their position. In their view, zero-rated services are better than no connectivity at all (Carew, 2015). It is difficult to disagree with this argument in developing communities that would otherwise have no access. The main advantages of Free Basics include that social media and the Internet can improve the lives of people living in developing communities. There are two ways that this advantage can be brought about, first the ability of the Internet to scale to connect more people is endless while the power of connecting people to take action to improve the quality of their lives are enhanced. In developing countries that are often found to have civil unrest or natural disasters, social media platforms provide connectivity to access information, find survivors and raise money for aid (Careerride, 2016). Initiatives such as Free Basics have repeatedly stated that affordable Internet connectivity is basic human right and therefore the zero-rated services are able to expand coverage in developing communities rather than profit from it. The argument extends further that this basic right is more important than network neutrality (Careerride, 2016; Gerbhart, 2016).

The proponents of free basics mention the provision of basic needs and how the beneficiaries value. For instance, the following quote from Yim, Gomez, & Carter (2017).

Free Basics provides free access to essential internet services like communication, education, healthcare, employment, farming and more. Go meet the people who don't have internet, and think about how [we can] bring internet access to those people... (Yim, Gomez, & Carter, 2017, p. 2595).

There is a lack of 'on the ground' research that investigates usage patterns and aims to support or refute this notion (Yim, Gomez, & Carter, 2017). One way to understand the positive impact of Free Basics can be through user comments and organisational case studies.

Some of the users on the platform enjoyed the accessibility of Free Basics as one of them put it:

I love EAG modules because these are always available for me, I don't have to do anything." Since Free Basics is offered in multiple languages, EAG could provide modules in Russian, English, Urdu and Turkish: "Learning has never been this easy. EAG modules are available in different languages so interested to read them more. For girls in under resourced communities who want to learn, Free Basics has made it easier for them. (correspondence with Mehwish Ayyub, Dawood Global Foundation)

Critics of Free Basics state that while it is nice to provide free access to limited content, this is only addressing a symptom of the problem. Full Internet access must be provided at prices people in developing communities can afford. Similarly, they often express that lack of internet connection is not a basic human right, but a first world problem. There are more basic problems, such as child survival and nutrition, access to clean drinking water and electricity, in developing countries that need to be addressed first (Careerride, 2016; Yim, Gomez, & Carter, 2017).

The marketing of Free Basics has promoted the idea that the service is a gift for the poor in developing countries. Often, the users in African countries associate Free Basics and Wikipedia Zero as telecommunication promotions and not with the Internet. The reason for this is that the marketing is primarily driven by these companies to increase their market share in a particular country (Gerbhart, 2016). This is supported by research down by Kalyani (2016) that found that the only source of info on Free Basics is Facebook. The company has previously been criticized that they used misleading marketing strategies in Brazil and India when they advertise 'free internet' but not inform the user that Free Basics is not the full Internet service.

The last argument against Free Basics that is worth mentioning is the privacy concerns of users. Information has become a commodity in the 21st century, and often companies will collect information about the people visiting their websites or making use of their services. Both Facebook and Google's model is based on monetising this personal data. Online Behavioral Advertisement (OBA) is defined as 'the tracking of consumers' online activities in order to deliver tailored advertising.' FTC (2009, p. 1). There are several arguments for and against OBA as is the case with net neutrality. While OBA provides businesses with the opportunity to tailor their marketing to specific customers to improve service delivery, there is a concern that the surveillance that is necessary of the online behavior of internet users may contain sensitive personal information. The profiling of health records, finances and children's details has been criticized because sensitive data may end up in wrong hand s or being used for purposes that were not anticipated (FTC, 2009). Currently there is very little regulation in this area, which has left the customer unprotected. This is further disconcerting as Facebook controls all the proxies through which the web requests and responses of Free Basics are directed (Careerride, 2016; Yim, Gomez, & Carter, 2017). Facebook has previously admitted to manipulating the newsfeed of thousands of users with the goal to see if it affected the tone of the users' comments on the platform. The fear is then if Facebook can find a way to manipulate news feeds to shape public opinion, the company will be in a unique position of power (Yim, Gomez, & Carter, 2017).

Although Free Basics do provide access to information in developing communities, it represents only a version of Facebook and those websites and services willing to collaborate with the proprietary platform. The argument that the cost of the full Internet must be affordable to the member of the community if internet penetration is to improve still hold. This solution will provide Internet access to more people and will be more beneficial than the limited platform that Free Basics provide (Careerride, 2016). Simultaneously, telecom operators carry the cost of the data that is used within the Free Basics platform. These costs are ultimately passed onto the user which reduces the incentive for the telecom operators to bring down the cost of paid Internet access (Kalyani, 2016). Kalyani (2016) reported that users often prefer to use the full Internet for shorter periods, rather than the Free Basics platform.

SOLUTIONS AND RECOMMENDATIONS

In this section the chapter discusses the different theoretical lenses that are used including social capital and ICT4D developments of Free Basics specifically in Africa.

Figure 2. Statistics about Free Basics
Yim, Gomez, & Carter, 2017.

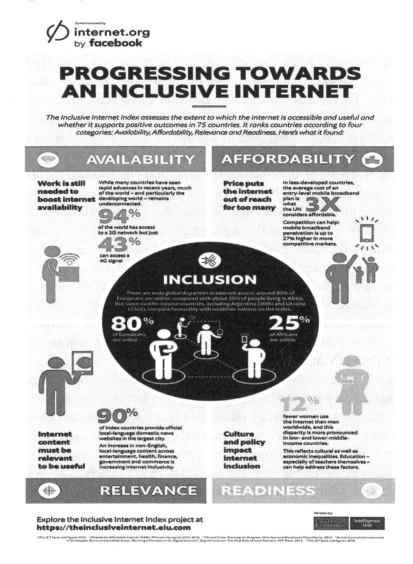

Donner and Toyama (2009) define ICT4D as the "name given to a range of activities which considers how electronic technologies can be used toward socio-economic development of developing communities" (p. 1).

ICT4D promote social capital through the development of projects using IT for both the individual and community. The social benefit of the Internet is often cited as the ability to keep in contact and exchange information with other users which is the purpose of social media sites such as Facebook and Wikipedia. The ultimate goal of Free Basics, current flagship project of zero-rated services, places it in the ICT4D arena (Yim, Gomez, & Carter, 2017). In this section, the analytical lenses of IT identify and social capital will be used to analyse the implications of Free Basic programs on ICT4D.

Social capital…is not a single entity but a variety of different entities, with two elements in common: they all consist of some aspect of social structures, and they facilitate certain actions of actors—whether persons or corporate actors—within the structure. Like other forms of capital, social capital is productive, making possible the achievement of certain ends that in its absence would not be possible (Coleman, 1988, p. 98).

The social network must have value if it is to impact on community development.

Putnam (2000) describes two different types of social capital: bridging and bonding. Bridging is defined as an inclusive, outward looking network which involves social connections among people from diverse backgrounds. The purpose of social capital is to improve and support broader identities and reciprocity such as religious organisations and youth service groups (Putnam, 2000). Bonding social capital is defined as exclusive, inward looking network involving people from similar backgrounds which reinforces the 'narrower self' and can be used for 'mobilizing solidarity'. This type of social capital also provides crucial social and psychological support (Putnam, 2000).

Nearly half of the world's population is under the age of 25. Investments in their health and well-being are crucial so they can make a positive transition into adulthood and fully contribute to the economic and social development of their families, communities and nations. But sexually-transmitted infections place a disproportionately heavy burden on young people who often have no access to comprehensive sex education and health services.

People hardest hit by health issues are also those less frequently reached by personalised dynamic media. Mobile penetration offers a means of communicating with nearly every person in Africa.There are currently a limited number of sources for mobile sexual reproductive health and gender information for youth

Bonding can be particularly useful for adolescent youth, especially in peer support and decision making. Tune Me is a sexual and reproductive health and rights mobile-optimized website aimed at improving the lives of youths in Sub-Saharan Africa by empowering them to make informed decisions around their bodies. Inspired by YoungAfricaLive (YAL), Tune Me is a mobile site designed for low- and high-end devices in environments where high data charges and poor network coverage combine to limit access to online services. YoungAfricaLive benefitted from being on Vodacom's Operator deck, contributing to its success. Zero-rating ensured that users who most needed the YAL service could access it for free and engage regularly.

Through social features and content designed to engage users rather than lecture, Tune Me aims to equip adolescents with the information and motivation they need to make better choices. YAL grew a 'safe sex-savvy' community by actively encouraging user-generated commentary around often sensitive topics. The ability to remain anonymous while at the same time posting very personal problems, questions and confessionals to the greater YAL community, was key in the product's effectiveness for an African market.

When using Tune Me you feel like you're talking to a fellow youth.....The stories there, I would say they sound or seem like they can touch you and might even feel as if that person wrote the story for you." Chiluba, 17, Zambia (Praekelt Foundation and Praekelt PBC, 2015)

Tune Me builds on these principles and serves as a mobile engagement platform that uses engaging content to create awareness of and demand for health services. Core content includes sexual and reproductive health and rights (SRHR) including HIV, family planning/pregnancy and contraception, gender-based violence (GBV), harmful cultural practices such as child marriage amongst important topics. Adapted from a global set of content, the stories are adapted and translated for local audiences to ensure relevance and improve engagement.

For Tune Me, which operates in several countries in Africa, including Zambia, Malawi, Zimbabwe, Lesotho, Namibia, Swaziland and Botswana, having access to Free Basics has helped youth share stories and discuss important sexual health and reproductive rights content. In Zambia, 9% of traffic (based on reports of activities in mid-June) came from Free Basics. While this number may seem small, consider the following user comments and feedbacks:

Like right now I don't have any data, any bundle or airtime and I can still access it. (Female user)

I like TuneMe because I can still use it even when I have no data bundle. (Male user)

You can even update your stories, like the competitions you have for story writing you can write free stories there and post them for free. (Female user)

Ellison et al. (2007) introduced a third type of social capital called maintained social capital, which illustrates "the ability to maintain valuable connections as one progresses through life changes" (p.1146).

The second theory that must be discussed in conjunction with social capital and ICT4D is Information Technology Identity theory (Carter, Grover & Thatcher, 2015). The theory postulates that IT identity starts to form when the user recognises the potential for self-expansion through a specific type of technology. According to the theory, the user may not understand or be aware what the full impact or consequence of the technology will be, but continue to engage with the technology. Carter et al (2012) found that there are 3 types of meanings that can be assigned to the use of mobile phones in young adults' self-identification process. The first is a functional meaning that focuses mainly on the functions of the phone. The second relate to the relational meaning where social ties are created and maintained through the device and lastly, self-identification meaning which focuses on the self where the mobile phone permeates all aspects of the daily life (Yim, Gomez, & Carter, 2017).

While the user is exploring or experimenting with the technology, the use of the technology will move through 3 stages. First there is an increased sense of efficacy on the part of the user which is followed by the technology becoming part of the social world of the user and ultimately the IT identity is formed. This identify allows the user to use the technology to solve daily problems and in the absence of the technology, the user experiences losses of technological capabilities and competencies, as if a part of the self is lost (Yim, Gomez, & Carter, 2017). In terms of the ICT4D goals the technology is used to promote innovative action and create patterns of behaviour amongst empowered individuals in the social group. Social capital is thus created through a bottom-up approach (Yim, Gomez, & Carter, 2017). While Free Basics do contribute to social capital, the degree of individuals' IT identify formation would certainly impact on these projects as the users may have different meanings assigned to the technology. In Africa it has been shown that users assign meaning to Facebook in a relational manner, while self-identification of the technology does not necessarily permeate their daily lives. These meanings will be influenced by the selected number and type of services offered as is the case with Free Basics (Gebhart, 2016, LaFrance, 2016). Technical barriers in African countries that can prevent the use of technology for ICT4D includes expensive connectivity and low bandwidth as discussed in the previous sections and electricity outages or the cost of the mobile phone. Educational barriers, including digital literacy and language literacy were also reported to influence the provision of Free Basics services (Gebhart, 2016).

FUTURE RESEARCH DIRECTIONS

Free Basics have been available in Africa for some time now and have shown to contribute meaningfully to the ICT4D arena. While there are some barriers that still need to be overcome, the potential of Free Basics to contribute to education for vulnerable groups in particular has been written about extensively in the literature. The argument that is often put forward that Free Basics violates net neutrality must be weighed against the access that is provided to educational resources for the Girl child project and SMEs that would otherwise not be possible without it. At the very least, the Free Basics programme provides an interesting insight into the unique problems that Africa faces in regards to Internet connectivity, but more research is needed to understand how the programme is affecting users on the ground.

FUNDING

This research received no specific grant from any funding agency in the public, commercial, or not-for-profit sectors.

REFERENCES

Ahmad, S., Haamid, A. L., Qazi, Z. A., Zhou, Z., Benson, T., & Qazi, A. I. (2016). A view from the other side: understanding mobile phone characteristics in the developing world. *Proceedings of the 16th ACM Internet Measurement Conference (IMC)*. doi:10.1145/2987443.2987470

Careerride. (2016). *Free basics- pros and cons*. Available on http://www.careerride.com/view/free-basics-pros-and-cons-26314.aspx

Carew, D. (2015). *Zero-rating: kick-starting Internet ecosystems in developing countries*. Policy Memo.

Carter, M., Grover, V., & Thatcher, J. B. (2012). Mobile devices and the self: developing the concept of mobile phone identity. In I. Lee (Ed.), *Strategy, adoption, and competitive advantage of mobile services in the global economy* (pp. 150–164). Hershey, PA: IGI Global.

Coleman, J. S. (1988). Social capital in the creation of human capital. *American Journal of Sociology*, *94*, S95–S120. doi:10.1086/228943

Donner, J., & Toyama, K. (2009). Persistent themes in ICT4D research: priorities for inter methodological. In *57th Session of the International Statistical Institute* (pp. 1–8). Durban: International Statistical Institute.

Dutta, S., Geiger, T., & Lanvin, B. (Eds.). (2015). *The global information and technology report 2015: ICTs for inclusive growth. Insight report.* World Economic Forum. Retrieved from: http://www3.weforum.org/docs/WEF_Global_IT_ Report_2015.pdf

Ellison, N. B., Steinfield, C., & Lampe, C. (2007). The benefits of Facebook 'friends:' social capital and college students' use of online social network sites. *Journal of Computer-Mediated Communication, 12*(4), 1143–1168. doi:10.1111/j.1083-6101.2007.00367.x

FTC. (2009). *FTC Staff Report: February 2009 Self-Regulatory principles For online behavioral advertising.* Available at: https://www.ftc.gov/sites/default/files/ documents/reports/federal-trade-commission-staff-report-self-regulatory-principles-online-behavioral-advertising/p085400behavadreport.pdf

Gebhart, G. (2016). Zero-rating in emerging mobile markets: free Basics and Wikipedia Zero in Ghana. *Proceedings of ICTD'16.* doi:10.1145/2909609.2909663

Hempel, J. (2015, September). Facebook renames its controversial Internet.org app. *Wired.* Retrieved from http://www.wired.com

International Telecommunication Union. (2014). *Measuring the information society report.* International Telecommunication Union. Retrieved from: https://www.itu.int/ en/ITUD/Statistics/Documents/publications/mis2014/MIS2014_without_Annex_4. pdf

Internet.org. (2015). *Where we've launched - internet.org.* Available on https://info. internet.org/en/story/where-weve-launched/

Kalyani, P. (2016). Studying the impact and awareness of free basics and net neutrality in reference to Internet usage in contemporary scenario. *Journal of Management Engineering and Information Technology, 3*(1), 1–15.

Keenan-Alspector, J. (2016). *What is free about Free Basics?* Boulder, CO: University of Colorado.

Knieps, G. & Zenhäusern, P. (2007). The fallacies of network neutrality regulation. *Diskussionsbeiträge // Institut für Verkehrswissenschaft und Regionalpolitik,* 115.

LaFrance, A. (2016, February 11). Facebook and the new colonialism. *Atlantic.* Retrieved from http://www.theatlantic.com/technology/archive/2016/02/facebook-and-the-new-colonialism/462393/

Lele, A. (2016). *Facebook's Free Basics: A digital apartheid – Analysis*. Available at http://www.eurasiareview.com/08012016-facebooks-free-basics-a-digital-apartheid-analysis/

NDP 2030. (n.d.). *Our future – make it work, National Development Plan 2030*. Pretoria: The Presidency.

OECD. (2006). Internet neutrality: a policy overview. OECD Working Party on Telecommunication and Information Services Policies, OECD Report, DSTI/ICCP/TISP(2006)4/FINAL.

Praekelt Foundation and Praekelt PBC. (2015). *Tune Me – project showcase*. Retrieved from https://www.praekelt.org/projects/

Praekeltfoundationblog. (2015, November 16). *Praekelt Foundation Incubator for Free Basics*. Retrieved October 19, 2017, from http://blog.praekeltfoundation.org/post/133335778822/praekelt-foundation-incubator-for-free-basics

Progressive Policy Institute. (2015). Retrieved from: http://www.progressivepolicy.org/wpcontent/uploads/2015/03/2015.03-Carew_Zero-Rating_Kick- Starting-Internet-Ecosystems-in-Developing-Countries.pdf

Putnam, P. D. (2000). *Bowling alone:tThe collapse and revival of American community*. New York: Simon and Schuster. doi:10.1145/358916.361990

Sen, R., Ahmad, S., Phokeer, A., Farooq, Z.A., Qazi, I.A., Choffness, D., & Gummadi, K.P. (2017). *Inside the walled garden: deconstructing Facebook's Free Basics program*. Academic Press.

Sen, R., Pirzada, H. A., Farooq, A., Sengupta, S., Choffness, D., & Gummade, K. P. (2016). On the free bridge across the digital divide: assessing the quality of Facebook's Free Basics Service. *Proceedings of the IMC*. doi:10.1145/2987443.2987485

Shangaza. (2015). *Free Data Bundles with Safaricom Airtel & Mt*. Retrieved from: http://shangaza.net/blogs/1/73/free-data-bundles-with-safaricom-airtel-mtn

Willems, W. (2016). *Beyond Free Basics: Facebook, data bundles and Zambia's social media internet*. African Elections, Featured, International Affairs, Media, September 2017.

Yin, M., Gomez, R., & Carter, M. (2017). Facebook's 'free basics' and implications for development: IT dentify and social capital. *Proceedings of the 50th Hawaii International Conference on System Sciences*.

Chapter 3
Exploring the Possibility of Using TV White Spaces in Africa

Benny Nyambo
University of Zimbabwe, Zimbabwe

Benard Mapako
University of Zimbabwe, Zimbabwe

Michael Munyaradzi
University of Zimbabwe, Zimbabwe

ABSTRACT

The people living in remote parts of the underdeveloped world usually do not have access to affordable internet, either because it is too expensive to lay fibre to these areas or mobile data is just too expensive to use every day. There has always been a need to find a way to bring fast, cheap, and reliable internet access to these people. This is where the TV white spaces (TVWS) or unused TV band spectrum comes in. TVWS refers to the gaps found between TV channels. It can be used to provide cheaper and reliable broadband to remote areas. Wi-Fi typically covers short distances and has trouble passing through obstacles. TVWS, on the other hand, can travel long distances and can penetrate obstacles. This makes TVWS suitable for long distance internet provision in remote areas. This chapter explores the possibilities and advantages of delivering broadband to remote areas of underdeveloped nations using TVWS with the intention of poverty reduction. The concept of TV channels digitalization also frees the whole analogue TV spectrum and allows it to be used in TVWS technology.

DOI: 10.4018/978-1-5225-3179-1.ch003

INTRODUCTION

Full participation in today's society is heavily reliant on access to modern information and communication technologies (ICTs). Thus, a well-developed, well-maintained and affordable information infrastructure that allows access to, and manipulation of the dematerialised economy is the backbone of a knowledge society. The eradication of poverty and other development challenges will require a transformation of all our basic institutions and this can be expedited with the use of ICT. It is unfortunate that over 3.9 billion people around the world do not have access to fixed regular Internet (Darkwa, 2016). However finding lasting solutions for this problem is difficult because of the cost associated with providing Internet to remote, rural and sparsely populated areas.

One of the most feasible technology for such areas would be wireless communication networks. In wireless communication networks, the radio frequency (RF) spectrum is a very expensive resource that is mostly regulated with the main aim of reducing interference between devices. Various wireless technologies that can be used include wireless cellular networks, Wi-Fi, microwave, WiMax and TV White Spaces (TVWS). Whilst the other technologies have been found feasible, they have high costs associated with their installation and operation. This would make them not very applicable to rural Africa were capital is very limited. TV White spaces is being considered widely as a possible solution to supplying affordable and reliable Internet access to rural, remote African locations.

TVWS refers to the unused frequencies that have been left lying idle after the migration of TV broadcast from analogue to digital. Previously, these were kept clear to avoid interference with neighbouring channels. TV networks would place these spaces of unused spectrum in between their channels in order to protect broadcasts from interference. These low-signal frequencies, can penetrate walls and can travel long distances without the need for amplifying the signal. These features make TVWS spaces a very suitable candidate to end the connectivity problem in Africa. This is because they enable TVWS based connectivity to reach wide areas and larger populations than GSM and LTE mobile base stations that are currently being used by Mobile Network Operators (MNOs).

Bridging the Digital Divide in Africa

In every country, there exist two classes of people in terms of access to information and communication technologies. The first group are those people who have access to the best information and communication technology as well as relevant training to use the technology. The other group consists of those people who, for one reason or the other, have limited access to information and communication technology or even relevant training in these technologies. The differences between the people in these two groups of people is called the digital divide (Marlien Herselman, 2002). Former UN Secretary-General Kofi Annan once pointed out that access to communication technologies is important just like other fundamental human rights and that the digital divide is a pressing humanitarian issue: "Today, being cut off from basic telecommunications services is a hardship almost as acute as these other deprivations, and may indeed reduce the chances of finding remedies to them" (Yu, 2002).

The Internet has the potential to positively impact and transform people's lives and bring benefits in a great number of areas, including health, education, financial services, transport, energy, agriculture, and more. However, we still have a long way to go towards providing ubiquitous affordable and reliable Internet access in Africa. As of 2017, at the household level Internet penetration is estimated at 31.2% in Africa as compared with 88.1% North America (Miniwatts Marketing Group, 2017).

With regard to broadband access, the divide follows similar patterns, but inequalities are even more accentuated, with less than 10% of the world's population having broadband access. Average broadband speeds vary by a factor of more than 40, from 256 kbps to more than 10Mbps. Access inequalities are even more visible when disaggregated by disadvantaged groups, especially in developing countries - particularly the rural population, women, oppressed cultural groups, people living in remote small island nations, and in the least developed countries generally. (Jensen, 2013). The greatest connectivity shortfall is exhibited in Least Developed Countries ("LDCs"), where 85% of the population is still offline set against only 22% in Developed Countries. In Africa 74.9% of the population offline. The reasons for being offline or for limited Internet use are manifold: many do not have access because they live in remote or difficult-to-reach areas and do not have access to digital or other basic infrastructure such as electricity or transport. Some do not see the benefits of being connected, often because of limited awareness, cultural impediments or limited relevant digital content. Still, others are illiterate, and many are too poor to afford even the most basic of Internet packages and devices. Existing inequalities in terms of income and education, particularly prominent among women, and other factors exacerbate the problem. To tackle the large offline populations, ITU within its Connect 2020 Agenda has made it a goal to bring 60% of the world's population online by 2020. (ITU, Connect 2020 Agenda, 2017) (Philbeck, 2017). The key challenges in meeting the ITU Connect 2020 agenda targets (ITU, Connect 2020 Agenda, 2017) are finding replicable solutions that can be scaled to connecting the large rural offline populations at minimal costs, and finding effective strategies for narrowing the usage gaps (including the gender gap) across all regions. While a significant amount of initiatives have been implemented, targeting both the rural/urban divide and the usage gaps largely at the local, community or national level, it is unlikely that large-scale rural 'almost free' solutions will be deployed within the next three years. Therefore, by default, most people to come online by 2020 are likely to come from more urban areas or areas that are already covered by infrastructure.

The offline population is disproportionately female, rural, poor, illiterate and elderly. Of the 3.9 billion people that are still unconnected, 58% are female, roughly 60% are rural and at least half come from countries with a GNI/capita of less than US$ (PPP) 6,500. Africa is the region with the highest rural population at 62%. In addition, many spend far in excess of 5% on ICT access and services as a proportion of GNI/ capita, the affordability threshold set by the UN Broadband Commission for Sustainable Development. Moreover, the elderly and individuals with low educational attainment are groups that are largely excluded from Internet use. While Internet penetration for people over the age of 75 remains well below 10 percent, individuals with low educational attainment often remain unconnected. There are a multitude of factors that influence if and how many people are on- or offline within a particular country. These include first and foremost the status and degree of infrastructure roll-out, the state of national development, the regulatory and enabling environment and corresponding policies, and demographic and socio-economic status. In this regard, ITU's MIS16 report highlights a strong link between Internet uptake, education, and income across both the developed and developing world. Moreover, the geographic location is also a significant determinant of Internet uptake. A large proportion of the rural population, especially in the developing world, remains unconnected. In this regard, lower levels of income and lower levels of education that are often prevalent in rural areas exacerbate the problem. Data on rural and urban Internet use is patchy. Still, for most countries it holds true that rural Internet use is almost always lower than urban Internet use. To this effect, the McKinsey Report "Offline and falling behind: Barriers to Internet Adoption" (2014) finds that urbanization is a key driver of Internet penetration.

While lack of infrastructure is still a key reason for being offline, including supporting infrastructure such as power, the demand-side barriers that include the lack of ICT skills, relevance (content, services and apps, cultural awareness or barriers such as gender, inclusion) and affordability (service and device costs as well as costs of electricity for e.g. recharging and taxes) should also be given attention. ITU data shows that while 84% of world population live within coverage of 3G and 53% live within coverage of 4G networks, and while 66% of world population lives within a 100 Km reach of fibre transmission networks, only 39% of total population have 3G or 4G connections and only 11% have fixed broadband subscriptions. Consequently, there is not only an infrastructure or access gap, but also an Internet usage gap.

As regards affordability, 57% of the world population currently cannot afford the Internet, because the costs of end-user devices, services, access and ancillary costs (including usage and device taxes) are still too high for many. The A4AI

Affordability Report 2015/2016 also highlights patent fees as one key driver of high smartphone costs. Income levels are generally too low for a large proportion of the offline population and it's particularly prominent in African rural areas, where 62% of people located. In relation to relevance, there is a significant number of individuals that do not connect because they do not perceive a benefit from, trust or have an interest in being online. Others are prevented from going online for lack of relevant content, services or apps, or for cultural reasons or lack of skills. Regarding capability, currently, only 44% of the global population have attended secondary education, a key determinant of Internet use as highlighted above.

The impact of lack of ubiquitous Internet access is that, a lot of people who have low incomes in Africa will not be able to participate fully in the digital revolution. They cannot find new ways of making a living, make more efficient use of available resources, access online learning materials, gain knowledge of health issues or use online government services, or to maintain regular contact with friends, peers, and family. People living in rural areas are particularly disadvantaged because they cannot take advantage of the 'death of distance' that the Internet provides, and they spend much time and their limited money traveling to urban centres for simple transactions. Outside main centres throughout Africa, schools, small businesses, local government offices, NGOs, libraries, clinics, colleges and many institutions that are fundamental to day to day social and economic development, still don't have affordable, reliable and fast internet. Without dependable access, the institutions and the public will not be confident about relying on the services provided over the Internet -as we come to depend more on connectivity for carrying out many day-to-day activities, service interruptions need to be minimised through having at least two physically independent connections to the Internet.

WHAT ARE TV WHITE SPACES?

Radio waves are the lowest frequencies in the electromagnetic spectrum, used mainly for communications. They have wavelengths between 1 millimetre and 100 kilometres (or 300 GHz and 3 kHz in frequency). They are divided into long waves, medium waves, VHF, and UHF. Long Wave are around 1~2 km in wavelength. Some radio stations broadcast in this range. Medium Wave are around 100m in wavelength and are used by some radio stations especially "AM" stations. Very High Frequency (VHF) has wavelengths of around 2m and "FM" radio stations, civilian aircraft and taxis are found in this range. Ultra-High Frequency (UHF) has wavelengths of less than a metre and it is used for television transmissions, police radio communications, and military aircraft radios.

The applications of radio frequencies at various frequency ranges are: AM Radio: around 10MHz, FM Radio: Around 100MHz, Television: Many frequencies from 470MHz to 800MHz, and others, Cellular phones: 850MHz, 1900MHz, and others, Wi-Fi: 2.4GHz (UHF) and Wi-Fi: 5GHz (SHF), Satellite: 3.5GHz, and WiMAX 10-66GHz. Recent studies have shown that by and large in most frequency bands in almost all areas the spectrum is under-utilized. Among all the under-utilized chunks of spectrum, of particular interest are the Low VHF (Channels 2, 5 and 6), High VHF (Channels 7 to 13), Low UHF (Channels 14 to 51) and High UHF (Channels 52 to 69). The amount of spectrum under-utilized in the TV bands is much larger than that available for the current unlicensed applications. This sub-GHz band provides much more superior propagation characteristics as compared to the higher frequency bands, and this makes the TV spectrum extremely lucrative for wireless service providers. TV White Spaces (TVWS) are vacant, unused or interleaved frequencies located between broadcast TV channels in VHF/UHF range (54 MHz – 806 MHz). In general, any part of the spectrum that is unused is termed as a white space. In many countries like USA, UK, Europe and Australia, digital switch-over in TV bands has recently resulted in relaxed regulatory regimes, where unlicensed spectrum use is allowed, provided that non-harmful interference to incumbent systems is guaranteed (Dominique Noguet, 2011). As a consequence, TV White Space (TVWS), has been regarded to meet regulatory and actual deployment-driven requirements. Various IEEE802 groups, (IEEE802.22 IEEE802.11af) have carried out standardization actions to exploit TVWS and enable rapid availability of white space devices (WSD) on the market.

A White Space Device (WSD) is wireless device that operates in the TVWS frequency range. The low-signal frequencies, from around 400 MHz to about 800 MHz, can penetrate walls and other obstacles more easily than the traditional broadband technologies. While a traditional Wi-Fi router has a relatively limited range, around 100 meters under perfect conditions, and can be blocked by walls or other environmental barriers, TV White Space technology can cover an expanse of about 14 kilometres in diameter before they need to be boosted. This means that fewer towers or base stations are needed to cover a wider area. Regulatory agencies across the world are developing regulations to allow the use of TVWS by unlicensed wireless devices. Care has to be taken that these devices do not interfere with any licensed services (Tuncer Baykas, 2012). In the future many heterogeneous, and independently operated, wireless networks may utilize the TVWS.

Broadcast television services operate in VHF and UHF licensed portion of the radio spectrum. Regulation in most countries prohibits the use of unlicensed devices in TV bands with the exception of remote controls, medical telemetry devices, and wireless microphones. World over TV stations are required to convert from analogue to digital transmission. This digital television transition, also called the digital switchover (DSO) or analogue switch-off (ASO), is the process in which analogue television is converted to and replaced by digital television. This primarily involves the conversion of analogue terrestrial television to digital terrestrial. This may also include analogue cable conversion to digital cable as well as analogue to digital satellite. This ASO will definitely give a boost to the range of available frequencies to use in TVWS since nearly all the TV broadcast frequencies will be available for use in TVWS.

Digital Switchover (DSO)

TV broadcasting has always only involved transferring sound or video streams by means of analogue signals, up until the only1990s. This happened in a linear process in which elements were transmitted in serial, one element after another. This has a disadvantage of consuming lots of bandwidth. A lot of capacity is taken up on wireless electronic frequencies in order to carry analogue signals. This means that only a limited number of stations could be accommodated on the radio spectrum. This was compounded by the fact that other frequencies were not suitable for audio transmission, were better used for TV or cellular telephony, or were reserved for military communications only. This was the same story in TV, where one station was allocated one frequency and there was no sharing of spectrum. In effect, the result was a limit to the number of stations in a country.

With the advent of digital electronics, sound, video, text and still images, could be stored and transmitted in the form of binary digits. In this way, digital data can be manipulated in various useful forms through software.

Digital data can be compressed through algorithms. In this way, more content can be electronically stored on smaller space than previously and more content can be transmitted in the same bandwidth than in analogue TV. Many digital television technologies today use MPEG4 compression and in digital radio, MP4 compression is used. Digital communication gives us much greater efficiencies in the use of bandwidth. With compression, data can be broken up into in many separate and simultaneous "packets" which can be re-assembled in the right order at the destination. The most significant advantage of all this for broadcasting is that more radio and TV channels can be allocated into the exact same frequency space than is possible under analogue transmission. A digitised signal can allow for up to ten TV channels to be broadcast, whereas a single analogue channel would require the whole frequency using a technique called multiplexing which several streams of broadcast content into the single signal.

The space freed-up is known as the "digital dividend" allows for some of the vacated bandwidth to be used for other purposes. For instance, broadcasters can introduce multiple sound-tracks and language subtitling as part of the video channel on digital TV. In the case of digital radio, multiplexing can facilitate an ensemble of up to 50 channels on a single signal.

A TV broadcaster can increase the compression (and quality) of most of its TV channels for a particular event, to avail bandwidth for a resource-hungry High Definition (HD) broadcast of that specific occasion. Digital broadcasting allows for creating channels within channels. Depending on the type of their licensing, a TV broadcaster can run radio services at certain times of the day and switch to TV or data streams at others. Digital content can also be stored on the receiving device, providing the user with the power to pause and even rewind up to a point.

Against this whole backdrop, digital migration is the process by which broadcasting around the world today is switching from inefficient analogue transmission to more efficient digital transmission. Without digital transmission, you don't have digital migration, even if production and reception are digital. Radio and TV stations will have to move to digital transmission for them to start talking about DSO. Both broadcasters and the audiences need to be digitally migrated for the success of this endeavour.

Digital Switchover is expected is expected to be lengthy and a lengthy overlap will take place where analogue and digital transmission will be used together for some time. This is because a long process is needed in which broadcasters, signal distributors, regulators, manufacturers, governments and the public align themselves so that the digital transition will work successfully. Millions of people are saddled with analogue sets that were never designed to receive digital signals directly. There is a need for them to buy a Set Top Box or upgrade to a digital TV set before DSO is done otherwise millions will be left without access to broadcasting.

Digital Migration in Africa

Digital migration in Africa has been happening very slowly. This is because, driving digital migration is the agenda of the developed world. The general agreement though, especially in Southern Africa, was that all African countries have to meet the 2015 deadline for finishing the process whilst allowing for an additional five years to some 30 African nations. As argued earlier, the decision was mainly in response to the interests of the European sector, because there is certainly no major pressure to free up airwave spectrum in Africa, and nor are there strong consumer electronics industries or consumer markets in African countries.

More than two-thirds of the countries on the African continent are exempt from the 2015 deadline, and instead have a 2020 switch-off date. However, up until the end of 2016 (ITU, 2017) most of the SADC countries were still to finish the DSO process. Many African countries believe that the pressure for digital migration in developed countries is not demand driven but mainly supply-side driven. Despite the advantages highlighted above, digital migration in Africa, is believed to be a solution in search of a problem. The other school of thought that can be made is that the longer African countries wait, the more they can benefit from standardisation and cheapening of equipment elsewhere.

The ITU decided that, unless those signals have been switched to digital, it will no longer intervene to protect a country's TV broadcast signals in any instances where these are being swamped by a neighbour's, after the defined cut-off date. This issue of signal swamping or cross-border interference with signals is not a serious issue in most African countries where huge percentages of the African population still do not even receive any TV broadcasting signals. In other cases, African audiences welcome spill-over across borders, which may offer a little more choice. So for some African countries, they can probably still continue analogue TV long after the deadline without incurring any serious disadvantages in terms of aggressive neighbouring broadcasters bothering their national signal space. The few disputes that may occur will not necessarily even require ITU intervention to resolve.

It is also believed that to give Africans more and better video choices do not depend exclusively on TV digital migration. The choice is also not between digital TV and the analogue dark ages. There are many options to advance digital communications across many fronts, and no reason why digital TV transmission should get the lion's share of limited resources. The point being made here is that the world of broadcast and digital possibilities is a lot bigger than only digital migration. It is with this background that DSO in Africa is not being taken as an emergency. Most countries are proceeding as and when resources permit them.

Even though African broadcasters are not exactly clamouring for more TV channels, digital migration of analogue will free up some spectrum for cellular telephony expansion and for wireless broadband (TVWS). It is our view that if and when African countries decide to finish their DSO it will be a great day to reap the whole fruit of TVWS since huge tracts of radio spectrum will be available for use. All this spectrum can be used to provide affordable broadband to remote rural areas and even in urban areas.

WHY IS TVWS IMPORTANT?

As the world becomes more reliant on the Internet for communication, information, health services, and business relations, it has become clear that Internet connectivity should be seen as a basic human right. Unfortunately, due to environmental obstacles, lack of financial incentives and distance from major service providers, Internet penetration has been so low in remote areas that have low population density. This results in expensive and complex networks with a lack of options for those living in these rural communities.

Current trends in e-commerce involve buyers and sellers meeting in cyberspace and transacting business in real time. Sellers advertise their products and buyers search and buy stock and in most cases, this is delivered to their homes. The internet has become a marketplace where buyers, sellers and even transporters meet and transact business without meeting physically. Unfortunately, in Africa, all these interesting innovations and development are most times excluding the rural population. In Africa, rural populations are still lagging behind in terms of Internet and digital technologies. Obstacles to low internet users in Africa includes low computer literacy, limited telecommunications infrastructure, sustainable energy and the high cost of internet services. Although there has been rapid mobile penetration in recent years, there is still low Internet usage in rural areas.

Large percentages of African population live in rural areas. Agriculture is the main source of living in these areas. The people in these areas rely on selling their farm produce and in most cases, their biggest markets are in urban areas. Farmers transport their produce to urban areas with the hope of getting clients. Most times there is no prior communication with possible clients or at least market research or understanding before farm produce is sent to markets. These people are mostly physically cut off from the rest of the world in terms of internet connection. Internet connection and computer literacy can make a huge impact in including the African rural population in the e-commerce revolution engulfing the world. It is expected that if these farmers have regular communication with clients and are in touch with market variations, they will definitely improve their sales. The Internet can also be a source scientific and commercial knowledge for farmers. There is a lot of free farming tutorials on the internet, but lack of internet access will mean that rural farmers in Africa never have access to such information. Africa remains the region with the lowest penetration of e-commerce (UNCTAD, 2005). Since most African economies and agriculture-based, an increase in internet usage is expected to will impact these economies in a good way.

It is believed that low and middle-income countries could raise economic growth by 1.4% for every 10% increase in broadband penetration, ITC (2015). The cost of broadband remains an obstacle to internet access in rural South Africa, but by reducing the cost of broadband access millions of Africans could get online. This creates new opportunities for education, healthcare, commerce and the delivery of government services across the country. It is important to seek ways in which we can reduce the digital divide in Africa. The digital divide is related to low internet penetration and high cost of broadband services. Investment in infrastructure and modern technologies such as ICTs is expected to improve the situation caused by the physical remoteness of poor rural communities, (Rhodes, 2003). TVWS is a technology that can help in increasing connectivity in Africa's rural areas. When TVWS connectivity is achieved in most African countries, it will add up to the existing broadband internet access coverage in rural and underdeveloped areas.

The TV White Space networks enable greater internet penetration, providing more bandwidth for less money, and this allows students, farmers and SMEs to use bandwidth-intensive applications for low costs.

Benefits of TV White Spaces

Using TV broadcast spectrum for broadband connectivity has three main advantages as listed in (Roberts, 2015):

- **Greater Distances:** For TV white spaces networks, the signals travel over longer distances, unlike in the conventional wireless networks where the signal travel shorter distances. This is primarily because it transmits in the lower frequencies. Wavelength is around 0.5 meter and common obstacles like leaves and raindrops are much smaller than the wavelength. Also, the Ground wave component follows the earth well in hilly terrain and thus TVWS experiences lower free-space loss (proportional to the square of the frequency) thereby improving the maximum range of transmission. This makes TVWS a perfect fit for rural Africa where there are sparse or no infrastructure at all (Microsoft, 2016). Conventional Wi-Fi signal can cover a distance of approximately 100 meters whilst a TVWS signal can cover several kilometres. In (Roberts, 2015) they report experiencing long distances of up to above 14 kilometres whilst transmitting 10 Mbps.
- **Penetrates Common Obstructions:** TVWS radios operate at lower frequencies, and its signals can easily penetrate walls and obstructions while other wireless technologies like Wi-Fi cannot pass through walls. In (Roberts, 2015) they report a simple experiment in a building (covering an area of 67.6656 square km over 4 floors) they were able to cover all parts of the building using a single TVWS base station operating at 20 dBm with a 2 dBi gain antenna. However using Wi-Fi, the building required 150 Wi-Fi Access Points to provide high-speed access. Microwave links require line-of-sight between the points being connected. In areas with rugged or forested terrain, tall towers are required to provide line-of-sight connection, making microwave an expensive and unfeasible solution for rural African locations. TV White Space technology can provide an alternative solution since it utilizes signals that can penetrate obstacles and cover uneven ground without requiring additional infrastructure. So it is expected that it will be cheaper to

provide internet access over TVWS since it requires less hardware than other conventional wireless technologies.

- **Greater Efficiencies:** Since the TVWS signals travel farther than Wi-Fi, a TVWS deployment would cost less, and would consume less power than Wi-Fi or mesh based topologies to cover sparsely populated communities in Africa. As we show later in this section, TVWS deployments are also more economical than LTE for these scenarios. This brings us to to the question of why TVWS spectrum attractive? It is basically a cost-effective way to provide broadband to areas that would be too expensive to serve by other means.

TVWS can be found beneficial to the African economy through various application areas of the economy as explained by (Calabrese, 2006):

- **Rural Broadband Deployment:** The favourable propagation characteristics of the TVWS allow for wireless broadband deployment with a greater range of operation and has the ability to pass through buildings, weather, and foliage at lower power levels. This ensures that TVWS can be successfully be deployed to provide broadband service in rural, remote areas, in less densely populated and bad weather areas, as well as where there is little or no telecommunication infrastructure nor electricity installed.

- **Auxiliary Public Safety Communications:** The ability of TVWS to cover long distances will make it so suitable for providing communication during emergency situations. The TV white spaces could be used to provide auxiliary services to support already existing public safety communications on licensed networks in cases like earthquakes and floods. This is possible since TVWS will not need a lot of infrastructure to be installed.

- **Educational and Enterprise Video Conferencing:** TVWS can be used to give schools in rural areas with mobile, high-speed Internet for their regular school requirements like internet and video conferencing. This will expose them to opportunities that are already enjoyed by schools in urban areas. Combined with TVWS broadband connectivity, activities such as video conferencing could help enable distance learning for students in remote areas for whom classroom-based learning is not enough.

- **Personal Consumer Applications:** The improved signal reliability of TVWS and range of the TV broadcast spectrum in both rural and urban areas could be used to provide new consumer applications which take advantage of these attributes. Wireless local area networks using could enable new capabilities that bring safety, convenience, and comfort to consumers in their homes. Low power and battery operated WSD could provide improved energy efficiency through intelligent home automation and power monitoring or home security with robust low-power wireless video feeds.

- **Mesh Networks:** TVWS could be used in mesh networking of WSD, whereby information is relayed locally from device to device. Mesh networking is "self-configuring," and most times "self-healing" such that any failure of a single device will cause a "re-route" as opposed to a network failure, thereby enabling reliable communications. Mesh networks can use TVWS to make sure that, unserved or remote communities could readily and cost-effectively create their own network extensions as alternative means of Internet connectivity. In addition, because mesh networks are easily deployed, they can offer a means of communications if existing networks fail due to disasters.
- **Enhanced Local Coverage and Communications:** Localities could use the TV white spaces to enable mobile video services. These services could provide information of special interest to the local community; coverage of local sporting events; and new methods for local advertisers to reach customers in a more targeted and valued manner.

How Does TVWS Work?

The most common implementation of TVWS networks is accessed using smart, radio-enabled devices that report their location to a cloud-based TVWS spectrum database. The database informs the device about the available TVWS channels, and the maximum power level it is permitted to use at its current location. The database maintains a list of all protected TV stations and frequencies across a country, so the devices can avoid causing interference to TV broadcasts and wireless microphone signals. This technology is truly dynamic: as different TV channels become available, TVWS devices can opportunistically switch from one group of channels to another. TVWS translates to greater network capacity, allowing a greater number of users in a given area while, at the same time, protecting television reception from interference. All of this engineering is invisible to the consumer, who simply experiences more ubiquitous broadband connectivity.

Figure 1 depicts a block diagram of a typical TVWS network. From left to right, the components include off-the-shelf 802.11 b/g/n/ac Wi-Fi access points (APs), which connect directly to the TVWS customer premise equipment (CPE); using standard Cat5 or Cat6 cable.

The CPE, in turn, communicates with the TVWS base stations (BS) through a TVWS air interface protocol, e.g. IEEE 802.11af, which can be located within several hundred meters of the CPE or many kilometres away, depending on the use case, availability of mounting radio facilities, and the location of fibre access.

Figure 1. TVWS network architecture
Roberts, 2015.

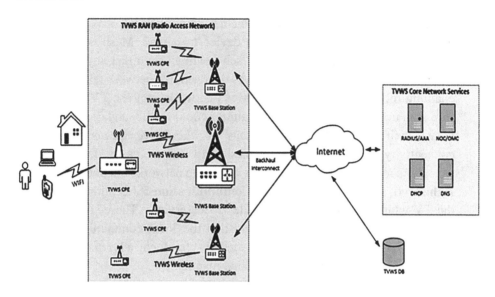

The CPE site configuration is simple and easy to install: a high gain directional UHF antenna is pipe or mast mounted at the service location. The TVWS radio attaches behind the antenna to the same pipe mount and an RF jumper connects to the antenna while Cat5 cable drops to the Wi-Fi AP or Ethernet switch. Radio power is provided via Power over Ethernet (PoE). Because of the low power draw (typically < 20 W) of the CPE (or BS) radios it is possible to use a solar power system in the event that electricity is not present at the site.

Each TVWS BS can consist of one or multiple sectors and radios. A typical BS configuration would have multiple sectors, just like any GSM or LTE BS, in order to illuminate 360 degrees around the site, which is ideal for point to multipoint implementations of white spaces. If the capacity requirement calls for more than one channel per sector, a duplexer can be used to multiplex another radio onto an existing sector antenna. Once channel bonding is available as a radio feature, duplexers can be eliminated. Given that the TVWS Effective Isotropic Radiated Power (EIRP) is limited to 36 dBm or 4 Watts, and the conducted power of a present-day TVWS BS is only 100 mW per radio, high gain panel antennas are used to help boost the effective signal in the directions of interest. The gain of antennas can be reduced for radios that can transmit at higher power.

The output of each BS radio is connected to a site aggregation router, and the output of the router points towards the Internet, whether locally available, or hundreds of miles away using fibre or a point-to-point or even VSAT backhaul systems.

From an architectural perspective, there is an advantage to mounting the BS as close as possible to the CPE. Furthermore, given the low cost of high quality, high capacity unlicensed microwave backhaul radios, there is a good reason to keep TVWS access equipment within a confined area. This is not to say that long-range TVWS communications is not possible or even desirable, just that there are the typical telecommunications trade-offs involving cost, performance, and feasibility that always need to be made.

On the backend, any commercial TVWS deployment will require core services, including some sort of Radius/AAA for customer provisioning and billing; Network Operations Centre and Operation and Maintenance Centre tools for network management and control; and DHCP/DNS for IP addressing allocation and management. Finally, the regulator in each country will either own or outsource TVWS database functionalities to ensure that all assigned UHF channels are accounted for and protected from interference. When a TVWS radio queries the DB for channel availability at its location, only unassigned channels are returned.

TV White Space database (Wikipedia, 2017b), is an entity that controls the TV spectrum utilization by unlicensed white spaces devices within a determined geographical area, while protecting incumbent broadcasting services. TV White Space database was first brought as a way to overcome the technical hurdles faced by spectrum sensing techniques to precisely detect very weak primary signals. Spectrum is deemed available, or unavailable, to unlicensed usage depending on criteria that are regulator specific and thus the database operation can significantly vary between countries. Regulations on white space spectrum utilization are important since they pose limits to the amount of white space spectrum that can be reclaimed by White Space technology for wireless broadband access. Having a certain degree of spectrum accessibility is crucial to the relevance and the successful adoption of TVWS as a technology.

Planning a TVWS Network

When designing a TVWS network all the traditional radio network planning tools and procedures apply. To address coverage, we get a good visualization of the network and terrain characteristics by plotting the proposed fibre POP, BS towers and CPE endpoints using any of a myriad of planning tools, such as Radio Mobile, Atoll, or EDX. In many cases, the fibre POP will be located some distance from the area which is intended to be served by TVWS. Extending the POP is cheap and easy as there are many affordable high quality and high capacity point to point licensed and unlicensed microwave solutions. Once plotted, we use the path profile tool to verify Line of Sight (LOS) on all links. Even though TVWS operates in the UHF band, those signals will not penetrate mountains and can still be blocked. If terrain or man-made obstacles appear challenging on a path, we always verify LOS with a physical path survey. Another method we use is to erect a test transmitter and conduct a field survey. We also optimize the link by raising BS and CPE antenna heights as much as possible. The same tools mentioned above generally also can calculate a link budget to ensure that the terrain and link range allow ample signal strength at the receiver to provide the desired throughput.

REGULATION OF RADIO SPECTRUM

Since the beginning of the 20th century, the use of radio has been the most strictly regulated medium of communication. Essentially everything is forbidden which is not explicitly authorized by your country's government. Today, students of comparative law will immediately recognize this as the "authoritarian" model, and it is found even in the most liberal democracies. Two decades ago, in most countries, unlicensed radio was simply illegal. In a few others, it was a daring exception to the norm of licensed services. Now, thanks largely to Wi-Fi and RFID's global acceptance, most countries have license-free bands. And in a few places (Europe and the US), license exemption is increasingly recognized as the new norm, with licensed radio services a shrinking part of the wireless ecosystem.

In 2002, the FCC surprised everyone by asking whether new applications might be allowed to use TV white spaces on a license-exempt basis. 12 "White spaces" are areas where the assignment of specific TV channels is forbidden in order to protect stations using those channels elsewhere. Note that the white spaces are actually larger than the areas of broadcast coverage. One reason why TV white spaces are so large is that the band planners assumed only TV stations would use these channels and TV stations transmit at high power so they need to be widely separated. However, it is possible for low-power devices to operate completely within a white space so their signals do not impinge on the broadcast coverage areas.

This was the insight that led the FCC to suggest opening white spaces to low-power uses.

With the advancement of regulations worldwide, regulators are now allowing secondary devices access to unused, but licensed spectrum starting with TVWS in VHF/UHF bands. Secondary users use this spectrum when it is available, while the primary licensed users retain their licensing rights. Primary users, are protected from secondary user interference and they have priority over their licensed spectrum which they may access at any time. In the United States of America, this scheme has been driven by the Federal Communications Commission (FCC) which has set the rules for the unlicensed TVWS in order to protect primary users such as TV broadcast stations and wireless microphones. There is a problem of coexistence of multiple WSDs using different wireless technologies and different operators and service providers (Tuncer Baykas, 2012) without conflict. This need to be addressed by regulators if TVWS operation is going to be successful. With proper technical and regulatory specifications, TV White Spaces (TVWS) is capable of making internet connectivity technically possible and affordable in rural Africa.

TVWS USE IN AFRICA

Microsoft, Google, Spectra Link wireless, Uhuru one, Wave Tek, COSTECH, TENET among others are some of the companies running pilot studies and installations of TVWS in Africa. (Dynamic Spectrum Alliance, 2015) and (I. Opawoye, 2015) document some real-life stories where TVWS has been deployed and tested, mostly as pilot studies.

Mozambique

Since 8th of August 2015, the Institute of National Communications of Mozambique (INCM) in partnership with the Universal Access Fund (FSAU), the Network Start-up Resource Centre (NSRC), the Abdus Salam International Centre for Theoretical Physics (ICTP), Internet Solutions (IS) and the University Eduardo Mondlane Center of Informatics (CIUEM), were conducting a TV white spaces pilot project financed by the Universal Access Fund of Mozambique. Its aim was to study and establish if cognitive radios are capable of delivering free access to the Internet to the rural schools and the library at the University Unitiva located in the municipality of Boane.

Botswana

Microsoft in collaboration with the Botswana Innovation Hub, the Botswana-UPenn Partnership (BUP), Global Broadband Solutions, Vista Life Sciences, BoFiNet, Adaptrum and USAID-NetHope, in March 2015 launched a TVWS pilot project known as Project Kgolagano. The project provides internet for telemedicine services to local hospitals and clinics so that they can have access to specialised medicinal help from Gaborone and around the world. This project is operating with the support of the Botswana Ministry of Health and the Ministry of Infrastructure, Science, and Technology.

Namibia

In Namibia, Microsoft also partnered MyDigitalBridge Foundation in partnership and Adaptrum in TV White Spaces (TVWS) pilot project called the 'Citizen Connect'. They were supported by the Millennium Challenge Corporation (MCC) and Millennium Challenge Account (MCA). Their intention was to provide a blueprint of a countrywide broadband internet connectivity. This project was TVWS network and was deployed over a 62km x 152km (9,424 km^2) area covering three regional councils, and connecting 28 schools in northern Namibia.

Accra, Ghana

Accra TVWS pilot network was the first of its kind in West Africa. In March 2014, SpectraLink Wireless, under authorization from the Government of Ghana's National Communications Authority (NCA), and in collaboration with the Meltwater Entrepreneurial School of Technology (MEST) deployed a pilot network to offer free wireless broadband access for its community of Entrepreneurs in Training.

The successful network deployment of the company's leading-edge TV white space technology is the first of its kind in West Africa and has proven the viability of SpectraLink's platform in delivering high-speed Internet connectivity through this medium. The purpose of the pilot with MEST has been to test the efficiency of using TV white spaces for Internet radio networks, in an urban environment that presents multiple sources of interference. The network has been successfully tested on channels adjacent to active television channels, over a 10 km link, with no interference observed.

Koforidua, Ghana

In 2013, SpectraLink Wireless, in collaboration with Microsoft and Facebook, are connecting Koforidua Polytechnic and other universities in Ghana to wireless broadband and cloud-based services through TV white space technology. The pilot is supported by Microsoft's 4Afrika Initiative which aims to improve the region's competitive positioning by facilitating technology access, while ensuring students have reliable Internet access. The networks use TV white space-enabled radios from 6harmonics to connect campus buildings, as well as hostels where students live, to ensure pupils have access to fast wireless broadband and cloud-based services, such as Office 365. The project is operating under the first TV white space pilot license issued by the Ghana National Communications Authority.

Polokwane, South Africa

In July 2013 Microsoft, 6harmonics and The Meraka Institute, who research and develop geo-location spectrum databases, partnered with the University of Limpopo in South Africa to provide the institution and five schools in an 8km radius with internet access using TVWS. The main idea of the pilot will be to show that TVWS can help in providing low-cost internet access countrywide. This is the South African Government's goal which needs to be achieved by 2020.

Cape Town, South Africa

In March 2013, Google partnered with the CSIR Meraka Institute, Tertiary Education and Research Network of South Africa, e-Schools Network, the Wireless Access Providers' Association, Comsol Wireless Solutions, Carlson Wireless, and Neul to embark on a six-month TVWS was launched in Cape Town. The TVWS network consisted of multiple base stations, which delivered broadband Internet service to ten schools within a 10-kilometre radius. The aim was to study if broadband can be offered over white spaces without interfering with licensed spectrum holders. Each school received dedicated 2.5 Mbps service with failover to ADSL in order to prevent downtime during school hours. The network used Google's spectrum database to determine white space availability in order to prevent interference with other channels.

Zomba, Malawi

The University of Malawi, in partnership with the Malawi Communications Regulatory Authority (MACRA), and the International Centre for Theoretical Physics in Trieste, has launched a white-spaces pilot project in the city of Zomba, in southern Malawi. The pilot, which got underway in September 2013, has connected a number of different institutions including a school, a hospital, an airport and a research facility.

Dar es Salaam, Tanzania

UhuruOne and Microsoft are partnering with the Tanzania Commission for Science and Technology (COSTECH) to supply 74,000 students with affordable wireless broadband access, devices, and cloud-based services in a project called Broadband4Wote project is designed to assess the commercial feasibility of wireless broadband using TV White Space technology. The Open University of Tanzania, Institute of Finance Management, College of Business Education and Dar es Salaam School of Journalism and Mass Communication are all connected to the network which focuses on TV White Space capabilities in urban settings.

Nanyuki, Kenya

Since February 2013, Microsoft, in collaboration with the Government of Kenya, Mawingu Networks and Jamii Telecom Limited, and with support from the Communications Authority of Kenya (CAK), conducted a pilot TVWS project that utilizes Adaptrum and 6Harmonics and solar-powered base stations to deliver low-cost internet to schools, healthcare clinics, government offices, and some small businesses near Nanyuki, Kenya.

Use of TVWS and other innovative uses of spectrum for fixed wireless access can help meet these goals in the following ways (Jensen, 2013):

1. **Reducing Internet Access Costs:** Internet service providers able to make innovative use of radio spectrum can help to create more competition in markets for Internet access. This will put pressure on the existing/incumbent carriers which rely on their market dominance to maintain high-profit margins or inefficient business practices. Mobile operators, in particular, have become the 'new incumbents', often operating in cartel-like fashion even if there is nominal competition. These 'monopolistic' practices do not only keep prices high, they also limit network neutrality and innovation.
2. **Providing More Ubiquitous Access:** The lower radio frequencies used by TVWS can help by reaching greater distances than higher frequency systems which are less cost-effective. In addition, greater competitive pressure provided by new fixed wireless providers will also increase the incentive for carriers to make more infrastructure investments in unserved areas.
3. **Providing More Reliable Access:** In the developed world 'permanent' connectivity would most often be provided by a DSL or cable-TV service, complemented by a mobile broadband service. In Africa and other developing regions, a fixed wireless solution such as TVWS could be complemented by a WiFi for mobile broadband connection. In this way TVWS can provide an alternative physical path to the Internet, ensuring that vital services continue in the event of a service interruption on one of the links.

With the growth in the use of wireless technologies generally, radio spectrum has become a particularly vital part of the Internet ecosystem. The use of TVWS and other dynamic spectrum-uses are particularly appropriate for developing countries - where there is plenty of unused broadcast spectrum, bitrate expectations are lower and there are large numbers of people living in areas unserved by existing infrastructure. The explosive growth of mobile access has tended to draw attention away from the provision of fixed access (which offers higher speeds and lower subscription costs), and as a result fixed last-mile infrastructure has tended to take a lower priority in public policy, and current policy and regulatory practice has not responded to the problem with much creativity.

Rural communities are especially vulnerable to poorly managed spectrum because they are less likely to have any fixed line alternatives. But although there is also more spectrum available in rural areas because there are much fewer existing spectrum users, this has not translated into better spectrum access.

Lack of awareness by national policymakers of the need for low-cost spectrum for wireless operators is a key factor, along with lack of capacity to update spectrum plans as new technologies emerge, as well as resource constraints in spectrum regulation enforcement. Among the most visible of these problems is linked to the slow move from analogue to digital TV in developing regions, delaying the availability of the important 700-800 MHz wavebands, which are particularly suitable for high-speed wireless broadband services. Allocation of the 2.6 GHz waveband is important for broadband in urban areas and is also subject to allocation delays in many countries. Use of dynamic shared and unlicensed spectrum technologies such as TVWS and WiFi could have a major role to play in meeting connectivity needs immediately, without having to wait for the analogue to digital switchover, which now appears that it will not take place in many developed countries before the 2015 deadline proposed by the ITU.

Currently, the high cost of spectrum licenses is a major constraint on deploying new wireless services, limiting the deployment of wireless Internet services, and increasing end-user costs. High spectrum prices are also linked to the continued dominance of the mobile operators. Having paid millions of dollars to the state for these licenses, the mobile operators are able to convince governments to limit the entry of other new wireless players in the market. Many mobile operators have claimed that the license fees were paid on the basis of a limited number of market players and that the market size is insufficient to support more operators. This has been reinforced by the fact that different approaches to spectrum management for increasing access are usually overlooked by most regulators and smaller and local ISPs.

Of particular importance is that the dynamic spectrum-use model can also be applied to other frequencies to increase the efficiency of spectrum use more generally, and help reduce the burden on regulators for spectrum management. The few TVWS trials that have taken place have already demonstrated that very large portions of the allocated spectrum bands are not actually in use, and this has thrown into question the whole premise of 'spectrum scarcity', upon which current allocation models are based. Hopefully, as more on the ground spectrum-use information becomes available from more developing countries, and from more sources than just the (often poorly resourced) national ICT regulator, such as through crowdsourcing, there will be better awareness of the increased potential of the radio spectrum resource.

In this respect, TVWS is a point of entry for highlighting issues of spectrum management generally, and can bring together a wide range of stakeholders to work together on solutions to the access problem. As highlighted by the history of TVWS support in the US where NGOs first pushed for its use, civil society has an important role to play in bringing attention to dynamic spectrum use. With a technology-neutral agenda, civil society groups are not biased toward a particular access solution and can be a trusted partner in helping to guide the adoption of the most effective mix of technologies.

Maximising the Impact of Innovative Spectrum Use

It is important to note that TVWS and other dynamic spectrum technologies are part of a larger 'connectivity ecosystem' and will not reach their full potential unless other needs for the access ecosystem are also addressed at the same time. In developing countries these needs are many but the most important of these are:

- **Low Barriers to Entry for New Internet Providers (Licensing):** High licensing costs for spectrum usually exclude smaller players who may wish to enter the market, and mobile operators are often resistant to any new applicants. Even more of a constraint in some countries is that new licenses to operate Internet services are simply not available, leaving the market to the incumbent and the existing mobile operators.
- **Efficient Interconnection:** There is a need for good interconnection with existing networks, so that smaller dynamic spectrum providers can offer their customers services that is at par with those of the existing larger players. This requires an efficient exchange of local traffic with other Internet providers & Content Distribution Networks (CDNs) by ensuring the presence of well-run Internet Exchange Points (IXPs) with participation from all the major Internet providers. This should also include interconnection mechanisms with the traditional voice operators for carrying out Voice over IP (VoIP) calls.
- **National Fibre Backbones:** With good national fibre backbone infrastructure, the more remote areas which are most likely to benefit from TVWS and other wireless technologies will able to connect affordably and with sufficient capacity. Governments need to encourage more investment in this infrastructure by encouraging competition and also ensuring cost-based access to existing fibre optic networks. This may also require implementation of infrastructure sharing regulation for existing providers. This helps in reducing the costs of the cost of laying fibre lies in the civil works.

- **Low-Cost Access Devices:** Low-income groups are particularly constrained in being able to afford the necessary equipment to access the full potential. To support better access for these communities, public financing schemes may need to be adopted with low-interest loans or guarantees, and by minimising import duties on equipment.

- **Public Support for the Extension of Connectivity:** To remote and rural areas. The use of universal service funds which take a proportion of revenues from existing operators to support network deployment in underserved areas has become a well-accepted vehicle for this. The regulator deducts the national average cost of providing a connection and gives the deference to the operator who must install the connection within a specified time period. A reverse auction for the provision of service in under-serviced areas is another such mechanism.

- **Public Access Facilities Are Needed:** For those who cannot afford access in the home or at work. This can often be achieved by equipping libraries and community centres with the necessary equipment.

- **Online Payment Systems:** Without widely available electronic payment systems for the unbanked, those in rural areas will not be able to take advantage of one of the most desirable features of the Internet - e-commerce. Unfortunately, most of the payment systems adopted to date rely on mobile networks – other alternatives need to be made available.

- **Local Content Development:** Support is needed for building relevant local applications in order to maximise the demand for networks, such as for e-Governance and civil-service networking.

- **Effective Consumer Protection:** To reduce the risks of accessing the Internet, effective protection will be needed against such as aspects as spam, fraud, and hate speech, especially against women and minority groups.

CONCLUSION

Several countries in Africa have low penetration of Internet connectivity. In this chapter, we have described how TVWS technology can be used to bridge the digital divide. We realised that the digital switchover that is currently going on in broadcasting will create and opportunity for more radio spectrum that can be used for TVWS technology. However African countries are not migrating to digital transmission at the same rate with the whole world with most of them with ongoing projects. Various reasons were presented for dragging of feet, however, there is a general agreement that by 2020 all African states would have made the DSO. We hope that by this date, a lot of African states would have appreciated the potential of

TVWS for an affordable alternative source of broadband especially for rural sparsely populated areas. We discussed TVWS pilot projects in different African countries. All these pilot projects have reported promising results for the deployment of TVWS in Africa. This is very encouraging and it is hoped that African governments will put favourable regulatory environment to ensure easy deployment of TVWS in rural Africa. This will definitely bridge the digital divide in Africa and boost the economies in Africa. In future, we need to find ways of helping African governments in legislating for easy access of TVWS in remote rural areas. There is also a need to investigate ways to achieve higher speeds on a TVWS link using a single radio, e.g. using channel aggregation and MIMO.

REFERENCES

Calabrese, M. (2006). *Examples of Consumer Benefits from TV 'White Spaces' Legislation*. Retrieved September 10, 2017, from https://www.newamerica.org/oti/policy-papers/examples-of-consumer-benefits-from-tv-white-spaces-legislation/

Darkwa, O. K. (2016, July). *The role of tv white space technology*. Retrieved from The Ghananian Times: http://www.ghanaiantimes.com.gh/role-of-tv-white-space-technology/

Dominique Noguet, M. G. (2011, November 15). Advances in opportunistic radio technologies for TVWS. *EURASIP Journal on Wireless Communications and Networking, 170*, 1–12.

Dynamic Spectrum Alliance. (2015). *Worldwide Commercial Deployments, Pilots, and Trials*. BristolUnited Kingdom: Dynamic Spectrum Alliance.

ITU. (2017a, September 13). *Connect 2020 Agenda*. Retrieved from Connect 2020 Agenda: http://www.itu.int/en/connect2020/Pages/default.aspx

ITU. (2017b). *Status of the transition to Digital Terrestrial Television Broadcasting: Summary*. Retrieved from http://www.itu.int/en/ITU-D/Spectrum-Broadcasting/Pages/DSO/Summary.aspx

Jensen, M. (2013). The role of TV White Spaces and dynamic spectrum in helping to improve internet access in Africa and other developing regions. In E. A. M. Zennaro (Ed.), TV White Space: A pragmatic approach (pp. 83-89). ICTP-The Abdus Salam International Centre for Theoretical Physics.

Marlien Herselman, K. B. (2002). Analysing the role of ICT in bridging the digital divide amongst learners. *South African Journal of Education, 22*(4), 270–274.

Microsoft. (2016, December 30). Retrieved from http://research.microsoft.com/en-us/projects/spectrum/pilots.aspx

Miniwatts Marketing Group. (2017, June 30). *World Internet Users and 2017 Population Stats*. Retrieved September 13, 2017, from World Internet Users and 2017 Population Stats: www.internetworldstats.com/stats1.htm

Opawoye, I., Faruk, N., Bello, O. W., & Ayeni, A. A. (2015). Recent trends on TV White space deployments in Africa. *Nigerian Journal of Technology, 34*(3), 556–563. doi:10.4314/njt.v34i3.19

Philbeck, I. (2017). *Connecting the unconnected, working together to archive Connect 2010 Agenda targets*. Davos: ITU.

Rhodes, J. (2003). Can E-commerce enable marketing in an African rural women's community based development organisation? *Informing Science, 6*, 157–172. doi:10.28945/523

Roberts, S. P. (2015). Connecting Africa using the TV white spaces: from research to real world deployments. *The 21st IEEE International Workshop on Local and Metropolitan Area Networks, 21*, 1-6.

Tuncer Baykas, M. K. (2012). Developing a standard for TV white space coexistence: Technical challenges and solution approaches. *IEEE Wireless Communications, 19*(1), 10–22. doi:10.1109/MWC.2012.6155872

Wikipedia. (2017a). *IEEE 802.22*. Retrieved from https://en.wikipedia.org/wiki/IEEE_802.22

Wikipedia. (2017b). *TV White Space Database*. Retrieved from https://en.wikipedia.org/wiki/TV_White_Space_Database

Yu, P. K. (2002). Bridging the digital devide: Equality in the information age. *Cardozo Arts & Entertainmnet, 20*(1), 1–52.

Chapter 4

Fostering Affordability of ICT Access in Developing Countries Through Infrastructure Sharing:
The Devil Is in the Detail

Ngonidzashe Zanamwe
University of Zimbabwe, Zimbabwe

Taurai Rupere
University of Zimbabwe, Zimbabwe

Benard Mapako
University of Zimbabwe, Zimbabwe

Benny M. Nyambo
University of Zimbabwe, Zimbabwe

ABSTRACT

Infrastructure sharing has been viewed as a plausible route to affordable ICT access in the wake of duplication of ICT infrastructure in developing countries. In spite of this belief in its effectiveness, getting ICT operators to share infrastructure can be inhibited by several challenges relating to regulatory approach, competition between players, and lack of consensus between regulators and business. This chapter uses evidence from Zimbabwe to assess how infrastructure sharing can be implemented in developing countries where coverage competition is yet to give way to service provision-based competition in the wake of disproportionate investment by network operators. It suggests that instead of push factors alone, infrastructure can best be shared when business' commercial interests and regulators' quest for affordable universal services coincide to form a win-win situation built on both push and pull factors.

DOI: 10.4018/978-1-5225-3179-1.ch004

INTRODUCTION

Infrastructure sharing has been seen as a way of improving the affordability of ICT access, enabling faster rollout and reducing environmental degradation (Hatsu, Mabeifam and Paitoo, 2016; Namisiko, Sakwa, and Waweru, 2015; Mahendra, 2013; ICASA, 2015). In developing countries, it is considered as a way of ensuring Return on Investment (ROI) on ICT infrastructure in sparsely populated rural areas (ICASA, 2015). Regulatory bodies and consumer pressure groups applaud it for fostering universal access and affordable access cost. In spite of these advantages, it is inhibited by the competitive strategies often employed by Mobile Network Operators (MNOs) that aim quick ROI.

This situation is worsened by the nature of the mobile ICT sector, which includes high capital intensity and high operating cost. While both Capital Expenditure (CAPEX) and Operating Capital Expenditure (OPEX) are high, the tariffs tend to keep reducing as hardware and software technologies improve. This has also happened against a background of tightening ICT regulation that has seen the introduction of stricter cost models. It is also happening against a background of fast depreciation of capital infrastructure as technologies get phased out after short lifespan and newer ones get introduced due to rapid changes in technological innovations (Mahendra, 2013). This motivates MNO to seek quick ROI by beating competitors who may be lagging behind in infrastructure investment.

The need to manage the conflict of interest between regulatory bodies' quest for affordable and universal access and the MNOs' quest for profit and ROI has resulted in the use of several levels and models of infrastructure models. These levels can be broadly classified as passive, active and backhaul models of infrastructure sharing (KPMG, 2009) and they can be implemented using mandatory or optional and voluntary approaches. These challenges are worse when trying to enforce infrastructure sharing in an asymmetrical network among existing MNOs who view network coverage as a competitive urge as opposed to situations where a state-owned network is to be shared. Asymmetric networks are dominated by one network that owns disproportionally more infrastructure than others (Garcia & Kelly, 2016), as is the case in Zimbabwe.

While infrastructure sharing is seen as a way of reducing CAPEX, OPEX and hence telecommunication tariffs and concomitant environmental degradation emanating from infrastructure duplication, Postal and Regulatory Authority (POTRAZ) is not finding it easy to get stakeholder buy-in. This in spite of the fact that the Telecommunications Act of 2001 empowers them as the regulatory board to direct and compel licensees on issues of national interest. Cognizant of the negative effect of high intensity of regulation on infrastructure investment, regulators tend to be cautious. For instance, POTRAZ took some commendable best practice steps to establish the appropriate way of introducing mandatory infrastructure sharing in Zimbabwe. These include a consultative survey, followed by consultation paper and a stakeholder workshop. During this process, the biggest MNO and Internet Access Provider (IAP) Econet Wireless and Liquid Telecoms, pulled out of the process because it threatened their interests.

The two ICT giants are jointly owned by the self-exiled Strive Masiiwa who according to Velamuri (2003) fought a four-year legal battle against the state for it to acquire a mobile network license. Econet Wireless Zimbabwe is the only privately owned MNO after the acquisition of Telecel in 2016 by the state. It is the highest tax-payer (Takavarsha & Makumbe, 2012) and it owns about 53% of the base stations in Zimbabwe (POTRAZ, 2016).

Before we critic the role of regulators in developing countries, we must appreciate the technical, and political challenges they face. Technically POTRAZ wants to avoid a shared network that may break down and disrupt the entire telecommunication service in a country bedeviled by intermittent Internet and energy supply. On the political front infrastructure sharing, is inhibited by mistrust between a dominant MNO which competes with three MNOs that belong to a government resisted its inception and attempted to close it (Zimbabwe Independent, 2010). Zimbabwe also has indigenisation laws that limit foreign ownership and inadvertently competition.

This paper is a case study of Zimbabwe's challenge with infrastructure sharing. It discusses the challenges experienced in Zimbabwe and it attempts to present key lessons that other developing countries may employ should they seek to introduce infrastructure sharing. This is done by answering a research question which says, how can the tariff reduction benefits of infrastructure sharing be achieved without compromising the business interests of MNOs? After this introduction, the rest of the paper is organized as follows the next section looks at the literature review followed by the methods and approach section then the findings and discussions with the conclusion ending the paper.

LITERATURE REVIEW

Infrastructure sharing is defined as the use of part or parts of a network infrastructure by more than one MNO (SAPHYRE, 2010 cited in Hatsu et al., 2016; BTA, 2012). There are different kinds of infrastructure sharing models that are being used by MNOs in developing countries. These include passive, active and backhaul infrastructure sharing approaches. Passive infrastructure sharing consists of sharing towers, BTS shelters, power as opposed to active infrastructure sharing which includes the sharing of radio access networks (RANs)-spectrum, switches, antennae and Backhaul consists of the sharing of Core network elements such as switching centres, GPRS service nodes, transmission equipment and all links connecting elements of the core network (KPMG, 2009).

Other studies classify these models as five different technical levels of infrastructure sharing (Loizillon, 2002). These include level 1 which shares site passive elements, level 2 where antennas are shared and level 3 which includes base station sharing. Level 4 is where MNOs share radio networks and finally level 5 where cored network is shared. Onishi and Tsuna (2010) describe three models of joint ownership or usage of mobile network infrastructure. These include, type 1 where the Mobile Virtual Network Operator (MVNO) where a company elects to provide telecommunication services using leased infrastructure instead of building its own. Type 2 'roaming' where an MNO uses parts of another MNO's network for areas where it does not have infrastructure i.e. usually overseas. The final one is type 3 where a company builds its network and leases out part of it with other MNOs while it also leases other MNOs infrastructure. This paper uses evidence that was collected in a country where types two and three are mainly being used.

Advantages of Infrastructure Sharing to the User

The regulatory bodies' interest in infrastructure sharing emanates from its benefits to the subscriber. The main advantage of infrastructure sharing to the end user is the resultant tariff reduction. The subscribers get to pay lower tariffs because the MNOs will transfer less infrastructure capital expenditure (CAPEX) and operating expenses (OPEX) to the subscribers since they incur less of these costs than it is in situations where each MNO goes it alone. A recent study shows that MNOs can spend about 25000 USD on CAPEX per month. Other studies posit that operators can reduce CAPEX by 16% to 20% (KPMG, 2011) OPEX by about 60% (Hatsu et al., 2016). POTRAZ, however, estimates that an overall cost saving of 15% to 30% can be achieved from passive infrastructure sharing in Zimbabwe (Nhundu, 2015). Such a huge cost saving should result in a significantly lower tariffs for the end user.

There are also some non-commercial advantages that compel both regulators and telecommunication consumers to favour infrastructure sharing. These include less noise, environmental and health effects associated with duplication of telecommunication infrastructure (Hatsu et al., 2016). In the case of base stations, this could include the fumes from generators used for generating electricity in un-electrified places and as standby facilities in developing countries like Zimbabwe where continuous electricity supply is not guaranteed. It also includes reduction of digging of sidewalks where underground cables are installed. Infrastructure sharing is also favoured for compelling network operators to seek other value-added services instead of depending on superior network coverage. Such benefits accrue to mature networks where there is no more room for expansion (Mahendra, 2013).

Advantages of Infrastructure Sharing to Business

The advantages of IS to telecommunication operators include, cost reduction, improved rollout speed and access to geographic sites that are already occupied. Some of these advantages depend on the model being used, whether it is passive (also known as tower sharing) or active infrastructure sharing. Passive infrastructure sharing is favoured by MNOs because it allows them to pursue their own service-based differentiation strategies while they enjoy CAPEX and OPEX reduction (Onishi and Tsuna, 2010). These include high quality of service, loyalty bonuses, promotions and discounts of various kinds.

Infrastructure sharing can reduce CAPEX and OPEX in ways that can increase the rollout speed of network infrastructure. This will also improve the network coverage of ICT infrastructure and enable the MNOs to meet capacity demands that may come with increased data traffic (Namisiko et al., 2015). The reduction of OPEX can reach 60% (Hatsu et al., 2016) while OPEX reduction can be from 16% to 20% (KPMG, 2011). It also allows the sharing of strategic geographic sites the highest hill which would otherwise be monopolized by the first MNO to enter a specific area (Mahendra, 2013) as a permanent first-mover advantage. Other players would never manage to get access to such strategic places if the first mover refuses to share such areas with competitors. Infrastructure sharing would, therefore, be an equalizer to an otherwise incontestable advantage. This could be done through joint use of passive or active infrastructure or co-location i.e. the sharing of space in the area used for transmission

While the above advantages may encourage its adoption, infrastructure sharing has some inhibiting disadvantages. For starters, it has the potential to discourage investment in quality infrastructure since investors will not enjoy differentiation based on the quality of infrastructure. Litigation between operators over breaches of confidentiality increase if operators who may be forced into a marriage of convenience share infrastructure. Instead of enabling affordable tariffs, it may also compel operators to engage in market splitting arrangement (Ornelas, 2016).

Conditions Shaping the Strategy of Infrastructure Sharing

The strategy adopted for the deployment of infrastructure sharing depends on market conditions, network symmetry, regulator's behaviour as well as the market's competitive structure (Garcia and Kelly, 2016).

Market conditions refer to the market's potential to enable a quick return on investment. For instance, less densely populated rural areas inhabited by low-income subscribers compel MNOs to reduce capital and operating cost through infrastructure sharing. Network symmetry is about the similarity of the MNOs roll our cycles which incentivises them to merge their network, deconstruct redundant site so as to compete on service differentiation. However, if the network is asymmetrical, the operator with a larger network may be reluctant to share so as to dominate the market on network coverage. Also critical is the regulator's behaviour, because if new entrants that benefited from existing infrastructure expect similar benefits in future, they tend to postpone investing in new technologies (Grajek, et al. (2009). Finally, market competitive structure encourages infrastructure sharing if operators are compelled to compete on product differentiation instead of network coverage (Garcia and Kelly, 2016).

According to KPMG (2009), the conditions motivate infrastructure sharing include mature networks, growing networks, high cost regional and rural networks still being rolled out, new entrants looking to build scale, and pressure for cost reduction. Mature networks refer to networks where competitive advantage is no longer based on better network coverage. Garcia and Kelly (2016) refer to this as the market's competitive structure. Growing markets are markets where there is a constantly increasing need to expand the network. Infrastructure sharing is also motivated by regulatory mandate to meet universal service obligations to enter high-cost regional/rural areas by their license. Under such circumstances, operators find it profitable to reduce both CAPEX and OPEX by sharing the cost of obligatory roll out to such areas of low ROI. Another driver of infrastructure sharing is when new entrants looking to build scale in the shortest possible time. They will have to share existing infrastructure with incumbents. Finally, KPMG (2009) present pressure on costs in times when operators need to save CAPEX in an increasingly competitive market. In such a situation the sharing of infrastructure will free their resources for in differentiation of service.

Business Models for Infrastructure Sharing

The benefits of infrastructure sharing can also be assessed in terms of the business strategy being adopted by the MNOs. An MNO may decide between pursuing outright collaborative, competitive strategy or a hybrid that employs both at different spheres or technical levels of the business (Loizillon et al., 2002). An MNO engaging in infrastructure sharing can be viewed as a collaborating business in an extended business value chain (Bititci, Veronica Martinez, Pavel Albores and Kepa Mendible, 2003). Bititci et al. (2003) posit that the motive of such a company is not collaboration for its sake but it is rather the advantages emanating from it.

After establishing their competitive strategy, i.e. plan for deploying its resources, how to achieve sustainable competitive advantage and the necessary trade-off (Jekassi and Enders, 2005), a telecommunications company must be able to determine whether and how it should engage in passive or active infrastructure sharing. For instance, an MNO will have no choice but seek to share both passive and active infrastructure with a view to compete at product differentiation level.

Hatsu et al. (2016) argue that since achieving such competitive advantage requires higher investment in costly infrastructure, Infrastructure Sharing (IS) may be preferred as a way of achieving this. A firm may also gain an urge over its competitors through product differentiation i.e. the provision of a unique and superior customer experience. This may include high product quality, special features and high after sale service. Since such high quality and higher revenue per unit can only be achieved through more cost, infrastructure sharing can be helpful.

Based on the literature reviewed above, this section presents success factors for infrastructure sharing as a first step towards the creation of a reference model. It represents the regulator's influence on business i.e. (MNOs), consumers and market conditions.

The Regulator's Influence

The regulator can influence MNOs' willingness share as well as the sharing strategies they adopt. For example, resultant strategies like; assets sharing strategy (where two or more operators in the same sector share assert necessary for the final product) may be influenced by regulatory intensity. Other strategies include mutualisation strategy (where an infrastructure provider builds and operates for all to share) or cooperation strategy (where agents from different sectors share without competing with each other). High-intensity regulation may discourage investment if new entrants anticipate mandatory regulation to continue (Grajek et al., 2009). The regulator may use infrastructure sharing for achieving competitive access to infrastructures, reduce market failures and increase social welfare through universal access obligation (Garcia and Kely, 2016).

Business (MNOs)

Since MNO exists to make profits for its shareholders (Bititci et al., 2003), it may achieve competitive advantage by reducing CAPEX and OPEX through sharing infrastructure. In a competitive environment, it may have a competitive advantage by producing at a lower cost than its rivals or by offering differentiated products at a premium price that exceeds the extra cost incurred for differentiation. In situations where superior network coverage allows an operator to charge a premium price, it would rather not share infrastructure (Garcia and Kely, 2015).

Consumers

The consumer and their advocacy bodies may exert pressure on both regulators and operators to foster universal access obligation through infrastructure sharing.

Market/Network Conditions

Highly competitive markets, network maturity raise the propensity to share infrastructure while they focus on service differentiation. This is unlike new markets where operators are concerned with market share through network coverage.

METHODS AND APPROACH

This paper uses interpretive research approach articulated by Klein and Myers (1999). Evidence was collected using in-depth interviews with selected stakeholders. A purposively selected sample of 19 stakeholders from Zimbabwean's telecommunications sector was interviewed. The sample included 3 mobile network operators, 13 data and Internet companies, 2 consumer advocacy groups and 1 telecommunications regulator. This diverse sample was meant to acquire multiple interpretations of the views of the stakeholders.

The data and Internet providers were selected for their role in supporting MNOs and their involvement in the ongoing debate on infrastructure sharing in Zimbabwe. Consumer pressure groups were selected for their advocacy role on behalf of the consumers of mobile Internet and mobile telephony services that are provided by the MNOs and data and Internet providers. The data and Internet sample consists of Internet Access Providers (IAPs) as well as Internet Service Providers (ISPs). While about three-quarters (eight) of the sample doubled as both IAPs and ISPs about a quarter (five) of the data and Internet companies were ISP who served to inform the research on the role of IAPs that provide both consumers and themselves.

The interviews were electronically recorded using a mobile device and transcribed using MS Word. The analysis draws from Grounded Theory Methods coding and constant comparative analysis (Urquhart, 2007). We used selective coding (Glaser, 1992) for analyzing each interview before proceeding to the next one in order to refine the research guide and to identify the core categories as articulated by Strauss and Corbin (1998). The main categories that we identified were enablers and inhibitors of infrastructure sharing. This selective use of GTM techniques for generating concepts is presented by Urquhart et al. (2010) as one of the common optional approaches to the full use of the GTM.

FINDINGS

Both MNOs and the regulator agreed on the need for infrastructure sharing in Zimbabwe. They view it as a way of reducing operating costs for MNOs as well as reducing tariffs for consumers as stated by one respondent 'I agree with POTRAZ if there is infrastructure sharing, it will improve quality of service because Econet has the latest technology and Telone has the undersea fibre. If there is sharing of this infrastructure the cost will be less and it will have the effect of making the tariffs lower.'

There also agreed that the MNOs that are resisting infrastructure sharing have a right to ensure that they get their ROI. The players in the field view this as an issue that deserves speedy attention as one respondent put it. 'the issue of infrastructure sharing is something that has to be dealt with a lot of speed and I think the argument that people like Econet have been using is, it's an investment which we did, we need a return on our investment. There should be a way of mitigating it.'

Zimbabwe's biggest investor in infrastructure thinks that the current standoff on infrastructure sharing is because the regulator has not concluded the matter. According to an Econet executive, '...the ball is in the court of POTRAZ we are waiting to hear from them.'

They also suggest that it must be done in a way that respects their need to get a ROI as well as the interests of all stakeholders. LIQUID telecoms suggested that some infrastructure sharing is already going on very well. While criticizing the proposed mandatory infrastructure-sharing as bad for their business interests, they claimed that infrastructure sharing was good for them since they have excess capacity. As the respondent put it:

The sharing is there and there is nothing wrong with the sharing. Ours is an open access network and the capacity that we have is too much and we want to share it. The problem with this model is the mandatory....' He added that in spite of any commercial agreement they may have, the mandatory model will make it impossible to cut off a defaulter: 'It doesn't matter that you have commercial agreements ...... the point is you can haggle on the commercial agreement but if it's mandatory I can't cut you off.

On the contrary, a respondent from a consumer advocacy group wanted the regulator to make it difficult to disconnect a defaulting MNO. The respondent suggested that consumer connectivity and interoperability should not be affected MNO by disagreements over commercial issues. In the respondent words,

… who do they want to cut? It's the consumer of the defaulting company..... even their own customers will not be able to call their friends on the other network. You see, there won't be any interoperability there.

Another informant who concurred with the idea of respecting their mutual business interests also expected the regulator to enable them. As the respondent put it, '….from my personal view it (Infrastructure Sharing) is a viable route. Let's consider what they have invested because they have used some funds to invest, but if we are taking the infrastructure sharing route …. it's an issue of agreeing on the prices like let's have this on the table and they (Regulator) approve.'

She added that the leasing party must not charge exorbitant prices that will end up raising costs. In her own words, she said, 'they can't be charging rental fees which are exorbitant, just some prices that are much more agreeable to what the market wants because that is another cost that pushes prices to rise.'

The need for price regulation was supported by a Mobile Virtual Network Operator (MVNO) who lamented the lack of uniformity in the pricing of the same service. He said,

… they (conditions) are so not agreeable because each provider will, … say I want fiber link from one provider to the other and you get very different prices as one is charging this way and the other is charging that way. They just look at the face and say is this the client that wants to be connected?…and then they charge…. so there is no uniformity within the industry.

Econet was worried about the mandatory model because its competitors were state-owned and they did not want a model that made it difficult for them to challenge government-owned telecommunication companies if they default. He suggested that the ministry of ICT which is also the parent ministry of the regulator will not be impartial since it is also in charge of the state-owned TELCOS. He said:

… let's be very clear here, if it happens to be Telone not paying and we know that the Minister and POTRAZ (telecoms regulator) belong to one Ministry. The Ministries first and foremost responsibility is to ensure that Telone operates as viable. He is looking at Telone as his family and us as the extended family. So if one does not pay and he is the one who made it mandatory for us to connect Telone, he will not make Telone pay us.

The executive added that since they were already sharing infrastructure on business terms it was unhelpful to make it mandatory. He recommended that the regulator should instead give guidelines that regulate what they were already doing on voluntary commercial terms. He emphasized it saying: 'Why do you want to make it mandatory, why not give us guidelines and we will conform because we are already sharing.' To emphasize the point that infrastructure sharing was already happening he gave examples;

... we connected the whole Northern part of ZESA riding on their power pylons. We have already connected ZESA from Harare, Kariba to Mutorashanga all their power stations like Chetsi, Bindura, we have connected them to Hwange power station. We even bought them the equipment to monitor the faults and they are doing that using our fiber.' What more infrastructure sharing do you want and we high-cost. Business practice and requirements drove us to do that.

Another issue that seemed to inhibit infrastructure sharing was network asymmetry. One operator had more infrastructure than the other networks put together. This leaves the player with very little reason to reduce their competitive advantage by sharing with others. According to a respondent for an IAP that supports MNOs, ISPs and other IAPs:

... if you combine Telecel and Netone their towers are not even at half of Econet. Oh yes, we will say we are sharing not like half and half but we will share on a commercial basis without being forced. Mandatory is going to help the one that does not have enough

The idea that disparities in infrastructure ownership makes it unfair to impose mandatory sharing was also raised by an MNO executive who said, '.... If I have 10 dairy cows and you have 2, why do you expect us to share the milk equally?' He further explained the nature of the standoff saying:

When we were discussing with POTRAZ we asked them to put it in the document that we can cut those who do not pay and they said we can't because it's a commercial agreement. So we said sharing is mandatory according to a statutory instrument but payment is no longer mandatory because it's a commercial agreement. If the sharing is mandatory, the punitive action to correct the lack of payment should also be also statutory? So that's where we have a problem.

A MODEL FOR INFRASTRUCTURE SHARING IN DEVELOPING COUNTRIES

Regulator's Leadership

This refers to the need for the regulator to exercise an appropriate and balanced level of leadership which will not generate negative outcomes on the market. We found that after the Zimbabwe telecommunications companies, presented their preferences to they expected the regulator to chart the way forward. Even as they called for the regulator's leadership they did not expect that to affect their business models or in the case of Econet disregard, the voluntary sharing that was already

Figure 1. A model for infrastructure sharing in developing countries' discussions

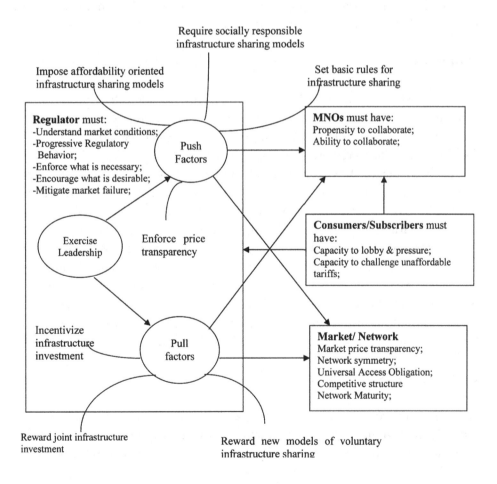

going on before the regulator attempted to impose mandatory sharing. Our analysis of the situation obtaining in Zimbabwe also showed that such leadership needed to employ both push and pull factors.

Push Factors

These are factors which forcible force MNOs to effect due to unbearable and controllable conditions. The need to employ push factors emanates from the fact that social responsibility remained low and would not improve until measures were taken to encourage it. For instance, tariffs remained high because the current voluntary infrastructure sharing was not universal. There was little propensity to practice social responsibility when it affected profitability. For instance, entering areas of low ROI and practicing environmental stewardship were costly endeavours that required some imposition of universal service obligation. There was also a need to impose price transparency because TELCOS were charging different prices for similar services. The enforcement of basic pricing rules is also justified by the concern that some high tariffs being charged to others could defeat the affordable universal access.

Pull Factors

These are factors that attract MNOs through various operations like incentives and benefits. Given the negative effects of over-regulation, we propose more use of pull than push factors. Pull factors refer to the use of incentives, concessions, and benefits for encouraging Infrastructure Sharing and reward compliance. Since TELCOS have already been found to be engaging in voluntary Infrastructure Sharing, pull factors could encourage more of it in order to yield desired outcomes. Since Infrastructure Sharing keeps evolving from passive to active sharing, it will be desirable to reward innovations in adopting a new model of Infrastructure Sharing. Pull factors may also be used for rewarding investment in new infrastructure because operators may be tempted to stop investing in infrastructure when it no longer guarantees competitive advantage. We also recommend the use of pull factors to reward joint investment in infrastructure that will be shared. Such incentives must target MNOs and investors that wish to build infrastructure for other users to rent. This creates network symmetry by making sure that infrastructure is owned by many players.

Consumers/Subscriber Action

As stated in the conceptual framework, telecommunication service consumers and their advocacy groups may exert pressure on both regulators and MNOs to observe social responsibility. In the Zimbabwean case, we found that consumer advocacy groups were opposed to the disconnection of defaulting MNOs because they wanted to protect interoperability. Such voices are critical in that they lead to the development of a model that is customer-centric.

DISCUSSIONS

Many developing countries may be facing the challenges that Zimbabwe encounters in regulating infrastructure sharing except for those that strategized in advance. Burgeoning literature shows that, the benefits of infrastructure sharing accrue to networks that are competing on differentiation instead of network coverage. This also happens where there is an increasing need to expand, where there is growing competition and need to enter (rural) areas of low return on investment (Garcia & Kelly, 2016). While the Zimbabwean domain shows aspects of these, the regulator has not exploited them.

While POTRAZ also views the risk of a shared network that may break down and disrupt the entire country as an inhibitor of active infrastructure sharing, they also face an asymmetrical network that is dominated by one company that is competing with state-owned operators. On the socio-economic front, Zimbabwe has indigenization laws that limit foreign ownership and inadvertently multi-national competition.

There is also evidence that suggests that regulating ICT deployment too early has negative effects on innovation. For instance, mobile money systems like M-Pesa are believed to have benefited from the absence of regulation (Morawczynski, 2009). This paper shows that Zimbabwe is finding it difficult to use infrastructure sharing for ensuring affordable access and for reducing negative effects of lack of it while balancing the interests of all stakeholders. They, therefore, need to overcome them using a raft of measures that combine push and pull methods with a view to benefit both MNOs and subscribers.

They are drafting a draft regulation on infrastructure sharing and they are using USF for constructing base-stations that allow infrastructure sharing. For infrastructure sharing to be acceptable to providers, it must reward their investment in existing infrastructure through licensee to licensee contracts that are economically feasible. To protect the consumer, such arrangements must guarantee interconnectivity and uninterrupted access.

Since mandatory sharing is being resisted for not guarantying payment by all users while voluntary sharing may interrupt connectivity and interoperability by disconnecting defaulters, a creative mix of both mandatory and voluntary sharing is necessary. As one MNO suggested, 'no one approach suits Zimbabwe it will have to be a hybrid approach.' To break the current non-compliance infrastructure sharing, stakeholders suggest that POTRAZ must restrict installation in wired areas and direct investment in un-entered areas. Experts recommend that their approach to infrastructure sharing must follow a national broadband plan since it shows the desired infrastructure plan against the existing network. This will then determine where new infrastructure should be installed and restrict further duplication in networked areas.

The main impediment of infrastructure sharing in Zimbabwe seems to be its immature network. This is because those that have invested heavily in infrastructure are reluctant to share while those that haven't support it. Policymakers must find how to shift a developing network from competing on coverage to competing on product differentiation. Such a scenario is necessary because, at that state of network maturity, MNOs will be compelled to share infrastructure (KPMG, 2009).

When we asked how to foster network maturity one operator advised that there was no need because it was already happening. In his own words, ' …..coverage is no longer a big issue, we used to take a whole page in the newspaper to say Rusape we now have you covered, it's no longer necessary.' This shows that even while coverage is no longer that critical, other factors like network asymmetry are inhibiting Infrastructure Sharing. The MNO with more infrastructure is resisting mandatory sharing because it dilutes the benefit of network asymmetry. They prefer a voluntary model that allows them to disconnect defaulter that fail to pay them. As one executive aptly put it, 'The moment you say XX give YY that and its mandatory and YY does not pay me, what happens?'

An issue of concern to consumer advocacy bodies in Zimbabwe is how to avoid termination of services when a partner fails or refuses to pay for their use of a shared network. The dominant operator does not trust that a state-owned enterprise will respect their payment obligations while they belong to the same ministry as the regulator. They, therefore, need a legal provision that will protect them in case of such challenges. Having faced challenges with ministerial directives that were only resolved legally they wanted to be protected from future directives. This suggests that the proposed infrastructure sharing model needs to protect current and future investors in infrastructure.

Zimbabwe National Policy for Information and Communications Technology (2016) section 7b) takes cognizance of the need to encourage investment. The government is however aware of and unhappy with the current model which operators want to perpetuate 'Currently, ICT providers share infrastructure on a purely contractual basis with the regulator playing a limited oversight role in enforcing sharing. This has resulted in unnecessary duplication of infrastructure and wastage.' Section 7, Ibid. The operator sees the proposed mandatory infrastructure sharing without legal safeguards to their business interests as an impediment to investment. To resolve such a conflict, the regulator takes leadership without over-regulating

KPMG (2009) also sights regulatory push factors like enforcement of the rollout of coverage to high cost rural areas as a driver for infrastructure sharing. This is effective where regulators can enforce such requirements. A key player in the sector advised that the regulator does not enforce such universal service obligation since it is difficult to enforce because, 'there nothing you can do when they show that they don't have the resources.' An MNO suggested that it was the regulator's responsibility to deploy the Universal Service Fund (USF) to these areas. Another respondent added, 'what our network (ECONET) has already contributed to the USF is more than enough for covering these areas. To date, we have contributed over sixty million dollars'

The Zimbabwean MNOs are yet to extend their network coverage to some rural areas yet 70% of the population lives in these sparsely populated rural areas. The low-income people who live in rural spend less on communication. As one operator put it, '...there are still areas to enter but we first consider, if there is need to enter an area that is below 5% capacity utilization.' Such areas require higher CAPEX (because of their remoteness) yet they yield less revenue to the MNOs than the densely populated urban areas. As a result, the extension the mobile network coverage by each MNO to rural areas has been slow. This is an area where regulatory push factor must address the inhibitors of infrastructure sharing because of the strength of other factors. We suggest that since their licensing requires universal access, it must be enforced.

CONCLUSION

It must be concluded that the regulator needs to adopt a model that combines both voluntary and mandatory aspects. They must also conform to the contextual issues affecting the players in their country, their fears and their lack of confidence in a regulator must be addressed. The regulator also needs to give pricing guidelines in order to avoid exorbitant pricing that may result in exorbitant price. Future research must, however, investigate the priority of each of the above factors.

REFERENCES

BTA. (2012). *Guidelines for sharing of passive communications infrastructure.* Retrieved From:www.researchictafrica.net/.../Draft_Guidelines_for_Passive_ Communication_Infrastrure

Garcia, J. M., & Kelly, T. (2016). *The economic and Policy Implications of Infrastructure Sharing and Mutualisation in Africa. World development report. Background Paper*. Academic Press.

Glaser, B. G. (1992). *Basics of grounded theory analysis*. Sociology Press.

Hatsu, S., Mabeifam, U. M., & Paitoo, P. C. (2016). *Infrastructure sharing among Ghana's mobile telecommunication networks*: Benefits and challenges. *American Journal of Networks and Communications*, *5*(2), 35–45. doi:10.11648/j.ajnc.20160502.14

Independent, Z. (2010). *Econet threatened with closure*. Retrieved from: https://www.theindependent.co.zw/2010/06/17/econet-threatened-with-closure/

Jekassi, I., & Enders, A. (2005). *Strategies for e-business*. Hallow, UK: FT Prenticehall.

Klein, H., & Myers, M. (1999). A Set of Principals for Conducting and Evaluating Interpretive Field Studies in Information Systems. *Management Information Systems Quarterly*, *23*(1), 67–94. doi:10.2307/249410

KPMG. (2011). *Passive Infrastructure Sharing in Telecommunications*. Retrieved from: https://www.kpmg.com/BE/en/IssuesAndInsights/ArticlesPublications/Documents/Passive-Infrastructure-Sharing-in-Telecommunications.pdf

Mahendra, R. (2013). *"Commons" in the Telecoms Sector: Competition Policy Challenges in a Small Economy*. Working Paper Series No. 03/13. Retrieved From: http://www.fnu.ac.fj/new/images/CBHTS/Working_Paper/2013/wps_03_13_commons.pdf

Meddour. (n.d.). *On the Role of Infrastructure sharing for Mobile Network Operators in Emerging Markets*. Retrieved from: https://arxiv.org/ftp/arxiv/papers/1211/1211.7113.pdf

Morawczynski, O. (2009). Exploring the Usage and Impact of Transformational M-Banking: The Case of M-PESA in Kenya. *Journal of Eastern African Studies: The Journal of the British Institute in Eastern Africa*, *3*(3). doi:10.1080/17531050903273768

Namisiko, P., Sakwa, M., & Waweru, M. (2015). Effects of Network Infrastructure sharing Challenges on Open Information Communication Technology Infrastructure Sharing among Mobile Service Providers in Kenya. *I.J. Information Engineering and Electronic Business*, *3*(3), 11–19. doi:10.5815/ijieeb.2015.03.02

Nhundu, N. (2015). *Is Infrastructure Sharing a game changer in Zimbabwe*. Academic Press.

Onishi, T., & Tsuna, Y. (2010). Introduction and Expansion of Infrastructure Sharing among Japanese MNO, Will Infrastructure Sharing be the key to cost cuts in a saturated market. Mizuho Industry Focus, 91.

Ornelas, I. (2016). *Legal Framework for Infrastructure Sharing in Ghana*. Retrieved From: https://www.google.co.zw/?gws_rd=cr&ei=KGHrV--tCIXXa_rUm_AO#q =LEGAL+FRAMEWORK+FOR+INFRASTRUCTURE+SHARING+IN+GH ANA%2C+pdf

POTRAZ. (2016). *Post and telecommunications Communications Regulatory Authority of Zimbabwe. Post and telecommunications sector report*. First Quarter of 2016.

Takavarasha, J., & Makumbe, J. (2012). The effect of politics on ICT4D: A case of econet wireless's struggle for a license in Zimbabwe. *International Journal of E-Politics*, *3*(3), 40–60. doi:10.4018/jep.2012070103

Urquhart, C. (2007). The evolving nature of grounded theory method: The case of information systems discipline. In A. Bryant & K. Charmaz (Eds.), The Sage handbook of grounded theory (pp. 311-331). London: Sage.

Urquhart, C., Lehman, H., & Myers, M. (2010). Putting the 'theory' back into grounded theory: Guidelines for grounded theory studies in information systems. *Information Systems Journal*, *20*(4), 357–381. doi:10.1111/j.1365-2575.2009.00328.x

Velamuri, S. R. (2003). *Resisting political corruption: Econet Wireless Zimbabwe* (Research Case Study). Retrieved May 18, 2011, from http://ssrn. com/ abstract=1009452

Walsham, G. (2001). *Making a World of Difference: IT in a Global Context*. Chichester, UK: Wiley.

Chapter 5
Affordable Access to Internet and ICT:
A Solution via Telecentres

Jay Pancham
Durban University of Technology, South Africa

Richard Millham
Durban University of Technology, South Africa

ABSTRACT

Telecentres were conceived and designed in order to provide internet access to designated disadvantaged groups that could not otherwise afford this access. In this chapter, the concept of telecentres, with its goal of affordable internet access for the community, is introduced. A few of the common challenges faced by telecentres and their evolving business models are discussed. The problem of monitoring, with its related aspect of affordability is discussed. In order to provide uniform data on usage and user profiles, a common set of data attributes for telecentre operational monitoring is obtained through a literature review of telecentre data collection projects and through interviews with local telecentre managers. Traditional monitoring methods for telecentres, such as through questionnaires, are evaluated as to the timeliness of their data and their associated cost which impact telecentre affordability. The common set of attributes form the basis of an electronic monitoring system with its advantages of continuous data collection and lower costs.

DOI: 10.4018/978-1-5225-3179-1.ch005

INTRODUCTION

In this chapter, we explore the affordability and sustainability of Internet access, particularly through the use of community telecentres in order to address the digital divide between those who have and those who do not have access to Internet. These telecentres, usually located in disadvantaged areas, provide Internet at a lower cost, through shared access and equipment, than otherwise would be the case. The impact of telecentres on their communities, within the world and within the South African context, is given.

Some of the challenges that telecentres encounter are briefly discussed along with their evolving nature, including the business model upon which they were initially based. The use of continuous monitoring of telecentres as a way to mitigate some of these identified challenges is proposed.

In order to ensure that limited ICT resources are allocated to telecentres optimally, an effective monitoring model of Information Technology (IT) usage and user profiles is needed. Traditional monitoring methods for telecentres are introduced and evaluated. The shortcomings of these traditional methods are identified and a more responsive solution, continuous real-time electronic monitoring, is suggested. An aspect of this solution, the consolidation of diverse telecentre business procedures and data items, into a common set of processes and data attributes is conducted in order to facilitate the gathering of a common set of data and uniform data reporting.

BACKGROUND

Digital Divide and Telecentres

One of the most important concepts to understand when trying to understand the need for telecentres is the subject of the digital divide. Although the digital divide is often referred to as the gap in society between those who have access to the Internet and those who do not, definitions of this digital divide do vary and focus on different characteristics such as discrepancies in usage and skills (Min 2010); (in)equality in the of use of IT (Gomez 2012); and educational level and economic status, along with the importance of rural as opposed to urban settings (Mossberger, Tolbert and Hamilton 2012). This chapter adheres to the broad definition of digital divide as the difference between those who have access to IT and those who lack this access; this definition is further specified in that it localises this gap to the varying opportunities of people to be able to utilise computers and the Internet (Van Dijk, 2005).

Similar to definitions of the digital divide, definitions of Telecentres vary by researchers (Pather and Gomez 2010; Gomez and Baron-Porras 2011; Gomez, Pather and Dosono 2012; Seman et al. 2013). This chapter describes Telecentres using the most common definition of Telecentres as provided by the (Telecommunication Regulatory Authority. Sultanate of Oman 2012). This common definition denotes a Telecentre by its intent of permitting people to access IT services in a public place and with regards to the IT and telecommunication services that it offers (Telecommunication Regulatory Authority. Sultanate of Oman 2012). Examples of IT services offered by Telecentres typically include internet access and word processing facilities (Colle 2005; Jacobs and Herselman 2006).

Although it is recognised that the internet is one of the ways identified as being able to provide a positive impact on peoples' lives through the realisation of benefits in areas including health, financial services, and education, the ITU 2017 paper shows that the majority (53%) of the world's population does not have access to the Internet, with four-fifths of this group living in Africa and the Asia-Pacific regions. Furthermore, 57% of the world's population finds Internet too costly in terms of access, requirements for end-user devices, and auxiliary costs (ITU, 2017).

In order to bridge this digital divide, one of the most auspicious methods is in the deployment of Telecentres. Telecentres are physical spaces that supply and enable public usage of IT services and of internet access(Razak, Hassan and Din 2010) By splitting the cost of accessing the Internet (in terms of access, equipment, and other related costs) among many of its clientele, the cost for an individual to access the Internet was intended to be reduced. (Prahalad and Hammond, 2002) To address this issue of affordability in the short term, ITU recommends supplying public free access through telecentres. An example, Pakistan has pledged to the World Economic Forum 2017 that by 2020, that they will provide access to the Internet to all of their nation's currently underserviced groups through the construction of 200 telecentres (ITU, 2017)

Challenges and Evolving Nature of Telecentres

Although the types and nature of telecentres can be very diverse, many of the telecentres face a common set of challenges. A few of these challenges will be identified and discussed along with how the nature of how telecentres have changed subsequently. In addition, continuous monitoring of telecentres and their assets will be proposed as a method to mitigate a few of these challenges.

Through the provision of ICT services and Internet, one of the initial goals of telecentres was to promote economic empowerment of often disadvantaged communities through the improved access to information on health services, business, and educational opportunities and to encourage income generating activities and employment for residents of these communities. (Sumbwanyambe et al, 2013) However, telecentres often failed due to a combination of human, political, and technological factors. One of these technological factors was the growth of mobile phone usage and infrastructure which made access to the Internet more affordable outside the telecentre. (Attwood et al, 2013) Given the technological advancements of the mobile phone, some researchers have argued that telecentres are no longer a meaningful medium through which Internet access can be supplied (Gomez, 2012) Pancham proposed selling Telecentre Internet access to groups of mobile phone users as a replacement for potentially more costly data bundles bought through their mobile phone providers. (Pancham, 2016) In addition to technological changes, Telecentres were handicapped by policy failures, unaffordable prices, and poor management, among many other reasons. (Sumbwanyambe et al, 2013) Another constraint was that the telecentre intended clients had low incomes and were often dispersed over a wider geographical area. (Attwood et al, 2013)

An example of poor management was where a telecentre was furnished by a government agency but Internet access was managed through software and hardware maintenance was conducted via remote access from a commercial vendor. The software created numerous problems up to the point that it had to be removed. It later emerged that the government agency representative did not properly evaluate this software before it was installed. Another example was a telecentre that operated on a semi-business basis. Although the telecentre was equipped by the government for the community, the sustainability of operations depended on local revenue generated. This telecentre offered computer literacy classes to the local community on a strict deposit before class enrolment basis. The local telecentre manager stated that "(t)he cost for a 'Computer Literacy' course is R20 an hour, for 30 hours. They pay not less than a 30 percent deposit. When people don't pay on time we charge them 10 percent extra, this often encourages them to pay on time." (Attwood et al, 2013) Despite the manager's strict business practices, the same manager lacked a clear business plan for his telecentre's sustainability and the telecentre eventually closed (Attwood et al, 2013)

Another problem facing telecentres was the unaffordable cost of telecentre usage. Some telecentres charged up to USD $3 per hour for Internet access, which was beyond most of their clients' affordability. (Sumbwanyambe et al, 2013) In addition to the cost of telecentre usage, many client had to walk for three hours to reach the telecentre and others had to pay up to R60 for a one-way trip to the telecentre. With half of the potential clients of this telecentre having R100 or less per month as disposal income, these costs undoubtedly prevent regular visits to the telecentre. (Attwood et al, 2013)

Faced with high fixed costs and a declining intended client base, many telecentres adopted new business models. In South Africa, many telecentres relied on different enterprise schemes and on distance education students [whose Internet access fees would be billed directly to the educational institution]. (Sumbwanyambe et al, 2013; Sithole, 2014) Many telecentres offered accredited computer training (often through a third party) as another revenue stream. One telecentre offered a computer refurbishment service. Other telecentres facilitated some local entrepreneurs whose business relied on the telecentre. In one case, a telecentre user began her own business using the telecentre to keep in touch with her suppliers and to market her product to new groups of people. In another case, a Telecentre user used the facilities at the telecentre to build a business writing CVs for locals (Attwood et al, 2013)

Besides the adoption of new business models to try to keep telecentres sustainable, telecentres still face a reoccurring set of challenges in terms electricity outages, internet connectivity, and theft. One telecentre lacked internet access for months at a time. (Attwood et al, 2013) In order to mitigate some of these reoccurring challenges, a number of methods, including continuous monitoring, have been developed. An asset tracking system which records telecentre assets and tags telecentre equipment has been developed. In case of theft, it is possible to use these tags, via GPS tracking, to locate this equipment. Through this method, a possible deterrent and way to reduce theft is possible. If internet connectivity is lost, the start and end times of the particular period of loss will be recorded. In the case of electricity loss, the start and end times of this loss period will be recorded [using UPS for start of loss and equipment start-up, after electricity restoration, for end times]. (Pancham, 2016) Consequently, continuous monitoring, using the methods stated, can serve to maintain records of equipment inventory and track down missing assets as well as record instances and duration of electricity and Internet connectivity losses. With hard data in place in terms of periods of electricity and Internet connectivity loss, the telecentre manager would be better able to approach the electricity and Internet providers and address these issues. (Sithole, 2014)

The Impact of Telecentres

Although Telecentres possess challenges such as financing, sustainability, monitoring and reporting of activities which have been recognised by several researchers including (Hunt 2001) and (Benjamin 2009), Telecentres also have recognisable positive impacts throughout the world. These impacts include access to training, internet and office applications (Razak, Hassan and Din 2010) and improved ICT literacy levels attained by centres that provide in-depth training to their staff and users in Malaysia (Rajapakse 2012). Telecentres have also facilitated online collaboration between customers and vendors in Nigeria resulting in business growth (Achimugu et al. 2009). Additional Telecentre impacts include expanding e-governance services in India (Naik 2011) and help with homework and transcription (Bayo, Barba and Gomez 2012). Other general positive social impacts of public access computing include improved opportunities for enhanced learning, stronger personal interpersonal relationships originating from a feeling of inclusion within the global community, and enabling the public to access more sources of and a greater volume of information than would otherwise be possible. Thus, because Telecentres provide significant facilities to supply access to technologies in regions that have limited or no access to IT, these examples illustrate the various benefits that this access brings, particularly within developing countries.

South African Context of Telecentres

In order to better understand the role of Telecentres with their associated facets of sustainability and affordability, a more intensive investigation of Telecentre operations in a particular country, South Africa is provided. South Africa was selected because it suffers tremendously from the digital divide between advantaged and disadvantaged areas within its own nation. Attempts to address this divide within South Africa through the use of Telecentres encounter common problems that are faced by Telecentres world-wide.

(Benjamin 2001)'s initial study of South African Telecentres recognised several problems frequently encountered by South African Telecentres including poor technical support, negligible funding, and equipment failure; these problems are threats to a Telecentre's sustainability. Compounding these problems, no monitoring mechanism exists that would record user profiles and usage statistics or to indicate equipment or internet connection failure. (Benjamin 2001) Consequently, there is no sustainable model for Telecentres that could be deployed on a large scale throughout South Africa. (Benjamin 2009)

Given that there is no monitoring mechanism that can be used to monitor telecentre operations and supply the information needed to analyse user profiles and usage statistics in real time, there is no way to determine the impact that Telecentres have had so far on rural communities in South Africa. This impact has yet to be explored and interpreted; future work that Benjamin recognised as far back as 2001. (Benjamin, 2001)

The requirement for monitoring and reporting on Telecentre activities, along with documenting the impact that Telecentres have on South Africa, has been incorporated into the strategic plan of Universal Service Access Agency of South Africa [USAASA] (2011). USAASA is the central government body in South Africa that is responsible for the management of its country's Telecentres. One of the strategic goals of USAASA is to monitor and assess the amount to which universal access to the Internet has been achieved in South Africa. Specifically, one of the chief performance aims of USAASA is to develop a monitoring and evaluation mechanism for Telecentres. (USAASA 2011)

As per (Gomez 2012), efforts by the South African government to increase access to IT services and to the internet have been sluggish. The lack of progress in these efforts can be partly ascribed to Telecentre challenges which often do not operate effectively because of equipment failure and/or lack of internet connectivity. Recent strategies of the South African government towards their Telecentre policy have led to outsourcing Telecentre operations to private organisations. (Sitole 2014) In order to make informed decisions regarding proper resource allocation and investment viability of certain Telecentres, USAASA requires continuous real-time monitoring data of their Telecentres. In addition, this monitoring data would assist USAASA to pinpoint and then address particular Telecentre matters (including electrical or internet outages).

ISSUES: TELECENTRE MONITORING

This section emphasises the need for a typical monitoring model that will deliver timely, reliable, and accurate Telecentre user and usage data. In order to produce a set of uniform data (Whyte, 2000), a set of business processes common to telecentres together with its related attributes must be identified.

Research Indicating the Need for Telecentre Monitoring

Ahmad and Shiratuddin (2010) defines Business Intelligence (BI) as a process of turning data into information and then into knowledge that can be used for good decision making. Factors affecting Telecentres is dependent on such a BI approach (Rahmat et al. 2013). With the advancement of technology this accurate, real time information needs to be gathered automatically rather than manually from the source to provide timely BI at all levels. This BI will inform and support important decisions on allocation of assets, and where they are most needed resulting which impacts directly on the sustainability of Telecentres. In other words, BI can be used to allocate telecentre resource optimally in order to assist in sustainability. Given that telecentres are most often set up by governments and Non-Governmental Organizations (NGOs) with limited resources, their sustainability after their establishment is of primary concern. (Prahalad and Hammond, 2002)

Sustainability involves identifying and then using these resources optimally. One of the arguments for telecentre usage and shared usage of resources corresponds to both sustainability and to increased affordability for their clients. With shared usage, both the infrastructure and running costs are split amongst many clients and, consequently, the price of usage is significantly reduced. (Prahalad and Hammond, 2002)

An example given of shared usage reducing costs is provided by n-Logue, an Indian company, which connects hundreds of franchised village kiosks throughout rural India. The approach connects hundreds of franchised remote village kiosks to the national phone network and for Internet access. Each kiosk provides a phone, Internet services and other ICT services; each kiosk might serve 30 000 to 50 000 clients. Capital costs for this system were \$400 per wireless "line" in 2002 but these costs were projected to reduce to at least \$100 per line due to new incoming technology. The 2002 costs, per user, may total less than \$1, which is very affordable for their clientele. (Prahalad and Hammond, 2002)

Real-time monitoring of telecentre usage and user profiles can provide useful BI information as to the actual demographics and potential interests through the use of client usage data. Current ad-hoc queries based on data collected via questionnaires and interviews have a reliability challenge as this data relies on human participant input which could entail bias. This information, collected from real-time monitoring systems in turn, can be used to identify potential demographical markets for products. The recognised product-demographical markets form the basis of target marketing by companies. (Sheth, 1999) Given actual monitoring data and subsequent identified demographical-product markets, a much more solid case can be made to appeal to potential private sponsors and advertising companies. The revenue generated from this advertising can form an important third-stream income for telecentres (Sithole 2014) which enhances their financial sustainability and improves the average affordability of their services to their clients.

Past Traditional Methods of Telecentre Monitoring

In order to understand how real-time monitoring is a novel concept, one must first look at traditional methods of telecentre monitoring that have been employed in the past. In traditional telecentre monitoring, data from Telecentres is generally gathered on an ad-hoc basis. Harris (2007) observed the lack of monitoring from Telecentre management plans as well as irregular monitoring being done. This problem of irregular monitoring is further reiterated by (Gomez, Pather and Dosono 2012) by observing specific studies that record only snippets of evidence from a few selected Telecentres via infrequent studies instead of a comprehensive continuous study that provides a thorough understanding of the impact of Telecentres. Some observations, as noted by these researchers, are the breakdown of resources or poor usage within the first year on the one hand whilst experiencing overuse in the form of long queues of users at Belhar and Bonteeuwel Telecentres in Cape Town, South Africa on the other hand. Continuous monitoring of activities would have identified such issues of unbalanced equipment usage and problem cases at an early stage.

At present traditional manual data collection practices are used to collect data from Telecentre users, operators and managers worldwide. The vastness of implementing manual methods is seen in (Gomez 2012) where he collected data from 250 000 centres across 25 countries by using semi-structured interviews, questionnaires with open and closed questions, interviews with experts and operators, visits to sites, surveys of users, literature reviews, and focus group interviews. In one such study 799 user surveys were completed and analysed in South Africa. In another study, (Rajapakse 2012) conducted face-to-face, semi-structured, and in-depth interviews in seventeen Telecentres across Sri Lanka. Such data collection methods highlight the challenges of investment of time and cost associated with collection, analysis and managing this data. Another important aspect is that these traditional methods require trained staff to assist the researchers. (Gomez et. al., 1999)

As indicated by Gomez, each survey warrants vast resources. Another such study conducted by (Pather and Gomez 2010) looked at the success levels of public access to ICT programs in 25 countries. This international research also further reiterates the considerable resources required by manual methods of data collection in the absence of an effective automated monitoring model. Another problem with these surveys is that only snapshots of the status quo at the time of the survey are provided. (Gable 1994) As a result, data is inevitably outdated and therefore the time and cost of assimilating the data within a survey is prohibitive and produces obsolete conclusions. Consequently, the need for a more responsive model that collects data on a real-time basis that produces timeous and accurate data, is strongly established.

A qualitative study of Telecentres in South African by (Sopazi and Andrew 2008) used face to face interviews for a full day and thereafter observations and interviews over a period of four months. Another issue noted was the possible biases in the answers given besides the high cost of interviews and of non-participatory observations. An example of outdated data discovered only after the interviews were completed was the case of internet access that was only available two years after the opening of a Telecentre. This case exemplifies the delay deriving conclusions from traditional manual methods of collecting data. Results from this study, along with the burden of work, and time spent, when using manually-based methods, all go to demonstrate the high time and cost factors attributed to traditional data collection practices.

Another observation by (Hudson 2001) is that useful insights and lessons learned on usage, user profile and services offered are identified from stories and anecdotes as their sources of information on Telecentres. Useful insights are difficult to collect from anecdotes and could also be open to subjective interpretations as well as being multidimensional which makes synthesis difficult. (Moore and Stilgoe 2009) In addition, brainstorming and focus groups need a well-trained moderator and suffer from the limitation of certain participants shying away from contributing for various reasons. Interviews and questionnaires may include bias from respondents as well as researchers. Questions can be ambiguous and questionnaires and interviews are time consuming and costly. These factors may result in substandard data being collected which can lead to poor and sometimes incorrect decisions.

Traditional analysis of the data collected also poses difficulties. (Bailey 2009) used thematic content analysis together with interviews to study factors which appeared to impact the social viability of Telecentres in developing contexts. His study categorised and discussed the different issues that affect sustainability. Another study by (Cheuk, Atang and Lo 2012) used in-depth semi-structured interviews to study community perspectives regarding the Telecentre in Bario Borneo, Malaysia. During this interview process two interviewers per interviewee were used, one to focus on the questions whilst the other documented all responses. Such a process indicates the costly and time consuming aspects of using multiple resources to accomplish a common aim. Moreover, distilling common themes from qualitative responses is problematic, and non-uniform, due to the richness of these responses. (Burnard 1991)

These are only some of many such manual surveys carried out by many researchers over the decades to gather information on users and usage of Telecentres. This qualitative data can be used to alert management and other stakeholders to problems, but they will need more reliable quantitative data for overarching, accurate and usable information going into the future. Therefore it can be concluded that traditional methods of data collection have major disadvantages (Lethbridge, Sim and Singer 2005) including cost, effort, record keeping, effort required to analyse the data, and resulting problems with the accuracy and reliability of reports.

If a more responsive monitoring model were implemented, data would be obtained more quickly, accurately and timeously and many challenges with traditional Telecentre monitoring methods would be avoided. An electronic monitoring model is such a responsive model that delivers information at real-time for management to respond quickly to problems eliminating the need for a researcher to be on site.

Moreover, traditional monitoring lacks consistency in terms of when data is collected and what data is collected. In addition, the lack of a systematic gathering and methodological process in data collection leads to unnecessary time being spent, and additional costs incurred which in-turn leads to difficulties in reporting on user and usage profiles. The literature search did not reveal any formal Standard Operating Procedure (SOP) or work flow, which had been documented to address this monitoring gap. (Gomez, Pather and Dosono 2012) in their discussion of Telecentres in South Africa highlighted this lack of standardised processes and their indicators which made it more difficult to discover important information from

Telecentre operators sufficient to allow USAASA to monitor their developments efficiently. Furthermore, USAASA has never developed criteria for key terms that would permit it to plan effectively. (Parkinson 2005)

More Responsive Monitoring Model Is Needed

(McConnell et al. 2001; Sey and Fellows 2009; Pather and Gomez 2010) identified support processes for management of Telecentres as one of the areas that is missing in the Telecentre operational process. Even programs that were meant to demonstrate the potential of ICTs through trial projects often did not have robust monitoring and evaluation systems, adversely impacting on effective implementation. (Harris 2007) An example of this is the research on the requirements and expectations of Telecentre operators in Latin America and the Caribbean showed that monitoring was done at the end of a long-term project rather than commencing directly after implementation, and this resulted in incomplete data. (Gomez and Reilly, 2002) Evidence of non-usage and of demand for services only are identified when researchers happen to conduct research on such facilities – and the results of this research are often delayed. This lack of real time evidence makes decision making on sustainability very challenging, while at the same time this evidence is becoming ever more important due to the changing needs of users and the introduction of the cutting-edge technologies. The importance of improved methodologies for continuous monitoring and evaluation of Telecentres and the illustration of aspects that contribute to the sustainability of Telecentres in Malaysia is demonstrated in Razak (2009).

Traditional means of data collection requires the continuous active participation of the researcher and is extremely time consuming and resource intensive (Veeraraghavan et al. 2006). In their reporting of their research, they recognized the prerequisite to use a software based logging tool in order to understand the software usage of kiosks. This tool was subsequently implemented to gather detailed usage data for Kiosks in Maharashtra and Uttar Pradesh, India. Their software logging tool collected data on sites visited, hardware and software configurations and applications used. Information obtained from the data gathered from such systems can support community centre staff and enable management to provide and improve service to users. (Jacobs and Hersleman, 2006)

The crucial need for an effective and efficient procedure that will perform continuous monitoring is dependent upon an electronic, validated model. The need for this model that will take into account the common processes and data is evident.

(Veeraraghavan et al. 2006) tested a software tool which collected data on sites visited, hardware and software configurations, and the applications used. By interrogating the data gathered, information on number of users, applications used, time spent, and sites visited and internet searches could be obtained. Results from this research show that for certain types of requests the tool appeared to deliver more reliable information than did surveys. For example, the manual survey reported an increase in customer traffic on particular days whereas the information gathered from the tool did not show this consistent bias; 53% of the kiosks surveyed reported higher customer traffic than did the tool; in 69% of the cases the survey reports overstate usage and in the remaining 31% of cases the survey understates traffic by between half an hour and four hours per day. Thus, there is a variation in application usage between the survey and the tool results. Given this disparity of reporting of results, electronic monitoring, through software, seems to produce more systematic and reliable results.

However, in this implementation a weaknesses identified in the data collection process was that the data collected was via a memory stick rather than an online system due to the limitation of the network resources. The consequence of the manual process to transfer data was that it became time consuming, error prone and labour intensive. An additional shortcoming of this tool was that the user login was based on the continuous idle time exceeding a certain value, based on a heuristic. Furthermore, this design did not gather data on user profiles and therefore cannot be used to compare usage with user profiles. However the similarities of the model used by (Veeraraghavan et al. 2006) and the design of the model by Pancham (2015) in which the attributes and processes are the same, shows that there is a common need and applicability of the model.

(Veeraraghavan et al. 2006) emphasises the issues acknowledged in the earlier collection of data by researchers and the attempts to design electronic data collection tools in this regard. Most of the attributes used are common to those identified by authors in section, "Common Set of Attributes". The verified model produced by Pancham (Pancham, Millham and Singh 2013) is an attempt to present an all-inclusive model using the common attributes used in their software tool as well as the common attributes identified by the authors in section, "Common Set of Attributes". The application of such a model will lead to the continuous collection of data that is independent of the researcher.

SOLUTION: DEVELOPMENT OF A COMMON MONITORING MODEL

In order to develop a real time monitoring model, it is imperative to ensure that the telecentres, which are being monitored, share common business processes and use common data attributes to ensure that the data that is being collected, via monitoring, is in a uniform format that can easily be collected for analysis.

Common Business Processes

Business processes are defined as a combination of related activities within an enterprise that delivers a service or product (Rodríguez et al. 2011). The work by (Veeraraghavan et al. 2006) on the commonality of Telecentre business processes demonstrates the potential for a universal monitoring model.

Common Set of Attributes

As outlined in section, "Common Business Processes", these Telecentre business processes generate data on which decisions are based. As highlighted by (Gomez, Pather and Dosono 2012) a common design model would provide real time Telecentre data through uniform processes to enable sound business intelligence on Telecentre operations to be gathered. This research shows that a common design model that gathers data through common processes would be key to provide for the needs of real time data collection.

After studying the types of data gathered by Telecentre researchers, a common set of data attributes emerged, including service usage, gender, occupation, age, and number of visitors (Alasow, Udomsade and Niyamangkoon 2010; Cheang and Lee 2010; Lashgarara, Karimi and Mirdamadi 2012; Rajapakse 2012). Other researchers collected additional attributes including distance of user to Telecentre and qualification of user (Cheuk, Atang and Lo 2012; Gomez 2012). Though data on these attributes were collected manually, the process faced many challenges such as inconsistency (Burnard 1991), exhaustive resource usage, and high cost. (Gomez, Pather and Dosono 2012)

Consolidating the Attributes

In order to arrive at a set of common attributes used by researchers in their study of telecentres, the authors composed a list of telecentre researchers and then organized a matrix on the attributes which their studies utilised. By inspecting this matrix, a list of common attributes used in telecentre research can be derived.

Table 2 contains a list of researchers (listed by the respective number in Table 1) together with the attributes used by researchers in their studies. The columns labelled 1 to 12 correspond to the authors in Table 1. The 'Y' in the corresponding cell indicated whether the author used the attribute in their research.

This process of common attribute identification, amongst many Telecentre studies, provides a uniform data format for consistency in business intelligence analysis. In conjunction with identifying a common set of attributes, the diverse nature of Telecentre business, with their processes, must be standardised and combined into

Table 1. List of researchers on telecentres

No.	Author
1	(Hudson 2001)
2	(Rajapakse 2012)
3	(Cheuk, Atang and Lo 2012)
4	(Abdulwahab and Dahalin 2012)
5	(Naik, Joshi and Basavaraj 2012)
6	(Cheang and Lee 2010)
7	(Hassan *et al.* 2010)
8	(Razak, Hassan and Din 2010)
9	(Gomez 2012)
10	(Alasow, Udomsade and Niyamangkoon 2010)
11	(Gomez, Pather and Dosono 2012)
12	(Lashgarara, Karimi and Mirdamadi 2012)

Table 2. Attributes on telecentres used in researcher's studies

No.	Attribute	1	2	3	4	5	6	7	8	9	10	11	12
1	Reliability	Y											
2	Technical Assistance	Y											
3	Target group	Y											
4	Gender	Y	Y	Y		Y	Y	Y		Y	Y	Y	Y
5	Suggestions	Y											
6	Application usage	Y							Y				
7	Issues in app usage	Y											
8	Usage frequency	Y											
9	Frequency of users	Y	Y				Y	Y			Y	Y	Y
10	Services offered		Y				Y				Y	Y	Y
11	Service usage		Y		Y	Y	Y	Y			Y	Y	Y
12	Internet URL Usage		Y		Y								
13	Age		Y	Y			Y	Y		Y	Y	Y	Y
14	Income			Y		Y	Y		Y				
15	Qualification			Y			Y		Y				
16	Occupation		Y	Y			Y		Y		Y	Y	Y
17	Location to Telecentre			Y	Y		Y			Y			
18	Expenses					Y							
19	Resources		Y				Y	Y			Y	Y	Y
20	No of Visitors		Y				Y				Y	Y	Y

a common model. (Xiaodong 2007) This standardisation of processes reflect the Business Process Reengineering (BPR) method that transforms diverse business processes into standardised and more efficient set of processes that can be automated and integrated into electronic systems. (Stoilov and Stoilova 2006)

The standardisation of data attributes and processes leads to an automated electronic operational Telecentre monitoring model. The implementation of this model subsequently guides optimal resource allocation and decisions on telecentre sustainability. With resource optimally assigned, a telecentre's costs are reduced and this reduction is reflected in increased user affordability

FUTURE RESEARCH DIRECTIONS

With the increasing deployment of electronic telecentre monitoring software throughout South Africa and the world, there will be an increase in real-time, accurate monitoring data of telecentres. With proper business analysis of this data, better resource allocation and better service to clients could be provided and more advertising revenue could be generated. With data analysis, optimal resource allocation can occur with the movement of equipment from underused telecentres to overused telecentres resulting in better customer service and reduced wastage. With reduced wastage and increase in third stream revenue (such as advertising), the cost to the telecentre client can be reduced. Furthermore, with more sustainable and affordable telecentres available, their impact on the community will increase. One area of future study will be the impact of electronic monitoring of telecentres, with its subsequent effects, on further community development.

CONCLUSION

In this chapter, we briefly looked at the digital divide of Internet access and how Telecentres, a community-based facility that provides Internet access and other services, could help address this issue. Some of the challenges that telecentres face were identified and discussed. Given these challenges, a number of telecentres had to adopt new business models to remain sustainable. In addition to these new business models, a continuous telecentre monitoring model with asset tracking was proposed as a method to mitigate a small selected set of these challenges.

The need for telecentre monitoring for proper business decision making was argued. Traditional methods for telecentre monitoring were evaluated and their disadvantages in monitoring were indicated. This decision making required continuous gathering of a uniform data set so that clear, accurate, and consistent reporting could be made. The researchers, through literature analysis of existing telecentre studies, identified a set of common data attributes and business processes that were incorporated into a model. This model was then verified and partially validated by (Pancham, Millham and Singh 2013) for use in Telecentres to provide continuous telecentre monitoring. At present, this tool is being deployed to Telecentres throughout South Africa.

REFERENCES

Achimugu, P., Oluwagbemi, O., Oluwaranti, A., & Afolabi, B. (2009). Adoption of information and communication technologies in developing countries: An impact analysis. *Journal of Information Technology Impact*, *9*(1), 37–46.

Ahmad, A., & Shiratuddin, N. (2010). *Business Intelligence for Sustainable Competitive Advantage: Field Study of Telecommunications Industry*. Paper presented at the Annual International Academic Conference on Business Intelligence and Data Warehousing, Singapore. doi:10.5176/978-981-08-6308-1_38

Alasow, Jumnongruk, Niyamangkoon, & Surin. (2010). *Notice of Retraction People attitude towards telecenter utilization in Roi Et Province of Thailand*. Paper presented at the International Conference on Education and Management Technology (ICEMT).

Attwood, H., Diga, K., Braathen, E., & May, J. (2013). Telecentre functionality in South Africa: Re-enabling the community ICT access environment. *The Journal of Community Informatics*, *9*(4).

Bailey, A. (2009). Issues affecting the social sustainability of telecentres in developing contexts: A field study of sixteen telecentres in Jamaica. *The Electronic Journal on Information Systems in Developing Countries*, *36*(4), 1–18.

Bailey, A. N., & Ojelanki. (2010). Community mediation and violence prevention through telecentre usage: ICTs mediating the 'Border Line'. *Proceedings of SIG GlobDev Third Annual Workshop*.

Baron, L. F., & Gomez, R. (2012). Social network analysis of public access computing: Relationships as a critical benefit of libraries, telecenters and cybercafés in developing countries. *Proceedings of the 2012 iConference*. doi:10.1145/2132176.2132225

Bayo, Gomez, & Ricardo. (2012). *Better Learning Opportunities through Public Access Computing*. Paper presented at the the Prato CIRN Community Informatics Conference, Prato Italy.

Benjamin, P. (2001). *Telecentres and Universal Capability (PhD)*. Aalborg, Denmark: Aalborg University.

Benjamin, P. (2009). Does 'Telecentre' mean the centre is far away? Telecentre development in South Africa. *The Southern African Journal of Information and Communication, 1*, 32–50.

Cheang, S. L., & Jeong-Dong. (2010). *Evaluation telecenter performance in social sustainability context: A Cambodia case study.* Paper presented at the 6th International Conference on Advanced Information Management and Service (IMS).

Cheuk, , Azuriaty, Lo, & May-Chiun. (2012). Community Attitudes towards the Telecentre in Bario, Borneo Malaysia: 14 Years on. *International Journal of Innovation, Management and Technology, 3*(6), 682–687.

Colle, R. D. (2005). Memo to telecenter planners. *The Electronic Journal on Information Systems in Developing Countries, 21*(1), 1–13.

Gable, G. G. (1994). Integrating case study and survey research methods: An example in information systems. *European Journal of Information Systems, 3*(2), 112–126. doi:10.1057/ejis.1994.12

Gomez, R. B.-P., & Fernando, L. (2011). Does public access computing really contribute to community development? Lessons from libraries, telecenters and cybercafés in Colombia. *The Electronic Journal on Information Systems in Developing Countries, 49*, 1–11.

Gomez, R. P., & Dosono, B. (2012). Public access computing in South Africa: Old lessons and new challenges. *The Electronic Journal on Information Systems in Developing Countries, 52*(1), 1–16.

Harris, R. W. (2007). *Telecentre evaluation in the Malaysian context.* Paper presented at the the 5th International Conference on IT in Asia, Kuching, Sarawak, Malaysia.

Hassan, S., Yusof, Y., Seman, M. A. A., & Sheik, W. R. (2010). *Impact Analysis on Utilization of Telecenter: The Case of Telecentre in Baling.* Academic Press.

Hudson, H. E. (2001). Telecentre evaluation: Issues and strategies. In C. L. D. Walker (Ed.), Telecentres: Case studies and key issues (pp. 169-181). Vancouver: The Commonwealth of Learning.

Hunt, P. (2001). True stories: Telecentres in Latin America and the Caribbean. *The Electronic Journal on Information Systems in Developing Countries, 4*(5), 1–17.

ITU. (2017). *Connecting the Unconnected Working together to achieve Connect 2020 Agenda Targets.* A background paper to the special session of the Broadband Commission and the World Economic Forum at Davos Annual Meeting 2017. Accessed 21 August 2017, http://broadbandcommission.org/Documents/ITU_ discussion-paper_Davos2017.pdf

Jacobs, S. H., (2006). Information access for development: A case study at a rural community centre in South Africa. *Issues in Informing Science and Information Technology, 3,* 295–306. doi:10.28945/892

Kumar, R. (2004). eChoupals: A study on the financial sustainability of village internet centers in rural Madhya Pradesh. *Information Technologies and International Development, 2*(1), pp-45. doi:10.1162/1544752043971161

Lashgarara, , Mirdamadi, & Mehdi. (2012). Effective factors on the villagers use of rural telecentres (case study of Hamadan province, Iran). *African Journal of Agricultural Research, 7*(13), 2034–2041.

Lethbridge, T. C., Sim, S. E., & Singer, J. (2005). Studying software engineers: Data collection techniques for software field studies. *Empirical Software Engineering, 10*(3), 311–341. doi:10.1007/s10664-005-1290-x

McConnell, S. R. D., Doehler, M., & Wong, W. (2001). *Telecentres Around the World: Issues to be considered and lessons learned.* Retrieved from http://portal. unesco.org/ci/en/file_download.php/053c2bb713f94903fc72a2a910a4e495Telece ntres+around+the+world.pdf

Meddie, M. (2006). Rethinking telecentre sustainability: How to implement a social enterprise approach-Lessons from India and Africa. *Journal of Community Informatics, 2*(3), 45–57.

Min, S.-J. (2010). From the digital divide to the democratic divide: Internet skills, political interest, and the second-level digital divide in political internet use. *Journal of Information Technology & Politics, 7*(1), 22–35. doi:10.1080/19331680903109402

Moore, A. S., & Stilgoe, J. (2009). Experts and anecdotes the role of "anecdotal evidence"in public scientific controversies. *Science, Technology & Human Values, 34*(5), 654–677. doi:10.1177/0162243908329382

Mossberger, K. T., & Caroline,, J., & Hamilton, A. (2012). Broadband Adoption| Measuring Digital Citizenship: Mobile Access and Broadband. *International Journal of Communication, 6,* 37.

Naik, G. (2011). Designing a sustainable business model for e-governance embedded rural telecentres (EGERT) in India. *IIMB Management Review*, *23*(2), 110–121. doi:10.1016/j.iimb.2011.04.001

Naik, G., Joshi, S., & Basavaraj, K. (2012). Fostering inclusive growth through e-governance embedded rural telecenters (EGERT) in India. *Government Information Quarterly*, *29*, S82–S89. doi:10.1016/j.giq.2011.08.009

Pancham, J., & Millham, R. (2015). Design phase consistency: A tool for reverse engineering of uml activity diagrams to their original scenarios in the specification phase. In Computational Science and Its Applications-ICCSA 2015 (pp. 655-670). Heidelberg, Germany: Springer.

Pancham, J. (2016). *Determining and Developing Appropriate Methods for Requirements Verification and Modelling of Telecentre Operational Monitoring in a Developing Country* (Unpublished Master's Thesis). Durban University of Technology, Durban, South Africa.

Pancham, J., Millham, R., & Singh, P. (2013). *A validated model for operational monitoring of telecentres' activities in a developing country.* Paper presented at the Public and private access to ICTs in developing regions, 7th International Development Informatics Association Conference, Bangkok, Thailand.

Parkinson, S. (2005). *Telecentres, access and development: experience and lessons from Uganda and South Africa.* Warwickshire, UK: IDRC.

Pather, S. G. (2010). *Public Access ICT: A South-South comparative analysis of libraries, telecentres and cybercafés in South Africa and Brazil.* Paper presented at the AMCIS, Lima Peru.

Prahalad, C. K., & Hammond, A. (2002). What works: Serving the poor, profitably. World Resources Institute.

Rahmat, R., Ahmad, A., Razak, R., Din, R., & Abas, A. (2013). Sustainability model for rural telecenter using business intelligence technique. *International Journal of Social Human Science and Engineering*, *7*(12), 1356–1361.

Rajapakse, J. (2012). *Impact of telecentres on Sri Lankan society.* Paper presented at the the 2012 8th International Conference on Computing and Networking Technology (ICCNT), Gyeongju, South Korea.

Razak, N. A., Hassan, Z., & Din, R. (2010). *Bridging the Digital Divide: An Analysis of the Training Program at Malaysian Telecenters.* Academic Press.

Rodríguez, A., Fernández-Medina, E., Trujillo, J., & Piattini, M. (2011). Secure business process model specification through a UML 2.0 activity diagram profile. *Decision Support Systems*, *51*(3), 446–465. doi:10.1016/j.dss.2011.01.018

Seman, , & Haji, , Khairudin, Iadah, Mat, Zulkhairi Md, & Yasin. (2013). Community Characteristics for Self-Funding and Self-Sustainable Telecenter. *Global Journal on Technology*, *3*, 1666–1671.

Sey, A. F. (2009). *Literature review on the impact of public access to information and communication technologies*. Retrieved from 2009: http://library.globalimpactstudy. org/sites/default/files/docs/CIS-WorkingPaperNo6.pdf

Sheth, J. N., Mittal, B., & Newman, B. I. (1999). *Consumer behavior and beyond*. Harcourt Brace.

Sopazi, P. N. A. (2008). Evaluation of a Telecentre Using Stakeholder Analysis and Critical Systems Heuristics: A South African Case Study. *Scientific Inquiry*, *9*(1), 19–28.

Stoilov, T., & Stoilova, K. (2006). *Automation in business processes.* Paper presented at the International Conference Systems for Automation of Engineering and research-SAER.

Sumbwanyambe, M., Nel, A., & Clarke, W. (2011, May). Challenges and proposed solutions towards telecentre sustainability: a Southern Africa case study. In *IST-Africa Conference Proceedings* (pp. 1-8). IEEE.

Telecommunication Regulatory Authority, Sultanate of Oman. (2012). *TRA Position paper on Telecentres*. Retrieved from https://www.tra.gov.om/pdf/563_ trapositionpaperontelecetnersen.pdf

Townsend, L. S., Sathiaseelan, A., Fairhurst, G., & Wallace, C. (2013). Enhanced broadband access as a solution to the social and economic problems of the rural digital divide. *Local Economy*, *28*(6), 580–595. doi:10.1177/0269094213496974

USAASA. (2011). *USAASA Business plan 2011 - 2012*. South Africa Retrieved from http://www.usaasa.org.za/export/sites/usaasa/resource-centre/download-centre/ downloads/USAASA_Business_Plan_2011-2012.pdf

Van Dijk, J. A. (2005). *The deepening divide: Inequality in the information society*. Sage Publications.

Veeraraghavan, R., Singh, G., Toyama, K., & Menon, D. (2006). *Kiosk usage measurement using a software logging tool.* Paper presented at the Information and Communication Technologies and Development. doi:10.1109/ICTD.2006.301870

Whyte, A. V. (2000). *Assessing community telecentres: Guidelines for researchers.* IDRC.

Xiaodong, L. (2007). A review of SOA. *Computer Applications and Software, 24*(10), 122–124.

KEY TERMS AND DEFINITIONS

Affordability: The cost of a product or service relative to the consumer's ability to pay.

Attribute: A description that denotes the property of an entity, such as an object or element.

Digital Divide: The gap that separates the segment of the population who have ready access to modern information and communications technology and the segment of the population that lacks this access or has a very restricted access.

Monitoring: Keeping consistent surveillance over an entity. In this chapter, we are continuously keeping track of operations with their resultant data in telecentres.

Sustainability: The ability of an entity, in this case a telecentre, to be maintained without requiring outside assistance, particularly financial.

Target Market: A specific category of consumers that a product or service is directed towards.

Telecentres: Public places that allow the public to access IT services, including the internet, and that provide ICT-related services, such as photocopying.

Section 2
Applications and Case Examples

Section 2 presents case examples about how affordable access has been achieved using some of the methods discussed in this book. In addition to case examples, some domain-specific issues that call for improved access as a route to a more inclusive world are presented. For example, in Chapter 7, Indira Ananth discusses the use of mobile phones by street vendors, and in Chapter 8, Alsaeed and Boakes highlight the need for access to e-services by displaced communities.

Chapter 6
A Model for Economic Development With Telecentres and the Social Media:
Overcoming Affordability Constraints

Abraham G. van der Vyver
Monash University, South Africa

ABSTRACT

In 2000 the General Assembly of the United Nations accepted their Millennium Declaration. Two of their main foci are the eradication of poverty and the economic upliftment of disadvantaged societies. In Thailand, three initiatives contributed to the eradication of poverty. The "One Tambon, One Product" (OTOP) that was launched in 2001 has as its mission to stimulate the economy by creating small economic hubs in each subdistrict (Tambon). The OTOP initiative grew exponentially and a total of 85,173 products have been registered by 2010. The growing network of telecentres helped to close the digital divide. It also anchored many of the OTOP projects. In the third instance, the social networks redefined the business environment and created new communication platforms to promote entrepreneurial hubs. The researcher combined field studies with content analysis of the social media in order to establish to what extent these drivers of poverty eradication have been integrated.

DOI: 10.4018/978-1-5225-3179-1.ch006

INTRODUCTION

In September 2000 the General Assembly of the United Nations accepted their Millennium Declaration that *inter alia* made provision for poverty eradication and the protection of the environment (United Nations, 2000). A year later the road map for implementing the Millennium Declaration was formally unveiled. It made provision for eight goals, supported by 18 quantified and time-bound targets and 48 indicators, which became known as the Millennium Development Goals (MDGs) (The World Bank, 2013). The main foci are the protection of children's rights, the eradication of poverty and the economic upliftment of disadvantaged societies. Gold (2005) applauded the goals because "they underscore the fact that tailored interventions in many sectors are essential if human development is to be achieved". "By 2015, the leaders pledged, the world would achieve measurable improvements in the most critical areas of human development." (Unicef, n.d.).

In Thailand a new initiative named "One Tambon, One Product" (OTOP) was launched in 2001. The initiative is based on the highly successful "One Village One Product" (OVOP) project that originated in Japan in 1979 (Shakya, 2013, 9). The main aim of the Thai project was to stimulate the rural economy by creating small economic hubs in each subdistrict (tambon). Each *tambon* (a municipal subdistrict) proposes one product to be its showcase. The OTOP initiative grew exponentially and a total of 85,173 products have been registered in 2010 (Shakya, 2013, 15).

The OTOP initiative was not the only huge success that occurred in Thailand since the turn of the century. The telecentre movement not only gained huge momentum, it was also creatively diversified to empower a large array of disadvantaged groups. The telecentres helped to bridge the huge digital divide that resulted from affordability, adoption and utilization. The integration of the OTOP initiative with the telecentre movement and its impact on the affordability of ICT services and initiatives will be addressed in the chapter.

Last but not least followed the formation of a tsunami of social networks. Facebook, Twitter, Linkedin, and Whatsapp, to name but a few, conquered cyberspace, in a short space of time. "Today's consumer is more connected than ever, with more access to and deeper engagement with content and brands, thanks to the proliferation of digital devices and platforms (Nielsen, 2014). Those with outdated or no devices and those who could not afford access could still not share in the opportunities created by the new digital economy.

It didn't take long before both the OTOP initiative as well as the telecentre movement jumped onto the social bandwagon to make use of these newly founded communication platforms. Affordability issues could now be addressed by way of co-operative Internet access and collective economic activities. online.

Dean-Swarray, Moyo and Stork (2013) painted a realistic picture of the present state of the art regarding the implementation of affordable ICTs:

In many developing economies, ICTs have become the focus as a means of reducing poverty, promoting businesses and encouraging competitiveness in the global economy. It is envisaged that ICTs enable informal businesses to save money and travel time, compare prices, transact with existing customers and increase their customer network (Donner, 2007). While ICTs have become more affordable in recent years, and the informal sector has employed ICTs as a means to conduct business, the gap in the use of these devices is still great.

LITERATURE REVIEW

Research Perspectives

A number of important research perspectives are reflected in the economic and technological developments that Thailand experienced since the turn of the century. Heeks (2002, p.5) views the classic contingency theory as the starting point of resistance against the normative approach that dominated ICT4D in its early years. "Contingency sees no single blueprint for success and failure in organizational change. Instead, it recognises that there are situation-specific factors for each DC [developing country's] information system which will determine success and failure and, hence, strategies for success" (Heeks 2002, p.5). He also links contingency with the adaptation concept. "In the context of overall organisational change, this is mainly described in terms of the need for adaptation of organisational structure to the organisational environment (Butler 1991). In the context of DC information systems, too, there is an 'environment' to which the information system can be adapted (Heeks 2002, p.5). Information systems for development have been affected by the intimate three-way association of ICTs, modernisation and Western rationalism (Heeks 2002, p.9). This resulted in large gaps between systems design assumptions and practical realities (Heeks 2002, p.12). He branded these gaps "design-reality gaps" and used it as a basis for his analysis of ICT failures. "Design—reality gaps are not static, but change constantly throughout the phases of an IS project." (Heeks 2002, p. 13). He sees local improvisation as the solution to these gaps. Heeks (2002, p.13) recommended "changing the (often 'imported') IS designs to make them closer to DC organizational realities"

Avgerou (2009, p.3) presented two perspectives regarding the nature of the IS innovation process: as transfer and diffusion and as social embeddedness. The first is rejected by the latter. "The transfer and diffusion perspective examines IS innovation as the diffusion of IS knowledge transferred from advanced economies and adapted to the conditions of developing countries" (Avgerou 2009, p.3). Heeks (2009, p.4) pointed out that telecentres were introduced in Europe and North America to bring the Internet to rural and/or impoverished areas. This concept soon spread to developing countries where it surfaced in many forms. The social embeddedness perspective takes the view that IS innovation in developing countries is about constructing new techno-organizational structures within a given local social context. It focuses attention on the embeddedness of IS innovation in the social context of various organizational settings of developing countries (Avgerou (2009, p.3). The positioning of a telecentre as a communication hub within a small economic development zone, i.e. a Thai OTOP region, illustrates such a new techno-organizational structure. So too does the digital doorway concept that was described by Van der Vyver and Marais (2013).

Gomez and Pather (2012, p. 4) advocate an enabling perspective. They pointed out that too much emphasis has been placed on tangible impacts and benefits while the intangible ones have been neglected (Gomez and Pather 2012, p. 4). "We suggest therefore that examples of intangible impacts which need to be evaluated could include empowerment, self-esteem, and sense of self-worth, at the individual level, and social cohesion and strengthening of social fabric, at the collective level (Gomez and Pather 2012, p. 4). They referred to Songco (2002) who highlighted the intangible aspect of empowerment. "In this study it was found that given that the poor often feel marginalized and their lives can be characterized by a sense of powerlessness and instability, even the perception of benefits can assist in empowerment, which is likely to lead to proactive initiatives by the poor themselves (Gomez & Pather 2012, p. 10). With regard to cohesiveness, they subscribed to Reimer (2002) who stated that "only cohesive people can respond collectively to achieve valued outcomes and to deal with the economic, social, political, or environmental stresses (positive or negative) that affect them" (Gomez & Pather 2012, p. 10). Eyring, Johnson and Nair (2011) pointed out that such a challenge calls for the design and implementation of a new business model. They postulate that "(w)hat's often missing from even the savviest of these efforts is a systematic process for reconceiving the business model (Eyring, Johnson and Nair, 2011). The establishment of economic cohesion is the main purpose of the creation of the OTOP model that is the main topic of the next section.

The OTOP Model

Economic development in Thailand is driven by the creation of small regionalized subeconomies based on one product range/service for which that region/district is known. This concept did not originate in Thailand. "The 'One Village One Product' (OVOP) movement was initiated in Oita Prefecture, Japan, in the late 1970s, and aimed to vitalise the prefecture's rural economy. The word prefecture means district. The original concept of OVOP was to encourage villages in Oita to each select a product distinctive to the region and to develop it up to a nationally and globally accepted standard" (Natsuda, Igusa. Wiboonpongse, Cheamuangpan, Shinghkharat & Thoburn, 2011, p.1). "OVOP development is seen as a way of enhancing local communities' entrepreneurial skills by utilising local resources and knowledge; creating value adding activities through branding of local products; and building human resources in the local economy" (Natsuda *et al.* 2011:1-2).

In order to reduce the gap between the have's and the have not's that was widened by the meltdown of the Asian economies from 1997 the government of Thailand introduced a set of policy guidelines based on the Sufficiency Economy concept (Curry & Sura, 2007, p.88). "Sufficiency's theme is that a successful development strategy must be an integrated mix of rural, agricultural and community based-private sector initiatives supported by governmental technical assistance designed to enhance productivity, increase personal income and generate higher levels of community income" (Curry & Sura, 2007, p.88).

In order to execute the Sufficiency concept, Thailand followed in the footsteps of the Japanese and introduced their own initiative named One Tambon, one Product (OTOP). "Initially, it was the government under Prime Minister Thaksin that officially launched the OTOP Development Policy in 2001 as a measure to revitalize and diversify the rural economy as a part of national economic restructuring" (Kurokawa, Tembo & te Velde, 2010:10). Curry and Sura (2007) explained OTOP in the following way:" local communities form private sector enterprises that produce and market finished products made from local resources and made by local workers whose skills are improved with assistance that increases their technical and marketing attributes. It is a publicly inspired program that depends upon whether private agricultural and forestry enterprises are successful in terms of profitability and market survival." "The central government played an active role in providing funds, awards and trainings, conducting OTOP product championship for brand-making, and in building web sites for OTOP groups (Kurokawa, Tembo & te Velde, 2010, p.10).

In the same vein as the OVOP-model, the OTOP-model centers around a prominent product or service of the tambon to anchor economic development in that region. Noknoi, Boripunt and Lungtai (2012) confirmed that OTOP uses local wisdom and community skills, and aims to support unique locally made products, by utilizing the indigenous skills and craftsmanship of the community combined with available natural resources and raw materials. Six product categories have been identified in the OTOP policy, namely (1) fresh and processed food, (2) alcoholic and non-alcoholic beverages, (3) clothes and garments made of natural and mixed fibers. (4) ornamental products including hats, scarves, bags and necklaces, (5) decorative and handicraft items produced from Thailand's forest resources and (6) herbal products made of natural ingredients (Curry & Sura, 2007). The success of the OTOP initiative moved government to utilize it as a national brand. (Noknoi, Boripunt & Lungtae, 2012). A network of OTOP shops has been established spanning all over Thailand from small rural villages to elaborate product exhibition areas at all the Thai airports. The OTOP system provided managerial hubs that served as platforms for marketing and training. Marketing agents collected products from the various small suppliers at central points. Training was also provided at these central points, thereby turning each OTOP node into a coordinating unit. By simplifying the logistics of product distribution the members of an OTOP node could all benefit from the affordable services.

The implementation of the OTOP model posed massive communication challenges to all the stakeholders. Keeping the disadvantaged communities informed of opportunities and progress was by far the biggest problem. They needed regular access to ICTs in order to conduct their operations. New developments in computerization as well as the advent of the Internet offered a lot of promise, yet "frustrating stories of systems which failed to fulfil their initial promise are more frequent" (Avgerou and Walsham 2000:1). Gomez and Pather (2012, p.1) pointed out that "Ten years ago, however, much cynicism followed the euphoria, fueled in part by the many anecdotal stories of failure and success of ICT experiences in development that characterized much of the ICTD environment during the first few years of the new millennium.

At the turn of the century the Thai public sector suffered from a tainted reputation regarding the computerization of services. "Failure cases seem to be the norm in Thailand at all governmental levels" (Kitiyadisai 2000). The fast growing network of telecentres proved to be a solution to many of these problems. Based mostly on public-private partnerships, this network anchored a turnaround strategy regarding access to ICTs in that it made Internet access not only achievable, but also affordable for the citizen on the street. This was an important milestone in the economic renaissance in Thailand.

Telecentres

The advent of telecentres was a result of the digital divide. The term Digital Divide usually refers to the discrepancy between information and communication technology (ICT) "haves" and "have-nots" (Scadia, 2002). According to Deichman et al. (2006, p.47) "there are three dimensions at play when measuring the digital divide". It reflects the basic access to and use of technology, the factors that affect the use of technology, and the advanced application of technology.). Lu (2001) added that the digital divide was also used to describe social disparities in Internet access, the access of educational or business opportunities as a result of differences in access to online information.

Ayanso and Lertwachara (2015, p. 389) are of the opinion that costs, i.e. affordability "associatedwithaccessingandutilizingICTsremainsamongthemostchallenging impediment[s] for individual consumers in developing countries looking to take advantage of available information technologies."

The most common approach adopted by governments and donors to provide access to computers and to the Internet to disadvantaged communities has been the implementation of telecentres in both the developed world as well as the developing world (Andrade & Urquhart, 2010, p. 354). Heeks (2009:4) commented that "Naturally, ICT4D 1.0 [the first phase in ICT4D] was not solely restricted to telecentre projects. But the telecentre was the archetype for this period, stretching from the mid/late-1990s to the mid/late-2000s." "Telecentres are characterized by shared facilities for people who can not individually afford them because they are too expensive and/or too complicated to use (Ariyabandu, p. ii). Affordability is thus at the heart of the telecentre network. Rao (1998) defined the role of telecentres in India in the following comprehensive manner: "Telecentres, known more popularly as community information centres, are public-access information and communication initiatives that serve as a community-gathering place where people can access communication technology and applications, learn new skills, tackle local social issues, face common challenges and empower their neighbours. Since the Rao-definition was formulated in 1998, it does not make provision for telecentres to offer Internet access. In a more recent definition a typical telecentre is described as a place providing "connectivity and access to information via a range of information and communication technologies including phone, fax, computers and the internet" (Bailur, 2007:62). The researcher who conducted this study did include Internet access as a prerequisite for a viable telecentre. When Internet access became more freely available, the emphasis shifted to is affordable Internet access as Parkinson (2005) illustrated in her study on telecentres in South Africa and Uganda. She made the following finding:

Another clear issue is affordability. Both end consumers and local access centres, whether run by entrepreneurs or NGOs, struggle with the high cost of equipment and telecom services. These costs can limit the spread of ICTs and undermine their potential value. Affordability itself is a very elastic term, since it is often difficult to place a clear value on an ICT service – it depends on what it is used for. The International Telecommunication Union, for example, suggests 3 per cent of income should be spent on ICT-related services; but in Khayelitsha, based on people's own reported spending estimates and census figures, people were spending over 25 per cent of their incomes just on phone services! What then, is an affordable rate? (Parkinson, 2005, p.389)

Five years later the United Nations in their report on information economy posted the following report:

While coverage, affordability and electricity remain major concerns as barriers to ICT uptake, education and awareness are key bottlenecks, especially for using data services. Lack of skills inhibits greater use of computer and the Internet, especially among the poor and in rural areas. Governments should facilitate demand through developing relevant capabilities, promoting digital literacy and supporting the development of applications by the relevant stakeholders. (United Nations, 2010, p. 35)

The 2015 report contains the following positive developments:

Connectivity has greatly improved, notably as a result of the widespread uptake of mobile telephony and the social media as well as the rising levels of Internet usage enabled by the deployment of fibre-optic networks. (United Nations, 2015, p. xii)

While the rapid diffusion of mobile technology continues to transform the ICT landscape, the challenge embedded in the 2010 Information Economy report remains valid. It stated that (u)niversal, ubiquitous, equitable and affordable access to ICT infrastructure and services, constitutes one of the challenges of the Information Society and should be an objective of all stakeholders involved in building it" (United Nations, 2010, p.43).

With the advent of mobile and laptop technology, attention shifted away from the public provision of access to the internet to personal ownership of ICT devices. There is, however, still a large segment of the world's population that is dependent on public access points. The World Development Report of 2016 held that "(w)orldwide nearly 21 percent of households in the bottom 40 percent of their countries' income distribution don't have access to a mobile phone, and 71 percent don't have access to the internet. Adoption gaps between the bottom 40 percent and the top 60 percent and between rural and urban populations are falling for mobile phones but increasing for the internet (World Development Report, 2016, p.7).

Recent research by Proenza (2015) found that public or shared access venues were also used in large numbers by those who had personal ownership of ICTs and accessed the internet from home, office or school. Apart from providing better equipment and faster connectivity, public access venues serve an important social function: for almost one-third of users surveyed in six countries (Bangladesh, Brazil, Chile, Ghana, the Philippines, and China), they were a place to be with friends or other people. Telecentres serve as hubs that facilitate the sharing of ideas and opportunities i.e. collaborative spaces. Telecentres also create a safe environment for marginalized groups like women and minors in the following ways: a) venue layouts that are open and promote social interaction as opposed to privacy in browsing b) places which provide access to software and hardware for storage, printing, and other skilled activities and c) places which provide training or facilitate learning activities and classes.

Thai Telecentres

The economy of Thailand is earmarked by a huge economic divide between the cities and the rural areas. The cities have experienced spectacular growth, resulting in Thailand meeting most, if not all, of the United Nations' Millennium Development Goals (MDGs) well in advance of 2015 (Intaratat 2008). The rural areas, on the other hand, have not benefited from this wave of economic development and have remained poverty-stricken. The Thai government has been constantly upgrading its policy documentation to keep up with the digital revolution. Thailand's approach to the application of ICT in social and economic development is laid out in the IT 2010 Policy Framework, which has met with cabinet approval; and the ICT Master Plan 2002-2006, drawn up in response to rapid technological developments. Both these policy documents are in accordance with the 9th National Economic and Social Development Plan. The master plan lays out administrative, monitoring, and assessment mechanisms, setting targets and achievement indicators for the overall plan, as well as for each strategy (Intatarat 2008). The ICT plan, as incorporated in the National Economic and Social Development Plan, intends to achieve its objectives under three main categories i.e. 1) Knowledge Management, 2) Access to Information and Knowledge and 3) Knowledge Application for Self-sufficiency and Sustainable Development. This is sought to be achieved by five main national strategies on: e-Government, e-Commerce, e-Industry, e-Education, and e-Society (Intaratat 2008).

Even though the Telecentre initiative was introduced to Thailand in 2002, the implementation thereof only started in earnest in 2007. Disseminating the concept was a brain child of Thailand's Ministry of Information and Communication Technology (MICT). Their objective was firstly to reduce the digital divide, and secondly to capitalise on the opportunity to establish ICT infrastructures all over the country. According to Intaratat (2008), the MICT sponsored telecentre programmes in Thailand started small with 20 telecentres in 2007 as a pilot project. Forty more were added in 2008 and 140 more in 2009, bringing the total to 200 telecentres in all 79 provinces of Thailand. The grand plan of the MICT is to create 1,000 telecentres by end of 2010 (Intatarat, 2008).

Even after the target was reached, telecentres, nevertheless continued to spread like mushrooms and flourish. By 2013 there were already 1879 such centres all over the country (Boonperm, 2013). Most of them offered Internet access to members of the community who do not own a mobile device. At these telecentres disadvantaged members of the community can access the social media as well as the websites that could facilitate their access to economic opportunities. During 2013, 700 000 (4% of the population) made use of the services of telecentres (Thailand National Statistical Office, 2013).

Kalyanamitra (2012, p.1) pointed out that a regular telecentre in Thailand is not only computer lab or internet café but a learning center as well. Thai telecentres are based on the principle that training is the catalyst that can give members of a disadvantaged community access to jobs. Helping disadvantaged communities to become economically active is an important objective of the telecentre network. Since a number of telecentres in Thailand are formally or informally embedded in some form of integrated business model, these linkages were also investigated.

The Conventional Media

After the commercialization of the Internet in 1995 it didn't take long before every institution that mattered had a website. These sites varied from ordinary display sites to elaborate interactive communication platforms. The multitude of multimedia options that flooded the market was incorporated into these websites.

A new type of website named a blog became a force in cyberspace. "A blog, a sort of online journal and interactive Web site, is another great way to engage and build a community while generating more easily measurable online activity than typically garnered from other social media venues" (Schlinke & Crain, 2013, p. 89). A website can also act as a host to blogs. The website of Telecentre Europe act as a host for several highly active blogs. On 13 December the site contained references to ten blogposts. One of these bloggers, Lize de Clerq has already written 63 content pieces on her blog. Her latest contribution "Can telecentres play a role in women's access to ICT-related jobs" is referenced to Facebook by another blogger, Iva S. Walterova. The reference features in the Community Activity section of the Telecentre Europe website.

"With blogs housing long-form content, a de-emphasis of links and keywords in search engine results, and the increasing adoption of tablets and mobile phones, user expectations around what constitutes a functional Web site have shifted. Users navigate to a Web site to learn how to contact the firm, where it is located, services offered, and to access links to the firm's alternate online venues. The focus is on visual appeal, ease of use, and ease of navigation" (Schlinke & Crain, 2013, 89).

The Social Media

The establishment and growth of virtual social networks such as LinkedIn, Facebook, Twitter and YouTube, and, in general, all kinds of virtual communities, has dominated the ICT domain in the first decade of the new century. A detailed understanding of social networks and virtual communities is essential for interpreting current changes in the economic and business environment. The networking potential promoted by the new innovations, "drives all of society and corporations to work faster, create and manage more interdependencies, and operate on global markets" (Kalpic & Bernus, 2006, p. 41).

The social media has become the primary communications platform in an economy where the importance of networks, partnerships and alliances between firms and other agents is paramount. The value of Facebook as a tool for commercial marketing and management is well-documented.. A study on social networking sites shows that 64 percent of users visit a site on the internet if they see that one of their friends did the same (Palmer and Koenig-Lewis, 2009, p. 168). Hansson, Wrangmo and Søilen (2013, p. 114) also acknowledge the importance of WOM [word-of mouth], or word of web (WOW), on Facebook.

It speaks for itself that the use of Facebook is not only restricted to for-profit organizations. Nonprofit organizations use Facebook to interact with stakeholders, educate others, and build relationships (Waters et al., 2009). Both these dimensions are applicable to the Thai economic model that is earmarked by rapid intergration.

According to Kemp (2016) 56% of the Thai population of 68 million people enjoy Internet access. Of those 56% access the social media (Kemp, 2016). 86% of the Internet users visit it daily while 7% only visits it once a week (Kemp, 2016). The 2016-figures reflect a 21% rise in Internet users and a 19% increase in social media users since 2015 (Digital Kemp, 2016). The average Thai who has access to the social media spends 2 hours and 52 minutes per day on these platforms.

Although most users who visit a company's Facebook profile are mainly looking to get information about product news and updates, and see if there are any campaigns running, they also view video's and communicate with other customers or potential customers. Successful integration of social media by a company gives the customers the feeling that they belong to a group with a common interest (Hansson, Wrangmo and Søilen (2013, p. 114).

Testimonials and endorsements can add credibility to a product and/or campaign. They can take the form of spontaneous remarks or strategically-designed content. "Hiring a celebrity to endorse a product is a popular promotional option for many marketers, but endorsements from friends, family, colleagues, or anyone that the consumer actually knows at an interpersonal level are the most trusted kind. (Li, Lee and Lien, p.122).

The micro-blogging tool, Twitter, was launched in 2006. By 2009 it had registered 58, 5 million users (Schönfeld, 2009). Jansen *et al.* (2009) described Twitter as a form of electronic word-of-mouth (WOM). Twitter is an information sharing platform using which users can broadcast short messages – known as tweets –not exceeding 140 characters to the pool of users that have subscribed to them. Moreover, Twitter provides a search facility, where by recent tweets can be retrieved for the user query and are displayed in reverse-chronological order (Twitter.com).

Despite the overwhelming interest in the social media, it needs to be remember that they are still only communication platforms that can only contribute if they are used to promote real development projects and programs.

Provide broad definitions and discussions of the topic and incorporate views of others (literature review) into the discussion to support, refute, or demonstrate your position on the topic.[1]

METHODOLOGY

Creswell (1998, p.485) defines case study as "an in-depth exploration of a bounded system (e.g., an activity, event, process, or individuals) based on extensive data collection involving multiple sources of information rich in context". "The central notion is to use cases as the basis from which to develop theory inductively. The theory is emergent in the sense that it is situated in and developed by recognizing patterns of relationships among constructs within and across cases *and* their underlying logical arguments" (Eisenhardt and Graebner, 2007, p. 25).

The researcher strung a number of case studies together. The inclusion of multiple case studies in one research design is supported by Yin (1994, p. 14). Eisenhardt and Graebner (2007, p. 25) explained that "each case serves as a distinct experiment that stands on its own as an analytic unit."

The problem statement addressed in the study is validated by a statement of Karanasios (2013, p.318) who alluded to the fact that "(w)hile there is mounting evidence on the positive national level economic benefits of Information Communication Technologies (ICT) in developing countries, one area where knowledge could be improved is how ICT and information has led to a re-orientation and transformation of human activity. That is, changes in activities in terms of how they are conducted, the actors, actions and laws/norms and the labour that contributes to the activity and how ICT introduced in one activity impacts on other activities and the creation of new activities." The researcher is of the opinion that the forging of a linkage between a telecentre and an OTOP activity, whether achieved by pre facto design or post facto business process reengineering offers a researchable platform in this field, however in order to achieve optimal marketing integration the social media will have to be incorporated in the promotion cycle.

The researcher used four of the six recommended sources of evidence that Yin (1994, p.80) recommend i.e. documentation, interviews, observation and participant observation. They visited a number of telecentres in Bangkok and Chiang Mai during the period 2010-2013. These telecentres all offered Internet access as well as a training facility. Although some of the telecentres served the general community, a significant number of them were aimed at serving special interests, i.e. the disabled, the aged and the prison population. Semi-structured interviews were conducted with telecentre operators, users and other stakeholders. Interviews were conducted at the telecentres shown in Table 1.

A number of OTOP centres were also visited by the researcher. Semi-structured interviews were conducted with managers and/or personnel at these centres. Prof

Table 1. Telecentres visited during data collection in Thailand

Type	Owner	City	Interviews and Language	Presentation and Language
Telecentre for the Disabled	Foundation of Disability Empowerment	Bangkok	2 Managers, 2 residents (T)	-
Telecentre for the Aged	The Family Development Centre	Bangkok	2 Managers (E & T)	1 x T
Telecentre in the Female Prison	Klongprem Prinsoner Jail	Bangkok	2 Managers (E & T)	-
Telecentre at the School under the tree	Pakdee Community Telecentre	Bangkok	1 Manager & 3 learners (T)	
Telecentre linked to silverware industry	Pradittorakarn Artisan Telecentre	Bangkok	1 Manager (T)	-
Telecentre at school	Kotharam Temple Telecentre	Bangkok	2 Managers (T)	
Telecentre that are linked to recycled plastic industry	The Family Development Centre / the Garbage Bank Centre	Bangkok	2 Managers (T)	-
Telecentre at training centre for young ladies	Foundation of Young Girls Development	Chiang Mai	1 Manager (T), 1 Sponsor (E)	-
Multi-purpose telecentre linked to longan industry	Prathat Ha Duang Temple Telecentre	Lee	1 Mayor (T) 1 Manager (T)	1 x 7 Officials (T)
Telecentre for young Buddhists	Prathat Hariphoonchai Temple	Lamphun	-	-

Kamolrat Intaratat from Sukhothai Thammathirat Open University in Bangkok, Thailand acted as the interpreter for all these interviews. Comments made during interviews were documented and supplemented with field notes. The OTOP centres shown in Table 2 were visited.

The researcher also scanned the social networks and detected a number of relevant locations. The collection shown in Table 3 will be discussed in the chapter.

Table 2. OTOP centres visited during field work in Thailand

City	Product
Lee	Longan (fruit), coffee, confectionary
Lamphun	Multiple products
Bangkok, Suvarnabhumi *Airport*	Multiple products
Bangkok	Herbal products
Chiang Mai, Wualai village,	Silverware
Chiang Mai	Ceramics: child and animal figurines
Bangkok	Bamboo products
Bangkok	Marionettes (ceramic heads and elaborate textile costumes).

Table 3. Social media sites and postings examined

Platform	Site	Type	Content	Likes/Visits
Facebook	Official fan page of OTOP Thailand (translated)	Celebratory (10 years of OTOP)	Background, mission, photo's of celebrities and events, pictures and recipes	1760
Facebook	Thailand OTOP	Communication	Comments (in Thai)	62
Facebook	OTOP Namkian	Marketing	Mission, comments, photo's	229
Twitter	Telecentre.org	NGO	Disability, social inclusion. gender equality	1404 Followers 2310 Tweets
Website	Telecentre.org	Promotion	News and other announcements – a global community	No counter
Website	Thai Tambon Dot Com	Marketing	Fairs, products, channels	430096

TELECENTRE CASES

The cases are categorized according to the type of telecentre and/or special interest that are served by the telecentre.

Multi-Purpose Telecentre

A multi-purpose telecentre offers an array of services to the citizens of a town, tambon or user group. Apart from Internet connectivity these services can include training, a linkage to an OTOP product or service as well as a hub for community engagement. All of the above services are either provided at affordable rates or free.

The researcher visited one decentralized example of such a centre in the town of Lee in the North of Thailand. The visit was preceded by a meeting with the town council, chaired by the mayor. The mayor explained through an interpreter that the council is fully committed to an integrated approach where the telecentre will be directly linked to the OTOP model. The mayor not only took personal charge of the integrated process, he also featured as the face of the project in/on promotional material for the project.

The researcher also visited a construction site where the building that will host the joint OTOP/telecentre activities is at present being constructed. The telecentre will serve as a marketing and liaison hub for the marketing and distribution of the OTOP products identified for this region. The region is famous for religious tourism as well as an exotic fruit known as the longan. A special brand of coffee and cacao is manufactured from this fruit. It is sold from an OTOP centre which is at present situated next to the main road but will form part of the integrated business centre that is at present under construction. Once completed the business centre will serve as a co-operative that offers participating business units the opportunity to gain leverage for purchasing and marketing. By pooling resources at purchasing time, the participants can receive volume discounts. Such an OTOP cooperative can purchase advertising and pay for other marketing at advantageous rates.

Religious Telecentre

In the town of Lamphun that is also situated in the Northern part of Thailand the researcher was taken to a telecentre that was set up to train young monks. It is called "the Monk School". This telecentre is situated in the educational zone of the temple. Although it is an inclusive system, it did contribute to the empowerment of these religional leaders of the future.

Training Telecentre Focusing on Disadvantaged Females

The researcher attended a workshop for young entrepreneurs at a telecentre training venue in the outskirts of Chiang Mai. This training centre called the Foundation for Young Female Development had been established to offer training to disadvantaged young females including girls from the remote rural villages as well as the urban poor. The telecentre where the training took place is equipped with all the relevant ICTs. The workshop for 40 people between the ages of 15 and 25 was fully sponsored by Microsoft, ASEAN Foundation, The Thailand Research Center of Communication and Development Knowledge Management CCDKM, and the Asian-Pacific Telecentre Network (APTN). The course content for this week-long event consisted of a number of business and IT modules. Product selection, marketing, basic database development as well as website design formed part of this impressive initiative. A qualified systems designer from a local company took charge of the training.

School-Based Telecentre

During 2011 the researcher visited a school-based telecentre on the outskirts of Bangkok. During the week the computing facilities were used for formal scholastic activities but during weekends they were used for the provision of affordable ICT training for members of the communities. Volunteerism proved to be the most important variable in the model. A local lawyer who happens to be an alumnus of the school manages the training program. He made his services available at no cost whilst a local radio station announced the upcoming courses free of charge. "Word of mouth" plays an important role to inform the local communities of the activities of the telecentre with children attending the school acting as main message carriers. Members of the local community who attended the courses have to pay a nominal fee. A website administered at the school offers opportunities to the local business fraternity to get involved in e-commerce.

Culturally-Driven Telecentre

The researcher visited an example of such a telecentre in the centre of Bangkok. This centre, The Family Development Center, is run under the auspices of the Ministry of Human Security and Welfare Development. The centre that is well supported by the aged focused on cultural activities like dancing, cooking, and the manufacturing of cultural artifacts. Dancing lessons in traditional forms as well as Western styles were offered as well as classes in traditional Thai cooking. The telecentre not only offered computer training to the local community, it also served as an information hub from which the centre's activities were promoted. Cultural artifacts which consisted mostly of handcrafts could be purchased at the centre. A website was created to facilitate efficient and affordable marketing.

Telecentre for the Disabled

One of the best examples of the use of a telecentre for the empowerment of the disabled is situated in central Bangkok. The Foundation of Disability Empowerment is only one of organizations whose main objective is to empower disabled people especially the physical disabled. This small telecentre offer ICT skills training on all levels. It also served a very effective marketing platform for the handcrafted articles that the disabled produce during working hours.

Telecentre for Prisoners

During 2012 the researcher paid a visit to a telecentre that was situated within a prominent female prison in Bangkok, the Klongprem Jail. The telecentre served as an ICT training facility for the prisoners as well as the officials of the correctional facility. The main function of this telecentre, however, is to act as a marketing hub for handcrafts and other products that were produced by prisoners during their time of incarceration. The telecentre was unfortunately closed down soon after the researcher's visit when prison officials discovered that certain illegal activities (drug-trafficking) were co-ordinated from the telecentre. At the time of publication, the telecentre has been reopened to fulfill its fundamental functions.

Manufacture-Driven Telecentre

This type of telecentre supports an industrial cluster consisting of home-based workers, vocational groups as well as small and medium enterprises operating in a tambon or larger region. The researcher visited one in suburban Bangkok known as the Praditorakan Artisan Community. It is linked to the silverware industry. Silverware varying from small trinkets to large candelabras are manufactured in small plants and cottage industries. The telecentre act as a business centre from where manufacturing, marketing and order taking are co-ordinated. Representatives who serve the numerous flea markets in Thailand and surrounding countries gather at this telecentre to formulate and implement business plans. An interactive website serves as a platform for e-commerce. This model is also applied for the marketing of various medicinal, cosmetic, and herbal products that are unique to the Thai society.

Community Centre-Based Telecentre

Although most telecentres have been established to serve their community in one way or the other, some centres form part of general community centres. It is situated on the same premises as sports and other recreational facilities. It is during a visit to such a centre that the researcher came across a remarkable school-under-a-tree. The researcher conducted informal interviews with 8 girls who set up their own school at a table under a tree. Since the telecentre did not offer 24/7 connectivity, they used the downtime to discuss aspects of the curricula they followed. During the times that the telecentre did offer connectivity they accessed the Internet in order to download their course material. The girls even wore similar school uniforms in order to motivate them to take their project serious. All the girls came from backgrounds that did not allow them to enroll into the formal schooling system.

MEDIA CASES

Telecentre.org

The telecentre.org website is the homepage of the Telecentre Foundation. It serves as a high level international anchor for worldwide telecentre activities. In their profile they describe themselves as follows:

Telecentre.org is a global program managed by Telecentre.org Foundation that supports the establishment and sustainability of grassroots level telecentres (Telecentre.org). On the website, telecentres are defined as: "public places of access to the Internet and other digital technologies that help promote personal and social development—offer crucial services, skills and opportunities to people living in remote and rural locations around the world. (Telecentre.org)

The program that displays the characteristics of an online community is funded by sponsors and donations. Microsoft is listed as one of the three major sponsors of the program. An appeal for donations does also appear on its homepage. The funds are used to finance the Foundation's three major initiatives, The Telecentre Academy, Sparklab, and Telecentre Women.

The Telecentre Academy (TCA) TCA provides value-added training and certification for the entire online community (www.telecentre.org). "SparkLab is leading the evolution of telecentres, from public access points to a global network of entrepreneurship and innovation hubs for socio-economic development" (Telecentre. org). The TC Women's main intitiative is the Digital Literacy Campaign, "a global collaboration between TCF and International Telecommunications Union (ITU), that empowers one of the sectors most vulnerable to poverty and its consequences — women" (www.telecentre.org). By the end of 2016 1,2 million women would have received training in ICTs (www.telecentre.org).

A recent example from the site reads: Samjhana Bhandari posted a status

Nepal Children and Women Welfare Society is a free Digital Literacy, ICT in Education & Entrepreneur training facilitator.

Twitter @telecentreorg

The Telecentre.org program is strongly linked to Twitter. Regular Twitter feeds keep this online community interactively informed of progress and events in this domain. An analysis of ten Tweets that were posted during 20-31 December 2013 provides proof of relevance and variety. Two Tweets were posted by individuals and eight by organisational sources. Telecentre.org contributed 4 Tweets, the European Commission and Telecentre Women Phillipines one each. Two of the Tweets contained feedback on projects while two more contained notifications of publications. The publication of the book "100 Outstanding Woman Telecentre Managers" was announced in one of the notifications. Two tweets had photographs embedded and another one referenced a DVD that contained a testimonial on a program for the disabled. News of a consultative session that was held with telecom operators in Pakistan regarding the establishment of telecentres was also embedded in a Tweet. One tweet was vague and contained only sketchy detail on a youth investment.

The following are examples of tweets:

Connecting people for development: Why public access ICTs matter http://bit. ly/2oXE65w via @taschagroup (it contains a reference to a research report of the University of Washington titled Connecting people for development: Why public access ICTs matter).

Another tweet from the Telecentre Foundation reads:

TelecentreFoundation @telecentreorg 4 Feb 2016

More

RT This is why @telecentreorg is here for! More than 3 BILLION people have NO Internet access. Learn more. The tweet contains a link to a news report.

Tweets are often used to promote telecentres. The following is an example.

Nabil Eid @nabileid1 21 Dec 2015

More

#Smart #Technologies = #Smart #Solutions for #Inclusion #PWD #accessibility #Innovation @telecentreorg #Spark #ICT4D

Tweets can also be used to provide contact detail of community organizers. The following example illustrates this:

Antonio Santos @akwyz 18 Dec 2015

More

#AXSchat video (captions) with @nabileid1 Nabil, Regional Community Coordinator for the MENA region at @telecentreorg https://youtu.be/9AnuQZKMt08

Facebook Sites of OTOP THAILAND

OTOP Thailand has mostly been used to promote events like the OTOP festival of 2014. Of the last seven postings that were analysed, seven dealt with activities during the 2012 OTOP festival when the program was in its 10th year of existence. Postings mainly dealt with festive activities like on stage entertainment, comedy, cooking the local cuisine, and a parade. Celebrities featured prominently as well as awards. Participants engaged by way of likes and dislikes. The most popular posting generated 32 responses.

Several other OTOP sites also serve mainly as promotional platforms. The OTOP City Thailand page recently displayed the following posting that advertised a mobile application (see text below).

Ae Athikhom Otop City Thailand (group)

Do you have any products or shops?

Owns a brand or own business.

Interested in trying to add a distribution channel.

Sell and product ads via app

Yes, sir!

THEORETICAL INTEGRATION

After the announcement of the Millennium Development Goals, economic development in Thailand took on an evolutionary pattern. The relatively successful implementation of telecentres in Thailand proved that the much-needed economic cohesion is often based on the intangible benefits that marginalized communities experience. The strengthening of social fabric at the collective level that Songco (2002) as well as Gomez and Pather (2012) emphasized occurred at telecentre level when the disadvantaged communities were given affordable access to ICT facilities. The sustainability of these centres are effectuated by volunteerism as well as a willingness to donate some of their limited personal income to create educational opportunities for their dependents. The latter factor underscores the importance of affordability.

The OTOP model that was established in parallel with the growing telecentre network provided income-generating opportunities to the same marginalized communities. Although by no form of social engineering these two models converged into the development of a new ICT-driven model for economic development. The first orchestrated example that the researcher came across was in the town of Li in Northern Thailand.

The third force that impact on economic development in Thailand is the social media. Although its integration into the economic development domain in Thailand is in a very early stage, its immense potential can't be denied. It is also a manifestation of the social embeddedness perspective of Avgerou (2009) that is based on constructing new techno-organizational structures within a given local social context. The development triangle formed by telecentres, the OTOP model and the social networks constitutes a unique local improvisation that challenges Heeks's design-reality gap. The researchers established that the success of this model rests heavily on characteristics that forms part of the national psyche of Thailand to wit their sense of community involvement, affordability and volunteerism. Increased ubiquity of mobile technology is creating new opportunities for enterprises to contribute to development and to reduce poverty (United Nations, 2010, p.11). In order to leverage ICTs further as a tool for poverty reduction, it is important to enhance usage and the sophistication of applications, particularly using the capabilities of high-speed wireless data networks (United Nations, 2010, p.20).

FINDINGS

Curry and Sura (2007) reiterated the following caution that was issued in 2004 by the Office of the Prime Minister of Thailand: Although it is becoming more successful, OTOP program is not a "silver bullet" that can eradicate completely rural poverty in Thailand. The program rests on the existence of four basic conditions. "First, local agriculture and forestry resource bases are substantial and readily accessible, second, communities are well organized and experienced and comfortable with cooperative activities, third, local people have strong workplace attributes, and fourth, communities are experienced in gaining "outside" financial and technical assistance from government and more advanced private companies" (Curry & Sura, 2007, p.85). It is against the backdrop of this sensible set of comments that the researcher considered his findings. After careful consideration they reached the following findings.

Telecentres linked to OTOP activities have a better chance to become sustainable. Such telecentres don't function as standalone business entities and therefore don't only rely on ICT activities to balance the books. The telecentre theoretically becomes a division of the OTOP business unit and is funded as such. It contributes to the marketing and promotion of the OTOP products that anchor that particular business unit. It also serves as a communication platform from which OTOP participants can access the social media. Since the OTP business unit is run on cooperative principles, all the marketing and communication activities become more affordable. Logistical costs are shared and economies of scale secure cheaper sourcing of raw materials.

Telecentres can play an important role in the empowerment of the disabled communities. The telecentre activities co-ordinated by the Foundation of Disability Empowerment in Bangkok support this finding.

Telecentres can also contribute a great deal to add value to the lives of disadvantaged communities. The case studies dealing with the telecentres for the aged as well as the one for female prisoners validate this finding.

Telecentres can be implemented to serve major social responsibility causes. By linking a telecentre to the recycling industry through The Garbage Bank, a major environmental cause is served.

Telecentres can serve as hubs for local development activities. Stakeholder partnerships negotiated within the local context provide solid platforms for addressing local needs and circumstances. The case study in Lee proved that co-ordination of local interests can work to the benefit of all the stakeholders involved.

Volunteerism plays an important role in successful telecentre utilization. Telecentre champions often have day time jobs. They dedicate their weekends to teach at telecentres. This phenomenon was detected at Kotharam Temple Telecentre on the outskirts of Bangkok.

Telecentres seems to be well-integrated into the framework that is offered by the Telecentre.org community. Furthermore, the strong Twitter support that this community enjoys, provides interactive support that seems to be lacking in the OTOP structures.

SOLUTIONS AND RECOMMENDATIONS

The embedding telecentres into the OTOP-model will undoubtedly improve the chances of an OTOP-initiative to become sustainable. This feature, albeit present in a number of isolated cases, is not yet part of the present OTOP planning model. Since the Thai government is actively involved in the promotion of the OTOP brand, it will be to their benefit to incorporate telecentres in their promotional drives. The same goes for the usage of the social media. Both telecentres and the social media can contribute affordability to the value chain.

The Telecentre.org program offers an impressive platform to link into the international telecentre community. Their Twitter platform has proved itself as a highly effective interactive communications channel. Both these initiatives can be integrated into the OTOP model.

The Young Entrepreneur program can become the future bedrock of the OTOP initiative. The telecentre network can be used as a training platform for this program. The researcher found that the course content is ideally suited to serve as a launching pad for young people who want to enter the SME business environment. The mix of technology and business skills that are taught in the curriculum met all the requirements for sensible market entry while the sponsorship from Microsoft bodes well for the expansion of the training program. The use of the social media needs to be included as an integral part of the course, preferably as a standalone module.

Volunteerism proved to be one of the fundamental pillars of such an integrated approach. It is important to note that volunteerism doesn't always happen spontaneously. It needs to be stimulated and engineered. Competent individuals need to be informed of opportunities to contribute. Invitations to experience the activities in telecentres often trigger involvement in the form of volunteerism. The social media is ideally suited for the promotion and co-ordination of volunteerism.

An integrated approach based on holistic contextualism that makes provision for broad stakeholder involvement can serve as a platform for successful sustained economic development and affordable growth initiatives. The political will to get involved in development initiatives as well as constructive involvement of the private sector and the local communities seem to be the variables that determine the ceilings of success. Stakeholder partnerships as well as volunteerism need to be actively promoted in order to maximize positive outcomes. The social media can play a prominent role in these initiatives by providing seamless and affordable communication platforms.

The program needs to be embedded in the social media in order to facilitate interactive communication between stakeholders.

The researcher is of the opinion that the both Young Entrepreneur program and the integrated OTOP/telecentre model have got the potential to be exported to other developing countries. It is recommended that the model and the program be used as flagship export models by the Thai government. If these initiatives can be constructively integrated into the social media they offer vast opportunities for affordable expansion and interactive involvement.

CONCLUSION

The findings of this study underscore the viewpoint of Park and Lejano (2013) that successful and affordable ICT4D implementation needs a wide range of requirements, and this can be only satisfied through strategic alliances. The high levels of volunteerism as well social cohesion that earmark the Thai culture form the base of many productive strategic alliances. Major stakeholders like government in all spheres, religious institutions and the local communities seem to bond seamlessly into these alliances.

The researcher is of the opinion that the model in which a telecentre is linked to some form of market activity offers a highly sustainable and affordable option for economic empowerment of the disadvantaged communities. Although the researcher found little proof that this model has been formalized in the policy domain, it would be in the interest of Thai policymakers and politicians who are responsible for the stimulation of the Thai economy to develop and introduce this telecentre/OTOP model in their framework of development planning. OTOP activities not only relieve the economic burden on the linked telecentre, it create the proverbial win/win platform of cooperation. This platform can be vastly strengthened by linking it to the social media. Social platforms like Twitter, Whatsapp, and Facebook can play an important role in stimulating affordable organizational communication processes.

The Young Entrepreneur program, if effectively linked to the social media, and introduced on a national scale, can play an important role in guaranteeing sustainability to the OTOP success story. The youth's propensity to live close to the social media validates this vision.

REFERENCES

Andrade, A. D., & Urquart, C. (2010). The affordances of actor network theory in ICT for development research. *Information Technology & People, 23*(4), 352–374. RetrievedSeptember42016. doi:10.1108/09593841011087806

Ariyabandu, R. (2009). *Role of Telecentres as Knowledge Networks: Successes and Challenges*. Bangkok: ESCAP.

Avgerou, C. (2009). Discourses on innovation and development in information systems in developing countries research. In E Byrne B Nicholson & F Salem (Eds.), *Assessing the Contribution of ICT to Development Goals*. Dubai, UAE: Dubai School of Government. Retrieved on 1 May, 2014, from http:// www.ifip.dsg.ae

Avgerou, C., & Walsham, G. (2000). IT in developing countries. In C. Avgerou & G. Walsham (Eds.), *Information Technology in Context*. Aldershot, UK: Ashgate.

Ayanso, D. I., & Lertwachara, K. (2015). An analytical approach to exploring the link between ICT development and affordability. *Government Information Quarterly, 32*(4), 389–398. doi:10.1016/j.giq.2015.09.009

Bailur, S. (2007). Using Stakeholder Theory to Analyze Telecenter Projects. *Information Technologies and International Development, 3*(3), 61–80.

Boonperm, J. (2013). *Telecentres: helping to develop a knowledge-based society that can be self-sufficient. Community ICT Learning Centre*. Chiang Mai: ITU.

Butler, R. (1991). *Designing Organizations*. New York: Routledge.

Creswell, J. W. (1998). *Qualitative inquiry and research design. Choosing among five traditions*. Thousand Oaks, CA: Sage.

Curry, R. J. Jr, & Sura, K. (2007). Human resource development (HRD) theory and Thailand's sufficiency economy concept and Its "OTOP" Program. *Journal of Third World Studies, 24*(2), 85–94.

Dean-Swarray, M., Moyo, M. & Stork, C. (2013). ICT access and usage among informal businesses in Africa. *Info, 15*(5), 52-68.

Deichmann, J. I., Eshghi, A., Haughton, D., Masnghetti, M., Sayek, S., & Topi, H. (2006). Exploring breakpoints and interaction effects among predictors of the international digital divide. *Journal of Global Information Technology Management, 9*(4), 47–71. doi:10.1080/1097198X.2006.10856432

Donner, J. (2007). Customer acquisition among small and informal businesses in urban India: Comparing face-to-face mediated channels. *The Electronic Journal on Information Systems in Developing Countries, 32*. Retrieved from www.ejisdc.org/Ojs2/index.php/ejisdc/article/view/464

Eisenhardt, K. M., & Graebner, M. E. (2007). Theory Building from Cases: Opportunities and Challenges. *Academy of Management Journal, 50*(1), 25–32. doi:10.5465/AMJ.2007.24160888

Eyring, M., Johnson, M. W., & Nair, H. (2011, January). New business models in emerging markets. *Harvard Business Review*. Retrieved from https://hbr.org/2011/01/new-business-models-in-emerging-markets

Gold, L. (2005). Are the Millennium development goals addressing the underlying causes of injustice? Understanding the risks of the MDGs. *Developmental Review*, 23–42. Retrieved from http://www.trocaire.org/resources/tdr-article/are-millennium-development-goals-addressing-underlying-causes-injustice

Gomez, R., & Pather, S. (2012). ICT evaluation: Are we asking the right questions? *The Electronic Journal on Information Systems in Developing Countries, 50*(1), 1–14.

Hansson, L., Wrangmo, A., & Søilen, K. S. (2013). Optimal ways for companies to use Facebook as a marketing channel. *Journal of Information, Communication and Ethics in Society, 11*(2), 112–126. doi:10.1108/JICES-12-2012-0024

Heeks, R. (2002). Failure, Success and Improvisation of Information Systems Projects in Developing Countries. *Development Informatics. Working Paper Series.* Manchester: Institute for Development Policy and Management, University of Manchester. Retrieved on 3 April 2011, from http://unpan1.un.org/intradoc/groups/public/documents/NISPAcee/UNPAN015601.pdf _wp42.htm

Heeks, R. (2009). *The ICT4D 2.0 Manifesto: Where Next for ICTs and International Development?* Retrieved on 3 April 2011, from http://www.sed.manchester.ac.uk/idpm/research/publications/wp/di/di_wp42.htm

Intaratat, K. (2008). Telecentres in Thailand: The Way Thus Far. *Telecentre Magazine.* http://www.telecentremagazine.net/articles/article-details.asp?

Jansen, B. J., Zhang, M., Sobel, K., & Chowdury, A. (2009). Twitter power: Tweets as electronic word of mouth. *Journal of the American Society for Information Science and Technology, 60*(11), 2169–2188.

Kalpic, B., & Bernus, P. (2006). Business process modeling through the knowledge management perspective. *Journal of Knowledge Management, 10*(3), 40–56. doi:10.1108/13673270610670849

Kalyanamitra, W. (2012, January). ICT telecentre: new model of social development for rural communities in Thailand. Graduated Volunteer Institute Journal.

Karanasios, S. (2013, May). Framing ICT4D Research Using Activity Theory. *Proceedings of the 12th International Conference on Social Implications of Computers in Developing Countries*, 318-333.

Kemp, S. (2016). *Digital in 2016. We are Social.* Retrieved 1 December, 2016, from http://www.slideshare.net/wearesocialsg/digital-in-2016

Kitiyadisai, K. (2000). The implementation of IT in reengineering the Thai Revenue Department. *Information Flows, Local Improvisations and Work Practices, Proceedings of the IFIP WG9.4 Conference 2000.*

Kurokawa, K., Tembo, F., & te Velde, D. (2010). *Challenges for the OVOP Movement in Sub-Saharan Africa – Insights from Malawi, Japan and Thailand.* JICA-RI working paper 18 of 2010. Nepal: JICA.

Leerapong, A., & Mardjo, A. (2013). Applying Diffusion of Innovation in Online Purchase Intention through Social Network: A Focus Group Study of Facebook in Thailand. *Information Management and Business Review, 5*(3), 144–154.

Li, Y-M., Lee, Y-L. & Lien, N-J. (2012). Online social advertising via influential endorsers. *International Journal of Electronic Commerce, 16*(3), 119–153.

Lu, M.-T. (2001). Digital divide in developing countries. *Journal of Global Information Technology Management, 4*(3), 1–4. doi:10.1080/1097198x.2001.10856304

Natsuda, K., Igusa, K., Gush, K., Wiboonpongse, A., Cheamuangpan, A., Shinghkharat, S., & Thoburn, J. (2011). *One village, one Product – Rural Development Strategy in Asia. The Case of OTOP in Thailand.* Retrieved 22 August, 2014, from http://www.apu.ac.jp/

Noknoi, C., Boripunt, W., & Lungtae, S. (2012). Key Success Factors for Obtaining a One Tambon One Product Food Five-Star Rating in Phatthalung and Songkhla Provinces. *European Journal of Economics, Finance and Administrative Sciences, 48*, 96–103.

Palmer, A., & Koenig-Lewis, N. (2009). An experimental, social network-based approach to direct marketing. *Direct Marketing: An International Journal, 3*(3), 162–176. doi:10.1108/17505930910985116

Park, S. J., & Lejano, R. P. (2013). ICT4D Partnership: A Review and Reframing. IFIP Working Group 9.4: 12th International Conference on Social Implications of Computers in Developing Countries. Mona, Jamaica: University of the West-Indies.

Parkinson, S. (2005). *Telecentres, Access and Development*. Bourton-on-Dunsmore: ITDG.

Proenza, F. J. (Ed.). (2015). *Public Access ICT across Cultures*. Cambridge, MA: MIT Press.

Rao, S. S. (2008). Social development in Indian rural communities: Adoption of Telecentres. *International Journal of Information Management*, 28(6), 474–482. doi:10.1016/j.ijinfomgt.2008.01.001

Schlinke, J., & Crain, S. (2013, March). Social media from an integrated marketing and compliance perspective. *Journal of Financial Service Professionals*, 85-92.

Schonfeld, E. (2009). Twitter finds growth abroad with 58.4 million global visitors in September. *TechCrunch*. Retrieved 23 August, 2014, from: http://techcrunch.com/2009/10/26/twitterfinds-growth-abroad-with-58-4-million-global-visitors-in-september

Sciadas, G. (2005). *From the digital divide to digital opportunities: Measuring infostates for development*. Montreal: ORBICOM International Secretariat.

Songco, J. A. (2002). *Do Rural Infrastructure Investments Benefit the Poor? Evaluating Linkages: A Global View, A Focus on Vietnam*. Washington, DC: World Bank.

Telecentre Foundation. (2016). *Digital Empowerment, Entrepreneurship, and Innovation*. Retrieved 1 February, 2016, from www.telecentre.org

Thailand National Statistical Office. (2013). *Information and Communication Technology Survey in Household*. Retrieved May 3, 2015, from http://web.nso.go.th/en/survey/ict/ict_house13.htm

The World Bank. (2013). *World Development Indicators 2013 released*. Retrieved 18 May, 2015, from http://www.worldbank.org/en/news/press-release/2013/04/18/world-development-indicators-2013-released

Unicef. (n.d.). *Millennium Development Goals*. Retrieved 17 November 2014, from http://www.unicef.org/mdg/index_aboutthegoals.htm

United Nations. (2000). *Resolution 55/2 of General Assembly. United Nations Millennium Declaration*. New York: UN.

United Nations. (2010). *Information Economy Report. ICTs, Enterprises, and Poverty Alleviation*. New York: UN.

United Nations. (2015). *Information Economy Report. Unlocking the potential of e-commerce for developing countries*. New York: UN.

Van der Vyver, A. G., & Marais, M. (2013). Evaluating Users' Perceptions of the Digital Doorway: A Narrative Analysis. *Information Technology for Development*. doi:10.1080/02681102.2013.841629

Waters, R. D., Burnett, E., Lamm, A., & Lucas, J. (2009). Stakeholder engagement and social networking sites: How nonprofit organizations are using Facebook. *Public Relations Review*, *35*(2), 102–106. doi:10.1016/j.pubrev.2009.01.006

Whyte, A. (2000). *Assessing community telecentres: Guidelines for researchers*. Ottawa: International Development Research Centre. Retrieved 12 December, 2013, from http://www.telecentre-europe.org/

World Development Report. (2016). *Digital Dividends*. Washington, DC: World Bank Group.

Yin, R. K. (1994). *Case Study Research, Design and Methods* (2nd ed.). Newbury Park, CA: Sage.

KEY TERMS AND DEFINITIONS

Digital Divide: Digital divide is a term that refers to the gap between demographics and regions that have access to modern information and communications technology, and those that don't or have restricted access. This technology can include the telephone, television, personal computers, and the internet.

Multimedia: Multimedia consists of a combination of different content forms such as text, audio, images, animations, video, and interactive content.

OTOP: A system that allocates a specific product range to a geographical area for production and distribution to fit in with a national economic development plan.

Poverty: Poverty is a state or condition in which a person or community lacks the financial resources and essentials to enjoy a minimum standard of life and wellbeing that's considered acceptable in society.

Social Media: The social media refer to an array of websites and other online platforms that are used by large groups of people to share information and to develop social and professional contacts with the use of multimedia applications.

Stakeholder: A stakeholder is an individual, entity, or organization that can affect or be affected by the organization's actions, objectives, and policies.

Telecentre: A telecentre is a community centre that offers shared access to information and communication technologies (ICTs) for the purpose of community level development and poverty reduction. Telecentres are being promoted as an answer to the problems of the digital divide, whereby large sections of society do not enjoy access to ICTs and are therefore at risk of being excluded from the socio-economic benefits that such access brings.

Chapter 7

Missed Call or an Opportunity:
Understanding Mobile Phone Literacy Among Street Vendors in Chennai

Indira Ananth
Loyola Institute of Business Administration, India

ABSTRACT

The mobile phone has come to be recognized as one of the key instruments of ICT. Its easy acceptance as a communication device enhances its usage. India is one of the fastest growing markets for the government has been keenly promoting a digital India programme with a vision to transform India into a digitally empowered society and knowledge economy. There has been much focus on mobile phones and their applications in the light of delegalisation of notes in India. It has gained attention in the scenario of moving to a cashless economy. It has brought into focus more sharply the need for mobile phone literacy. This chapter discusses the use of mobile phones among street vendors in Chennai, a capital city and the fourth largest urban agglomeration in India. The study found that most owned a basic mobile phone. The vending business continued to be practiced in old ways with no new management skills. The business was run and was highly dependent on cash payments. The respondents did not consider the mobile phone as an important tool for daily business.

INTRODUCTION

There has been much focus on mobile phones and their applications in the recent past. It has been discussed in greater earnest in the light of the recent delegalisation of notes in India, which came very suddenly. It has gained attention in the scenario of the

DOI: 10.4018/978-1-5225-3179-1.ch007

need to move towards a cashless economy. In this context, it would be worth a while to look at how much the mobile phones have made inroads into the Indian economy as it has been identified as one of the instruments that can be easily disseminated among the public, especially among those working in the unorganized sector.

The Government of India has on its part, since the mid-1990s taken up ambitious projects to implement and take forward the e-governance initiatives. The e-initiatives are mainly focused on the development of information systems in the country. They laid emphasis on citizen-centric services, prominent among them being railway computerization, land record computerization and others. The National level e-Governance Plan was initiated in 2006. This plan focused on thirty one Mission Mode Projects to cover domain areas such as agriculture, land records, health, education, passports, police, courts, municipalities, commercial taxes, treasuries among others. In many instances the so-called citizen-centric projects remained remote and made less than the desired impact. This was attributed to the lack of absorption capacity among the end-users. A study of the projects by the Department of Information Technology, Government of India (2008) also showed that the varying degree of impact in the various initiatives could be explained by the extent of computerization and the re-engineering done in them for easy implementation.

Across the world a lot of thrust has been given, to promote inclusive growth that covers electronic services, products, devices and job opportunities. This is true of India also. India's imports of electronic goods are expected to reach US $400 billion by 2020. It seems the country is at the tipping point where technology could be effectively leveraged to meet the aspirational needs of its 1.2 billion citizens. So what then is the common thread that binds the e-initiatives and ICTs?

The common use of Information and Communication Technologies (ICTs) tends to refer to the newer technologies of phone and internet, but the term ICT could be best used to include traditional communication media such as radio and television. Digital convergence is gradually bringing devices to the market that include the traditional media such as phones with radio, media centers with computing capability and television, which increasingly blurs the distinction between old and new ICTs. The OECD (2005) has a broad umbrella definition for ICT, which includes the internet and mobile phones under ICT.

An earlier OECD (2003) study clearly identified that ICTs could facilitate economic growth in developed countries. The ways in which this had been experienced was: (i) the technological innovation and high volumes of demand generated by an ICT production sector; (ii) the use of ICTs throughout the value chain contributing to the multi-factor productivity and (iii) the ICT investment that had contributed to 'capital deepening' in the countries. In case of the developing countries, it was seen that concentrating on ICT production and service sectors led to noticeable poverty reduction, though the poor seemed to benefit less than the non-poor. If the poor had to benefit, it would have to be brought about through pro-active policies.

Coming to mobile phones, it can be seen that it is one technology which has had the fastest adoption rates across the world. Today more households in developing countries own a mobile phone than having access to electricity or clean water, and nearly 70 per cent of the bottom fifth of the population in developing countries own a mobile phone (WDR, 2016). People are more connected today, helping in bringing more opportunities for businesses, households, and governments.

About the mobile phone, the four characteristics that instantly fascinate the user are its varied facets: (i) the ability for two-way communication; (ii) availability for 24 hours in a day; (iii) perception of shrinking of geographical distances with a touch of a button; and (iv) low transaction costs.

Till recently mobile phones were seen only as a communication tool but with the advent of smartphones and mobile applications, more business opportunities have opened up and are being successfully implemented. The use of mobiles is a great democratizing tool which at once reaches all sections of society. One of the most important consequences of the use of mobile phones among the economically weaker sections of the society is that it can bring down transaction costs as it can help in mitigating infrastructure constraints. It can empower people to harness their creativity and ingenuity.

It was estimated that at the end of 2015, there would be more than seven billion mobile subscriptions and the number of internet users would reach 3.2 billion. As per HDR 2015, if Internet access in developing countries were the same as in developed countries then an estimated US $2.2 trillion in GDP could be generated. This would be in the way of more than 140 million new jobs, of which 44 million would be created in Africa and 65 million in India. Long-term productivity in developing countries could be boosted by up to 25 per cent.

The HDR 2015 encapsulates the effects of spread and adoption of digital technologies as 'seizing the future in the digital revolution is not chance or fate – it is a matter of skill and foresight'. It also aptly recognizes that the digital technologies need not any more be associated only with high-tech industries, but also that which is influencing a whole range of informal activities from agriculture to street vending.

India is one of the fastest growing markets in the world with a considerable opportunity for broad-based services offering through mobile phones. The number of telephone subscribers in India at the end of March 2016 was 1,058.86 million, of which wireless (mobile) subscribers accounted for 1,033.63 million (97.6 per cent). This clearly shows the faster growth in wireless telephony as compared to wire line telephony in the country (TRAI, 2016). Urban subscribers formed 58 per cent of the total telephony subscribers. Even so, the influence of mobile phone can be considered from the perspective of universal access with three key components, which are availability, accessibility, and affordability. The universal access policies would need to increase access to telecommunications. This would need to be designed on a shared basis, such as a community or at a village level rather than on an individual basis.

This chapter looks specifically at the street vendors in Chennai, the capital city of Tamil Nadu in Southern India. Street vending as an occupation is of historical importance. It has been the cornerstone of many cities' cultural heritage. It has existed for hundreds of years in India too. It is to be recognized that urban vending is not only a source of employment but provides 'affordable' services to the majority of the urban population.

Street vending forms part of the informal/unorganized sector. In India, as per National Sample Survey Organisation (NSSO) study of 2004-05, the workforce employed in the informal sector in India was estimated to be about 422 million workers representing nearly 92 per cent of the total workforce of about 457 million. The National Commission for Enterprises in the Unorganized Sector (NCEUS), 2007 categorized workers according to the level of income in the unorganized sector, and found that around 75 per cent self-employed workers belong to the poor and vulnerable group.

In India, the National Policy on Urban Street Vendors, May 2006 recognized three basic categories of Street Vendors. The first is street vendors who carry out vending on a regular basis with a specific location. These are vendors who have a permanent space somewhere in a market or near the roadside which is either allotted to them or which they have bought themselves. The location of their business gives them identity where they are found selling their goods during the working hours on all working days. The second is street vendors who do not carry out vending on a regular basis. They do not have a specific location, for example, vendors who sell goods in weekly bazaars during holidays and festivals and so on. When these kinds of vendors with temporary space sell in the city, they find it difficult to run the business as they have poor social and legal protection. Many a time they may be considered as encroachers and regarded as public nuisance. The third is mobile street vendors. These vendors can be seen with head loads or with a mobile cart. They basically move around with their wares, generally on a regular route. These vendors provide goods at the customer's doorstep.

The total number of street vendors in India is estimated at around 10 million. It is estimated there would be nearly 200,000 to 250,000 street vendors in the other two major metropolitan cities of India, Mumbai and Kolkata respectively. Overall, the number of vendors is expected to constitute approximately 2 per cent of the population of a metropolis. The street vendors even though constituting only a small percentage of the city's population, form an integral part of the economic and social system. They cater to the needs of the lower and middle-income groups of the population, which is the major chunk of the total population. So their influence on the society is considerable. But it is seen that the way they run their business has not changed for years. They still adopt informal methods which are most often not very productive. Even though technology has penetrated into every section of the society, it is quite evident that in the world of street vending, they continue to rely on old methods to run their business which caters to their personal needs.

This chapter has as its objectives the following: (1) to understand the diffusion of mobile phones among the street vendors – to see what kind of mobile phones are popular and found useful; (2) to understand the impact of mobile phones on the personal and business lives of street vendors – to gauge the proficiency in using the mobile phones for various purposes.

BACKGROUND

The extant of studies show the use of mobile phones in micro and small business operations in developing countries and its contribution to their livelihood. Today the penetration of mobile phones in the world is unparalleled by any other communication technology. Adoption of mobile phones throughout the developing world has been more rapid than any other communication technology in history (Castells et al., 2007). Waverman *et al* (2005) estimated that 10 more mobile phones per 100 people could increase GDP per capita growth by up to 0.6 per cent. Similarly, a 2012 Deloitte Report argued that in middle or low-income countries, a 10 per cent increase in mobile phone penetration is linked to GDP growth of 1.2 per cent (Deloitte, 2012).

Further to the economic contribution, much effort has been spent in examining the social, political, and cultural impact of mobiles. GSMA (2015) asserts that mobile phones and access to the internet can have a social and political impact. Mobile phones can, for example, provide communications and basic services to the disadvantaged populations. McKinsey (2013) suggests that if mobile enabled internet access achieves an impact on the same scale as mobile telephony has in Africa, it could have transformational effects on sectors such as retail, agriculture, education, and healthcare. The Arab States Mobile Observatory (GSMA, 2013) comments that mobile services impact positively on the living standards of people across communities in a practical manner, increasing social capital.

There is growing literature on the spread of mobile technology in developing countries and the tangible effects on socio-economic development, though not many in number (Donner, 2008). The study by ICRW, 2012 showed that mobiles more than computers or the internet has allowed women to build entrepreneurial success. In the context of migrant workers, Qiu (2008) showed that working-class ICTs had diffused widely and the migrants' socio-economic status significantly affected ICT connectivity.

In India, TISS (2015) study has shown that there is a clear correlation between mobile phone ownership and both economic and wider measures of social well-being. However putting a mobile in the hands of an individual is unlikely by itself to improve that person's livelihood, but needs to be strengthened further with education on related techniques and tools (Vodafone Public Policy, 2009).

Warshauer (2003) showed that increased capabilities occur if individuals or groups have the internal capacity like education, health, political freedoms to be able to use new technology resources. Surveys of mobile phone use at the bottom of the pyramid (BoP) suggest that ICTs enabled communications to build human capabilities and freedoms while providing economic services, as well as personal, family, social interaction and community relationships (Spence & Smith, 2009). LIRNEasia research indicated that 90–100% of people surveyed in the BoP in 2006, in countries such as Pakistan, Bangladesh, India, Sri Lanka, Thailand, and the Philippines had used a mobile phone in the past three months.

However, it is important to recognize that mobile phones alone are not capable of raising people out of poverty or encouraging democratic governance. UNDP (2012) refers to mobile phones as catalytic tools for enhancing and broadening development programmes. They can add immense value when they are deployed strategically. There is no doubt that the information technology helps a large section of people to leapfrog to reach a higher level of development. But it seems a key determinant that affects the progress is 'capabilities'. A person's advantage is determined by their capabilities, that is to say, what they can or cannot do, or can or cannot be (Sen, 1985). So in some cases, ICTs can simply represent a new way in which inequalities are further entrenched. They can have adverse effects such as being a new source of social exclusion. It could raise a new form of deprivation also, which is now referred to as 'digital poverty'. This is defined as 'the lack of goods and services based on ICT' (Barrantes, 2007).

Hence as stressed by Amartya Sen, the relationship of people to the resources that they have and the commodities that they require in meeting their basic sustenance requirements will influence the way they take it forward.

USE OF MOBILES AMONG STREET VENDORS

Mobile Phones in India

Mobile phones in India can be broadly classified into three kinds – (i) Basic Phones - these devices have no touchscreen, qwerty or advanced operating system; (ii) Multi-media Phones - these may have touch screen or a qwerty keypad but lack an advanced operating system that can be found in a smart phone and (iii) Smart

Phones - these devices which may or may not have a touch screen but have an advanced operating system. Those mobile phones having android, windows, iOS operating systems and having the capability to allow third party applications would fall under this category. While smartphones are growing more aggressively, basic phone shipments still continue to be over 85 per cent of mobile handset shipments on the back of a feature-packed, low-price proposition. Expert estimates suggest that over 70 per cent of data users and 50 per cent of traffic still comes from basic phones, making it a segment that one cannot ignore.

While mobile internet use is possible on all of these mobile phones, the quality of user experience is better on a smartphone. The adoption of smartphones in India has been happening at a relatively slow pace, especially when looked at in the context of the 700 million active mobile subscribers. One of the primary reasons could be the high price of smartphones and the slow surge of 3G connections. Feature phones are more prominent in India, accounting for over 90% of all internet capable devices. While smartphones were growing more aggressively, feature phone shipments continued to be over 85% of mobile handset shipments on the back of a feature-packed, low-price proposition.

About Chennai

India has 29 States and 7 Union Territories. Tamil Nadu is in the South of India. It is one of the most rapidly industrializing and urbanizing States. As per the Census 2011, 48.4 per cent of the state's population lived in urban areas. This was an increase of over 27 per cent from the year 2001. Chennai is one of the 32 districts of Tamil Nadu which is fully urban (100 per cent). It had a population density of 26,903 persons per square kilometre in 2011. This is next only to the cities of Delhi and higher than Mumbai and Kolkata. In 2011, Chennai was the fourth largest urban agglomeration in India with a continuous urban spread over the three districts of Thiruvallur, Chennai, and Kancheepuram.

The per capita income in Chennai at constant prices grew from Rs.37676/- in 2004-05 to Rs.57706/- in 2010-11. In 2011, as per the Overview for the Twelfth Five Year Plan 2012-17 of the Government of Tamil Nadu, the Human Development Indicators (HDI) calculations for the state showed that Chennai remained as one of the top five districts in the states. Chennai had an HDI of 0.817 which was the highest among all districts. But its per capita income was Rs.57387/- in 2008-09 and sex ratio of 986 was well below the other districts.

Chennai has witnessed unprecedented growth in recent years, principally due to the information technology boom. Chennai City alone accounts for 10.94 per cent of the State income, while the Chennai Metropolitan Area accounts for 16.21 per cent of the State income from all other sectors. Nearly 90 per cent of the people are engaged in the tertiary sector. With respect to the informal sector, as per Census 2001, it was estimated that persons in informal sector would be about one million in the Chennai City. These persons are predominantly in low wage paying sectors like rickshaw pulling, repair of bicycles, personal services, etc. Occupations with better wage conditions include construction, manufacturing and repair activities. What is of particular interest is that in Chennai, nearly 92 per cent of the population were connected, that is they had a telephone connection, mobile or otherwise.

The survey discussed here was conducted among street vendors in the capital city of Chennai in the year 2014. For the purpose of the study, a proportional random sampling was done by dividing the whole of Chennai City into 5 zones. Further within each of the zones, respondents were chosen at random who were interviewed using a structured questionnaire. The questionnaire was divided into three main sections. The data collected included: (i) basic social background of the respondents such as their age, education, and marital status; (ii) business details which included the respondents understanding about business; (iii) mobile literacy which covered the usage of mobile phones by the respondents and looked at what functionalities other than basic calling option the respondents generally used.

Profile of the Street Vendors

The study surveyed 250 vendors. The study did not predetermine the ratio of male and female vendors - 77 per cent of the respondents were male. The street vendors were aged between 25 and 45 years. 35 per cent were in the age group of 30 to 40 years. Most had some form of formal education. Nearly 42.4 per cent had discontinued studies while studying in classes 6 to 10. The majority of the vendors (86 per cent) were married with two or more children in the family. In some cases there were elderly dependent members. The street vendors were largely in the business of selling fruits and vegetables followed by small accessories. The wares were sourced from the locally well-known bigger markets. The purchases were primarily based on cash payments. The average monthly income earned in the business was in the range of Rs.7000/- to Rs.15000/-. Most vendors were satisfied with their vocation. They did not sense any challenge in their occupations.

Profile of Mobile Use

Table 1 gives the profile of the mobile used by the street vendors surveyed. It was seen that all the street vendors owned a mobile phone. All were first-time users of phones. They had never before owned a landline. All vendors were using it in their regular daily activities. 80 per cent of the respondents said that the mobile had become a necessity.

Table 1. Profile of mobile phone used

	About Mobiles Used	No. of Respondents
1. Mobile used for (years)	Less than 2	22
	3 to 5	91
	6 to 8	34
	9 to 10	69
	More than 10	29
	Total	250
2. No. of times mobile has been changed	Less than 2	70
	2 to 5	77
	6 to 10	31
	11 to 15	33
	More than 15	33
	Total	250
3. Type of mobile	Basic	149
	Intermediate	56
	Low-end smartphone	36
	High-end smartphone	3
	Total	250
4. The cost of mobile (Rs.)	Less than 2000	149
	2000- 5000	62
	5000-10000	27
	More than 10000	3
	Total	250
5. Type of Service	Prepaid	219
	Postpaid	31
	Total	250
6. Purchased by	Family	49
	Self	190
	Total	239
7. Share mobile with (no. of persons)	None	220
	1 to 3	21
	Total	241

continued on following page

Table 1. Continued

	About Mobiles Used	**No. of Respondents**
8. Purchase decision based on (influenced by)	Social group (friends)	67
	Brand Value	52
	Features	43
	Low budget	81
	Total	250
9. Expenditure on mobile services (Rs.)	100 – 200	67
	200 - 300	46
	300 – 500	33
	500-1000	42
	More than 1000	32
	Total	250

Source: Primary data.

59 per cent owned a basic feature model, which cost them less than Rs.2000/-. Less than 10 per cent of the street vendors spent more than Rs.5000/- on a mobile phone. More than 95 per cent of the respondents had owned a mobile phone for more than 3 years. Nearly 29 per cent had used a mobile phone for more than 10 years.

It was also seen that nearly 60 per cent of them had changed their phones after two to five years of use. The purchase decision was mostly influenced by the cost of the phone instrument and the budget which was pre-decided. The other important factor was the opinion of the social circle of friends. The phone was most times bought by the individual for personal use. It was not owned by the family. The instrument was almost never shared with anybody.

Survey showed that the respondents aged between 40 to 45 years had the least urge to change their phones. Those vendors aged between 25 to 35 years changed their mobile phones more often to keep in touch with technology in the market. It was also seen that the second purchase and after was always a higher-end model. It seems that those in the younger age group were more adept in understanding the functions associated with the higher-end mobile phones.

Nearly 45 per cent of the street vendors incurred an expense of Rs.100/- to Rs.300/- on any of the available mobile services in the market. While those in the age group of 40 to 45 years spent about Rs.100/- to Rs.200/- per month, those between 25 and 30 years spent about Rs.500/- to Rs.1000/- as their mobile expenses per month. These were expenses incurred on payments for services which they made on a pre-paid basis.

Table 2. Profile of mobile phone user

	Profile of Mobile Use	No. of Respondents
1. Difficulty of handling	Very easy	91
	Easy	86
	Moderate	34
	Difficult	28
	Very difficult	5
	None	6
	Total	250
2. Texting proficiency (SMS)	None	6
	Don't use	140
	Receive only	55
	Send / receive	49
	Total	250
3. Proficient to save new contact	None	6
	No – use address book	14
	No – others help	56
	Yes	174
	Total	250
4. Aware of use of memory card	None	6
	No	72
	Yes	172
	Total	250
5. Number of calls received per day	None	6
	Zero	107
	Less than 3	81
	3 to 5	32
	5 to 10	9
	More than 10	15
	Total	250
6. Number of calls made to supplier/customer		None
7. Regional language use preferred?	None – do not know	6
	No	147
	Yes	97
	Total	250

continued on following page

Table 2. Continued

	Profile of Mobile Use	No. of Respondents
8. Practice of giving missed calls	None – do not know	6
	Don't give	166
	Because of low balance	50
	Only among family	22
	Only for business	6
	Total	250
9. Improvement in business because of using mobile phone	None – can't say	6
	No	199
	Yes	45
	Total	250

Business Utility of Mobile

The majority of street vendors found it easy to handle the mobile phone.

Table 2 gives the profile of the mobile phone user. Nearly 60% of the respondents were using only a basic feature mobile phone with only calling and message (SMS) facility. Less than 20% of those surveyed said they ever used the instrument for texting any messages. What is however interesting is that nearly 40% never ever received any phone call on the mobile.

With a bit of prodding during the interviews, it came out that those who were proficient only with making phone calls bought only a basic feature model. They had made the purchase without any preference for color display or screen size. Interestingly, more than half of the respondents did not use SMS as a mode of communication with their mobile phones. In those cases, where they used SMS, the respondent preferred an advanced model with a larger screen for visibility. And those more adept and starting to use other services like the internet were increasingly opting for a more advanced handset.

With regards to the preference for native language to use the mobile, it decreased as the respondents acquired a higher educational qualification. This is quite clear from the fact that those literate and comfortable with English had no need to use the mobile phone in the regional language.

With regards to the businesses, the survey showed that the street vendors were following in the footsteps of the father or other senior members of the family. They could not however say when the families had come into the business. Many times to tide over urgencies, they borrowed from local pawnbrokers and other money lenders at high-interest rates. The survey found that the street vendors were not using any calculators in their daily business and were not aware of how to use the calculator in their mobile.

Most of the vendors (69.6 per cent) knew how to save contacts in the address book in their mobile phones. However, those in the older age group of 40 to 50 years did not know how to save the contacts. In fact they did not know how many contacts were stored in the device. They seemed to need help to retrieve and see the contact on the mobile screen. They also could not distinguish between personal and business contacts.

Most of the vendors, irrespective of their ages, did not see any gain or felt that the mobile phone was important for any business operation. None of them had made any calls to either the supplier or customer. Nearly 80 per cent of the respondents across all age groups felt that mobiles were not useful in their business. Most vendors said that mobile phones did not increase their daily business transactions. Very few vendors were using any message boosters, rate cutters for voice call and internet boosters, or were not even aware of these.

Interestingly, nearly 60 per cent also said that they did not use the mobile phone for a 'missed call'. A missed call being the practice of calling and disconnecting the call before the receiver answers. This is commonly used to inform the receiver to call back.

IMPLICATIONS FOR POLICY

It seems that the implications for policy arise because of the fact that the ways of business as practiced by the street vendors are far from the expected ordinary management practices. They had continued in the same profession of vending as their parents. The business was run only on a cash payment mode. This was done in case of both suppliers and customers.

Diffusion of Mobile Phones

The mobile phone was a popular device. It was owned by all the street vendors in the survey.

This is in keeping with the market which shows that basic feature phones are more prominent in India, but in stark contrast to the United States of America which has more smartphone consumers. As of 2015, only 26.3 per cent of India was using smartphones. The adoption of smartphones in India has been slow. This is glaring, especially when looked at in the context of the 700 million active mobile subscribers. The primary reasons cited for this were the high price of smartphones and the slow surge of 3G connections.

With regards to the three key components of universal access, namely, availability, accessibility and affordability, the study clearly showed that: (i) Mobile phones are easily available. The street vendors used the most basic feature model. Those in the younger age group of 25 to 35 years were aware of the other models of mobiles available in the market. (ii) With respect to the other two, accessibility and affordability - the usage pattern of mobile phones among the street vendors lay in the intersection of the issues that affect its accessibility, to mean whether everyone can use it and affordability, whether everyone can afford to use it. The survey showed that those more adept and those starting to use the internet were increasingly opting for a more advanced handset. As the price of the mobile has a direct correlation with the model features, proficiency in the use of the mobile has an impact on the price they are willing to pay for the handset.

The affordability of the smartphone plays a key role in understanding the issue of accessibility. It constitutes the understanding of using all the services that can be designed for this segment. This would be dependent on how fast the smartphones become cheaper so that it becomes available universally. The next step or the challenge would be to design the mobile applications which can match the skill levels of the users.

While it is possible to access the internet using the basic feature model, multi-media model or the smart phones, the quality of user experience is without question better on a smartphone. Access to internet leads to better user engagement on smartphones as demonstrated by several research efforts. It is seen that a smartphone user consumes 35 times more data than a basic phone user. And consequently, increased engagement leads to better monetization opportunities for businesses through advertising and commerce.

Keeping in mind the reach of mobile phones and internet, there is a huge opportunity to promote and market products through them. For companies, it is seen that revenues through digital media promotion are already on the rise. They are showing a 30 per cent increase compared to previous years. This can trickle down through the population groups towards the less privileged segments of the society. In general, it is observed that most businesses today set aside 10 per cent of the spending on digital media for marketing through mobile phones. For businesses dealing with financial services and related instruments there is opportunity to design products that are simple and easy to adopt. This would give a great fillip for a cashless economy that can be further promoted through mobile phones.

Proficiency in Using the Mobile Phones

Proficiency in using the mobile phones has a bearing on two key issues of accessibility and affordability. The accessibility here can be understood with respect to the street vendors' competency levels in using the mobile. The street vendors in the survey did not seem to use either the 'missed call' method of contacting people or using SMS for exchanging information. In fact, in contrast to many studies, street vendors were not using mobile phones for being connected. This finding is different from the study of slum-dwellers in Delhi, Ahmedabad and Kolkata, other large urban cities in India which showed that use of mobile phones had positively impacted their economic well-being. The benefit derived from the use of mobile phones was higher than the expenses they incurred in using the facility (Vodafone, 2009).

The finding in this study is also in contrast to the five unusual ways in which majority of middle-class Indians are supposed to be using the mobile phones (BBC, 2014). Whereas in the BBC study, the mobile phone was variously being used for giving a missed call; as a torch; as a radio; an alternative to youtube; as a scanner or copier – by taking photos of documents, this survey found that the vendors were not using the calculators in their daily business. They were not aware of the use of calculator in the mobile phone. This finding however seems to very similar to the findings in another study by MaduraMicroFinance in Chennai which found that the micro-entrepreneurs had very little numerical literacy skills.

Street vending as a business was run based on old contacts. These were based on personal relationships. There seemed to be no attempt made to keep a business relation using mobile phones. Infact, those surveyed said they made no business calls to either customers or suppliers. An interesting observation during the field visits to the market showed that none were even using the instrument as a radio.

The study result clearly shows that the street vendors need to be reached out to in other ways. Working in the midst of a bustling market and thriving economy of the fourth largest city like Chennai, they seem to be woefully unaware of the use of mobiles.

FUTURE RESEARCH DIRECTIONS

Mohammad Yunus (2008) predicts that "The future of poverty, as I see it, will be decided by the technological devices and services that are designed a priori for poor people."

There are opportunities for online payment portals. Studies need to be taken up to understand the feasibility of devising a financial service that can be configured in basic feature phones that are popular among the street vendors. Therein lies the challenge as most street vendors only use a basic model which cannot support external applications or third party applications, especially because all promotions or exchange as such are nowadays conveyed only be through text messages. This is a skill which they may need to be trained in as not all of the vendors surveyed showed much proficiency in the use of text messaging.

The street vendors do not find the mobile operations difficult, but as they move towards smartphones there is a need to understand how they can be trained to use the various applications. There is an opportunity for designing training programs for improving digital literacy for users in the unorganized sector. The street vendors as micro-entrepreneurs could be a promising business opportunity for ICT companies', if learning and development could be designed for various products that are relevant to both.

Though many among the surveyed vendors had changed their mobile phones, prices remain a constraint and most would not really want to buy a higher-end model.

But more importantly, the study shows that there is a need to seriously look at the nature of business activities among the street vendors. The use of mobile phones and the kind of mobile phones used is dependent largely on the income levels of the street vendors. The current business levels are barely sustainable. The vending activities that the vendors are involved in show no scope or need of higher technology intervention. This could change if the business activities are further improved. This can be done only by looking at their business and management skills. The opportunity at the present juncture lies in promoting micro-insurance activities, banking facilities or use of mobile phones as mobile wallets.

CONCLUSION

The street vendors were aged between 25 and 45 years. While most had some form of formal education, nearly 40 per cent had discontinued school at a very early stage. The majority of the vendors were married. They had two or more children in the family. Many had elderly dependents too. The street vendors were largely in the business of selling fruits and vegetables followed by small accessories. The average monthly income was in the range of Rs.7000/- to Rs.15000/-. The majority of (59 per cent) street vendors surveyed owned basic feature mobile phones. They had leap frogged to using the device without really having any experience of using a landline.

The street vendors found no use for mobile phones in their daily business activities. There was limited use or no visible use in the business activity for communicating with customers and suppliers. More than half of the respondents did not even use the SMS as a mode of communication. Interestingly they did not even use the mobile phone to make a 'missed call'.

With regards to the three key components of universal access, the study clearly showed that mobile phones are easily available. With respect to the other two, accessibility and affordability - the usage pattern of mobile phones showed that there was much scope for the use of all features in a better manner with a smart phone. But the high-end smartphones cost more. The younger street vendors had greater aspirational levels. If the ICT companies could research and design the mobile apps and related features in a friendly format it could capture this segment. It is seen that mobile phones have over time become cheaper and more easily accessible to everyone in the society. Hence accessibility relates to the affordability of the mobile phone.

Local city governments could also help in designing business districts in cities better to achieve an inclusive design in terms of both human and technical resources such that the street vendors could earn more to afford better devices which could improve their overall economic and social well-being.

REFERENCES

Barrantes, R. (2007). Analysis of ICT Demand: What is Digital Poverty and How to Measure It? In H. Galperin & J. Mariscal (Eds.), Digital poverty: Latin American and Caribbean perspectives (pp. 29-53). Ottawa: IDRC.

Castells, M., Fernanadez-Ardevol, M., Qiu, J., & Sey, A. (2007). *Mobile communication and society: A global perspective*. Cambridge, MA: MIT Press.

De Silva, H., & Zainudeen, A. (2017). *Teleuse on a shoestring: Poverty reduction through telecom access at the 'Bottom of the Pyramid'*. Retrieved from http://www.lirneasia.net/wp-content/uploads/2007/04/lirneasia_teleuse_cepa_-mar07_v30.pdf

Deloitte. (2012). *What is the impact of mobile telephony on economic growth? A Report for the GSM Association*. Retrieved from https://www.gsma.com/publicpolicy/wp-content/ uploads/2012/11/gsma-deloitte-impact-mobile-telephony-economic-growth.pdf

Donner, J. (2008). Research approaches to mobile use in the developing world: A review of the literature. *The Information Society*, 24(3), 140–159. doi:10.1080/01972240802019970

Government of Tamil Nadu. State Planning Commission. (2012). *Approach Paper for Twelfth Five Year Plan (2012 - 17)*. Retrieved from http://www.spc.tn.gov.in/fiveyearplans/approachnew.pdf

GSM Association. (2012). *Universal access: How mobile can bring communications to all*. GSM Association Universal Access Report. Retrieved from https://www.gsma.com/ publicpolicy/wp-content/uploads/2012/03/universalaccessfullreport.pdf

GSM Association. (2015). *The mobile economy Sub-Saharan Africa 2015*. Retrieved from https://www.gsma.com/mobileeconomy/archive/GSMA_ME_SubSaharanAfrica_2015.pdf

GSMA. (2013). *Arab states mobile observatory 2013*. Retrieved from https://www.gsma.com/publicpolicy/wp-content/uploads/2012/03/GSMA_MobileObservatory_ArabStates2013. pdf

Madura Microfinance. (2016, November 23). *Numerical literacy in microentrepreneurs*. Retrieved from http://maduramicrofinance.co.in/insights/2016/11/23/data-spotlight-numerical-literacy-in-microentrepreneurs/

Malhotra, A., Kanesathasan, A., & Patel, P. (2012). *Connectivity: How mobile phones, computers and the internet can catalyze women's entrepreneurship. India: A case study.* International Center for Research on Women. Retrieved from https://www.icrw.org/wp-content/uploads/2016/10/Connectivity-how-mobile-phones-computers-and-the-internet-can-catalyze-womens-entrepreneurship.pdf

Manyika, J., Chui, M., Bughin, J., Dobbs, R., Bisson, P., & Marrs, A. (2013). *Disruptive technologies: Advances that will transform life, business, and the global economy.* McKinsey Global Institute. Retrieved from https://www.mckinsey.com/business-functions/digital-mckinsey/our-insights/disruptive-technologies

Ministry of Communications and Information Technology, Government of India. (2008). *Impact assessment of e-governance projects.* National e-Governance Plan, Department of Information Technology, Ministry of Communications and Information Technology & Indian Institute of Management, Ahmedabad. Retrieved from http://www.iimahd.ernet.in/egov/documents/impact-assessment-of-egovernance-projects.pdf

Mobile Phone and Smartphone Users in India 2014-19. (2015). Retrieved from https://apsalar.com/wp-content/uploads/2016/03/India-Mobile-Users.jpg

National policy on urban street vendors: Report & recommendations. (2006). Retrieved from http://nceuis.nic.in/Street Vendors policy.pdf

OECD. (2003). *ICT and Economic Growth: Evidence from OECD countries, industries and firms.* OECD Publications Service. Retrieved from http://www.cla.org.pt/docs/OCDE_TIC.PDF

OECD. (2005). *Good practice paper on ICTs for economic growth and poverty reduction.* Retrieved from https://www.itu.int/net/wsis/docs2/pc3/contributions/co1.pdf

Qiu, J. L. (2008). Working-class ICTs, migrants, and empowerment in South China. *Asian Journal of Communication, 18*(4), 333–347. doi:10.1080/01292980802344232

Samarajiva, R., & Zainudeen, A. (Eds.). (2008). *ICT Infrastructure in emerging Asia: policy and regulatory roadblocks.* Los Angeles, CA: Sage.

Sen, A. K. (1985). Well-being, agency, and freedom: The Dewey Lectures 1984. *The Journal of Philosophy, 82*(4), 169–221.

Spence, R., & Smith, M. (2009). *Harvard Forum II: Information and Communication Technologies, Human Development, Growth and Poverty Reduction: A Background Paper.* Ottawa: IDRC.

Tata Teleservices Limited. (2015). *Mobile-owning households in Madhya Pradesh enjoy a 63 percent economic prosperity premium compared to those without a mobile.* Retrieved from https://www.tatateleservices.com/Downloads/NewsRoom/ttsl/The-Mobile-Multiplier-Study-Madhya-Pradesh-Press-Release.pdf

Telecom Regulatory Authority of India. (2016). *Highlights of Telecom Subscription Data as on 31ˢᵗ March, 2016* (Press Release No. 34/2016). Retrieved from http://www.trai.gov.in/sites/default/files/Press_Release_34_25may_2016_5_25-05-2016.pdf

Tushar Banerjee. (2014, February 12). *Five unusual ways in which Indians use mobile phones.* Retrieved from http://www.bbc.com/news/world-asia-india-26028381

United Nations Development Programme. (2012). *Mobile technologies and empowerment: enhancing human development through participation and innovation.* Retrieved from http://www.undp.org/content/dam/undp/library/DemocraticGovernance/AccesstoInformationandE-governance/MobileTechnologiesandEmpowerment_EN.pdf

United Nations Development Programme (UNDP). (2015). *Human Development Report 2015: Work for human development.* Retrieved from http://hdr.undp.org/sites/default/files /2015_human_development_report.pdf

Vodafone Group. (2009). *India: The impact of mobile phones.* Retrieved from http://www.icrier.org/pdf/public_policy19jan09.pdf

Warshauer, M. (2003). *Technology and social inclusion: Rethinking the digital divide.* Cambridge, MA: The MIT Press.

Waverman, L., Meschi, M., & Fuss, M. (2005). *The Impact of Telecoms on Economic Growth in Developing markets.* Retrieved from https://www.gsma.com/publicpolicy/wp-content/uploads/2012/11/gsma-deloitte-impact-mobile-telephony-economic-growth.pdf

World Bank Group. (2016). *World Development Report 2016: Digital dividends.* Washington, DC: The World Bank. Retrieved from http://documents.worldbank. org/curated/en/896971468194972881/pdf/102725-PUB-Replacement-PUBLIC.pdf

Yunus, M. (2008). *A Poverty Free World—When? How?* Romanes Lecture at Oxford University. Retrieved from http://www.muhammadyunus.org/index.php/news-media/ speeches/212-a-poverty-free-world-when-how

Chapter 8

Key Challenges for Sustainable E-Services in Unstable Societies:
The Case of Syrians

Abraheem Alsaeed
University of Portsmouth, UK

Rich Boakes
University of Portsmouth, UK

ABSTRACT

Refugees and displaced people who have been affected by disaster or political instability (uprooted from their homes in search of safety) are an interesting group of citizens when we consider e-government services since they face extra challenges of access to such government services. The chapter explores challenges faced by e-service delivery to refugee and displaced people which are often characteristic of unstable societies. This chapter reports on a study of Syrian refugees and displaced people using a survey exploring the use of e-services for citizens inside and outside of Syria. The authors apply institutional theory as a theoretical lens using the dimensions of economic, political, technical, and social to understand the context and issues of providing e-government services within this very challenging domain. The results indicate six themes influencing sustainable and effective support for e-services for such groups of people, namely importance of e-services, connectivity, awareness, e-service availability, financial constraints, and digital literacy.

DOI: 10.4018/978-1-5225-3179-1.ch008

INTRODUCTION

Electronic Government (hereafter eGov) define as a transformative agent upon political and civic activity. It utilizes provision and use of information, services, and communications by citizens and governments to improve the efficiency and effectiveness of service delivery and transactions in the public sector (Alsaeed, Adams, & Boakes, 2014). Seo & Bernsen (2016) point out that eService developed in many ways which have enhanced by the citizens' requirements. Alshehri, Drew & Alfarraj (2012) argue that Governments usually provide eServices to people within its authority, which depend on the people's needs and thus provide the opportunity for better development, especially, in terms of the varieties of service provided and their availability. Therefore, many governments have put financial investment and effort into developing and enhancing eGov for better use of the eService across people's categories (such as poor, old, young, displaced and settle ...etc.) (Chatfiel & Alhujran, 2009; Seo & Bernsen, 2016). In the race for successful eGov implementation, policymakers around the world are competing against each other for solutions to bridge the digital divide across societies. Although the digital divide element usually stands as a significant barrier to implementing eGov successfully, governments are trying to avoid excluding certain categories (for example elderly, disabled and vulnerable people) and are trying to include all people to adopt the eService (displaced people and refugees should not be exception), consequently, which lead to fill the gap of the digital divide. Helbig, Ramón Gil-García, & Ferro (2009) argue that using sophisticated information technologies in government has little social value if the people cannot use the service, or benefit from this innovation in a meaningful way. Otherwise, the negative impact would be an inevitable consequence if, however, a segment of the society left behind where everyone should be included (United Nations, 2012a). However, governments have not been so successful in providing eService to unstable societies or encouraging refugees to adopt or continuously use the eService provided, especially those people who are living in camps where they are isolated (Transtec S.A., 2015). The survey by the UNHCR (2016) reveals that the world is experiencing the largest humanitarian crisis since the Second World War with 65 million refugees and displaced people. The report, also, shows that developing countries are hosting 86% of the world's refugees. A recent survey from (Information Management Unit, 2016) states that the Syrian people have endured one of the most ferocious, barbarous and brutal conflicts of the 21st century which has lasted for five years and is still going. The survey reported over 250,000 people killed, over a million injured, 6.5 million displaced within Syria, 4.6 million refugees who have fled to neighbouring countries and the remaining population, which is about 13.5 million people are in an unbearable situation and much of them lack humanitarian support. Although some studies focusing on eService in developing countries and its benefits and challenges have shed light on the developments of eGov literature (Elsheikh, 2011; SWEISI, 2010; Al-Busaidy, 2011), there is little research that investigates the driving factors that prevents ordinary citizens, refugees and displaced people of adopting the eServices in unstable societies. This is considered to be an important aspect which unleashes new models of eService targeting new segments of the society which appeared as a result of the instability such as refugees and displaced people, as well as ordinary citizens. This report seeks to answer the question as to what the obstacles are that affect the use of eService in unstable societies and Syria is a good current example of such an unstable society as it is going in a period of unrest with many displaced people and refugees. It is a difficult, but important topic since it covers people often in distress and need of government services. Thus, the aim of this research is to explore obstacles to successfully adopt eService in unstable societies which would allow people to experience its benefits. This study will, also, identify a list of recommendations for the sake of increasing the effectiveness of the aforementioned eService. This is a very challenging domain, notably, for security issues, political instability and access to relevant affected citizens which limits what method can be applied. In order to answer the research question and to achieve the aim of our research, the article structured as follow. Section 2: briefly sheds light on the undertaking context and stating the current situation in Syria as they are the new challenges of eGov adoption. Section 3: briefly examines the benefits and challenges of eService in general and the impact of eService refugees and displaced people in particular as published in the literature. Section 4: outlines the research methodology used to collect and analyze the literature. Section 5: presents the empirical findings. Section 6: discussion and institutional classification are proposed. Section 7: presents the report conclusions and recommendations.

SYRIAN DISPLACED AND REFUGEES PEOPLE OVERVIEW

Syria is home to diverse ethnic and religious groups, including the majority Arab population. Syrian state was established after gained independence in April 1946 from French Occupation, as formed a parliamentary republic and later on, become a member of the United Nation. Syria was under Emergency Law from 1963 to 2011: this means suspending most constitutional protections for citizens, hence, the system of the government is considered to be non-democratic. In March 2011, Syrian people took to the street protesting against the Syrian Regime who is ruling the country, whose forces responded with violent crackdowns. The conflict gradually morphed from popular protests to an armed rebellion after months of military sieges, as consequences millions of people have fled their homes to seek refuge in the neighbouring countries and some other have been displaced internally (Sengupta, 2012). The Syrian Interim Government was formed by the opposition umbrella group, the Syrian National Coalition, in March 2012 and was recognised as the sole representative of the Syrian people by several nations (Schofield, 2012). This new situation placed Syria among the high level of the unstable countries which triggered an alerts for world nations and NGOs to consider the Syrian humanitarian crisis as a high priority and to provide the Syrian people (displaced internally and Refugees outside Syria) every possible help such as health, education, services, welfare, children protection and to support their need and to be considered as a new emerging society and to be treated as such. According to the UNHCR (2012), a number of two and a half million Syrian have fled Syria to neighbouring countries to seek refuge and about 4 million Syrians were internally displaced.

LITERATURE REVIEW

Policymakers considering concepts of eGov such as the effectiveness of multichannel service delivery; the importance of eService to vulnerable groups; digital divide; enhancing and increasing the internet connection as driving factors for sustainable development that will help for advance economic sustainability and social equity(United Nations, 2012a). Therefore, The scope and application of eGov have rapidly grown and evolved as it has been adopted worldwide. The (United Nations, 2010) defines eGov as "the use of ICT, and its application, by the government for the provision of information and public services to the people". Similarly (Wold Bank, 2011) defines eGov as the "use by government agencies of information technologies that have the ability to transform relations with citizens, businesses and other arms of government, These technologies can serve a variety of different ends; better delivery of government services to citizens, improved Interactions with business and industry, citizen empowerment through access to information, or more efficient government management", whereas the (European Commission, 2001) decrees that Information and Communication Technology (ICT) is "a powerful tool for good governance, with five key principles: Openness, Participation, Accountability, Effectiveness, and Coherence". Government to Citizens (G2C) Model allows a government to interact with its citizens and vice versa to deliver the best service solution by electronic methods (Zhi & Zhenhua, 2009). This implies all stages of the process, from browsing the provided information by the government up to the level of two ways transactions. (Ramlah, Norshidah, Abdul-Rahman, Murni, & Umar, 2010). Governments sought, in the run to achieve this potential, to find the latest and more stable solutions so that citizens may experience its benefits and be economically advantageous to the country. However, this will require a robust eGov strategy to achieve the successfulness. Table 1 summarised the recent literature in the eService domain.

Gant (2018) argues that eGov is the use of ICT in government to provide public services, to improve managerial effectiveness and to promote democratic values; as well as a regulatory framework that facilitates information-intensive initiatives and fosters the knowledge society. However, a study of developing countries best practices by (Azab, Kamel, & Dafoulas, 2009) suggests that the availability of an effective eGov assessment framework is a necessary condition for advancing eGov implementations, The potential benefits of implementing eGov (the International Telecommunication Union, 2009) particularly for those in developing countries and rural areas, can dramatically reduce transaction costs and improve internal planning mechanisms. Moreover, the introduction of eGov and its integration with services usually requires a government to streamline its administrative processes, thus improving efficiency and reducing costs. Although (Strachan, Wanous, & Mofleh, 2008) stated that "ICT in the developed world is entering into all aspects of life including public services, commercial activities, education, and health". The ICT infrastructure (which include providing internet services and reliable web services with the capacity to support widespread use) is recognized to be one of the main challenges for eGov Internetworking which is required to enable appropriate sharing

Table 1. Examples of recent literature in the eService domain

Researcher	Research Topic	Methodology	Contribution
(Seo & Bernsen, 2016)	Comparing attitudes toward e-government of non-users versus users in a rural and urban municipality	Quantitative research method questionnaire based-survey	Model to show different factors enhance the adoption of eService among users and non-users in rural and urban places, which contribute a more nuanced perspective to the e-government.
(Alshehri et al., 2012)	Analysis of eServices adoption in Saudi Arabia: Obstacles and Challenges	Quantitative research method questionnaire based-survey	Important challenges in the Saudi eGov context were found and a list of recommendations for a successful adoption of eService at
(SWEISI, 2010)	Exploration of Factors Contribute to a Successful Implementation of eServices an in Libya	Mixed method (quantitative and qualitative)	Roadmap to policymakers and key stakeholders in Libya which may assist in the successful implementation of e-Government services programmes.
(AlKhatib, 2013)	E-government systems success and user acceptance in developing countries	Quantitative research method questionnaire based-survey	A model provides decision-makers in developing countries an approach to determining which factors require attention of reap the highest benefits from e-Governments' projects

of information and open up new channels for communication and delivery of new services. Security is another important challenge. Alsmadi (2011) gives great attention to e-security where security has been widely recognized as one of the main obstacles to the adoption of Internet services and it is *"considered an important aspect in the debate over challenges facing Internet banking"*. Furthermore (Alsmadi, 2011) shed a light on the importance of the personal data that e-Gov portal could contain and the need for security implementation in order to protect such information, In the scope and vision of using and expanding the types of services eGov portals can offer to citizens, one of the major challenges and possible barriers is the security concern. In their study of the challenges to implementing a successful e-Gov, Khan et al. (2010)found that the level of ICT literacy and skills of eGov users in developing countries is very low, moreover, they suggested that citizens should be aware of the eService in order for the eGov to be adopted successfully. These researchers argued that eService would be improved by awareness from a Knowledge Management perspective. Sallard and Alyousuf (2007) argue that the widespread evaluation culture and experience in countries' administrations is very important due to the fact that eGov initiatives are designed and implemented by individual units in developing countries. A very a loose institutional links with other agencies as a result. Sallard and Alyousuf (2007) argue that this could prevent the development of a common culture and experience of implementation and evaluation across government. Dubai is an example where eGov faced several challenges from government departments regarding the quality of services (Sethi & Sethi, 2008). For example, some institutional departments exaggerated the claim of offering eServices but their services were of little value to customers, and some others focused on quantity rather than quality. In Syria (as in many other developing countries) a comprehensible design and implementation of eGov are crucial to encourage adoption and to help prevent the initiative from failing. (Dada, 2006) suggests that practitioners must understand the importance of the specific context within which they are working. This is true in the Syria case where (Heeks, 2002) commented on the same issue, saying that: "There is widespread recognition that this challenge must be met by the strategic building of national infrastructure". He suggests that everyone involved in the project must fully understand the eGov initiative and be aware of its objectives, otherwise it will face failure "they mainly end in failure; either partial or total". Heeks also highlights that such projects should consider the reality of citizen behaviour with their design: "stakeholders must be sensitized to the large gaps that often exist between project design and public sector reality". Furthermore, he argues that such services must be available: "for 24 hours a day during the seven days of a week citizens of any given country should have full access to government information at any moment and everywhere".

RESEARCH METHODOLOGY

One of the most important instruments for data collection is the Questionnaire-based survey as suggested by Neuman (2006), he also states that this method has been used for recording answers to a predetermined order questions from chosen participants which sought to answer a particular research question. Heeks & Bailur, (2007b) state that eGov research should increase the use of quantitative analysis with a strict collection. Furthermore, conducting a survey makes it possible to collect data from a large sample of participants (Choudrie & Dwivedi, 2006; Saunders, Lewis, & Thornhill, 2002) and more importantly is one of the few practical and safe methods to access relevant people in these displaced communities (safe but not easy). Thus, the survey is an appropriate and a suitable approach for this study.

Why Survey?

To understand the successful adoption of eGov services at the High level of instability it is necessary to find a suitable method and to be safe at the same time. The authors decided that survey is one suitable method allows us to know the opinions, attitudes, and beliefs of a sample group of people who are living in unstable societies. The survey focuses on the effective and efficient factors that the use of eServices would meet the Syrian citizen requirements. Therefore, the authors conducted an open-end questionnaire in order to cover as much eService related information from Syrian people (inside and outside Syria) refugees and/or displaced people as possible. The authors conducted both paper-based and virtual questionnaire, in order to, gain an insight of the availability, effectiveness, efficiency, and affordability of eServices that people in an unstable environment may use and comprehend the barriers that those people may face in adopting this technology. Furthermore, to test the attitude of the participants towards the current eService under the current circumstances in Syria, the problems they facing in using this technology and their evaluations for further improvements. Another reason for choosing this method due to the insufficient data was published on the aforementioned topic. Furthermore, the study was approved by ethics review committees at the University of Portsmouth.

Data Collection

Two samples of the survey were designed and distributed as follows, the first sample is to reach the Local Syrian Citizens who are living inside Syria (hereafter LSC-Sample). The second sample is to reach the Syrian refugees outside Syria (hereafter RSC-Sample). These samples give the opportunity to represent the majority of the Syrian people, hence, a clear picture of the majority about the topic would be revealed.

Furthermore, the authors have conducted the investigation for the second sample in different countries due to the large volume of the Syrian population which has fled to neighbouring countries such as Turkey, Lebanon, Jordan, Egypt, and the UK. This is especially important where could capture the attitudes from different groups, especially, the people who have experienced the use of electronic sources other than the one provided by the Syrian government. Therefore, the findings would give us an insight of different factors playing roles in the effectiveness of eService which meet the Syrian citizens' requirements during the political pressures (UNHCR, 2013; UNHCR Syria, 2015; UNHCR, 2014; Information Management Unit, 2016). But, due to the Syrian situation on the ground (visiting Syria is companied with varieties of dangers), the authors decided to choose the virtual survey method by sending it by email to a few friends who are still living in Damascus (two of them are members of staff at Damascus university; four employees at the Syrian government). They have (at their end) distributed the samples on our behalf. The survey was distributed to students, employees, professionals and ordinary people at some of the government departments such as the Immigration and Passports Department, Ministry of Higher Education, Damascus University and the City University (student accommodations). The survey was distributed, also, in the Town Centre (shopping centre with some shops, banks, restaurants, and children playgrounds) and Shelter centres in different places in the city. Damascus is considering a safe place compared to many Syrian cities, hence, it accommodates a large segment of the society, after they have been affected by the war in their hometowns, thus, wide categories of the population would be found in Damascus, as a consequence of the search for safe places. The Survey took longer than the time assigned to it, to be completed, due to a considerable challenge of getting access to displaced people. The Survey started on 20 April 2016 and was completed and translated from Arabic into English by end of August 2016. The people who worked on our behalf faced many difficulties, on the ground, including their availability and the willingness of the participants to take part in the survey. Each response has been given a unique id to avoid replication. During this time 1634 responses were received in total, but the total responses that were completed by the participants were only 415, the rest were excluded. Therefore, our dataset contains 415 entries for subsequent analysis and investigation.

Data Analysis

For the analysis phase, we used SPSS (version-22) Statistics software package. Figure 1, illustrates the different phases of the survey.

The result of the analysis was structured and grouped into main points to reflect the respondent point of views on each point which listed and discussed in turn. For example measuring the response of the Level of Awareness ranging from "not at

Figure 1. Stages of the survey

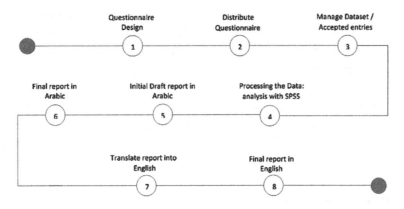

all aware", "Slightly aware", "Somewhat aware", "Moderately aware", "Extremely aware". On the other hand, to output the result of the aforementioned test, the authors used the descriptive statistics to provide a simple summary of the undertaken samples, also used the frequency distribution to summarise the individual values or ranges of values for the variables and finally, used a simple graphics as well to aid the data analysis. To ensure clarity and anticipate as many as possible responses, the questionnaire was written in Arabic and then translated into English

What Questions, Why?

The questions for this survey were utilized previous studies such as (Jait, 2012; SWEISI, 2010) with some amendments to suit our research. A set of questions were designed for this questionnaire where some used closed-ended questions and some other used open-ended questions to give the participants the chance to express their opinions in more detail.

The questions designed in two dimensions: the first one considers six variables namely: Importance of eServices, Connectivity, Awareness, eService Availability, Financial constraints and Digital literacy. The second dimension is concerned with the four institutional theory pressures which were namely: Politic, economic, social and technology where the discussion under each pressure highlights the influence of the above variables (first dimension), based on its definition, on the eService adoption. Furthermore, the above variables were derived from key themes recognized from the literature review study (Alsaeed & Adams, 2015) that are forming the main challenges faced eServices in the unstable countries such as political, socio-economic, technological, organizational, human infrastructure and financial challenges. However, the above variables were tested on different scales as well as the Likert scale which uses five points for measuring responses (Ogonek et al., 2016). Furthermore, to produce a clearer and more concise findings the authors designed and categorized the questions under the following main category: Education and Health during instabilities, Connectivity, Awareness, Sufficient online services and Digital literacy. Which means that the repeated and the unnecessary data will be rejected. Thus, it facilitated and determined the suitable data for further focus.

The authors have realized, after the analyse stage took place, that more questions needed to be addressed, thus, the authors have recovered those questions in the qualitative phase of our primary research (during the interviews of the conducted case studies)

Respondent's Profile

Out of the 415 completed questionnaires, about 64% of the responses came from Syria and the rest came from different countries that are hosting Syrian refugees such as Turkey, Jordan, Lebanon, Egypt and UK(paper-based used for this population as it was easy to access and no danger associated).

The majority of the respondents of the LSC-Sample which is about (69%) were males and about (50%) of their age group range between 23-30, (51%) had a university graduate qualification, (56%) were employed and (64%) considered their computer literacy to be medium. On the other hand, the majority of the respondents of the RSC-Sample which is about (65%) were males, (49%) age group range between 31-45, (40%) had a High School qualification, (86%) were unemployed and (51%) considered their computer literacy to be high. Figure 2 represents the size and the distribution of the gender among the samples.

Figure 2. Samples size and gender

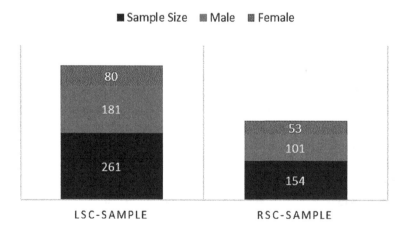

Out of the 261 responses from the LSC sample it shows that half of the responses age between 23-30 years old, the highest group comes second the group age between 18-22 years old with 15.3% out of the responses, the genders of the responses divided into 69.3% male and 30.7 female, more than half reported as a university graduates 51.0% and 29.1% have a high school degree and the rest have a postgraduate and below high school degrees. The computer literacy revels that 63.6% have a medium computer skills 13.0% low and the rest are high-skilled with the computer and out of the 55.9% of the responses reported as employed as shown in Table 2.

Out of the 154 responses from the RSC sample, it shows that 48.7% of the response's age between 31-45 years old, the highest group comes second the group age between 18-22 years old with 18.8% out of the responses, the genders of the responses divided into 65.6% male and 34.4 female. The high school education reported first with 39.6%, 29.2% university graduates and the rest between postgraduate and below high school. The computer literacy revels that 50.6% have high computer skills and 38.3% are medium skilled with the computer and out of the 86.4% of the responses reported as unemployed as shown in Table 3.

FINDING FROM SURVEY

From the participants' responses and by looking at their comment the authors can highlight the following enablers and barriers contribute to successfully adopt the eServices delivery in the given environments:

The Importance of eService in Education and Health During Instabilities

When participants of the LSC-Sample and RSC-Sample were asked about the most important eService(s), the results as revealed shown in Table 4 and Table 5. The emerged themes out of the respondents' comments are highlighted and further discussed next.

Education

The education sector in Syria is in a critical situation where students experience difficulties in accessing education with different aspects of needs. A report by (Information Management Unit, 2016) shows that 44% of the Syrian schools have stopped functioning due to a security reason where a huge amount of bombardment on schools' buildings found in the areas of conflict. Which led some respondents to stress that the lack of funding, using the school as a shelter and shortage of teachers

Table 2. LSC-Sample demographic responses

Variables	Frequency	Percent
Age		
18-22	40	15.3%
23-30	130	49.8%
31-45	27	10.3%
45-65	50	19.2%
Over 65	14	5.4%
Total	261	100.0%
Gender		
Male	181	69.3%
Female	80	30.7%
Total	261	100.0%
Education Level		
Below High School (BHS)	33	12.6%
High School(HS)	76	29.1%
University Graduate(UG)	133	51.0%
University Post Graduate(UPG)	19	7.3%
Total	261	100.0%
Employment Status		
Student	45	17.2%
Employed	146	55.9%
Unemployed	67	25.7%
Retired	3	1.1%
Total	261	100.0%
Computer Literacy		
Low	34	13.0%
Medium	166	63.6%
High	61	23.4%
Total	261	100.0%

have an impact on the education process as well. When the participants were asked about the most important eServices, the majority commented that education is very important, especially, for their children's future. Their comments revealed that a huge number of students have been dropped out of schools, due to lack of transportation in some areas as well as the burdens in purchasing books, stationery and other

Table 3. RSC-Sample demographic responses

Variables	Frequency	Percent
Age		
18-22	29	18.8%
23-30	20	13.0%
31-45	75	48.7%
45-65	25	16.2%
Over 65	5	3.2%
Total	154	100.0%
Gender		
Male	101	65.6%
Female	53	34.4%
Total	154	100.0%
Education Level		
Below High School (BHS)	39	25.3%
High School(HS)	61	39.6%
University Graduate(UG)	45	29.2%
University Post Graduate(UPG)	9	5.8%
Total	154	100.0%
Employment Status		
Student	0	0%
Employed	21	13.6%
Unemployed	133	86.4%
Retired	0	0%
Total	154	100.0%
Computer Literacy		
Low	17	11.0%
Medium	59	38.3%
High	78	50.6%
Total	154	100.0%

school materials and the lack of special equipment for the high number of disabled children. The Office for the Coordination of Humanitarian Affairs (2016) reported that "Children are withdrawn from school to be breadwinners, exposing them to exploitation, child labour, and recruitment into armed groups and early marriage" and "After five years into the crisis, 5.7 million children and adolescents in and

Table 4. eService priority: LSC Sample

LSC-Sample Which of the Following eService Is Most Important to You?		
Variables	**Frequency**	**Percent**
Civil Registration	34	13.0%
Travel Documents and Passports	21	8.0%
Vehicle registration and transport	13	5.0%
Education information	12	4.6%
Water and Electricity	18	6.9%
Other	163	62.5%
Total	261	100.0

Table 5. eService priority: RSC Sample

RSC-Sample Which of the Following eService Is Most Important to You?		
Variables	**Frequency**	**Percent**
Health information	14	9.1%
Civil Registration	44	28.6%
Travel Documents and Passports	10	6.5%
Education information	29	18.8%
Water and Electricity	36	23.4%
Other	21	13.6%
Total	154	100.0%

out of school" . eService in such environment would facilitate the continuation of students education and eliminate many of the aforementioned barriers via online learning. By having a connection to the internet, this would bridge education divides and widen access to quality education for all. Furthermore, a faster broadband connection would maximize the opportunity for e-learners. In addition, students can access from anywhere and at any time to education martial.

Health

People in the unstable country i.e. Syria could benefit greatly from a remote consultation that eService provides, with this technology, they also can gain access to a vital health information and healthcare services. In Syria, Over 11 million people are in need of health assistance (Information Management Unit, 2016), where the limited number of hospitals and health centres are unable to provide such services, especially with the war is still going and many of the health locations have been bombarded. Using mobile communication technology to access or to obtain health information even through a simple text message could work as powerful tools to improve health (United Nations, 2014a). Furthermore, social media may play roles to disseminate information about health treatments or physicians, medical information and advice. Some respondents from the LSC-Sample stress the importance of having an alternative solution for having to go to a distant location to get treatment. The lack of simple knowledge of some symptoms causes many deaths, where they were depending on local doctors who have either fled the country, detained or died as a consequence of the war.

Connectivity Considered as an Important Issue in Unstable Society

When the authors asked the participants about their opinion of the importance of connecting to the internet, the results revealed that 65% of the respondents from LSC-Sample felt that connecting to the internet is "Extremely Important". Furthermore, some comments from the participants show the attitude of how important to be connected, "the internet is a lifesaver" as stated by one of the responses. Furthermore, "Under the current situation in Syria, the internet plays crucial roles in terms of security and protection". On the other hand the result from the second sample (RSC-Sample) revealed that 55% of the respondents also "Extremely Important", "it is heartbreaking not to be able to be in contact with the loved one inside Syria, it is also important to be able to download some important documents through the internet coming from Syria, as the host country demanding for" as suggested by one of the participants. Connecting people who are living in unstable society play crucial roles in improving humanitarian services, such as Safety and security. From the RSC-Sample few responses revealed that they rely on the UNHCR published information related security and safety as shown in Tables 6 and 7.

Furthermore, it gives the chances for refugees and displaced people to be self-reliance. Some people highlighted through their comments about their online Jobs, where the work opportunity is restricted for refugees in some host countries such as Jordan.

People surveyed from the LSC-Sample 20.3% using 3G mobile broadband technology, 23.8% using the 2G cellular network on a basic phone, 16.1% Internet delivered via a phone line, 14.2% Satellite broadband Technology and 25.7% have no internet access at all. On the other-hand people surveyed from RSC-Sample indicate that they using 3G mobile broadband technology with a rate of 79.2% and the rest have no internet access at all as shown in Tables 8 and 9.

Table 6. Importance of connectivity from LSC Sample

LSC-Sample: How Do You Classify the Importance of the Internet in Your Life?		
Variables	Frequency	Percent
Not at all important	11	4.2%
Low importance	19	7.3%
Neutral	26	10.0%
important	35	13.4%
Extremely important	170	65.1%
Total	261	100.0%

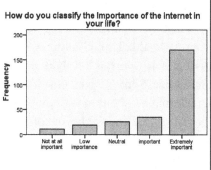

Table 7. importance of connectivity from RSC Sample

RSC-Sample: How Do You Classify the Importance of the Internet in Your Life?		
Variables	Frequency	Percent
Not at all important	5	3.2%
Low importance	6	3.9%
Neutral	20	13.0%
Important	38	24.7%
Extremely important	85	55.2%
Total	154	100.0%

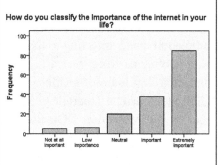

Table 8. Internet access type LSC Sample

LSC-Sample What Type of Access to the Internet Do You Have?		
Variables	Frequency	Percent
I use 3G mobile broadband technology	53	20.3%
2G cellular network on a basic phone	62	23.8%
Internet delivered via a phone line	42	16.1%
Satellite broadband Technology	37	14.2%
I have no internet access at all	67	25.7%
Total	261	100.0%

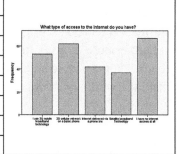

Table 9. Internet access type RSC Sample

RSC-Sample What Type of Access to the Internet Do You Have?		
Variables	**Frequency**	**Percent**
I use 3G mobile broadband technology	122	79.2
I have no internet access at all	32	20.8
Total	154	100.0

People Awareness of the Innovation

The awareness and usage among the population of the LSC-Sample are relatively low. According to the surveyed responses, 45.2 percent of the citizens were not at all aware of eServices, 10.3 slightly aware but not using them where 17.6 percent were moderately aware and 9.2 reported using the services and they are extremely aware. This indicates that half of the surveyed populations have not experienced the benefit of this technology, otherwise, a huge impact would reflect on the successfulness of the implementation. See Figure 3

On the other hand, awareness and usage are much higher among the population from the RSC-Sample. The result reflected that the majority of 35.7 percent of

Figure 3. Awareness from LSC-Sample

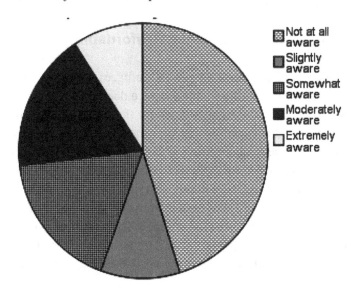

Figure 4. Awareness from RSC-Sample

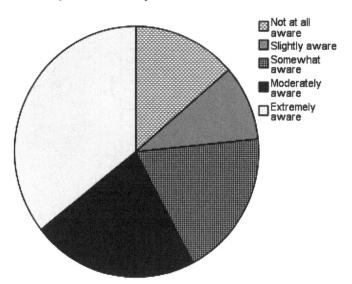

the responses are "Extremely aware", 22.1 percent moderately aware, 18.8 percent somewhat aware and 13.6 percent are not at all aware. This result indicates that a significant eServices implementation in place in the host countries and different strategy for delivering online services compared with the Syrian eGov strategy approach, See Figure 4. By raising the awareness of the benefits of eServices through social media, for example, this allows for more people to adopt this technology and greater rewards and benefit for all stockholder, as a result this resulted in maximizing the eGov capability and benefits.

Financial Constraints and Devices' Affordability

The biggest concerns of displaced people and refugees are the cost of connecting to the internet or the affordability to buy a device due to rules and regulations put by some host countries on the right to work for those people, their displacement that requires unpredictable expenses and their movements that also required extra funding. Furthermore, the frequent rising of the prices under the situation of the war inside Syria puts even further encumbrances on the citizens which prevent people from using the internet freely and without worrying about their bills.

The following question was asked people from both samples: What is the biggest concern(s) of using the eService and the internet? The responses from LSC-Sample revealed that the Cost of connecting to the internet is our most concerns by 72.8 percent, they also were concerns about the cost of Device Affordability by 27.2

Table 10. Financial constraints LSC Sample

LSC-Sample What Is the Biggest Concern(s) of Using the Internet?			
Variables	**Frequency**	**Percent**	
Cost of connecting to the internet	190	72.8	
Device Affordability	71	27.2	
Total	261	100.0	

Table 11. Financial constraints RSC Sample

RSC-Sample What Is the Biggest Concern(s) of Using the Internet?			
Variables	**Frequency**	**Percent**	
Cost of connecting to the internet	98	63.6	
Device Affordability	12	7.8	
Inaccurate information	6	3.9	
Violation of transaction security	27	17.5	
Violation of privacy	11	7.1	
Total	154	100.0	

percent as shown in Table 10. Responses from the RSC-Sample Sample (Table 11) show that Cost of connecting to the internet also was a huge issue with a majority of 63.6 percent, Device Affordability just 7.8 percent concern, people from this sample were worried about Violation of transaction security with rate of 17.5% due to the unfamiliarity of the host country languages, the emerging comments indicate that there are people exploiting them by using their data for their own benefit.

However, the financial constraint of using the internet is less painful when you divide the bill amongst the users, as stated by few comments.

Sufficient Online Services and Effective Functionality

The availability of eServices that the Syrian eGov provided seen as little by 28.4 percent of the respondents from the LSC-Sample, where there is no any indication of this issue from the RSC-Sample (the indication of eServices availability in host countries)(see Table 16 & 17). As the result of the survey shows that only 37.2 percent answered "YES" to whether the population of the LSC-Sample has ever visited any of the government websites and 62.8 percent answered "NO", this indicates that no many eGov institutions have implemented eServices or started to communicate with their citizen electronically, Table 12 indicating those results. As some comments from this Sample responses suggested that establishing kind of partnership and collaboration between the governmental sectors would make different in the eService delivery, especially, the duplicate and the redundancy of the Civil Registration, where the result shows that 13.0 percent from LSC-Sample seen this service is important but require a collaboration with different government arms to be fully effective, this also true for the RSC-Sample even more important to the people who are living outside Syria where the result revealed that 28.6 percent are cared for such eServices due to the demands by the most host countries for the refugees civil documentation, such as mirages certificate, Birth Certificate, personal identification, family cards .etc. as some responses noted (see Tables 4 & 5). The huge responses with a rate of 86.4 percent from the RSC-Sample that answered "YES" to whether they have ever visited any of the government websites (see Table 13). This indicates that the implementation of eServices in those countries have reached an advanced stage compared to the Syrian one, furthermore, also indicate that the people are aware of the different type of eServices and have adequate digital literacy to deal with modern technology

Table 12. Frequently visiting the government websites: LSC Sample

LSC-Sample Have You Ever Visited Any of the Government Websites?			
Variables	**Frequency**	**Percent**	
Yes	97	37.2	
No	164	62.8	
Total	261	100.0	

Table 13. Frequently visiting the government websites: RSC sample

RSC-Sample Have You Ever Visited Any of the Government Websites?			
Variables	**Frequency**	**Percent**	
Yes	133	86.4	
No	21	13.6	
Total	154	100.0	

Tables 14 and 15 show the most eServices that attract users and the most used eServices from both samples, for example, the 23.4% online payment from the RSC sample against the 14.6 from the LSC sample indicate the advanced eServices in the countries hosting refugees compared with the one running in Syria

Digital Literacy

Digital Literacy is considered as one of the major factors that contribute to eService adoption. The authors first asked the population from the tow samples on the amount of time in using the computer or other devices for surfing the internet, the survey reveals that 39.8% of the responses from the LSC sample using it when it needed and 22.2% on a daily basis, where 79.2% on daily basis from the RSC sample see Table 16 & Table 17.

With regards to digital literacy in helping with eServices, the results revealed that 12.3 percent of the LSC-Sample don't know how to use the eService and 10.4

Table 14. Attractive eServices: LSC Sample

LSC-Sample What the Reasons for Using the eServices?		
Variables	**Frequency**	**Percent**
Searching for information	33	12.6
Downloading documents	27	10.3
Online Payment	38	14.6
Other	163	62.5
Total	261	100.0

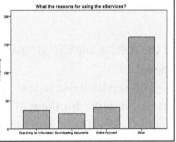

Table 15. Attractive eServices: RSC Sample

RSC-Sample What the Reasons for Using the eServices?		
Variables	**Frequency**	**Percent**
Searching for information	33	21.4
Submitting online application form	29	18.8
Downloading documents	20	13.0
Online Payment	36	23.4
Other	36	23.4
Total	154	100.0

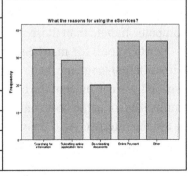

Table 16. Using the internet: LSC Sample

LSC-Sample How Often Do You Use the Internet?		
Variables	**Frequency**	**Percent**
Daily Basis	58	22.2
Twice or more a week	41	15.7
Weekly basis	58	22.2
Only when needed	104	39.8
Total	261	100.0

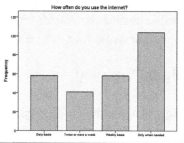

Table 17. Using the internet: RSC Sample

RSC-Sample How Often Do You Use the Internet?		
Variables	**Frequency**	**Percent**
Daily Basis	122	79.2
Weekly basis	14	9.1
Only when needed	18	11.7
Total	154	100.0

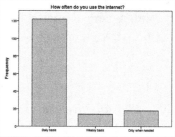

of the RSC-Sample also have the problem of using the system as shown in Tables 18 and 19.

The results indicate that there is a portion of the population required digital literacy in order for them to be able to start communicating with the government electronically. The level of literacy is varied among different social groups, youngster for example, whose find playing computer games very pleasurable time for them, it increases their digital literate indirectly, also different people from different background such as rich people who could afford the technology equipment and who be able to afford to attend training sessions might have a better knowledge of computer skills, moreover, refugees who are living in cities would have more computer-literate than those who are living in camps or in small primitive villages.

Furthermore, for many Syrian people who have fled the country to countries with different language than Arabic, they found it a huge barrier to use the eService, especially, since most of the computers and mobiles languages have been written in English and or in the host country language, this creates a new barrier for the people to use the internet. Also the way of connecting to the internet to use the eServices whether, from home PC, Mobile phones, local library or internet café shop may play

Table 18. Attitudes towards using eGov services: LSC Sample

LSC-Sample Reasons for Not Using Government's Websites?			
Variables	**Frequency**	**Percent**	
I have a negative attitude against them and don't trust the electronic transactions	7	2.7	
I prefer the traditional way of providing the service	36	13.8	
I don't know how to use the e-service	32	12.3	
I believe I don't need them	14	5.4	
eService Not available.	74	28.4	
Other	98	37.5	
Total	261	100.0	

Table 19. Attitudes towards using eGov services: RSC Sample

RSC-Sample Reasons for Not Using Government's Websites?			
Variables	**Frequency**	**Percent**	
I don't know how to use the e-service	16	10.4	
I believe I don't need them	5	3.2	
Other	133	86.4	
Total	154	100.0	

a huge role in elevating the standard of the digital literacy among the populations of the samples. The population of the LSC sample using a mobile phone to get access to information with 58.2% also more than half of the RSC sample population using mobile communication with a rate of 51.3% as shown in Tables 20.

CLASSIFYING AND DISCUSSION THROUGH INSTITUTIONAL THEORY

The institutional Theory was adopted as a theoretical lens to have a deeper perspective at the found barriers to eService adoption in unstable environments. Al-Busaidy (2011) argues that "it is evident that many studies have applied institutional theory

Table 20. Devices used: LSC Sample

LSC-Sample What Type of Device(s) You Use to Get Connected?		
Variables	**Frequency**	**Percent**
I have my own PC	42	16.1
I use libraries to have access	27	10.3
I use Internet Cafes	40	15.3
I use mobile phones	152	58.2
Total	261	100.0

RSC-Sample What Type of Device(s) You Use to Get Connected?		
Variables	**Frequency**	**Percent**
I have my own PC	43	27.9
I use libraries to have access	20	13.0
I use Internet Cafes	12	7.8
I use mobile phones	79	51.3
Total	154	100.0

to explore how the formal structured organizations such as government departments are institutionalized by economic, political or social contexts in terms of meeting the society requirements (e.g. values and beliefs)". Therefore, the authors examined the eService related changes (factors affecting the implementation) in the given environment through the influence of the main key pressures found by the institutional theory (Economic, Political, Technical and Social) that have been derived from the institutional theory's main pillars: cultural-cognitive, normative, and regulative; that expected to hinder the eGov implementation. Scott (2001) define that the institutions are "social structures that have attained a high degree of resilience. They are composed of cultural-cognitive, normative, and regulative elements that, together with associated activities and resources, provide stability and meaning to social life". Where the Regulative Institutions (Coercive) are the set of rules, agreements policies, and procedures where every member's behaviours with the institutions are influenced according to the rules of the institutional structure (Kondra & Hurst, 2009). Normative is legitimizing the normal social behaviour by imposing constraints on social actions and a consequence it operates as a system (Scott, 2001; Scott, 2008; Scott, 2004). On the other hand, Cultural-Cognitive (Mimetic) is the idea of having a duplicate copy of organizations in the same business domain when they share same goals, objectives, challenges, conditions, customers, suppliers... etc. The theory encourages the idea of "best practice" among organizations as long they share a set of operation similarities (Teo, Wei, & Benbasat, 2003). However, the theory is used primarily as a frame for classifying the internal and external institutional influences on eService implementation (Al-Busaidy, 2011). Therefore, the authors address the aforementioned identified challenges under the four key pressures (economic, technical, political, and social) in order to better comprehend the eGov service delivery aspects in unstable society.

Economic Pressures

The population of unstable societies can be affected economically by the adoption of eService, hence, the found variable is challenged by the current economic situation in Syria. The improvement of the eServices quality that the government provides requires a significant amount of spending and budget to maintain connectivity, implementing new channels for education and health care that resulted in providing more eServices, in turn required promoting through raising the level of awareness among users and diffusion through advertising, furthermore, improve the digital literacy among citizen also attracts more users which require budgeting as well. The economic impact would consequently attract more users for adoption, means enhancement of the eGov capability for the long run. As a return for the individuals under the Syrian current situation would promote self-reliance by broadening their opportunities for improving their own lives which result in a better economic return in both directions (users and providers).

Political Pressures

Although the civil war in Syria is still going and no any indication of any solutions, there is a normal daily life and almost all ministries and institutions of the government are fully functioning, especially, in the capital Damascus and some of the none affected towns and cities. Therefore, the political pressures in the role of leadership in defining a clear ICT strategy and operational plan have been held for the first two years of the conflict, where eGov was not the top priority of the top management. However, one example of the political pressures that was facing the decision makers up till year 2012, although there were several attempts to launch e-banking systems by the government in a partnership with private NGOs, the lack of uniform standard of communication and mechanisms of verification and traceability, coding and encryption and identification mutual data standard and information security regulations prevent of implementing this service. Therefore, political pressures have an influence on all aspects of the eGov, especially, affected the eService Availability in the country which is one of the examined variables above.

Social Pressures

The social pressures elicited by whether the eService could reach all people equally, regardless of their locations, gender, age, economic background or their educational background. This issue becomes even more challenging in reaching different people in unstable society. The situation is quite different as the pressures are more manageable in countries hosting refugees as there are no obstacles due to a securities reasons i.e. establishing a training program. The use newspapers, radio, and television in promoting and announcing new eServices or about the benefits of using existing service would raise the level of awareness among people that would enhance the communication and connectivity. As a result, this might place more demands for new and betterquality eServices that would result in citizen empowerment, increased the quality of life, increased privacy and security especially for displaced and refugee people.

Technological Pressures

Overcoming technological pressures allows users of enjoying the eService delivery through a single one-stop shop portal which contains an answer to most eService related queries where no issues of techniques are problematic. Furthermore, adopting a sensitive ICT-related procedure such as security and privacy, system reliability and availability and international standards is the core of building trust with users and attract even unsure people. Integrated model among different government agencies would overcome many duplication and bureaucratic behaviours that traditional services users experienced. The standards of eServices implementations give users predictions of similar functionalities in different situations which consequently would help in bridge some gap in the digital literacy and reduces financial constraints by beaning less connected to the internet which is expensive especially, for displaced people.

Form the above discussion, the authors can conclude that all above pressures are related to each other in a way that improving one would result in reducing the barriers that facing the others and vice versa.

CONCLUSION

This study explored challenges in adopting eServices facing the people in unstable societies. The authors have examined two samples of the Syrian populations (inside and outside Syria). The novelty of this research is reflected in a quantitative survey that the result of analyzing the associated data describe the current state of implemented eService in the Syria eGov, its benefit and the challenges facing displaced people and refugees in using this system through their interaction with the government electronically. The aim of the present research was to examine elements have emerged from the literature review that thought to have an impact on the successfulness of eService delivery which people in unstable societies may face. Through conducting a questionnaire-based survey and based on analysis the finding, we can conclude that the most common elements that will affect the success of the eService delivery system in Syria as considered to be an unstable country are: The importance of eServices, Connectivity, Awareness, eService Availability, Financial constraints and Digital literacy. Furthermore, we have adopted institutional theory as a theoretical lens to have a deeper perspective on the above challenges which classify them under four key pressures (Economic, Political, Technical and Social). The result of the investigation shows the different implementation of eService in a country classified as a high level of instability and other countries with different level of instability, through different challenges that are facing the respondents from each sample. However, greater knowledge and understanding is still needed in this realm, there is a need for sustainable solutions to support displaced people and refugees. Our work shows the importance of eServices in unstable societies and particularly to displaced people and refugees since it provides a life-line into information and services and enables integration of displaced people in local communities. From this work we are able to provide some recommendations and suggestions towards sustainable approaches as follows:

- Consider Mobile based technology as an alternative channel for eService delivery in an unstable environment, where mobile network reaches people in most locations which are not the case for a different network.
- Pay more attention to the rural area and provide services smiler to the one in the urban area, by providing the necessary infrastructure, this would bridge the digital divide among citizens.
- High-speed internet and provide people with adequate and reliable internet connection as well as cut the cost of connectivity down, hence, more people would consider joining the service.
- Establishing digital literacy training programs and pay attention to the education process as a whole, especially, for those who rolled out from schools as a result of the conflict.
- Considering Social media as a platform for dissemination of eServices information as well as utilizing the media including television and radio and newspaper to raise awareness among all.

- Involvements of NGOs in empowering the eService delivery by cooperating and collaborating with the government whether the Syrian one or the countries hosting refugees to provide the best of services.
- Advertising campaign focusing on emerging eService, especially in education and health.
- Highlight eServices benefits and advantages.
- System integration among government's arms and establishing culture of Collaboration and cooperation

REFERENCES

Al-Busaidy, M. (2011). *Evaluating the institutional factors affecting egovernment implementation.* Brunel University.

AlKhatib, H. (2013). *E-government systems success and user acceptance in developing countries: The role of perceived support quality.* Brunel University. Retrieved from http://dspace.brunel.ac.uk/handle/2438/7471

Alsaeed, A., & Adams, C. (2015). E-Service adoption in developing countries with instability status: The case of e-government in Syria. In *Proceedings of the European Conference on e-Government, ECEG* (pp. 393–402). Portsmouth, UK: Academic Press.

Alsaeed, A., Adams, C., & Boakes, R. (2014). The need for policies to overcome egov implementation challenges. *International Journal of Electronic Government Research*, *10*(3), 66–79. doi:10.4018/ijegr.2014070105

Alshehri, M., Drew, S., & Alfarraj, O. (2012). A comprehensive analysis of e-government services adoption in Saudi Arabia: Obstacles and challenges. *International Journal of Advanced Computer Science and Applications*, *3*(2), 1–6. Retrieved from papers3://publication/uuid/A1CEA70F-B951-4D95-9F49-566F06677E09

Alsmadi, I. (2011). Security challenges for expanding e- governments services. *International Journal of Advanced Science and Technology*, *37*, 47–61.

Azab, N., Kamel, S., & Dafoulas, G. (2009). A suggested framework for assessing electronic government readiness in Egypt. *eJournal of eGov*, *7*(1), 11–28.

Chatfiel, A. T., & Alhujran, O. (2009). A cross-country comparative analysis of e-government service delivery among Arab countries. *Information Technology for Development*, *15*(3), 151–170. doi:10.1002/itdj.20124

Choudrie, J., & Dwivedi, Y. (2006). Investigating factors influencing adoption of broadband in the household. *Journal of Computer Information Systems, 46*(4), 25–34.

Dada, D. (2006). The failure of e-government in developing countries: A literature review. *The Electronic Journal on Information Systems in Developing Countries, 26*(7), 1–10.

Elsheikh, Y. M. a. (2011). *A model for the adoption and implementation of web-based government services and applications. a study based on grounded theory validated by structural equation modelling analysis in a Jordanian context.* Retrieved from http://hdl.handle.net/10454/5378

European Commission. (2001). *European governance: A white paper.* Retrieved from http://ec.europa.eu/transparency/regdoc/rep/1/2001/EN/1-2001-428-EN-F1-1.Pdf

Gant, J. (2008). Electronic government for developing countries. International Communication Union, 2(52).

Heeks, R. (2002). *iGovernment: Working Paper Series* (No. 13). eGovernment in Africa: Promise and Practice. Manchester, UK: University of Manchester, Precinct Centre. Retrieved from http://idpm.man.ac.uk/wp/igov/index.htm

Heeks, R., & Bailur, S. (2007). Analyzing e-government research: Perspectives, philosophies, theories, methods, and practice. *Government Information Quarterly, 24*(2), 243–265. doi:10.1016/j.giq.2006.06.005

Helbig, N., Ramón Gil-García, J., & Ferro, E. (2009). Understanding the complexity of electronic government: Implications from the digital divide literature. *Government Information Quarterly, 26*(1), 89–97. doi:10.1016/j.giq.2008.05.004

Hubbard, B. (2013, July). Momentum Shifts in Syria, bolstering Assad's position. *The New York Times.*

Information Business Publications. (2013). *Syria energy policy, low and regulations handbook.* Washington, DC: Author.

Information Management Unit. (2016). *DYNAMO: Syria dynamic monitoring report.* Gaziantep: Assistance Coordination Unit.

International Telecommunication Union. (2009). *eGovernment implementation toolkit: A framework for e-government readiness and action priorities.* Author.

Jait, A. (2012). *Government e-services delivery requires citizens a wareness :the case of brunei darussalam.* Loughborough University.

Khan, G. F., Moon, J., Rhee, C., & Rho, J. J. (2010). E-government skills identification and development : Toward a staged-based user-centric approach for developing countries. *Asia Pacific Journal of Information Systems*, *20*(1), 1–31.

Kondra, A. Z., & Hurst, D. C. (2009). Institutional processes of organizational culture. *Culture and Organization*, *15*(1), 39–58. doi:10.1080/14759550802709541

Neuman, W. (2006). *Social research methods: qualitative and quantitative approaches* (6th ed.). Boston, MA: Allyn and Bacon.

Ogonek, N., Gorbacheva, E., Räckers, M., Becker, J., Krimmer, R., Broucker, B., & Crompvoets, J. (2016). Towards efficient egovernment: identifying important competencies for egovernment in european public administrations. Electronic Government and Electronic Participation. *Proceedings of IFIP EGOV 2016 and ePart 2016*, *23*, 155–162. doi:<ALIGNMENT.qj></ ALIGNMENT>10.3233/978-1-61499-670-5-155

Ramlah, H., Norshidah, M., Abdul-Rahman, A., Murni, M., & Umar, A. (2010). G2C adoption of e-government in malaysia: Trust, perceived risk and political self-efficacy. *International Journal of Electronic Government Research*, *6*(3), 57–72. doi:10.4018/jegr.2010070105

Saunders, M., Lewis, P., & Thornhill, A. (2002). Research methods for business students. Prentice Hall.

Scott, R. W. (2001). *Institutions and organizations*. Thousand Oaks, CA: Sage Publications.

Scott, R. W. (2004). Institutional theory. In G. Ritzer (Ed.), *Encyclopedia of Social Theory* (pp. 408–414). Thousand Oaks, CA: SAGE Publications Inc.

Scott, R. W. (2008). Approaching adulthood: The maturing of institutional theory. *Theory and Society*, *37*(1), 427–442. doi:10.1007/s11186-008-9067-z

Sengupta, K. (2012). *Syria's sectarian war goes international as foreign fighters and arms pour into country*. The Independent.

Seo, D. B., & Bernsen, M. (2016). Comparing attitudes toward e-government of non-users versus users in a rural and urban municipality. *Government Information Quarterly*, *33*(2), 270–282. doi:10.1016/j.giq.2016.02.002

Sethi, N., & Sethi, V. (2008). *E-government Imple- mentation: A Case Study of Dubai e-Government*. Singapore: In Nanyang Technological University.

Strachan, P., Wanous, M., & Mofleh, S. (2008). Developing countries and ICT initiatives: Lessons learnt from Jordan's experience. *The Electronic Journal on Information Systems in Developing Countries, 34*(5), 1–17.

Sweisi, N. A. A. O. (2010). *E-government services: An exploration of the main factors that contribute to successful implementation in Libya.* University of Portsmouth.

UNHCR Syria. (2015). *Protecting and supporting the displaced in syria: unhcr syria end of year report 2015.* Damascus, Syria: Author.

Teo, H. H., Wei, K. K., & Benbasat, I. (2003). Predicting intention to adopt interorganizational linkages: An institutional perspective. *Management Information Systems Quarterly, 27*(1), 19–49.

Transtec, S. A. (2015). *Independent programme evaluation (IPE) of UNHCR's Response to the refugee influx in Lebanon and Jordan.* Retrieved from www.transtec.be

UNHCR. (2013). *Syria regional response plan January to June 2013. Field information coordination support section.* Retrieved from http:/data.unhcr.org/syrianrefugees

UNHCR. (2014). *2014 Syria regional response plan: Strategic overview.* Retrieved from http://reliefweb.int/sites/reliefweb.int/files/resources/Syria-rrp6-full-report.pdf

UNHCR, & Accenture. (2016). *Connecting refugee: how internet and mobile connectivity can improve refugee well-being and transform humanitarian action/ united nations high commissioner for refugees.* London, UK: UNHCR's Division of Information Systems and Telecommunications (DIST) & Accenture Development Partnerships (ADP).

UNICEF. (2015). *Humanitarian response plan 2016 - Syrian Arab Republic.* Office for the Coordination of Humanitarian Affairs. Retrieved from www.humanitarianresponse.info/en/operations/syria

United Nations. (2010). *United Nations eGov development database: overview - United Nation eGov Database.* Retrieved from http://unpan3.un.org/egovkb/egovernment_overview/ereadiness.htm

United Nations. (2012a). *E-government survey 2012: E-Government for the People.* New York: Department of Economic and Social Affairs Division for Public Administration and Development Management. Retrieved from https://publicadministration.un.org/egovkb/Portals/egovkb/Documents/un/2012-Survey/Complete-Survey.pdf

United Nations. (2012b). *Implementation of general assembly resolution 66/253 b on the situation in the Syrian Arab republic report* (Vol. 46820). Author.

United Nations. (2014). *E-government survey 2014: e-government for the future we want*. New York: Department of Economic and Social Affairs Division for Public Administration and Development Management. Retrieved from https://publicadministration.un.org/egovkb/Portals/egovkb/Documents/un/2014-Survey/E-Gov_Complete_Survey-2014.pdf

World Bank. (2011). *E-government*. Retrieved from http://web.worldbank.org/wbsite/external/topics/extinformationandcommu nicationandtechnologies/extegovernment/0,menupk:702592~pagepk:1490 18~pipk:149093~thesitepk:702586,00.html

Zhi, J., & Zhenhua, Y. (2009). The local e-government practice in china: a survey of the G2C practice of "Changxing county". In *International Conference on information Management, Innovation Management and Industrial Engineering* (pp. 548 – 551). Academic Press.

Chapter 9
Scaling Mobile Technologies to Maximize Reach and Impact:
Partnering With Mobile Network Operators and Governments

Ambika Samarthya-Howard
Praekelt.org, USA

Debbie Rogers
Praekelt.org, South Africa

ABSTRACT

This chapter explores three existing financial approaches to scaling mobile technologies in low- and middle-income countries: user-paid services, reverse billing, and zero-rated platforms. As affordability is an impediment to internet access, key strategies focusing around the involvement of mobile network operators and governments are investigated in relation to sustainability, scale, reach, and impact for mobile technology projects in the world. Various examples under each type are explored as a starting point for understanding the risks and benefits of each approach. The chapter also discusses the importance of mobile initiatives in tackling social issues today.

INTRODUCTION

With more mobile phones than people in the world, it is possible, and critical, for social change organizations to effectively leverage mobile technologies and platforms to distribute information and services to marginalized and underserved communities

DOI: 10.4018/978-1-5225-3179-1.ch009

in low and middle income countries (LMICs). LMICs are defined by the World Bank based on gross national income. (World Bank, 2017) As an organization working in designing, developing, and creating mobile tools and content, Praekelt. org believes that, in order to reach those most in need, services must be accessible without charge to the end user. This requires understanding the various models of partnerships with mobile network operators.

Even on the basis of limited available evaluation studies, we know that mobile technologies have great promise for improving people's health and wellbeing. In Jeannine Lemaire's (2013) second report on scaling up m-health, the author cited a study, showing that two daily text messages to health care workers in Kenya improved pediatric malaria care by 24.5%, and a trial, which identified significantly improved anti-retroviral treatment (ART) adherence after weekly mobile text messaging. Unfortunately, many m-health evaluation studies are limited, as scale-up has been challenging and randomized control trials are not always financially feasible for program implementers.

One thing we have been able to observe via -health programs is the ability to identify gaps in the system, which can help improve care. A recent study published on the MomConnect maternal m-health initiative in South Africa (Barron, Pillay, Fernandes, Sebidi, & Allen, 2016) reported the efficacy of complaints lodged on the mobile platform in identifying iron supplementation shortages at clinics (anaemia contributes to mortality from obstetric haemorrhage, a leading cause of maternal mortality.) In at least two provinces, Gauteng and North West, reports of iron supplementation shortages led to improvements in the overall stock reordering systems at facility level. This is just one example of the power of mobile development interventions, specifically in public health, to support vulnerable communities.

Therefore, the question of access to mobile services when scaling these projects is paramount.

Mobile inventory (e.g., SMS, Voice, and Unstructured Supplementary Service Data/USSD) costs can be a significant challenge for mobile health projects in reaching scale and longevity. In a study on mobile for development, the GSM Association (GSMA), a trade body representing mobile operators globally, shared:

Scale will not be effective in decreasing costs if the SMS/USSD method of delivering services is utilised. As the number of users increases, the costs increase exponentially. Cost efficiencies through scale will only be effective if a maternal m-health programme were to operate via a data or SMS/USSD and data combination, as the incremental costs would be significantly less. (GSMA, 2014a, p. 31)

The epidemic of "pilotitis", or when mobile health projects do not scale behind pilot stage, exists in part due to the high cost of programs at scale and the lack of financial backing to ensure long term sustainability. Even if they show promising results around impact at the pilot stage, the cost of scale-up and lack of evidence on cost effectiveness make many donors reluctant to fund scale-up.

There are many ways to define scale. One way could be to define scale as reaching a certain quantity of people. In the context of underresourced and bottom-of-the-pyramid communities, this is not an effective measure of scale, as it ignores the potential disparities of who can access the service. We are defining scale both in terms of geographic reach and percentage of target population reached. For example, for MomConnect, a maternal health program targeting pregnant women in the public healthcare system in South Africa, an appropriate definition of scale would be that the program should be available in all nine provinces, at 90% of the facilities, and register 80% of the live births. In many areas of the developing world, scale can be defined as reaching the most vulnerable, underresourced communities. In this chapter, we are defining scale as a project that is operational nationally, reaching the majority of the target market in low and middle income countries. Depending on the environment, reaching the most vulnerable may create more impact, but, in regard to accessibility and partnerships, we are evaluating scale as maximizing the number of people reached.

The cost per user of the inventory of a platform can vary greatly depending on the country, channel of delivery of the program, and length of time for which a user will be engaged with the program. In our experience, the cost per user for most mobile programs which need regular engagement for a period of 6 months or longer is between $0.50 and $12. While during a pilot stage with a limited amount of users this cost may be marginal, an increase of a million users on a project makes this cost a significant ongoing financial commitment. It is also a significant cost when compared to the cost of other development interventions. For example, according to the World Health Organization (2014), it is recommended that governments spend an average of $44 per year per person on basic, life-saving health services.

The goal of health and social change organizations today is to explore models which will maximize the contributions and value of the various stakeholders involved in mobile health projects while addressing the needs of the poor (Hellström & Tröften, 2010). Since distribution plays a critical role in ensuring that social entrepreneurs, NGOs, governments, and other content providers are able to drive real-world impact at scale, different models for payment of inventory must be explored and weighed against each other.

Three categories of models can be used to pay for the inventory costs for mobile for development programs: payment by user, payment by implementing organizations which is known as reverse billing, or absorption of cost by the mobile network operator (MNO), known as zero-rating. Within each of these categories, various programs have taken a range of approaches. This chapter aims to explore these models, by providing concrete examples of the approaches which have been adopted and of their successes and failures, and to propose strategies that may be used in the future, as the mobile landscape changes and models of payment become more sophisticated.

Model 1: Payment by the User

Considering the relatively small cost per user for these services, one of the possible models for increasing financial sustainability is to transfer the cost of the service to the individual user. One of the solutions which has been proposed to ensure ongoing financial sustainability is to ask users to pay for subscriptions to services, rather than having the ongoing cost taken on by governments or donors. In order to make a case for this approach, many organisations have investigated willingness to pay with target communities. In a recent study by the GSMA (2014b) in South Africa, 37% of users showed a willingness to pay for maternal health messaging.

However, two major challenges arise when asking users to pay for this kind of service: firstly, paid-for services often exclude those most in need of services, and, secondly, ability to pay often does not translate into willingness to pay.

In a recent study conducting break-even and uncertainty analyses in evaluating costs and revenues of financial models for m-health scaling, the researchers noted that "especially in a resource-constrained setting, transferring costs to users may deter program use for the poorest and most vulnerable segments of the population" (Mangone et al., 2016, p. 9). The study shared the results of a willingness-to-pay survey of 1,332 m4RH users in Tanzania, where charging users to receive content "may limit program use to less than half (47%) of users who were willing to pay for the service" (Mangone et al. 2016, p. 9). M-health programs were developed to address communities which cannot even afford transportation costs for frequent clinic visits. How can we, then, expect these same communities to afford data costs for information they are not aware they are lacking?

The Aponjon service in Bangladesh is a global public-private health information service which was created by Mobile Alliance for Maternal Action (MAMA) of the U.S. Agency for International Development (USAID) in 2012 to help pregnant women, new mothers, and their families receive behavior change communication messages via mobile phone. Aponjon has attempted to address the problem of those most in need to pay for this and all user-paid services, by offering them free of charge for the persons who qualify. Qualification is worked out through a series of questions aimed at understanding the woman's ability to pay for the service. These questions do not only assess household income, but also household spending in order to better assess availability of funds for the service (Raihan, 2016, personal communication). Qualified users receive the service free of charge, while those who can afford the service pay for the inventory which is needed to deliver the service (approximately

2 taka, about $0.025, per message) to them, through a monthly subscription. This model has worked well for scaling the service with over 1.9 million users currently enrolled. However, the question of whether the service reaches those most in need is yet to be answered. Currently, only a relatively small percentage of the users of the service have qualified for the free-to-access offer. Nevertheless, no studies have been conducted to assess whether the impact of the service would be increased or decreased if the level for qualification was changed. The free-to-access service costs are provided by external donor funding, in this case primarily the USAID.

This ability to pay is not only related to household or individual financial levels to afford the service, but also to the availability at the specific moment when the registration of these funds or phone airtime is required. In this regard, significant issues have occurred with the uptake of our services. Indeed, between 2011 and 2014, while implementing the MAMA program in South Africa with our partners, the Wits Reproductive Health and HIV Institute (WitsRHI) and CellLife, we observed this first hand. When we did preliminary research in the clinics to assess if people would pay a nominal fee to register for the service (in this case the fee was 0.60 rand or approximately $0.04), the results showed that the majority of users were willing to pay this amount to register on USSD and then to receive 15 months of free messages. However, this data did not relate to the evidence we saw when we started the program. Registration was led by MAMA ambassadors at the clinic. While women were excited to hear about the service, the numbers of registrations per week were well below the anticipated volume. When the ambassadors were asked to give feedback, they reported that many women did not have airtime on their phones when they wanted to register, so they were not able to proceed.

The first attempt to rectify this issue was to provide women who did not have airtime a flyer with instructions on how to register, so that they could complete this operation when they had airtime. The increase in registrations with this action was negligible. When these women left the clinic, we lost them as potential users. Since at the time zero-rating or reverse billing of the USSD service was not available in South Africa, our next attempt to provide a solution consisted in using paper-based registration. Although the implementers were reluctant due to the challenges in data accuracy and scalability of this method, its adoption resulted in a substantial increase of registrations. The time and opportunity costs of waiting for a customer to have sufficient airtime or data can be prohibitive for m-health scale.

Another alternative which was explored to tackle this issue of availability of funds and ability to pay was to offer a free trial to the user. This not only would have ensured that users could easily register to a service, but it would have also increased the likelihood of users to subscribe because they would have had first-hand knowledge of the value of the service once they would have been asked to pay. GSMA's case study on m-health initiatives by Grameen Foundation in Nigeria and

Ghana (Bhandari, 2015) showed a large opportunity loss for new entrants of paid m-health programs and advocated for trials:

Incentives and marketing efforts are needed to attract and retain users. According to VAS2Nets, the platform gets about 4,000 hits per day that are not being converted to paying users. This means that people are dialing the short code to find out more, but are then not willing or able to pay the subscription fee of N30 per week. These potential customers need to be shown the value of Mobile Midwife, for example, through a free trial during which they can listen to sample voice messages and receive sample text messages. This type of "try before you buy" incentive is often necessary to convince people to subscribe to a service. (Bhandari, 2015, p.20)

Trial periods also offer an opportunity for mobile health programs to appeal to MNOs. An example of this is mDiabetes, a nation-wide diabetes prevention text messaging initiative being implemented in India by the U.S. nonprofit Arogya World in partnership with Nokia and supported by a consortium of partners in the U.S. and India. Arogya World is providing free access to mDiabetes content for an initial period of six months to Indian Nokia's customers who have the Nokia Life application on their phones and subscribe to Nokia's health channels. Once the six-month trial is over, customers can opt in to receive the diabetes awareness and prevention messages at a nominal fee. Between January 2012 and January 2013, 1.05 million consumers from across India opted in and were enrolled in mDiabetes through the Nokia Life platform. As of April 2013, mDiabetes has sent out over 45.9 million text messages through the program, with over 185,000 people having already completed the initial six-month program. mDiabetes creates a value-added service for Nokia, presenting a strong investment case, and uses their existing large-scale network of consumers on the Nokia Life platform to deliver diabetes awareness and prevention messaging. According to Arogya World, the marginal cost of enrollment is about $.40 per person, thereby presenting a potentially cost-effective model for chronic disease prevention (Lemaire, 2013). While in the context of the target demographics in India, forty cents per person may not be prohibitive, this may not be the same for many communities and demographics in Africa and Asia.

Model 2: Reverse Billing

With many questions still unanswered as to whether the models of user payment reach those who are most in need of life-saving services and information, many international development programs have opted for the reverse billed model of payment for inventory. In this model, the implementing organization, donor, or government that are involved in the program are billed for the inventory used by the program, while the user is able to access the service for free. Since reverse billing incorporates a sound business model for companies to offer free services to their customers, it is therefore available through most MNOs and simple to implement. Reverse billing can often be hard to scale, as it requires continued donor-based funding to cover inventory costs.

We have observed that in our projects, while we are often able to receive discounted rates from MNOs based on the scale of the service, even with these discounts, reverse billed costs can often account for 75% of the cost of the program. In some cases, MNOs may be willing to offer some free inventory through their Corporate Social Responsibility (CSR) programs, but the inventory is limited. An MNO may generously donate 50,000 messages to a social good program, but what happens when the program scales successfully and there are 50 million messages that need to be sent? While CSR interventions are a good source for initial funding, few of them are sustainable. "Very few CSR interventions are sustainable: the pilot is simply a part of the company's marketing plan once the press release been published and circulated the interest cease" (Hellström & Tröften, 2010, p. 65).

One widely known case for this is Text To Change, a mobile platform which sends and receives SMSs to provide and collect information in the developing world. The initiative has been successful in running an incentive-based system where participants receive free airtime as a way to sustain the project and reach results. Bas Hoefman, Founder of Text to Change, said about partnering with MNOs:

Orange is providing us with technical support in countries where they have operations; however, the partnership does not demand exclusivity-we are open to work with other existing operators within the region. I then must argue that Corporate Social Responsibility (CSR) is always a short-term association. To have a sustainable working relationship with the mobile operators we must ensure a win-win situation since the primary goal/core business of the operator is to provide network services and make profits. This is how it should be. I [would] rather have premium services and pay for it than a CSR project that doesn't have priority for the service provider because it is not profitable. (Lemaire, 2013, p.42)

Unfortunately, many public service health projects are not profitable for the MNO.

Ultimately, this will always leave us in the situation where supporters of the program, often global aid organizations and other donors, will have to pay large amounts of money to maintain a program at scale. Using donor money to this end can be controversial, as grant cycles are time-limited and funding a corporate entity is not often within the ethos of grant making organizations. Even with reduced rates, the knowledge that most SMSs only cost MNOs a cent to send while they are charging ten times that leaves many donors feeling queasy. Undoubtedly, once again this impacts the sustainability of the program.

This can be seen to contribute to the large number of pilots that have been unable to scale. In Lemaire's commissioned report for the Advanced Development for Africa (2013) the author stated: "Historically, 85% of funding for m-health was dedicated primarily to early-stage R&D or pilot programs" (p.6). In an earlier report she wrote that,

... despite the strong promise demonstrated by m-health tools and applications, the current landscape of m-health development in developing country contexts is characterized by a proliferation of unsustainable pilot projects that often expire once initial funding is exhausted. For example, in Uganda alone there were 23 m-health initiatives in 2008 and 2009 that did not scale up after the pilot phase. In India, there were over 30 m-health initiatives in 2009 that did not go beyond the pilot phase (Lemaire, 2011, p.12)

If the financial responsibility on users is not realistic for certain programs, then the burden on donors for scale-up is also not sustainable. There is another approach, in which the MNO covers the costs.

Model 3: Zero-Rating

The third model that has been explored in detail is that of zero-rating of services. In this model, the MNO waives the cost of the platform to both the user and the implementing organization. In many ways, this is ideal for the sustainability of mobile development programs, but significant challenges occur .

First, this kind of offering requires a very close partnership with the MNO. This partnership takes many forms, but invariably require a large amount of effort and time on the part of the implementing organizations. Secondly, MNOs are generally more comfortable with zero-rating data services, such as mobile Web sites, rather than transactional services, such as USSD, SMS, or Voice. This significantly reduces access to services in LMICs, and particularly for people most in need.

Despite these challenges, there have been a number of successful programs in this area, particularly with the involvement of large multinational organizations. Partnerships with MNOs are central to the success of these projects. Through sustained, integrated partnerships built on shared value, content providers and MNOs can and will bring life-changing mobile services to billions of people across the globe (Guildford, 2014). We will explore many variations of MNO relationships that can offer programs zero-cost platforms for scale.

Undoubtedly, building partnerships is easier if the target audiences can provide a viable business model and we can incentivize the MNO. A relevant great example is Switchboard, which, in partnership with mobile network operators Vodafone and

MTN, has created a free calling network for every doctor in Ghana and Liberia, and is expanding to Tanzania. Since 2008, physicians have been collaborating using the Switchboard network to improve patient care with over four million calls made. Physicians in Ghana were spending upwards of US$70 per month on calls to colleagues. Through Switchboard's mutually beneficial relationship, physicians gained a nationwide support network and telecoms gained new customers. The key to Switchboard's success was in designing a program for scale from the beginning by incorporating strong incentives for both partner and MNO participation. Switchboard's free calling networks save doctors money on calls to colleagues to seek advice or refer patients, providing them a significant incentive to switch carriers. This is especially valuable for a player such as Vodafone, which has only 18% market share in Ghana; yet, they have all 2,200 physicians as subscribers. While health practitioners make free calls to seek advice, they also make paid calls to friends and family–generating $1.5 million in revenue for Vodafone and MTN. Switchboard believes these creative business models are the key to nationwide m-health scale and expansion to new markets (Lemaire, 2013).

We can see how this business model may work for physicians. as they allow these professionals to save money, but could not be scaled for other demographics, such as poor pregnant mothers in rural communities. The model also rests on developing an exclusive partnership with a specific MNO provider, which would prohibit scale in other market contexts, and, of course, beyond one particularly national deployment. Also, the number of physicians in these countries is quite low in comparison to the market share held by youth or general populations. It is important to think creatively, but business models that have exclusive contracts are often not an option for many international nonprofit organizations.

The scope of the project can indicate costs as well as opportunities for scaling. Oftentimes, a higher volume of messaging involved with scaling a project can be leveraged with private sector actors for their support, as these entry points could service their business interests. Denigrating m-health partnerships with private sector messaging can be very tricky, on both a content and financial partnership level. Initiatives must tread lightly, understanding all the drawbacks to partnering with certain private sector actors, such as the exclusivity contracts of the above-mentioned case with Switchboard (Lemaire, 2011).

Advertising and incentive modeling opens up many questions around the ethics of reaching new vulnerable populations. Similar to the issues of data collection and selling, we have to be cautious that we are not breaching the end user's trust in order to scale a program or make it more sustainable. The goal is to create a more sustainable relationship by leveraging the network operator's technical capacity and core competencies to support the m-health intervention.

Around 45% of mobile operators around the world offer some type of zero-rating service (West, 2015). West (2015) shows that zero-rated programs represent effective ways to enable people who lack the financial resources for expensive data plans to use certain applications without having that usage charged towards their data cap, as well as in conjunction with free Wi-Fi networks or library-based devices. At a recent Internet Governance Forum, zero-rating programs were cited as a popular way to provide Internet service in developing nations. For example, Wikipedia offers a "zero" version of its informational website for mobile platforms to 350 million people in 30 developing nations, which attracts around 65 million page-views each month (West, 2015).

The role of zero-rating services on achieving scale was evident when Facebook moved from Facebook Zero to Free Basics. Free Basics, also often referred to as Internet.org, provides users with access to Facebook's "basic internet services", including Facebook, Facebook Messenger, and a suite of country specific Web sites related to education, finance, health, information, and news. While this is not synonymous with free and open Internet, it is a more comprehensive offering than Facebook Zero. By mid-2015 Facebook had partnered with more than twelve mobile operators in seventeen countries to provide free usage of its Internet.org mobile application (Futter & Gillwald, 2015). Several African nations have reported substantial upticks in Internet usage following the introduction of Facebook Zero, Facebook's zero-rated platforms. The number of Facebook users, for example, rose 154% in Nigeria, 85% in Ghana, and 50% in Kenya. For the continent as a whole, there was a reported 114% increase in Facebook users after the launch of Zero (West, 2015).

Zero-rating is a special form of differential pricing, where bandwidth cost is covered by either the ISP or content provider. Dr. Jeffrey A. Eisenach, Senior Vice President and Co-Chair of NERA's Communications, Media, and Internet Practice, presented an assessment of the benefits and costs of zero rating (Eisenach, 2015). Eisenach suggested that "zero-rating (in the context of network effects) is appropriately understood as a mechanism for achieving increased participation within relatively small communities, including within lower-income populations in developing economies" (p. 5). While many people have learned about zero rating specifically in the context of net neutrality debates, often citing contentious issues around Facebook's Free Basics platform, it can hold different meaning for nonprofit organizations, such as Wikipedia Zero, for instance, who are designing services with net neutrality principles in mind (Sambuli, 2016). Since we are investigating zero rating specifically around health information and non-profit, public well-being content, we will leave aside the issues around net neutrality in this chapter.

Research has also shown the impact of increased Internet accessibility on health services in particular. MAMA Bangladesh has shown, for example, 69% of mothers who accessed the site via zero-rated platforms such as internet.org received medical care, compared to 32% of nonusers. On average, site users had at least four clinical appointments during which they received medical care for their young child (West, 2015). One zero-rating service in Tanzania that has proved very popular is text messaging for mothers and pregnant women. Over a two-year period, 500,000 parents received 40 million text messages about "safe motherhood". This helped reduce infant mortality by 64% and maternal mortality by 55%. Airtel Tanzania supports this service on a zero-rating basis (West, 2015).

Outside of inventory costs, MNOs can also be instrumental in helping with the marketing of the service, another crucial financial burden for mobile development projects. The importance of partnering with a MNO in both marketing and distribution for mobile programs cannot be overstated. As Guildford (2014) mentions in his report on MNOs and the content distribution chain,

The depth of their partnerships can be particularly strong when the target population is in an emerging market or the content provider is not a for-profit firm. This is partly because MNOs in emerging markets frequently play a broader role in society than their counterparts in developed markets. The relationship is also deeper because content providers from the nonprofit and public sectors often lack commercial capabilities, and consequently they rely more on MNOs to undertake these activities. (p. 22)

When MNOs and project implementers can come to the table and develop partnerships together, they can often find mutually beneficial negotiating points.

A recent example of MNO involvement in scaling an existing project is VillageReach's partnership with Airtel, Africa's largest mobile carrier, to expand m-health services in Malawi in a new service, called Airtel Chipatala Cha Pa Foni (CCPF). VillageReach's blog describes CCPF as a combination of "a staffed health hotline with a mobile message service providing regular text or voice messages on reproductive, maternal, and newborn health topics tailored to the client's week of pregnancy or a child's age" ("Airtel to Support", 2015).

The merger leverages Airtel Malawi's customer base to expand the reach of VillageReach's services. According to the Acting Managing Director for Airtel Malawi, Charles Kamoto,

The initiative falls under Airtel Africa's mobile health (m-Health) portfolio, which has an overarching mandate to bridge the information gap about healthcare issues, raise awareness, enhance understanding about these issues and educate customers on how to lead a healthy lifestyle both in Malawi and across the continent. ("Airtel to Support", 2015).

The relationships between ICT for development and MNO partnerships has been widely discussed. During the Keynote Session at GSMA m-health Alliance Mobile Health Summit, Christian De Faria, SVP, Commercial & Innovation for the African operator MTN, recently spoke of the company's strategy to work with Sanlam Health as its strategic partner in developing and implementing m-health initiatives across all of the operator's twenty-one networks. While MTN brings infrastructure, distribution reach, and a "service mindset" to the table, De Faria said that Sanlam brings core medical knowledge and an understanding of the local medical operating environment. As Lemaire cited in her report: "We can sell airtime well, but we are not specialists in healthcare—our philosophy is to partner with companies that know", commented De Faria. "We have to complement each other and be respectful of the regulatory environment in every country. By partnering we know that the service we provide will be reliable and up to standard." Meanwhile Carlos Martinez Miguel—Head of Strategic Analysis & Planning at Spanish and Latin American operator Telefonica's Global Healthcare division—claimed that "network operators can be the ideal 'travel companions' for healthcare systems and providers." Stating that "strategic partners are required" for all m-health initiatives, Miguel said operators make good partners due to their experience in communications as well as customer service. "We have the ability to invest and offer end-to-end managed services" (Lemaire, 2011, p.31).

Yet, even with the understanding of the importance of this partnership, it is hard to achieve sustained MNO support. We have seen the impact of zero-rating in our work, such as Young Africa Live (YAL), a mobile platform where young people could talk about "Love, Sex and Relationships in the Time of HIV". Through a mutually conducive relationship with Vodacom, MNO agreed to not only zero-rate the service, but also to place the service on their operator deck VodafoneLive! in order to drive traffic. This combination of free access and consistent traffic made YAL one of the most active sites on Vodafone live and attracted over 1.85 million users to the platform, showcasing the importance of partnering with an MNO in scaling m-health platforms. Unfortunately, as with many partnerships, support for the program was dependent on key people at the company who eventually left or changed position. Due to the lack of additional funding to maintain the content on the platform, we closed the program after five years of growth and success.

One of the key incentives of deeper MNO partnerships, such as content integration with YAL, is to help drive to the service by providing integrated marketing. Human Network International has shown that the benefits of 30 years of airtime for the MNOs is correlated with a 28% increase in outgoing SMS and a 7-10% in subscriber-base penetration (Human Network International, 2015). This is for a service reaching over 150 thousand users monthly in Madagascar and over 84 thousand in Malawi. The benefits of MNO partnerships is clear, but often program implementers cannot carry the weight of building and sustaining these partnerships on their own. This is where governments can play a critical role.

A KEY ELEMENT ACROSS ALL MODELS: GOVERNMENT SUPPORT AND INVOLVEMENT

The key missing component in many of the above-illustrated solutions is government involvement. We believe that government integration is key in the sustainability of social good mobile programs that are supported on reverse billed or zero-rated platforms. Today, governments need to be engaged in creating a safe information national infrastructure, which is key to creating sustainability for mobile health and social good programs. A sustainable approach must serve the users' needs, the commercial needs of the MNO, and also the donors' or governments' needs. This is an extremely difficult balance to obtain and has not been entirely fully optimized, yet, in our opinion. Government involvement, public-private partnerships (PPP), and potentially new MNO technologies can all offer interesting opportunities for achieving this balance. This will also help us increase the impact of our messaging as we continue to iterate around the type and amount of messages sent based on feedback.

Even as early as 1995, according to The National Info Infrastructure Advisory Council,

... a national infrastructure links large numbers of individuals and institutions to one another and to an array of info & services, thus providing the potential to be a nation's most significant asset in the knowledge-based economy. To participate effectively in the economy of this century, all parts of society - individuals, as well as public and private organizations and businesses - will need to use info and info tech to communicate, collaborate, provide, and receive info of all kinds. An enhanced national infrastructure can make that possible. (Mutula, 2002, p.468)

In fact, as the report of the UN Secretary-General (United Nations, 2016) states on the progress of the Sustainable Development Goals (SDGs), SDG Goal 9 to "build resilient infrastructure, promote inclusive and sustainable industrialization and foster innovation" also includes the idea that infrastructure and economic development rely on information and communications technology.

We believe PPPs are the only way forward. Many mobile programs have owed these partnerships for their success-or lack of to their failure. An example is the Disease Surveillance and Mapping Project, which covers the implementation of a mobile disease surveillance and mapping project to aid Botswana's fight against malaria. This initiative is the result of a PPP formed between Hewlett Packard, the Clinton Health Access Initiative (CHAI), Botswana Ministry of Health (MOH), Central District Council Botswana, MNO Mascom, and Positive Innovation for the Next Generation (PING), which is a local Botswana nonprofit organization. The program goes as far as equipping health workers with mobile devices that collect malaria data and can be viewed in a geographic map of disease transmission, allowing for real-time disease outbreak data. It sends out SMS alerts of disease outbreak to all healthcare workers in the district and allows facilities to submit regular reports back to the Ministry of Health. By providing free data transmission for the project, Mascom sees an opportunity to build market share while fulfilling its strong commitment to social responsibility. Key, however, is the involvement of global nonprofit organizations, as well as the government of Botswana (Lemaire, 2013).

In the sustainable cost modeling study that we have cited earlier in this chapter, the researchers also concluded that "the government could also act as a key partner in helping to negotiate reduced costs, promoting the service as part of its existing promotional campaigns, or integrating the program into an existing service" (Mangone et al., 2016). A good example of this would be m-health in Tanzania. The Ministry of Health and Social Welfare of Tanzania leads the m-health Tanzania PPP, with support from the U.S. Government Center for Disease Control and Prevention, as well as numerous Tanzanian and international public and private sector partners.

The PPP focuses on addressing ministry defined public health priorities by convening partners and supporting national-scale solutions that work in concert with initiatives underway at the Ministry. The Wazazi Nipendeni free SMS service utilizes the multi-media campaign to reinforce awareness of the service and the shortcode, while employing a reverse-billing approach to enable pregnant women and their supporters to access the SMS service for free. (Lemaire, 2013, p. 16)

Indeed, the trend for PPP is noticeable: by 2013 USAID alone has formed nearly 700 PPPs, demonstrating a remarkable increase from around 50 PPPs existing in the 1980s (Sturchio, 2013).

The key is in leveraging the government's position to negotiate with private-sector investments. Specifically for the African context, with the dearth of public resources at the policy level, there is a need to create an enabling environment for the leveraging of private sector investments for the delivery of public services. In a recent policy paper on zero rating in the African context, the Department for International Development stated

The African MNOs offering zero-rated use of OTTs clearly see zero rating as a mechanism to induce data usage by the significant numbers of customers on the networks who have smartphones, but are not using, or who are underutilising, data services–with the idea that users drawn onto zero-rated platforms can eventually be drawn into paid services. Such a strategy is particularly appealing to late-entrant, nondominant MNOs seeking to boost market share and take market share from dominant operators. (Chair, Futter, Gillwald, Koranteng, Odufwa, Walubengo, 2016, p. 46)

Since many new markets in Africa are welcoming these approaches, government and nonprofit organizations can tap directly into these motivations when creating lasting partnerships. Government backing and support can be a great option for scaling with MNOs (Futter & Gillwald, 2015).

Money does not have to be the only incentive for MNOs to work with social good and international organizations. Another leverage point can be existing relationships. For example, VillageReach, has projects which have used the organization's long standing relationships with ministries as a bartering point with MNOs. From the beginning, airtime was the number one impediment to scale for VillageReach's Chipatala Cha Pa Foni. They partnered with GSMA, the trade body that supports mobile operators, to help broker deals with Airtel. Specifically for Malawi, Airtel wanted help in getting through government market barriers in a new market. VillageReach used their long-standing relationship with the government to help form deals beneficial to AIRTEL.

The way relationships with MNOs and governments develop within the context of freedom of information require the utmost attention. For example, recent partnerships with Facebook's Free Basics platform and MNOs have shown the extent to which government involvement can go to restricting Internet freedom.

The risk of censorship is amplified by the fact that many of the mobile providers partnering with Facebook on Free Basics are state-owned or partially state-owned. Kenyan mobile giant Safaricom, for instance, is 35 percent government-owned. Even those partners that are private companies are vulnerable to pressure from the government. In 2008, for instance, Airtel was one of several private mobile providers in Kenya that complied with government requests to hand over data on over 1,000 users accused of instigating violence after the election. (Nyabola, 2016).

We need to be cognizant of these risks when involving governments in mobile development projects, as cyber security and individual privacy rights are of critical importance.

CONCLUSION

Mobile social change programs, specifically those related to health, have shown results in improving the well-being of people, especially in low and middle income countries. Unfortunately, many m-health interventions struggle with ensuring consistent and sufficient financial resources over the long-term. Various models have been used to solve this problem, .

Many programs explore models such as user-pay services and reducing program costs through partnerships (Mangone et al., 2016). User-pay services may limit the reach of the program in specific poor and vulnerable communities. Also, as many of our projects have shown, ability to pay does not correlate to willingness to pay.

Another approach is reverse billing, in which inventory costs are covered by third party donors and/or nonprofit organizations. In this case, the implementers spend a great deal of time and effort on developing the partnership with the MNO and often even with discounted costs, funding for inventory is not sustainable in the long term with the structure of grant cycles.

A third model is that of zero-rated platforms, where MNOs provide their services free of charge to the program. Many zero-rated platforms work for Web data and do not cover USSD and SMS services, which for m-health programs represent the majority of costs.

The analysis of current successful global mobile health initiatives has highlighted that, regardless of the type of financial model, government involvement is key to the longevity of the program. As the Internet is becoming the place where both public and private services and information reaches people, a government's contribution in creating a safe information technology foundation can be key to creating sustainability and engagements in these programs. As we know, these spaces are increasingly areas where discussion, critique, and decision-making happen. We hope that rather than censoring these interactions, the government as well as private enterprises can use the feedback loops mobile communications provide to improve services and make systems more efficient.

This is going to become increasingly important as we look ahead to future communication channels, such as Internet Protocol (IP) Messaging, which is becoming increasingly popular in LMICs and provides an engaging and low cost alternative to channels such as USSD and SMS. For example, with 900 million users, Facebook Messenger is one of the most used chat apps in the world (Johnson, 2016). Messenger allows for larger character limits than SMS and none of the time-outs of USSD. Users send 60 billion messages per day using messenger-more than three times the global daily SMS volume.

Many implementers, including ourselves, have tremendous hope for what these channels will mean for mobile social change work. However, there are a number of unknowns that we need to tackle. The business incentives and model that MNOs will use for these platforms, such as Whatsapp, remains unclear. Will the model that has been used in previous channels such as WeChat remain the same or will we start to see a move to transactional costs as we have with SMS and USSD? MNOs could remain open to the zero rating of these channels or become reluctant and treat them like the way they handle the costs for SMS, Voice, and USSD as the IP market matures. These unknowns have the potential to further prevent the scale-up of mobile development programs. We believe that the time is right for governments to become involved in regulatory conversations with MNOs in order to ensure that we are not having the same challenges in the future as those we are facing currently in mobile development scale-up.

REFERENCES

Airtel to Support Free Health Hotline in Malawi. (2015, Nov 5). Retrieved from: http://www.villagereach.org/news-press/7387-2/

Barron, P., Pillay, Y., Fernandes, A., Sebidi, J., & Allen, R. (2016). The MomConnect mHealth initiative in South Africa: Early impact on the supply side of MCH services. *Journal of Public Health Policy, 37*(S2), 201–212. doi:10.1057/s41271-016-0015-2 PMID:27899795

Bhandari, P. (2015). *Connected Women: Grameen Foundation Case Study on Bringing "Mobile Midwife" to Nigeria.* Retrieved March 2015, from http://www.gsma.com/mobilefordevelopment/wp-content/uploads/2015/06/Connected-Women-Grameen-Case-Study-final.pdf

Chair, C., Futter, A., Gillwald, A., Koranteng, K., Odufwa, F. & Walubengo. J. (2016). *Much Ado About Nothing? Zero-Rating in the African Context.* Department for International Development.

Eisenach, J. (2015). *The Economics of Zero Rating.* NERA Economic Consulting. Retrieved March 2015, from http://www.nera.com/content/dam/nera/publications/2015/Economic sofZeroRating.pdf

Futter, A., & Gillwald, A. (2015). *Zero-rated internet services: What is to be done?* Broadband 4 Africa, Policy Paper 1, 2015. Retrieved Sept 2015, from http://www.researchictafrica.net/docs/Facebook%20zerorating%20Final_Web.pdf

GSMA. (2014a). *Maternal messaging mHealth programmes. Empowering and enabling decision makers to include mHealth services into their budgets.* Retrieved 2014 from http:// www.gsma.com/mobilefordevelopment/wp-content/uploads/2014/12/GSMA-mHealth- Programme-high-resolution.pdf

GSMA. (2014b). *Understanding the needs and wants of pregnant women and mothers.* Retrieved from http://www.gsma.com/mobilefordevelopment/wp-content/uploads/2014/07/Consumer-Research-Report.pdf?_sm_au_=ijVWr264Nr0mRQQq.

Guildford, M. (2014). To the next billion: Mobile Network Operators and the content distribution value chain. *Innovations, 9*(3-4), 21–31. doi:10.1162/inov_a_00213

Hellström, J., & Tröften, P. (2010). *The innovative use of mobile applications in East Africa.* Stockholm, Sweden: Swedish International Development Cooperation Agency (SIDA).

Human Network International. (2015). *Human Network International & its services* [PowerPoint slides]. Retrieved from http://www.slideshare.net/SandraGubler1/human-network-international-its-services

Johnson, K. (2016). *Facebook Messenger now has 11,000 chatbots for you to try.* Retrieved from http://venturebeat.com/2016/06/30/facebook-messenger-now-has-11000-chatbots-for-you-to-try/

Lemaire, J. (2011). *Scaling Up Mobile Health: Elements for the Successful Scale Up of mHealth in Developing Countries.* Retrieved from https://www.k4health.org/sites/default/files/ADA_mHealth%20White% 20Paper.Pdf

Lemaire, J. (2013). *Developing mHealth Partnerships for Scale.* Advanced Development for Africa. Retrieved from http://www.adaorganization.net/uploads/2/3/7/1/23713723/developing_mhealth_partnerships_for_scale_printer_friendly_low.pdf

Mangone, E. R., Agarwal, S., L'Engle, K., Lasway, C., Zan, T., van Beijma, H., & Karam, R. et al. (2016). Sustainable Cost Models for mHealth at Scale: Modeling Program Data from m4RH Tanzania. *PLoS One, 11*(1), e0148011. doi:10.1371/journal.pone.0148011 PMID:26824747

Mutula, S. M. (2002). Internet Connectivity and Services in Kenya: Current Developments. *The Electronic Library, 20*(6), 466–472. doi:10.1108/02640470210453949

Nyabola, N. (2016). *Facebook's Free Basics Is An African Dictator's Dream*. Retrieved from http://foreignpolicy.com/2016/10/27/facebooks-plan-to-wire-africa-is-a-dictators-dream-come-true-free-basics-internet/

Ohuruogu, V., Fernan Flores, P., & Foh, K. (2015). *GSMA: Mobile for Development: Catalysing mHealth Services for Scale and Sustainability in Nigeria*. Retrieved May 2015, from http://www.gsma.com/mobilefordevelopment/wp-content/uploads/2015/05/GSMA-Nige ria-Business-Framework-web.pdf

Sambuli, N. (2016). Challenges and opportunities for advancing Internet access in developing countries while upholding net neutrality. *Journal of Cyber Policy, 1*(1), 61–74. doi:10.1080/23738871.2016.1165715

Sturchio, J. L. (2013, Jan. 10). The Evolving Role of the Private Sector in Global Health. *Huffington Post*. Retrieved from http://www.huffingtonpost.com/jeffrey-l-sturchio/the-evolving-role-health_b_2432823.html

United Nations. (2016). *Progress towards the Sustainable Development Goals*. United Nations Economic and Social Council. Retrieved from https://http://www.un.org/ga/search/view_doc.asp?symbol=E/2016/75&Lang=E

West, D. M. (2015). Digital divide: Improving Internet access in the developing world through affordable services and diverse content. Washington, DC: Center for Technology Innovation, Brookings Institution.

World Health Organization. (2014). *WHO Global Health Expenditure Atlas, September 2014*. Geneva, Switzerland: Department of Health Systems Financing. Retrieved from http://www.who.int/health-accounts/atlas2014.pdf

World Health Organization. (2017). *World Bank Country and Lending Groups*. World Health Organization. Retrieved from https://datahelpdesk.worldbank.org/knowledgebase/articles/906519-world-bank-country-and-lending-groups

Chapter 10

ICT Affordability and Coping With Disaster:
Coping With Disaster

Carl Adams
University of Portsmouth, UK

Sam Takavarasha Jr.
University of Fort Hare, South Africa

ABSTRACT

This chapter explores the impact of a disaster on communities from a development perspective and the corresponding importance of access to ICT. Poorer communities are often most vulnerable to disasters, a situation that can affect the economic development of such communities for decades. The chapter uses the UN's Sendai framework to emphasize the role of ICT in supporting communities throughout the different stages of disaster situations, towards long-term recovery and development. Some key themes emerge in the chapter, notably access to technology is a key support mechanism; a longer-term temporal perspective of such disasters indicates there are likely to be different waves of "disaster" refugees; the initial ones being classed as humanitarian migrants with all the humanitarian supports that they attract; whereas longer term any resulting "refugees" would more likely be classed as economic migrants. The chapter also explores longer term support mechanisms such as the role of remittances.

DOI: 10.4018/978-1-5225-3179-1.ch010

INTRODUCTION: FROM DISASTER TO MIGRANTS

The impact of disaster events are often far reaching. Natural and manmade disasters have the potential to cause tremendous harm to communities impacting them over many years (Dillon 2014; Jensen and Youngs 2014; Lauras et al 2015; Schryen and Wex 2014). For instance, consider an earthquake and a following tsunami which can directly impact many communities over huge areas with devastating consequences on the life and wellbeing of communities. It can damage and destroy housing and key infrastructures, and take decades for communities to rebuild and recover. There have been several examples in the last few decades. The 2004 Indian Ocean earthquake that occurred on the 26th December with the epicentre off the west coast of Sumatra, Indonesia is one of the most dramatic examples. This 'Boxing Day' earthquake was one of the most powerful ever recorded and resulted in a very large tsunami that rapidly spread across the Pacific ocean, killing thousands of people in coastal communities in Malaysia, Indonesia, India, Sri Lanka and devastating Island states in the Pacific. It even smashed through coastal villages and communities in Somalia four and a half thousand kilometres away, resulting in over 170 deaths and more than 50,000 displaced people from Somalia alone (Wikipedia 2004). In addition to the immediate humanitarian disaster there is often longer term impact across wider sets of communities with an influx of refugees in adjoining communities, disruption to economic activity across whole regions or disrupting global supply chains.

James Daniell's (2014) work collates together details of over 35,000 natural disaster events around the globe since 1900 in his 'CATDAT Natural Disaster Socioeconomic Loss & Indices Database. As the CATDAT database show, the human cost of disasters is huge. The economic cost is similarly large. For instance an analysis of the impact of these events globally results in an estimated seven trillion US dollars economic damage caused by natural disasters since the start of the 20th century (Phys.org 2016; KIT 2016; Daniell 2014).

Of course there is often a disparity of the impact of such disaster events for different communities with the poorer communities often being most severely affected for longer periods of time. The poorer communities often lack the resources to be prepared for such events, have less resilient infrastructures to withstand a disaster event and have fewer resources to respond to and rebuild from such an event. However, there has been considerable global attention focused on how to better support and prepare nations for disaster events, such as the Sendai frame discussed in the next section.

The UN Response: Sendai Framework

The UN has been at the heart of trying to help nations prepare for and respond to disaster events. In 1994 the UN produced the "Guidelines for natural disaster prevention, preparedness and mitigation". After building on experiences of more disaster events and the various governments' responses to those the UN produced the 'Hyogo Framework for Action 2005-2015' (HFA 2005). This tried to help nations and communities build resilience against the *impact* of disasters, taking a slightly longer term perspective of impacts. The current UN's guidance is the Sendai Framework for Disaster Risk Reduction 2015-2030 (UN/ISDR 2014), which collated together further insights and experience from nations and communities dealing with disaster events. Perhaps one of the main differences in Sendai framework to that of previous guidance and frameworks is a shift towards *disaster risk management and reduction* as opposed to *disaster management* itself. So the focus is more on preparedness and planning. It also tries to engage contribution from multiple stakeholders within the global arena (Adams 2017). The rationale being that communities that are informed, aware of and prepared for potential risks from disaster events are more likely to successfully emerge from a disaster event. The UN also produced the Global Platform for Disaster Risk Reduction, with supporting regional platforms and mechanisms, to complement the Sendai framework and to encourage nations to set up their own disaster risk programmes.

The Sendai framework consists of seven global targets and four main areas for action (UN/ISDR 2014), these being:

Sendai Framework Global Targets

(a) Substantially reduce global disaster mortality by 2030, aiming to lower average per 100,000 global mortality rate in the decade 2020-2030 compared to the period 2005-2015.

(b) Substantially reduce the number of affected people globally by 2030, aiming to lower average global figure per 100,000 in the decade 2020 -2030 compared to the period 2005-2015.

(c) Reduce direct disaster economic loss in relation to global gross domestic product (GDP) by 2030.

(d) Substantially reduce disaster damage to critical infrastructure and disruption of basic services, among them health and educational facilities, including through developing their resilience by 2030.

(e) Substantially increase the number of countries with national and local disaster risk reduction strategies by 2020.

(f) Substantially enhance international cooperation to developing countries through adequate and sustainable support to complement their national actions for implementation of this Framework by 2030.

(g) Substantially increase the availability of and access to multi-hazard early warning systems and disaster risk information and assessments to the people by 2030.

Sendai Framework Areas for Action

Priority 1: *Understanding disaster risk*
Priority 2: *Strengthening disaster risk governance to manage disaster risk*
Priority 3: *Investing in disaster risk reduction for resilience*
Priority 4: *Enhancing disaster preparedness for effective response and to "Build Back Better" in recovery, rehabilitation and reconstruction*

Some of the key themes that emerge when examining the Sendai framework are the need for resources, particularly Information and Communication Technologies (ICTs) to underpin each of the preparedness stages. There is often limited availability of technology in many or the poorer countries or communities, and this is seen as one of the main challenges. There is recognition that the poorer countries need extra help and support:

Developing countries, in particular the least developed countries, small island developing States, landlocked developing countries and African countries, as well as middle-income and other countries facing specific disaster risk challenges, need adequate, sustainable and timely provision of support, including through finance, technology transfer and capacity building from developed countries and partners tailored to their needs and priorities, as identified by them. (UN/ISDR 2014,p14)

This requires input and support from the international community. For instance section IV of the Sendai framework covering 'International cooperation and global partnership', it emphasises the importance of technology and technology transfer

In addressing economic disparity and disparity in technological innovation and research capacity among countries, it is crucial to enhance technology transfer, involving a process of enabling and facilitating flows of skill, knowledge, ideas, know-how and technology from developed to developing countries in the implementation of the present Framework (UN/ISDR 2014, section IV).

Many of the key resources needed for monitoring, planning and interventions, as well as responding to an event, are information based. For instance, in collecting information on risk areas, and the needs and vulnerabilities of communities in those areas requires considerable information on the local contexts and the means of collating that information together. In being resilient to a disaster shock require, at least in a major part, active use of technology for disseminating information to inform planning, to be able to focus on main risk areas and coordinating activity. The same is true during and after a disaster event.

The next section will explore the result of a disaster or displacement event and how this impacts the people and communities affected.

The Disaster and Refugee Cycle: The Migrant 'Issue'

A major disaster event results in the need for humanitarian aid and support. In richer nations this can be mostly covered by the host nation, but in poorer countries support will likely be needed from the international community. Take for instance hurricanes in Caribbean region and the neighbouring USA. The USA is fairly well prepared for the impact of hurricanes with good infrastructure, lots of early warning mechanisms, insurance mechanisms and responses resources. With a few exceptions, such as the Katrina in 2005, the USA does not rely on international aid when a large hurricane hits. Whereas many of the mostly poorer island states in the Caribbean region can be completely devastated with key infrastructures wiped out, and consequently having to draw upon international support and aid.

Also after a major disaster there is usually a wave of refugee migrants to the surrounding local countries and communities. The 2005 Katrina hurricane example resulted with internal displacement of about 1 million people within the USA, some taking years to return. In poorer nations this usually means refugees extending to adjoining nations and communities (Collier 207), themselves which may have been affected by the disaster even and so putting further strain on those communities.

A continual challenge for many countries bordering regions facing risks of disasters is how to address the issues of such migrants. The migrants have an impact on local hosting communities as they stretch the local facilities and resources. The migrants also have an impact on the countries of origin as they deprive those countries of key skills and human capital – once people move from a risky disaster environment to a safer environment they will tend to want to stay in the safer environment.

As an example let us consider the Rohingya refugees from Burma. In South East Asia there has been a bubbling migrant crisis for decades with Rohingya refugees who have fled persecution and loss of statehood in Burma. This demonstrates that 'disasters' can be manmade geopolitical or conflict based as well as natural. The Rohingya refugees, or 'Asia's new boat people', impacted the local countries and communities of Indonesia, Malaysia and Thailand, and wider afield in the region to Australia (Guardian 2015). Interlinked with the refugees there are often economic migrants trying to get employment and a better life, in this case Bangladeshis mingled with the Rohingya refugees. The Guardian reporting on a regional meeting in Bangkok in May 2015 in response to thousands of refugee and economic migrants being stranded and abandoned at sea in the region, show some of the complexity of the problem space:

Malaysia and Indonesia agreed last week to provide the migrants shelter for one year. Indonesia says Rohingya can stay for a year but Bangladeshis will be repatriated. It is unclear what happens after a year, and both countries have called on the international community to help with resettlement options.

Thailand has offered humanitarian help but not shelter. More than 100,000 refugees, mostly from Burma's other ethnic groups, have been living in border camps for decades, and Thailand says it cannot afford any more. (Guardian, 2015).

It is a source of great pride in humanity when the international and surrounding communities do step up to the mark and provide direct and indirect support to refugees. The amount of work, contribution and support from charities and NGOs and the global general public that is often mobilised to help these mass refugees and migrants is often quite staggering (Adams 2017). The main burden of support often falls to the local neighbouring countries due to their close proximity, however this is often problematic as Collier (2017) identifies since the surround countries often have their own problems, especially if the event is geopolitical in nature.

The response to the Rohingya and Bangladeshis migrants by Malaysia and Indonesia is fairly typical in that they try to give different responses to the refugee migrants than to the economic migrants. In this case a limited safe haven for the Rohingy refugees while longer term solutions are explored, yet the Bangladeshis economic migrants are treated differently with more immediate repatriation. However, a deeper analysis shows the context to be more complex with the Bangladeshis migrants actually mostly claiming to also be Rohingy and who possibly share much history with previous migrations from Bengali and previous geopolitical upheavals going back to the Second World War. The distinction between the refugee and economic migrants may well be mute, since their plight is very much the same; both have current similar poor and desperate conditions and have similar geopolitical conflict backgrounds, just with different timescales. This reasoning points to perhaps a need to consider different 'waves of migrant' as a result of a disaster or geopolitical disruptive event.

The complexities of natural, manmade or geopolitical disasters can be very complex. Sometimes a refugee crisis can be long term. As an example, take the Palestinian refugees as a result of the 1948 Palestine War. This saw over 700,000 people displaced into adjoining countries in Lebanon and Jordan. These refugees are now 2nd and 3rd generation 'refugees' and are really integrated members of the host communities, though for some geopolitical reasons are given a refugee status. Part of these complexities is the engagement and involvement of the international community, an issue that Larry Thompson (2010) brings out in his book covering the mass *Indochina Exodus* post the Vietnam War period involving over a million people from three Indochinese countries - Vietnam, Cambodia, and Laos: Disasters and mass refugee and migrations are increasingly international issues.

One trend in the more recent migrant activities is the role of mobile technologies, media and social media in engaging the international communities. This has been evident in the recent migrations from the Northern African coast to Southern Europe where migrants (consisting of various refugees and economic migrants) use mobile technologies to inform rescue boats of as well as social media to engage the wider international community in their plight. There is also continual coverage in the wider media of newspapers, news websites and television. Technology is becoming an important tool for the migrants themselves.

The next sections will examine the role of technology in the post disaster stages, from the immediate disaster to longer term interventions.

Immediate Response: Connected for Information

The wide scale adoption of mobile and social media technologies provide a base to share information on potential disasters as well as disaster events as they unfold (Milliken and Linton 2015;Jennex 2010; Turoff 2002). For instance, monitoring networks have been used in flood monitoring (Assis et al 2016) and various other early warning systems have been used covering different areas of disaster risk such as extreme weather, earthquakes and volcanic activity (Zschau & Küppers 2002).

Often engagement in these systems for much of the population is through a connected mobile device. The Ushahidi platform (see https://www.ushahidi.com/) is a good example. Created in the aftermath of Kenya's disputed 2007 election, is a relatively simple but powerful app based platform enabling people to collect and share eyewitness reports of events. It has been used in the direct aftermath of the 2010 Haiti earthquake and the 2011 Christchurch, New Zealand earthquakes. Usahadidi, which is Swahili for 'witness' or 'testimony', has been used around the world for other citizen engagement projects.

Social media and crowdsourcing / open global principles are already starting to have an increasingly important role in disaster areas (Ramos et al 2015). The support typically covers direct aftermath of a disaster, for instance with the DigitalGlobe and FirstLook support mechanisms that sprang up in the immediate aftermath of the recent earthquakes in Napal. Poiani et al (2016) further describes how the use of social media and open street maps is used to help map both the impact of the Nepal Earthquake in 2015 and later to examine the needs of people affected.

Duffy (2012a,2012b) describes how social media can help build community disaster resilience and uses three dimensions for consideration, consisting of a) the initial disaster risk reduction (preparation and communication about preparation), b) the emergency management during a disaster event, and c) finally supporting community development after a disaster event.

Clearly these systems have likely saved lives by bringing humanitarian relief effort where it was most needed in a fashion not possible before. Having access to and being engaged with mobile technologies and social media during the unfolding of a disaster event is increasingly important for the ability to survive through the disaster and to recover from a disaster. Of course not having access to such ICT systems will likely put people at greater risk affecting their ability to communicate with others about their conditions and needs, and ability to participate in support others in need as well as receive support themselves.

One theme that emerges when examining humanitarian aid over long periods of time is the phenomena of 'donor fatigue' where aid donors stop donating to charities or humanitarian even, for instance as they get desensitised by the event or other priorities emerge. Interestingly, Pallas et al (2017) also found aid reduction at the country-level following similar donor fatigue type patterns. Access to humanitarian and charity aid provides support for only for short solutions post-disaster. Longer term solutions require development and rebuilding activity, which require the active engagement of the affected people. As the external interest and support wanes there is more needed from the affected local communities to rebuild their economy and society. Of course this will have its own challenges since the ability to recover from such a major disaster shock may be hampered by disruption to farming and production capabilities and the destruction of key infrastructure.

Sometimes that disruption is as a result of the aid and humanitarian activity. For instance, the USA is one of the biggest contributors to humanitarian aid after disasters through their food aid programme. However, the food aid consists mostly of food grown in the USA. This is great for getting good quality food quickly to areas needing it most, however the longer the food aid is given then the more it will likely disrupt and destabilise the local food production capability and supply chain. So the local producers find it even harder to sell their produce since there is a flood of 'free food' in their local markets (Barrett 2001; Bjerga 2013). Once the local food production supply chain has been disrupted it can take a long time to recover, for instance in lacking funds for seeds for the harvest in following years. It becomes even harder than before the disaster to have a functioning economy and community. It is in these times that a further wave of refugee migration often occurs as the new migrants seek routes to economic development both for themselves as well as their remaining relatives and community. This is a theme discussed in the next section.

Longer Term Support: Remittances, Connected for Development

Longer term support for communities that have faced stressful events such as a disaster or adverse geopolitical activity, or even extreme poverty, may also involve technology. As discussed earlier there may well be different waves of migrants after such events, the first being as immediate response to the event, while later waves may be due to lack of the affected communities being able to recover over time. Often there are waves of economic migrants trying to escape poverty for themselves or using economic migration to support their home community by sending back remittances. Many nations rely on remittances. The World bank 2016 'Migration and Remittances Factbook', captures some of the trends and reality for many of these nations:

Migrants are now sending earnings back to their families in developing countries at levels above US$441 billion, a figure three times the volume of official aid flows. These inflows of cash constitute more than 10 percent of GDP in some 25 developing countries and lead to increased investments in health, education, and small businesses in various communities. The loss/benefit picture of this reality is twofold: while the migration of highly skilled people from small, poor countries can affect basic service delivery, it can generate numerous benefits, including increased trade, investment, knowledge, and technology transfers from diaspora contributions. (World Bank 2016, page 5)

ICT Enabled Remittances

Remittances are defined in this study as both money (Kapur, 2003) and goods (Maphosa, 2005) sent by migrant workers to family and friends in their home country. There is also a phenomenon of social remittances that are discussed in literature. ICTs are a crucial tool for automating and facilitating remittances from international labour just as low cost flights have increased international travel (Bond, 2001; Mc Namara, 2003; United Nations, 2006; World Bank 2016)).

According to Kapur (2003), countries that are going through political and economic turmoil tend to experience increased emigration and remittances. For instance, remittances to Equado increased from 632m in 1997 to 1.4 billion in 2001 (Kapur, 2003). The remittance economy is associated with migrant economies and social refugee. This is because the hardships experienced in a war torn zone or a depressed economy tend to force the productive citizens to leave for safer places. When they migrate they are expected to maintain trans-disporic links with their home country in order to support the vulnerable people they left. This scenario places emigration from conflict zones and unstable economies in the 'new economics theory' which views emigration as motivated by 'push factors' like socio-economic failure and bad governance (Kapur, 2003).

The remittance economy of the information age is often referred to as ICT enabled remittances. This is because ICTs play a central role in facilitating the remittance of money and goods. Both the request for assistance and the transition of the remittances are highly dependent on ICTs. The people in the home country request for remittance through text messages, via social media or email if not voice calls to their relatives who relocated to foreign countries. The remittance sender in turn uses platforms like mobile money or Western Union which are also dependent of ICT platforms.

In view of this critical role of ICTs in the remittance economy, it is critical for both the sender and receiver of remittances to have access to affordable ICTs. This chapter focuses on the usefulness and availability of affordable ICT access to displaced populations. It presents this in the context of the use of ICTs for poverty reduction and development.

Some researchers claim that remittances contribute a larger income to developing countries than both foreign direct investment (FDI) and official development aid (ODA) (Mathison, 2005). Other reports however suggest that remittances are the second largest source of external funding after FDI. There is however some evidence that since the 1990s, remittances from international labour have exceeded ODA received by developing countries (McNamara, 2003; Maphosa, 2005; Mathison, 2005).

This is supported with research from the World Bank fact book remittance report (2016):

- *In 2015, worldwide remittance flows are estimated to have exceeded $601 billion. Of that amount, developing countries are estimated to receive about $441 billion, nearly three times the amount of official development assistance. The true size of remittances, including unrecorded flows through formal and informal channels, is believed to be significantly larger.*

- *In 2015, the top recipient countries of recorded remittances were India, China, the Philippines, Mexico, and France. As a share of GDP, however, smaller countries such as Tajikistan (42 percent), the Kyrgyz Republic (30 percent), Nepal (29 percent), Tonga (28 percent), and Moldova (26 percent) were the largest recipients.*
- *High-income countries are the main source of remittances. The United States is by far the largest, with an estimated $ 56.3 billion in recorded outflows in 2014. Saudi Arabia ranks as the second largest, followed by the Russia, Switzerland, Germany, United Arab Emirates, and Kuwait. The six Gulf Cooperation Council countries accounted for $98 billion in outward remittance flows in 2014. (World Bank, 2016, pV)*

This therefore makes remittance a higher contributor to poverty reduction and development than ODA. While ODA and FDI are prone to abuse by corrupt governments in developing countries, remittances are applauded for benefiting the needy people that they are sent to. Against this background we suggest that ICT enabled remittances must be seen as more human development than economic development oriented. This focus on human development instead of economic development is the ethos behind United Nations human development index (HDI) and gross domestic product per capita.

Clearly remittance activity is a very significant part of migration economic activity and offers long term solutions to displaced people post a disaster. However, access to ICT is an important part of having access to remittance capability, particularly access to mobile technologies enabling information about remittance needs to be disseminated as well as the means to send remittances. Cost of access to ICT is a significant problem to again the poorer communities, as also indicated by the World Bank fact book remittance report (2016):

The cost of remittances is the highest in Sub-Saharan Africa and in the Pacific Island countries (for example, it costs more than 20 percent to send $200 from Australia to Vanuatu, and 19 percent from South Africa to Zambia). As of the third quarter of 2015, the average cost worldwide remained close to 8 percent---far above the 3 percent target set in the Sustainable Development Goals. (World Bank, 2016, pVI)

Lack of affordable ICT impacts the ability for displaced people and migrants to fully participate in the remittance activity. This is directly impacting the ability to reach the UN's sustainable Development Goals.

CONCLUSION

Key Insights and Messages

The discussions above highlight the importance of access to ICT for people affected by a disaster or significant geopolitical disturbance event. There are clearly different phases to be considered, in line with the UN's Sendai framework, covering the preparation and preparedness of a community through a disaster event and towards sustainable development. It is also clear that 'disasters' are a development issue and that access to ICT is a significant contributing factor. This is supported by Fowler's (2017) discussion item 'Don't forget refugees and migrants when tackling risk':

Refugees and migrants must be included in efforts to reduce the risk of disasters, experts said this week at a European conference.

A special session of the European Forum for Disaster Risk Reduction spotlighted their vulnerabilities in the face of natural and human-induced hazards, but underlined that they also have an important role to play in curbing impacts.

There are some 250 million documented migrants globally, mostly living in urban areas, as well as 60 million people who are border-crossing refugees or who have been displaced within their own countries, the biggest level since the Second World War.

If authorities don't account for the needs of migrants before, during and after disasters, they won't be reducing risk.

It is interesting to note that Sendai framework doesn't explicitly focus on refugees and migrants, the focus being more on preparation and preparedness. It is more of a side issue, however refugees and migrants are key attributes of disasters affecting economic and societal stability both in the short term and long term.

The UN's Sendai framework focusses on preparation and preparedness for disasters, which also includes preparedness for dealing with a disaster event and recovering from a disaster, and general resilience. Priority 2 captures this explicitly *"Enhancing disaster preparedness for effective response and to "Build Back Better" in recovery, rehabilitation and reconstruction"* (UN/ISDR 2014, section V). As discussed above, the poorer communities do not have access to the same resources and mechanisms as the richer nations to do all the monitoring and preparation, or have effective responses and build back better. The result is often different waves of migration from these communities.

In addition the discussions above highlight there is often very little difference in the plight of disaster refugees and economic migrants, both having to face significant stress, poverty or risk if remaining in their home community.

To reiterate, the *Sendai framework areas for action covers four priority areas, these being*

Priority 1: *Understanding disaster risk*
Priority 2: *Strengthening disaster risk governance to manage disaster risk*
Priority 3: *Investing in disaster risk reduction for resilience*
Priority 4: *Enhancing disaster preparedness for effective response and to "Build Back Better" in recovery, rehabilitation and reconstruction*

These are mostly aimed at the pre-disaster stages, and technology is often an integral support mechanism to achieve those priority goals. However, as the discussion in the chapter identify, once a disaster event has occurred affecting poorer communities then it becomes increasingly difficult to recoup and recover. The poorer communities will likely effectively be knocked back and held back in their development potential. This is particularly so for poorer communities in areas affected by recurring disaster events, such a recurrent draught regions, flood regions, areas of high volcanic activity or geopolitical uncertainties. As global warming becomes more prominent then this situation is likely to extend to more poor communities around the globe. Breaking these cycles of economic and social development for the poorer communities of the world due to high risks of disaster events must be a focus for global policy makers in the coming years.

REFERENCES

Adams C. (2017). *Global disaster monitoring and learning methodology.* (Forthcoming)

Al-Husban, M., & Adams, C. (2016). Sustainable Refugee Migration: A Rethink towards a Positive Capability Approach. *Sustainability*, (8): 451.

Barrett, C. B. (2001). Does food aid stabilize food availability? *Economic Development and Cultural Change*, *49*(2), 335–349. doi:10.1086/452505

Bjerga, A. (2013). Obama Wants More Food Aid to Be Locally Sourced. *Bloomberg*. Available from http://www.bloomberg.com/bw/articles/2013-04-25/obama-wants-more-food-aid-to-be-locally-sourced

Coutts, A., & Fouad, F.M. (2013). Response to Syria's health crisis – poor and uncoordinated. *The Lancet, 381*(9885), 2242-2243.

Duffy, N. (2012a). Using social media to build community disaster resilience. *Australian Journal of Emergency Management, 27*(1).

Duffy, N. (2012b). Learning for disaster resilience. Earth: Fire and Rain - Australian & New Zealand Disaster and Emergency Management Conference, Brisbane, Australia.

Fowler, J. (2017). *Don't forget refugees and migrants when tackling risk.* Discussion paper, UNISDR. Retrieved from https://www.unisdr.org/archive/52560

Guardian. (2015). *South-east Asia migrant crisis: numbers are now 'alarming', talks told.* Retrieved from http://www.theguardian.com/world/2015/may/29/south-east-asia-migrant-crisis-numbers-are-now-alarming-talks-told

Hall, M. (2103). *The Syrian crisis in Jordan. Middle East Research and Information Project.* Academic Press.

Mills, D. (2014). *Aussies diplomat's incredible photos of the crisis in Syria ... and how he gave up a cosy office to make a difference.* Retrieved from http://www.dailymail.co.uk/news/article-2675841/Australian-worker-heading-relief-effort-worst-humanitarian-crisis-history-bringing-Syrian-refugee-crisis-control.html

Olwan, M., & Shiyab, A. (2012). *Forced migration of Syrians to Jordan: An exploratory study. Migration Policy Centre (MPC).* Badia Fiesolna, San Domenico Di Fiesole.

Pallas, C., Anderson, Q., & And Sidel, M. (2017). Defining the Scope of Aid Reduction and Its Challenges for Civil Society Organizations: Laying the Foundation for New Theory. *Voluntas*, 1–25.

Poiani, T. H., Rocha, R. S., Degrossi, L. C., & Albuquerque, J. P. (2016) *Potential of Collaborative Mapping for Disaster Relief: A Case Study of OpenStreetMap in the Nepal Earthquake 2015. Hawaii International Conference on System Sciences (HICSS)*, Kauai, HI. doi:10.1109/HICSS.2016.31

Ramos, I., Adams, C., & Desouza, K. C. (2015). Economic Resilience and Crowdsourcing Platforms. *Resilience and Information Systems (RIS) workshop, Pre – 23rd European Conference on Information Systems.*

Thompson, L. C. (2010). *Refugee Workers in the Indochina Exodus, 1975-1982.* Jefferson, NC: McFarland & Co.

Turoff, M. (2002). Past and future emergency response information systems. *Communications of the ACM, 45*(4), 29–32. doi:10.1145/505248.505265

UN. (2006). *International migration and development: Report of the Secretary General*. United Nations.

UN. (2014). *2014 revision of the World Urbanization Prospects*. Available from http://www.un.org/en/development/desa/publications/2014-revision-world-urbanization-prospects.html

UN/ISDR. (2004). *Living with Risk: A global review of disaster reduction initiatives*. Author.

UN/ISDR. (2014). *Sendai Framework for Disaster Risk Reduction 2015-2030*. Retrieved from http://www.unisdr.org/we/coordinate/sendai-framework

USAFID. (2004). *Celebrating 'Food for Peace' 1954-2004. U.S. Agency for International Development report 2004*. Author.

Wikipedia. (2004). *Countries affected by the 2004 Indian Ocean Earthquake*. Available from https://en.wikipedia.org/wiki/Countries_affected_by_the_2004_Indian_Ocean_earthquake_and_tsunami

World Bank. (2016). *Migration and Remittances Factbook 2016*. Retrieved from www.worldbank.org

Zschau, J., & Küppers, A. N. (2002). *Early Warning Systems for Disaster Mitigation*. Berlin: Springer.

Conclusion

This book has collated together a set of research covering issues related to access to Information and Communication Technologies (ICT) in some of the poorer economic developing countries of the world. What is clear from the chapters is that access to ICT is a development issue and a lack of access to such technology adversely affects poorer communities. In a globally connected world, ICT performs many roles and functions supporting and enabling communities and individuals to participate in economic activity, have access to information and educational resources, receive government services and, engage in a variety of community and social activities. The chapters bring out some of the complexities, challenges, and importance of addressing the digital divide that exists at the global level between the rich and poorer communities. This chapter hopes to bring together some of the key messages emerging from the research covered in the book.

DIVERSITY AND CONTEXT

This book has included a diversity of chapters covering a range of case examples and context as well as diverse issues, challenges, and approaches to solutions.

The chapters explore activities and issues across communities in Africa, the Middle East, the Indian subcontinent and Asia. Many common issues emerge, such as those relating to gender, education and the extra challenges of access for the rural communities. However, there are clearly many other context-specific issues that are relevant to the unique characteristics of local needs, capabilities and the geopolitical situation.

The focus of investigation within the chapters was varied. It covers from government to community level, while looking at private and nongovernment initiatives, from exploring the social and community aspects of the technological interventions. The chapters covered a variety of theoretical lenses using a diversity of investigation and research methods.

The collected works consequently provide a base for others to build on as they further explore this fascinating and important domain.

BARRIERS TO ACCESS

The majority of the chapters discuss some of the considerable barriers to access for many of the poorer communities. Rural areas and particularly the poorer communities in remote rural areas were consistently highlighted as having extra barriers to gaining affordable access to ICT. This is because the cost of providing infrastructure to sparsely populated and remote rural areas is comparatively much higher than providing infrastructure to urban areas. It is simply not cost-effective for Mobile Network Operators or infrastructure providers to provide the same access and infrastructure to these remote areas. A message that emerges from the chapters is the need for innovation in addressing these access barriers (and indeed several of the chapters discussed such innovations). The dominant models of service and infrastructure provision used in urban and richer communities simply will not work in the poorer remote communities. Hence the need for innovations and interventions discussed in this book.

In addition to infrastructural barriers, some demographic imperatives were identified in several chapters. These include, innumeracy, lack of information literacy and general lack of technological competency across the poorer communities. This compels us to investigate why marginalization and these deficiencies tend to co-exist between communities and within. For instance, the gender access gap was also a critical theme identified in the chapters. Females generally had less access to education, ICT literacy and financial resources (issues well discussed in Chapters 2 and 3). The lack of ICT and numeracy skills, and general education, has a knock on effects which can be classed as demand-side barriers. This has a negative impact on the acceptance of the interventions because people with limited skills and education may not be able to appreciate the relevance and potential that ICT access can provide.

Our endeavor to build a more equal world with ICTs calls a closer look at the inequalities highlighted in this book. The poorer communities have financial barriers which limit their access to technology on very limited budgets. They often have to spend proportionally larger amounts of their disposable income (assuming they have any) on technology. The extract cost of distribution of such technology to remote areas is also increasing the price of such technology adding further to access barriers. This calls for a focus on affordable innovations like community networks discussed in Chapter 1. A related barrier relates to access to electricity for powering their communication gadgets. Many of the poorer communities, do not have a robust and consistent electricity supply. Unlike counterparts in urban areas, they have to pay for charging their phones on a daily basis for them to remain connected. Similar issues of increased costs for many of the poorer communities can be found in other knowledge platforms like educational books. For instance, paper books are considerably more expensive in much of Africa than say Europe or America due to lack of infrastructure (say postal service), infrastructure, delivery costs, and high Intellectual Property charges.

The generic access barriers that emerge are that it is more expensive to provide access to the poorer communities and they are less likely to be able to pay for such access. The rural poor, the poor elderly and poor females in these communities have a further 'double whammy' of access barriers as it is proportionally more difficult and proportionally more expensive for them to have access to ICT resources - issues covered in several chapters, particularly Chapter 4. Further themes are the extra challenges small businesses and entrepreneurs face in these communities with limited and unreliable access to ICT making it more difficult as well as more expensive to participate in economic activity than in the richer communities of the world.

A further set of access barrier themes emerge in the chapters, that being the lack of access to ICT raises increased barriers in other areas of societal and economic activity. For instance, people can use ICT as a channel to maintain regular contact with friends, peers, and family, particularly for displaced people, as covered in Chapter 9, or remote workers that send remittances back to their home countries. Equally as critical is the use of ICT to access government services, health information as well as general information about resources, community activity, and opportunities. A common theme of ICT access is the ability to access the range of global educational resources and information. Clearly, as demonstrated in the chapter discussions, when considering barriers to access ICT we have to consider the wider access issues in how the lack of access affects individuals and communities.

OPPORTUNITIES TO IMPROVE ACCESS

What the discussions on 'access barriers' highlight is the potential for innovative solutions to providing affordable ICT access to poorer and disadvantaged communities. One interesting innovation is discussed in Chapter 3 where it examines the potential of using TV White Space technology and 'White Space' Device (WSD) that operates in the TV White Space (TVWS) frequency range - the result of moving towards digital TV switchover and freeing up bandwidth used in traditional analog TV. There is much potential in using the TV White Space technology in the more rural and remote areas since the technology can cover larger areas than Wi-Fi, WiMAX, and other wireless technologies.

Chapter 1 discussed some examples of community-based innovations and the role of governments and legislators in supporting such innovations. Chapter 3 discussed some new models of thinking to the problem space and options for innovation, such as the potential of zero-rating services e.g. Facebook's Free Basics platform. Similar discussions were in Chapter 9, where Ambika Samarthya-Howard and Debbie Rogers are looking at the potential providing "basic internet services" to communities giving limited but needed internet access to support education, finance, health, information, and news resources. In addition, other chapters capture the innovation taking place at the community level with locally initiated projects.

In Chapter 2 Takavarasha Jr, Adams and Cilliers examined an example of community-based access and entrepreneurship innovation taking place in developing community networks. The case study of a rural community network in South Africa shows innovations of providing complementary access to the mobile technologies coverage offered by Mobile Network Operators.

Another community innovation was discussed by van der Vyver in Chapter 6 with the OTOP initiatives, effectively creating small local economic hubs supported with social networks.

As the proverb "Necessity is the mother of invention" highlights, where there is a need then new inventions and innovations will emerge. The discussions in these chapters clearly identify a need along with some barriers to achieving those needs, all which point the emergence of innovative solutions.

SCALING, VIABILITY, AND SUSTAINABILITY

Building on from the discussion of diversity and context of the examples used in the book, a set of questions emerge on how projects can scale and have long-term sustainability. There are some really innovative approaches being adopted to address development needs of poorer communities.

There is always a challenge in taking a pilot project and scaling it up to wider use in other regions and other communities. A pilot project will often have pump-priming of resources such as money and expertise to get it going. It will also typically be initiated by willing and enthusiastic project champions. Taking a good project idea to other communities and locations without the extra boost of pump funding or without a natural project champion or the full buy-in of the local community will likely have many extra hurdles to gain success. In addition, there are considerable challenges after the pilot stage of a project to make it viable long-term. For instance, once the pump-priming of resources or support of the project champions or communities moves on then the project can often stall.

These issues are discussed in several of the chapters. For instance, Chapter 5 discusses some innovative approaches to achieve sustainability in such projects when they explored the "One Tambon, One Product" (OTOP) initiative in Thailand, which itself was building on a similar and successful initiative in Japan, the "One Village One Product" (OVOP). Some of the key messages from these projects was the need for buy-in from the top down. They also bring out the extra challenges in rural communities (the Tambons) and the successes based on each community generating their own initiatives. Similarly, in Chapter 5 they cover other sustainable initiatives based on the telecentre movement which also involved local engagement of communities, often blended with the OTOP initiatives.

Chapter 6 also looked at sustainability issues of telecentres but focused on much-needed information on the use of such centers. Accurate monitoring of use was identified as needed in helping to make decisions on telecentre use and investments, a key component in for corporate investment and for understanding sustainable success. Chapter 2 also touched upon scalability and viability of community networks in remote rural areas, an area clearly calling for engagement of stakeholders and opportunity for innovative solutions.

Scaling of successful initiatives was discussed in other chapters, some focusing on education, other focusing on the practicalities of scaling. Other themes of sustainability and viability were covered in Chapter 8 looking at support and integration of refugees and displaced people.

Other messages in the chapters are how to blend the inputs and activities from local communities, local and national government and the corporate world to address the local needs, challenges, and context. Long-term sustainable 'projects' need to be integrated into the social, government and economic activity of the community – and needs active engagement from those stakeholders. This thinking ties very much into some of the other chapters which raise the issue of the importance of having 'champions' for the initiatives. The champion, be they local, regional or national, will have a vision of how an initiative would address the needs of the communities, are able to generate interest and engagement from the various stakeholder groups.

RESEARCH METHODS

Another interesting observation on the chapter is the range and diversity of investigation approaches and research methods used to investigate the problems of affordable access to ICT. Case studies are used in several of the chapters though there are markedly different approaches to the case study research. For instance, chapter does an in-depth evaluation of the Zenzeleni project in Makhosi, South Africa. This is quite a detailed coverage of the background and context capturing many of issues as they evolve over the history of the project. The case study is informed by interviews and wider research around the example (records and literature reviewing) and captures much of the complexity of the context, issues, and challenges throughout the project. Chapter 5 also provides a complementary and equally solid case study approach, this time capturing multiple case examples including 10 diverse local telecentres in rural Thailand and 8 OTOP centers. The case examples were based on fieldwork visits. In addition, the case examples were supplemented with an application of the Social Media activity around these cases. So both chapters used a form of mixed methods and good analysis to tease out the underlying issues with the case study examples. Both also capture the richness of the historical context which provides key insights into the evolution of the projects, as well as the interplay with the different levels of government from national down to local level.

In Chapter 7 Dr. Indira Ananth, examines the sector level case of street-vendors in Chennai, the capital city of Tamil Nadu India. The study is interesting since the occupations considered i.e. street vendors are rarely covered in the literature, yet they have historical importance as a cornerstone of many cities' economic and cultural heritage. This chapter also used mixed methods including survey and interviews like Chapter 8 Alsaeed, and Boakes along with some focussed literature review. They then developed models to help analyze the context and emergent issues. Most chapters draw upon literature review to put their work in context as well as to be informed by burgeoning literature, and most try and develop models or frameworks to try parsimoniously articulate and evaluate the complexity of the topic being investigated.

Considering the range of research approaches and methods used in the book highlights the interesting opportunities of using a variety of research activity to investigate the topic of affordability of ICT to poorer communities. It is interesting to note that mixed methods are used frequently in the research presented here, which matches other thinking of doing ICT4D research in complex environments (Takavarasha et al., 2011).

THEORETICAL TOOLS AND LENSES

A variety of theoretical lenses and tools have been used in the chapters. In Chapter 7, Indira Ananth uses diffusion theories to examine the adoption of mobile phones. She also touches on the interplay between government support (free) vs market economy approaches and influences, effectively covering the base of much debate in development economics. In Chapter 2, Cilliers and Samarthya-Howard explore similar issues using the lens of Free Basics and the role of commercial enterprises (Facebook for instance) in providing 'free' access to services, again adding to the rich debate in development economics over the 'free vs paid' models of development. In

Chapter 10 Adams and Takavarasha also draw up models of development economics to explore the role and impact of technology.

In Chapter 9, Ambika Samarthya-Howard and Debbie Rogers provide an analysis of different payment models bringing in an innovation perspective, and interestingly the analysis covers blending of innovations such as paper and online support to increase mHealth registrations. The chapter also provides a gender perspective on the issues explored.

Amartya Sen's (1999) Capability Approach (CA) lens is used in a few chapters. Within this frame, Chapter 1 explores the freedoms and unfreedoms to pursue opportunities for the communities in their investigations. Indira Ananth in Chapter 7 also briefly refers to CA in considering the relationship of people to the resources that they have and the commodities that they need.

In Chapter 2 Cilliers and Samarthya-Howard adopt the "Social capital" lens, particularly Ellison et al.'s (2007) version which includes, maintained social capital, to articulate how Free Basics can be used to improve ICT access in developing countries. They complement this with Information Technology Identity theory (Carter et al., 2015) to help them explore ICT4D and understand how users recognize the potential for self-expansion through the application of technology. Some chapters use the construct of 'metaphor' as a lens to articulate the problem space. Chapter 8 uses Institutional theory, covering Economic, Political, Technical and Social attributes, as a lens to explore the factors affecting access to eServices for refugees and displaced people. Chapter 10 also exploring refugees and displaced people use theoretical support from development economics.

As can be seen from above there is much opportunity to draw upon a range of theoretical lenses to help explore the complex issues of affordability of ICT to poorer or disadvantaged communities. Clearly, for some of the chapters, the theoretical lens provided much support in articulating the very complex problem space, as well as to explore solutions. It is interesting to note that much of the applications of the different theoretical tools, and corresponding discussions, fall into the ground of the rich debates in development economics over the 'free vs paid' models of development.

TECHNOLOGY

A further interesting set of themes emerging in the book is the range of technologies that are being used to increase access to ICT and corresponding services. Mobile technologies in the form of 'cell phones' or 'mobile phones' and their wide-scale adoption is covered in several chapters. Similarly, the use and adoption of Social Media (SM) is well covered in other chapters.

There were also some innovative technological solutions considered in the book. Chapter 4 looked at various options to reach remote rural communities, including the use of TV White Spaces (TVWS), effectively the freed up bandwidth after analog TV signals get switched to digital during the 'digital change over'. The chapter considered several technological options highlighting there is much potential for innovation. Of particular interest is applying TVWS with other technologies, such as mesh networking and 'self-configuring' device to device networks. Other innovations were discussed in Chapter 5 exploring telecentres initiatives in Thailand. Different types of community networks are discussed in other chapters with some discussing technological infrastructure and options, others looking at the wider ecosystem, and others looking at different operating models.

Clearly, there is much potential to explore innovative provision to a variety of communities that face access barriers to affordable ICT. There is clearly a need for good technological solutions to address the issues of affordability of access to ICT. The chapters cover various approached that draw upon community-based solutions and effectively spreads the access costs between the community seems to off much potential in many contexts involving remote communities. This calls for community level and focused innovation as opposed to individual level innovation solutions that are dominant in the richer communities.

GAPS AND AREAS FOR FUTURE WORK

The research described in the chapters of this book provides an overview of some of the work covering activity within the area of affordable ICT access as a developmental issue. A range of issues and topics are covered but there is, however, much more that needs to be investigated – there are still many gaps in knowledge on how to adequately address the disparities in suitable access to ICT resources for many poorer and disadvantaged peoples of the world. We list here some possible gaps in knowledge that seems to need further work.

An examination of Chapter 8 covering the support for refugees and displaced people shows that there is more work that can be done to examine in greater depth the issues of refugees and economic migrants. Since armed conflicts and economic depressions are a major impediment to development and cause of poverty in developing countries, they need attention from the ICT4D researcher. The role of ICT for these communities seems more complex than conventional scenarios. This is because they need to fulfill extra communication and connection functionalities with home countries as well as providing a channel the other functionalities, that are required by other poor and disadvantaged groups. Displaced people and economic migrants need to keep in contact with the rest of their displaced communities and to maintain cross diasporic links with their home communities. Correspondingly, their home communities need to be linked into the remittance sending who often lack the option to visit their war-torn homelands. These extra issues cover the ICT addressable practicalities as well as the social and cultural issues that the displaces communities face.

A further gap area is in the affordability of ICT4D domain is the plight of particular disadvantaged groups, such as older people and females, issues covered by many other authors (e.g. Adams and Fitch 2006). Some of the chapters explicitly consider aspects of gender, the older and mostly illiterate communities and the remote rural communities. However, there is clearly much work that can be done to assess the interventions would improve the lives of these underprivileged groups.

Many of the chapters use case examples to describe different ICT innovations and how they have been deployed in developing countries. Some of the chapters also cover the issues of sustainability of affordable access. There is clearly a gap in how to bring sustainable innovation in ways that have long-term viability in providing affordable access to ICT and related key resources for the poorer and disadvantaged communities. This is because universal access projects are often funded by development agencies that have a short-term presence in these communities. It is therefore refreshing to note that some of the discussions and examples in the chapters of this book also point to community-based solutions that are championed by the communities that also own them. This again ties in with other works on successful community-based projects as articulated by Adams and Mouatt (2010a).

A further gap is in the relationship between the main influencing stakeholder groups including national and local government, regulators, education establishments, commercial enterprises, multinational and local corporations and NGOs (Adams and Mouatt, 2010b). In addition to this, is the key role that the project or initiative champions play from each of these main influencing stakeholder groups.

It is hoped that a variety of people will be able to use this work. There are practical implications of understanding which type of projects and initiatives may work in different contexts. The chapters hopefully also articulate some of the complexity of the issues around affordability of ICT access for disadvantaged groups, which can be used to better understand poverty reduction and development initiatives. It is also hoped that the collective work in this book provides a base for future researchers within the ICT4D domain to consider research activity, options, and theoretical tools that are appropriate for their research.

IMPACT ON ICT4D AND DEVELOPMENT THEORY

Though not always explicit many of the chapters in this book touch upon issues at the heart of the current debates in development theory, particularly over fundamental theories of how best to support development. This is the realm of discussions over socialism or capitalism, or discussion of neoliberalism and the freemarkets thinking dominant in much of the richer nations through the 1970s onwards (Harvey 2005) to debates over the end of capitalism as the strains and instabilities of unconstrained capitalism emerge (Harvey 2014). It is also the realm of Schmpeter's 'creative destruction' (Selwyn 2014) and the continued reshaping of global order, structures and prominence (Dicken 2007; Stopford, Strange and Henley 1991). This section hopes to give some background to these debates and put into context of affordable access to ICT.

Wiles (1962) and later Brett (2009) argue that theorists exploring change and development in least developing countries (LDCs) examine the geo-political and politico-economic structures and foundations of the countries. Effectively how the countries are set up and structured, including the roles, responsibilities, transparencies and freedoms of the various entities (from the citizens, to commercial organisation to government entities and leaders) all influence how their economies evolve. In Brett's (2009, p178) analysis he identifies five variables for considering models of politico-economic set-ups that are used to evaluate social changes within LDCs, these being:

1. Levels of personal autonomy that characterize social relationships
2. The degree of democracy or autocracy that characterizes the state-society relationship
3. The strength of the state's capacity to deliver services
4. The existence of economic markets as opposed to centralized command
5. The extent to which enterprises are privately of socially owned

As Brett identifies, sociologists usually focus on the first, political scientists on the next two and economists on the last two. These dimensions are clearly all interlinked, however we argue that from these perspectives there is a gap in mainstream development economic theory covering the role of technology. This becomes evident looking through the main chapters in this book which highlight the barriers, innovation, opportunity and impact of having affordable access to ICT. It is clear that an ICT lens provides a useful vista with which to understand development. Structure and mechanisms that provide barriers or enable access to affordable access to ICT will clearly have an impact on economic and wider development of the poorer and disadvantaged communities of the world.

Wiles (1962) provides a critical view of the concepts of the politico-economic set-ups of capitalism and socialism and argues that full free market capitalism still needs state intervention and direction, and that extreme socialism would require some free market activity. It is questionable if 'true and full free' markets actually really exist though at a global level there is much effort spent on trying to get encourage free market trade. This is evident with high level trade-negotiations under the World Trade Organization (WTO). The latest round of such negotiations is the Doha Development Agenda (DDA), or sometimes referred to as the Doha Declaration which started in a WTO meeting in 2001 in Doha, Qatar. The aims being to get consistent sets of rules to lower trade barriers around the world and so facilitate increased global trade. They started out as good principles from a 'free market' economic thinking by enabling open markets at a global level. They also had good aspirations from a development economics thinking perspective by potentially providing access to global markets to the poorer developing countries. In reality the 'free market' thinking from the dominant richer nations really translated to much self interest in being able to have more access to global market space while have natural barriers for the poorer countries to participate in the richer countries markets. The negotiations have been turning out to be a bit of 'bun fight' with many self interested groups wanting their own circumstances to shape the global trade rules for free trade. In 2008 there was a significant stalling of negotiations with disagreements over tariffs and subsidies, particularly over agriculture and industry, and particularly between the EU and USA, as well as other regions. Such subsidies and tariffs are seen as operating effectively as trade barriers. There is also contention between the richer developed nations (USA, EU, Japan and others) and the major developing countries (e.g. India, Brazil, China, and South Africa). The poorer nations have many worries and concerns over the potential for such global free trade to devastate or wipe out their own agriculture and industries if they open up their markets to big dominant international corporations. Local industries would not be able to compete against the purchasing power and resources of the multinational companies. Agriculture was of particular concern to the poorer nations since there is a real threat to local agriculture and agricultural diversity capability being impacted by cheap imports based on mono foods and GM crops. The result was the formation of the 'G33' a coalition of developing countries trying to coordinate representation in the Doha Round of World Trade Organisation negotiations, specifically in regard to agriculture. They have tried to address their concerns over by advocating the need to create a category "special products", particularly in agriculture, to allow developing countries to exempt certain products from tariff reductions and so provide "special safeguard mechanism" against import surges from richer countries. The G33 actually consist of more than 33 countries, currently consisting of over 40 countries, though the numbers may increase in further Doha negotiation rounds. The level playing field of global free market thinking and aspirations of the Doha Development Agenda (DDA) is turning out to be less achievable, but the overall *Neoliberalism* goals of free trade still has much potential particularly from a development perspective if barriers to global trade are reduced for the LDCs (Harvey 2005, 2014)

Further future stalling of the DDA is possibly with the nationalistic movements taking place across the EU, the USA and elsewhere in recent years. For instance Trump's 'America First' thinking may again set further barriers for those wanting to export into the USA at the same time the USA using their very significant geopolitical clout to make it easier for American companies to have unfettered free access to more global market spaces. A taste of what this might entail can be seen from an article in the Daily Signal (July 2016) which maps out what an American first free trade agreement should mean, including:

Focus on issues related to trade and commerce and not "monkey around with labor standards and environmental standards around the world," as former Ways and Means Committee Chairman Bill Archer put it. (Riley, 2016)

This vision of a 'free trade America first' may well mean a race to the bottom adversely affecting environmental issues and labor standards.

Similar arguments have been raised over humanitarian aid, for instance with the USA huge humanitarian activity based around food aid. Clearly this humanitarian support has saved many lives over many years giving quick response to communities facing the aftermath of a disaster, drought or other calamity. However it has also been accused of destabilizing local economies and food chains over longer periods of times since it floods the local food market with cheap USA produced food (Barrett 2001). This is in contrast to the article in the Daily Signal (July 2016) discussed above articulating what an American first model suggested by the Trump administration in the USA may looking like, including:

Limit the use of anti-dumping tariffs to cases where predatory pricing exists. Anti-dumping policies are a form of cronyism in which politically connected industries have the legal right to impose unnecessarily high prices on American businesses and consumers, and which other countries use to block U.S. exports. (Riley, 2016)

So possibly limiting 'dumping' by other countries but allowing other forms of dumping, such as under the banner of humanitarian aid, that favours the American agriculture industry.

Interestingly, as some of the example and themes developed in this book indicate, affordable access to global connected ICT may operate as a bottom-up or ground-up alternative to the DDA and other government level initiatives. The bottom-up us of affordable ICT can enable the poorer and disadvantaged communities to participate in the connected global economy a more level playing field and more quickly than these high level government initiatives. Of course it does require ensuring there is affordable access to ICT for these communities to enable them to participate in the global connected economy.

There is a further theme that emerges with rise of the international corporate body where the world seems to be dominated by very large multinational companies which can exert power and influence as great (or greater) as countries. This is demonstrated in Susan Strange's 'Mad Money' indicating the power and influence of the money markets and large corporations. Strange and Stopford and others (e.g. Strange 1996, 1998; Stopford, Strange and Henley 1991) argue there is a need for counter measures to the power of these very large mega corporations, and the global connected communities have been suggested as such counter measures (e.g. Adams and Hallsworth 2015a, 2015b).

The chapters and discussion in this book have potential to add to ICT4D and development theory, and indeed bring out the important roles that affordable access to ICT plays in economic, educational and social activity.

Carl Adams
University of Portsmouth, UK

Sam Takavarasha Jr.
University of Fort Hare, South Africa & University of Zimbabwe, Zimbabwe

REFERENCES

Adams, C., & Fitch, T. (2006). Social Inclusion and the Shifting Role of Technology: Is Age the New Gender in Mobile Access? In *Social Inclusion: Societal and Organizational Implications for Information Systems* (pp. 203-215). Springer.

Adams, C., & Hallsworth, A. (2015a). Virtual Non-productive value (NoPV) creation as a cause of economic instability. *AHE Conference*, Southampton, UK.

Adams, C., & Hallsworth, A. (2015b). Systemic problems in global finance: Non-productive value (NoPV) creation and storing rapidly increasing levels of value. *4th Global Conference on Economic Geography*, 19-23.

Adams, C., & Mouatt, S. (2010a). The rise of complementary currencies and corporafinance: E-commerce driven competition in the financial sector. *Journal of Internet Banking and Commerce, 15*(1), 1–13.

Adams, C., & Mouatt, S. (2010b). Evolution of Electronic and Mobile Business and Services: Government support for E/M-payment systems. *International Journal of Electronic Services and Mobile Applications*, 2(2), 43–54.

Barrett, C. B. (2001). Does food aid stabilize food availability? *Economic Development and Cultural Change*, 49(2), 335–349. doi:10.1086/452505

Brett, E. A. (2009). *Reconstructing development theory*. Palgrave Macmillan. doi:10.1007/978-1-137-05768-6

Carter, M., & Grover, V. (2015). Me, My Self, and I(T): Conceptualizing information technology identity and its implications. *Management Information Systems Quarterly*, 39(4), 931–957. doi:10.25300/MISQ/2015/39.4.9

Dicken, P. (2007). *Global shift: Mapping the changing contours of the world economy*. London: Sage.

Ellison, N., Steinfield, C., & Lampe, C. (2007). The benefits of Facebook "friends": Social capital and college students' use of online social network sites. *Journal of Computer-Mediated Communication*, 12(4), 1143–1168. doi:10.1111/j.1083-6101.2007.00367.x

Ferguson, N. (2011). *Civilization: The West and the Rest*. London: Allen Lane.

Harvey, D. (2005). *A Brief History of Neoliberalism*. Oxford, UK: Oxford University Press.

Harvey, D. (2014). *Seventeen Contradictions and the End of Capitalism*. London: Profile Books.

Mouatt, S., & Adams, C. (Eds.). (2010). *Corporate and Social Transformation of Money and Banking: Breaking the Serfdom*. Basingstoke, UK: Palgrave-Macmillan.

Riley, B. (2016) What it means to have a trade deal that puts America first. *The Daily Signal*. Retrieved from http://dailysignal.com/2016/07/15/what-it-means-to-have-a-trade-deal-that-puts-america-first/

Selwyn, B. (2014). *The global development crisis*. Cambridge, UK: Polity Press.

Sen, A. (1999). *Development as freedom*. OU Press.

Stopford, J., & Strange, S. (1991). Rival states, rival firms: Competition for world market shares. Cambridge University Press.

Strange, S. (1996). *The Retreat of the State: The Diffusion of Power in the World Economy*. Cambridge University Press. doi:10.1017/CBO9780511559143

Strange, S. (1998). *Mad Money*. Manchester University Press. doi:10.3998/mpub.10897

Takavarasha, S., Bednar, P., & Adams, C. (2011). Using mixed methods for addressing researcher's safety in a conflict area: An innovative use of mixed methods research in Zimbabwe. *International Journal of Mixed Methods in Applied Business and Policy*, *1*(1).

Wiles. (1992). *The political economy of communism*. Blackwell.

Glossary

2G, 3G, 4G, 5G: Stands for the "Generation" of the mobile network. A higher number before the 'G' means higher bandwidth or more power to send out and receive data over the mobile network. Much of the richer nations run on 3G and 4G with the 5th generation wireless systems proposed as the next telecommunications standards.

BoP, Bottom of the Pyramid: A socio-economic concept used in development works to categorise the large proportion of the world's poorest citizens on global income scales.

Digital Divide: Refers to the divide between people who have access to digital technology (usually associated with good access to the Internet) and the often poorer or disadvantaged communities that do not have access to such technologies. It is seen as a development issue since having access to such technologies also opens up access to a range of digital resources and information from education, government services, health, social interaction, communication and allows wider participation in economic activity.

Doha, Doha Declaration, Doha Development Round or Doha Development Agenda (DDA): Refers to a high level set of trade-negotiations of the World Trade Organization (WTO). They originally started in 2001, in Doha in Qatar, and have gone through successive rounds trying to get a consistent set of rules to lower trade barriers around the world and so facilitate increased global trade. It has gone through a few stalled negotiations since then, particularly in 2008 with disagreements over tariffs and subsidies, particularly over agriculture and industry with such subsidies seen as operating effectively as trade barriers. There is also contention between the richer developed nations (USA, EU, Japan and others) and the major developing countries (e.g. India, Brazil, China, and South Africa). Access to global connected ICT may operate (as developed in this book) as a ground up alternative to the DDA by providing the connected global economy a more level playing field for those with access to such ICT. See also G33.

Free Basics, or Free Basics by Facebook: Is an initiative by Facebook and others to offer internet access to poorer communities providing them with a limited set of basic services. This replaces or extends the previous Internet.org. There has been some controversy with the initial Free Basics with some accusing of violating net neutrality rules (i.e. limiting access to only certain resources). The Free Basics was opened up to the wider development community and further services have been added created by third-party developers.

G33: Is a coalition of developing countries trying to coordinate participation in the Doha Round of World Trade Organisation negotiations, specifically in regard to agriculture. They have similar concerns over barriers to global markets to the poorer developing countries. They advocate the need to create a category "special products" (particularly agriculture) allowing developing countries to exempt certain products from tariff reductions and so provide "special safeguard mechanism" against import surges from richer countries. The G33 actually consist of more than 33 countries, the latest Wikipedia entry includes 48 countries, though the numbers may increase in further Doha negotiation rounds.

GATT: General Agreement on Tariffs and Trade. An international organization established just after the second world war (WWII) to set up common rules for tariffs and reduce barriers for international trade. It was superseded with the World Trade Organization starting from the Uruguay round of GATT talks in 1986 and finally completing in 1994.

GDP: Gross Domestic Product.

GSMA: GSM Association is a trade body that represents the interests of mobile network operators worldwide.

HDI: Human Development Indicator.

HDR: Human Development Report.

HFA: Hyogo Framework for Action 2005-2015. The UN guidance on dealing with disaster events.

ICRW: International Center for Research on Women is a non-profit organization headquartered in Washington, D.C., United States, with a regional office in New Delhi, India. ICRW works to promote gender equitable development within the field of international development.

ICT: Information and Communication Technologies.

ICT4D: Information and communication technologies for development. This covers the application of information and communication technologies (ICTs) toward economic, social and political development of poorer and disadvantaged countries and communities. It is also associated with bridging the Digital Divide and by trying to provide equal access to technologies and digital resources across communities.

iOS: (originally iPhone OS) is a mobile operating system created and developed by Apple Inc. and distributed exclusively for Apple hardware.

LDCs: Least Developed Countries, Less Developed Countries. These are the countries with the lowest indicators of socioeconomic development as classified by the UN. The UN uses three criteria in their evaluation of LDCs status, namely level of Poverty, Human resource weakness (such as levels of nutrition, health, education and literacy) and Economic vulnerability.

MDG: Millennium Development Goals, a set of aspirational goals to achieve by 2015 decided at the UN Assembly of the leaders of 189 countries in September 2000. It is effectively a blueprint or roadmap endorsed the Millennium Declaration, a commitment to work together to build a safer, more prosperous and equitable world. The goals include 1. Eradicate extreme poverty and hunger; 2. Achieve universal primary education; 3. Promote gender equality and empower women; 4. Reduce child mortality; 5. Improve maternal health; 6. Combat HIV/AIDS, malaria and other diseases; 7. Ensure environmental sustainability; 8. Develop a global partnership for development. This was replaced with the Sustainable Develop Goals, a set of 17 goals to achieve by 2030.

MNO: Mobile Network Operators.

NCEUS: National Commission for Enterprises in the Unorganized Sector.

Net Neutrality: These are a set of rules aim to safeguard free expression on-line and to preserve the open internet and ensure that it could not be divided into pay-to-play fast lanes for some and slow lanes for everyone else. Many argue net neutrality rules are necessary to protect equal access to content on the internet. The net neutrality rules were approved by the Federal Communications Commission in 2015 under the Obama administration in the USA. The Trump administration in 2017 have set a target to reconsider net neutrality rules to be b=more favourable to bigger telecoms companies.

NSSO: National Sample Survey Organisation

OECD: Organisation for Economic Co-operation and Development.

OTOP: "One Tambon, One Product", an initiative in Thailand which aims to get local government regions and rural communities (Tambons) to select a product or service which they would excel at. So effectively the local government or community will be known for that one product or service. This built on a similar initiative in Japan, the "One Village One Product" (OVOP).

OVOP: One Village One Product initiative that was adopted in Japan in the late 1970's to develop local villages and communities. Each village or community will be known for that one product or service that they excel in.

SDG: Sustainable Develop Goals, a set of 17 goals to achieve by 2030. This replaces the Millennium Development Goals.

Sendai Framework: The UN's guidance for Disaster Risk Reduction 2015-2030 which collated together further insights and experience from application of their previous guidance (the 1994 "Guidelines for natural disaster prevention, preparedness and mitigation" and the 'Hyogo Framework for Action (HFA) 2005-2015'). The main change in the Sendai framework is a shift towards disaster risk management and reduction as opposed to disaster management itself.

SMS: Short Message Service – a text messaging service component of most mobile phones

Tariff: A government imposed tax on imports.

TISS: Tata Institute of Social Sciences, India.

TRAI: Telecom Regulatory Authority of India is an independent regulatory body established by the Telecom Regulatory Authority of India Act 1997 to oversee the telecommunications industry in India.

TVWS: TV White Space frequency range. This is analogue set of frequencies freed up after a country has moved towards digital TV.

UNDP: United Nations Development Programme.

WDR: World Development Report.

WiFi, or Wi-Fi: This is the most common technology for wireless local area networking enabling computers and devices to connect together wirelessly. It is based on the IEEE 802.11 standards.

WiMAX: Worldwide Interoperability for Microwave Access. This provides wireless broadband access over larger areas, competing with cable and DSL to deliver the 'last mile' of broadband access to communities. It a family of protocols based on IEEE 802.16.

WSD: 'White Space' Device that operates in the TV White Space (TVWS) frequency range. This is analogue set of frequencies freed up after a country has moved towards digital TV.

WTO: World Trade Organisation. The international organisation which administers multilateral trade agreements covering the rules of international trade. It evolved from the last of the GATT (General Agreement on Tariffs and Trade) organization round of talks starting in Uruguay in 1986 and finally completing in 1994, which shows some of the complexity of setting up international trade agreements.

Related References

To continue our tradition of advancing information science and technology research, we have compiled a list of recommended IGI Global readings. These references will provide additional information and guidance to further enrich your knowledge and assist you with your own research and future publications.

Abramowicz, W., Stolarski, P., & Tomaszewski, T. (2013). Legal ontologies in ICT and law. In *Digital rights management: Concepts, methodologies, tools, and applications* (pp. 34–49). Hershey, PA: IGI Global. doi:10.4018/978-1-4666-2136-7.ch003

Adamich, T. (2012). Materials-to-standards alignment: How to "chunk" a whole cake and even use the "crumbs": State standards alignment models, learning objects, and formative assessment – methodologies and metadata for education. In L. Tomei (Ed.), *Advancing education with information communication technologies: Facilitating new trends* (pp. 165–178). Hershey, PA: IGI Global. doi:10.4018/978-1-61350-468-0.ch014

Adomi, E. E. (2011). Regulation of internet content. In E. Adomi (Ed.), *Frameworks for ICT policy: Government, social and legal issues* (pp. 233–246). Hershey, PA: IGI Global. doi:10.4018/978-1-61692-012-8.ch015

Aggestam, L. (2011). Guidelines for preparing organizations in developing countries for standards-based B2B. In *Global business: Concepts, methodologies, tools and applications* (pp. 206–228). Hershey, PA: IGI Global. doi:10.4018/978-1-60960-587-2.ch114

Akowuah, F., Yuan, X., Xu, J., & Wang, H. (2012). A survey of U.S. laws for health information security & privacy. *International Journal of Information Security and Privacy*, 6(4), 40–54. doi:10.4018/jisp.2012100102

Akowuah, F., Yuan, X., Xu, J., & Wang, H. (2013). A survey of security standards applicable to health information systems. *International Journal of Information Security and Privacy*, 7(4), 22–36. doi:10.4018/ijisp.2013100103

Al Hadid, I. (2012). Applying the certification's standards to the simulation study steps. In E. Abu-Taieh, A. El Sheikh, & M. Jafari (Eds.), *Technology engineering and management in aviation: Advancements and discoveries* (pp. 294–307). Hershey, PA: IGI Global. doi:10.4018/978-1-60960-887-3.ch017

Al Mohannadi, F., Arif, M., Aziz, Z., & Richardson, P. A. (2013). Adopting BIM standards for managing vision 2030 infrastructure development in Qatar. *International Journal of 3-D Information Modeling*, 2(3), 64-73. doi:10.4018/ij3dim.2013070105

Al-Nu'aimi, A. A. (2011). Using watermarking techniques to prove rightful ownership of web images. *International Journal of Information Technology and Web Engineering*, 6(2), 29–39. doi:10.4018/jitwe.2011040103

Alejandre, G. M. (2013). IT security governance legal issues. In D. Mellado, L. Enrique Sánchez, E. Fernández-Medina, & M. Piattini (Eds.), *IT security governance innovations: Theory and research* (pp. 47–73). Hershey, PA: IGI Global. doi:10.4018/978-1-4666-2083-4.ch003

Alexandropoulou-Egyptiadou, E. (2013). The Hellenic framework for computer program copyright protection following the implementation of the relative european union directives. In *Digital rights management: Concepts, methodologies, tools, and applications* (pp. 738–745). Hershey, PA: IGI Global. doi:10.4018/978-1-4666-2136-7.ch033

Ali, S. (2012). Practical web application security audit following industry standards and compliance. In J. Zubairi & A. Mahboob (Eds.), *Cyber security standards, practices and industrial applications: Systems and methodologies* (pp. 259–279). Hershey, PA: IGI Global. doi:10.4018/978-1-60960-851-4.ch013

Alirezaee, M., & Afsharian, M. (2011). Measuring the effect of the rules and regulations on global malmquist index. *International Journal of Operations Research and Information Systems*, 2(3), 64–78. doi:10.4018/joris.2011070105

Alirezaee, M., & Afsharian, M. (2013). Measuring the effect of the rules and regulations on global malmquist index. In J. Wang (Ed.), *Optimizing, innovating, and capitalizing on information systems for operations* (pp. 215–229). Hershey, PA: IGI Global. doi:10.4018/978-1-4666-2925-7.ch011

Related References

Alves de Lima, A., Carvalho dos Reis, P., Branco, J. C., Danieli, R., Osawa, C. C., Winter, E., & Santos, D. A. (2013). Scenario-patent protection compared to climate change: The case of green patents. *International Journal of Social Ecology and Sustainable Development*, 4(3), 61–70. doi:10.4018/jsesd.2013070105

Amirante, A., Castaldi, T., Miniero, L., & Romano, S. P. (2013). Protocol interactions among user agents, application servers, and media servers: Standardization efforts and open issues. In D. Kanellopoulos (Ed.), *Intelligent multimedia technologies for networking applications: Techniques and tools* (pp. 48–63). Hershey, PA: IGI Global. doi:10.4018/978-1-4666-2833-5.ch003

Anker, P. (2013). The impact of regulations on the business case for cognitive radio. In T. Lagkas, P. Sarigiannidis, M. Louta, & P. Chatzimisios (Eds.), *Evolution of cognitive networks and self-adaptive communication systems* (pp. 142–170). Hershey, PA: IGI Global. doi:10.4018/978-1-4666-4189-1.ch006

Antunes, A. M., Mendes, F. M., Schumacher, S. D., Quoniam, L., & Lima de Magalhães, J. (2014). The contribution of information science through intellectual property to innovation in the Brazilian health sector. In G. Jamil, A. Malheiro, & F. Ribeiro (Eds.), *Rethinking the conceptual base for new practical applications in information value and quality* (pp. 83–115). Hershey, PA: IGI Global. doi:10.4018/978-1-4666-4562-2.ch005

Atiskov, A. Y., Novikov, F. A., Fedorchenko, L. N., Vorobiev, V. I., & Moldovyan, N. A. (2013). Ontology-based analysis of cryptography standards and possibilities of their harmonization. In A. Elçi, J. Pieprzyk, A. Chefranov, M. Orgun, H. Wang, & R. Shankaran (Eds.), *Theory and practice of cryptography solutions for secure information systems* (pp. 1–33). Hershey, PA: IGI Global. doi:10.4018/978-1-4666-4030-6.ch001

Ayanso, A., & Herath, T. (2012). Law and technology at crossroads in cyberspace: Where do we go from here? In A. Dudley, J. Braman, & G. Vincenti (Eds.), *Investigating cyber law and cyber ethics: Issues, impacts and practices* (pp. 57–77). Hershey, PA: IGI Global. doi:10.4018/978-1-61350-132-0.ch004

Ayanso, A., & Herath, T. (2014). Law and technology at crossroads in cyberspace: Where do we go from here? In *Cyber behavior: Concepts, methodologies, tools, and applications* (pp. 1990–2010). Hershey, PA: IGI Global. doi:10.4018/978-1-4666-5942-1.ch105

Aydogan-Duda, N. (2012). Branding innovation: The case study of Turkey. In N. Ekekwe & N. Islam (Eds.), *Disruptive technologies, innovation and global redesign: Emerging implications* (pp. 238–248). Hershey, PA: IGI Global. doi:10.4018/978-1-4666-0134-5.ch012

Bagby, J. W. (2011). Environmental standardization for sustainability. In Z. Luo (Ed.), *Green finance and sustainability: Environmentally-aware business models and technologies* (pp. 31–55). Hershey, PA: IGI Global. doi:10.4018/978-1-60960-531-5.ch002

Bagby, J. W. (2013). Insights from U.S. experience to guide international reliance on standardization: Achieving supply chain sustainability. *International Journal of Applied Logistics, 4*(3), 25–46. doi:10.4018/jal.2013070103

Baggio, B., & Beldarrain, Y. (2011). Intellectual property in an age of open source and anonymity. In *Anonymity and learning in digitally mediated communications: Authenticity and trust in cyber education* (pp. 39–57). Hershey, PA: IGI Global. doi:10.4018/978-1-60960-543-8.ch003

Balzli, C. E., & Fragnière, E. (2012). How ERP systems are centralizing and standardizing the accounting function in public organizations for better and worse. In S. Chhabra & M. Kumar (Eds.), *Strategic enterprise resource planning models for e-government: Applications and methodologies* (pp. 55–72). Hershey, PA: IGI Global. doi:10.4018/978-1-60960-863-7.ch004

Banas, J. R. (2011). Standardized, flexible design of electronic learning environments to enhance learning efficiency and effectiveness. In A. Kitchenham (Ed.), *Models for interdisciplinary mobile learning: Delivering information to students* (pp. 66–86). Hershey, PA: IGI Global. doi:10.4018/978-1-60960-511-7.ch004

Bao, C., & Castresana, J. M. (2011). Interoperability approach in e-learning standardization processes. In F. Lazarinis, S. Green, & E. Pearson (Eds.), *Handbook of research on e-learning standards and interoperability: Frameworks and issues* (pp. 399–418). Hershey, PA: IGI Global. doi:10.4018/978-1-61692-789-9.ch020

Bao, C., & Castresana, J. M. (2012). Interoperability approach in e-learning standardization processes. In *Virtual learning environments: Concepts, methodologies, tools and applications* (pp. 542–560). Hershey, PA: IGI Global. doi:10.4018/978-1-4666-0011-9.ch307

Barrett, B. (2011). Evaluating and implementing teaching standards: Providing quality online teaching strategies and techniques standards. In F. Lazarinis, S. Green, & E. Pearson (Eds.), *Developing and utilizing e-learning applications* (pp. 66–83). Hershey, PA: IGI Global. doi:10.4018/978-1-61692-791-2.ch004

Berleur, J. (2011). Ethical and social issues of the internet governance regulations. In D. Haftor & A. Mirijamdotter (Eds.), *Information and communication technologies, society and human beings: Theory and framework (festschrift in honor of Gunilla Bradley)* (pp. 466–476). Hershey, PA: IGI Global. doi:10.4018/978-1-60960-057-0.ch038

Bhattathiripad, V. P. (2014). Software copyright infringement and litigation. In *Judiciary-friendly forensics of software copyright infringement* (pp. 35–55). Hershey, PA: IGI Global. doi:10.4018/978-1-4666-5804-2.ch002

Bin, X., & Chuan, T. K. (2011). The effect of business characteristics on the methods of knowledge protections. *International Journal of Social Ecology and Sustainable Development, 2*(3), 34–60. doi:10.4018/jsesd.2011070103

Bin, X., & Chuan, T. K. (2013). The effect of business characteristics on the methods of knowledge protections. In E. Carayannis (Ed.), *Creating a sustainable ecology using technology-driven solutions* (pp. 172–200). Hershey, PA: IGI Global. doi:10.4018/978-1-4666-3613-2.ch013

Bin, X., & Chuan, T. K. (2013). The effect of business characteristics on the methods of knowledge protections. In *Digital rights management: Concepts, methodologies, tools, and applications* (pp. 1283–1311). Hershey, PA: IGI Global. doi:10.4018/978-1-4666-2136-7.ch063

Bogers, M., Bekkers, R., & Granstrand, O. (2012). Intellectual property and licensing strategies in open collaborative innovation. In C. de Pablos Heredero & D. López (Eds.), *Open innovation in firms and public administrations: Technologies for value creation* (pp. 37–58). Hershey, PA: IGI Global. doi:10.4018/978-1-61350-341-6.ch003

Bogers, M., Bekkers, R., & Granstrand, O. (2013). Intellectual property and licensing strategies in open collaborative innovation. In *Digital rights management: Concepts, methodologies, tools, and applications* (pp. 1204–1224). Hershey, PA: IGI Global. doi:10.4018/978-1-4666-2136-7.ch059

Bourcier, D. (2013). Law and governance: The genesis of the commons. In F. Doridot, P. Duquenoy, P. Goujon, A. Kurt, S. Lavelle, N. Patrignani, & A. Santuccio et al. (Eds.), *Ethical governance of emerging technologies development* (pp. 166–183). Hershey, PA: IGI Global. doi:10.4018/978-1-4666-3670-5.ch011

Bousquet, F., Fomin, V. V., & Drillon, D. (2011). Anticipatory standards development and competitive intelligence. *International Journal of Business Intelligence Research, 2*(1), 16–30. doi:10.4018/jbir.2011010102

Bousquet, F., Fomin, V. V., & Drillon, D. (2013). Anticipatory standards development and competitive intelligence. In R. Herschel (Ed.), *Principles and applications of business intelligence research* (pp. 17–30). Hershey, PA: IGI Global. doi:10.4018/978-1-4666-2650-8.ch002

Brabazon, A. (2013). Optimal patent design: An agent-based modeling approach. In B. Alexandrova-Kabadjova, S. Martinez-Jaramillo, A. Garcia-Almanza, & E. Tsang (Eds.), *Simulation in computational finance and economics: Tools and emerging applications* (pp. 280–302). Hershey, PA: IGI Global. doi:10.4018/978-1-4666-2011-7.ch014

Bracci, F., Corradi, A., & Foschini, L. (2014). Cloud standards: Security and interoperability issues. In H. Mouftah & B. Kantarci (Eds.), *Communication infrastructures for cloud computing* (pp. 465–495). Hershey, PA: IGI Global. doi:10.4018/978-1-4666-4522-6.ch020

Briscoe, D. R. (2012). Globalization and international labor standards, codes of conduct, and ethics: An International HRM perspective. In C. Wankel & S. Malleck (Eds.), *Ethical models and applications of globalization: Cultural, socio-political and economic perspectives* (pp. 1–22). Hershey, PA: IGI Global. doi:10.4018/978-1-61350-332-4.ch001

Briscoe, D. R. (2014). Globalization and international labor standards, codes of conduct, and ethics: An International HRM perspective. In *Cross-cultural interaction: Concepts, methodologies, tools and applications* (pp. 40–62). Hershey, PA: IGI Global. doi:10.4018/978-1-4666-4979-8.ch004

Brooks, R. G., & Geradin, D. (2011). Interpreting and enforcing the voluntary FRAND commitment. *International Journal of IT Standards and Standardization Research*, *9*(1), 1–23. doi:10.4018/jitsr.2011010101

Brown, C. A. (2013). Common core state standards: The promise for college and career ready students in the U.S. In V. Wang (Ed.), *Handbook of research on teaching and learning in K-20 education* (pp. 50–82). Hershey, PA: IGI Global. doi:10.4018/978-1-4666-4249-2.ch004

Buyurgan, N., Rardin, R. L., Jayaraman, R., Varghese, V. M., & Burbano, A. (2011). A novel GS1 data standard adoption roadmap for healthcare providers. *International Journal of Healthcare Information Systems and Informatics*, *6*(4), 42–59. doi:10.4018/jhisi.2011100103

Buyurgan, N., Rardin, R. L., Jayaraman, R., Varghese, V. M., & Burbano, A. (2013). A novel GS1 data standard adoption roadmap for healthcare providers. In J. Tan (Ed.), *Healthcare information technology innovation and sustainability: Frontiers and adoption* (pp. 41–57). Hershey, PA: IGI Global. doi:10.4018/978-1-4666-2797-0.ch003

Campolo, C., Cozzetti, H. A., Molinaro, A., & Scopigno, R. M. (2012). PHY/MAC layer design in vehicular ad hoc networks: Challenges, standard approaches, and alternative solutions. In R. Aquino-Santos, A. Edwards, & V. Rangel-Licea (Eds.), *Wireless technologies in vehicular ad hoc networks: Present and future challenges* (pp. 70–100). Hershey, PA: IGI Global. doi:10.4018/978-1-4666-0209-0.ch004

Cantatore, F. (2014). Copyright support structures. In *Authors, copyright, and publishing in the digital era* (pp. 81–93). Hershey, PA: IGI Global. doi:10.4018/978-1-4666-5214-9.ch005

Cantatore, F. (2014). History and development of copyright. In *Authors, copyright, and publishing in the digital era* (pp. 10–32). Hershey, PA: IGI Global. doi:10.4018/978-1-4666-5214-9.ch002

Cantatore, F. (2014). Research findings: Authors' perceptions and the copyright framework. In Authors, copyright, and publishing in the digital era (pp. 147-189). Hershey, PA: IGI Global. doi:10.4018/978-1-4666-5214-9.ch008

Cassini, J., Medlin, B. D., & Romaniello, A. (2011). Forty years of federal legislation in the area of data protection and information security. In H. Nemati (Ed.), *Pervasive information security and privacy developments: Trends and advancements* (pp. 14–23). Hershey, PA: IGI Global. doi:10.4018/978-1-61692-000-5.ch002

Charlesworth, A. (2012). Addressing legal issues in online research, publication and archiving: A UK perspective. In C. Silva (Ed.), *Online research methods in urban and planning studies: Design and outcomes* (pp. 368–393). Hershey, PA: IGI Global. doi:10.4018/978-1-4666-0074-4.ch022

Chaudhary, C., & Kang, I. S. (2011). Pirates of the copyright and cyberspace: Issues involved. In R. Santanam, M. Sethumadhavan, & M. Virendra (Eds.), *Cyber security, cyber crime and cyber forensics: Applications and perspectives* (pp. 59–68). Hershey, PA: IGI Global. doi:10.4018/978-1-60960-123-2.ch005

Chen, L., Hu, W., Yang, M., & Zhang, L. (2011). Security and privacy issues in secure e-mail standards and services. In H. Nemati (Ed.), *Security and privacy assurance in advancing technologies: New developments* (pp. 174–185). Hershey, PA: IGI Global. doi:10.4018/978-1-60960-200-0.ch013

Ciaghi, A., & Villafiorita, A. (2012). Law modeling and BPR for public administration improvement. In K. Bwalya & S. Zulu (Eds.), *Handbook of research on e-government in emerging economies: Adoption, E-participation, and legal frameworks* (pp. 391–410). Hershey, PA: IGI Global. doi:10.4018/978-1-4666-0324-0.ch019

Ciptasari, R. W., & Sakurai, K. (2013). Multimedia copyright protection scheme based on the direct feature-based method. In K. Kondo (Ed.), *Multimedia information hiding technologies and methodologies for controlling data* (pp. 412–439). Hershey, PA: IGI Global. doi:10.4018/978-1-4666-2217-3.ch019

Clark, L. A., Jones, D. L., & Clark, W. J. (2012). Technology innovation and the policy vacuum: A call for ethics, norms, and laws to fill the void. *International Journal of Technoethics*, *3*(1), 1–13. doi:10.4018/jte.2012010101

Cooklev, T. (2013). The role of standards in engineering education. In K. Jakobs (Ed.), *Innovations in organizational IT specification and standards development* (pp. 129–137). Hershey, PA: IGI Global. doi:10.4018/978-1-4666-2160-2.ch007

Cooper, A. R. (2013). Key challenges in the design of learning technology standards: Observations and proposals. In K. Jakobs (Ed.), *Innovations in organizational IT specification and standards development* (pp. 241–249). Hershey, PA: IGI Global. doi:10.4018/978-1-4666-2160-2.ch014

Cordella, A. (2011). Emerging standardization. *International Journal of Actor-Network Theory and Technological Innovation*, *3*(3), 49–64. doi:10.4018/jantti.2011070104

Cordella, A. (2013). Emerging standardization. In A. Tatnall (Ed.), *Social and professional applications of actor-network theory for technology development* (pp. 221–237). Hershey, PA: IGI Global. doi:10.4018/978-1-4666-2166-4.ch017

Curran, K., & Lautman, R. (2011). The problems of jurisdiction on the internet. *International Journal of Ambient Computing and Intelligence*, *3*(3), 36–42. doi:10.4018/jaci.2011070105

Dani, D. E., Salloum, S., Khishfe, R., & BouJaoude, S. (2013). A tool for analyzing science standards and curricula for 21st century science education. In M. Khine & I. Saleh (Eds.), *Approaches and strategies in next generation science learning* (pp. 265–289). Hershey, PA: IGI Global. doi:10.4018/978-1-4666-2809-0.ch014

De Silva, S. (2012). Legal issues with FOS-ERP: A UK law perspective. In R. Atem de Carvalho & B. Johansson (Eds.), *Free and open source enterprise resource planning: Systems and strategies* (pp. 102–115). Hershey, PA: IGI Global. doi:10.4018/978-1-61350-486-4.ch007 de Vries, H. J. (2011). Implementing standardization education at the national level. *International Journal of IT Standards and Standardization Research*, *9*(2), 72–83. doi:10.4018/jitsr.2011070104

de Vries, H. J. (2013). Implementing standardization education at the national level. In K. Jakobs (Ed.), *Innovations in organizational IT specification and standards development* (pp. 116–128). Hershey, PA: IGI Global. doi:10.4018/978-1-4666-2160-2.ch006

de Vuyst, B., & Fairchild, A. (2012). Legal and economic justification for software protection. *International Journal of Open Source Software and Processes*, *4*(3), 1–12. doi:10.4018/ijossp.2012070101

Dedeke, A. (2012). Politics hinders open standards in the public sector: The Massachusetts open document format decision. In C. Reddick (Ed.), *Cases on public information management and e-government adoption* (pp. 1–23). Hershey, PA: IGI Global. doi:10.4018/978-1-4666-0981-5.ch001

Delfmann, P., Herwig, S., Lis, L., & Becker, J. (2012). Supporting conceptual model analysis using semantic standardization and structural pattern matching. In S. Smolnik, F. Teuteberg, & O. Thomas (Eds.), *Semantic technologies for business and information systems engineering: Concepts and applications* (pp. 125–149). Hershey, PA: IGI Global. doi:10.4018/978-1-60960-126-3.ch007

den Uijl, S., de Vries, H. J., & Bayramoglu, D. (2013). The rise of MP3 as the market standard: How compressed audio files became the dominant music format. *International Journal of IT Standards and Standardization Research*, *11*(1), 1–26. doi:10.4018/jitsr.2013010101

Dickerson, J., & Coleman, H. V. (2012). Technology, e-leadership and educational administration in schools: Integrating standards with context and guiding questions. In V. Wang (Ed.), *Encyclopedia of e-leadership, counseling and training* (pp. 408–422). Hershey, PA: IGI Global. doi:10.4018/978-1-61350-068-2.ch030

Dindaroglu, B. (2013). R&D productivity and firm size in semiconductors and pharmaceuticals: Evidence from citation yields. In I. Yetkiner, M. Pamukcu, & E. Erdil (Eds.), *Industrial dynamics, innovation policy, and economic growth through technological advancements* (pp. 92–113). Hershey, PA: IGI Global. doi:10.4018/978-1-4666-1978-4.ch006

Ding, W. (2011). Development of intellectual property of communications enterprise and analysis of current situation of patents in emerging technology field. *International Journal of Advanced Pervasive and Ubiquitous Computing*, *3*(2), 21–28. doi:10.4018/japuc.2011040103

Ding, W. (2013). Development of intellectual property of communications enterprise and analysis of current situation of patents in emerging technology field. In T. Gao (Ed.), *Global applications of pervasive and ubiquitous computing* (pp. 89–96). Hershey, PA: IGI Global. doi:10.4018/978-1-4666-2645-4.ch010

Dorloff, F., & Kajan, E. (2012). Balancing of heterogeneity and interoperability in e-business networks: The role of standards and protocols. *International Journal of E-Business Research*, 8(4), 15–33. doi:10.4018/jebr.2012100102

Dorloff, F., & Kajan, E. (2012). Efficient and interoperable e-business –Based on frameworks, standards and protocols: An introduction. In E. Kajan, F. Dorloff, & I. Bedini (Eds.), *Handbook of research on e-business standards and protocols: Documents, data and advanced web technologies* (pp. 1–20). Hershey, PA: IGI Global. doi:10.4018/978-1-4666-0146-8.ch001

Driouchi, A., & Kadiri, M. (2013). Challenges to intellectual property rights from information and communication technologies, nanotechnologies and microelectronics. In *Digital rights management: Concepts, methodologies, tools, and applications* (pp. 1474–1492). Hershey, PA: IGI Global. doi:10.4018/978-1-4666-2136-7.ch075

Dubey, M., & Hirwade, M. (2013). Copyright relevancy at stake in libraries of the digital era. In T. Ashraf & P. Gulati (Eds.), *Design, development, and management of resources for digital library services* (pp. 379–384). Hershey, PA: IGI Global. doi:10.4018/978-1-4666-2500-6.ch030

Egyedi, T. M. (2011). Between supply and demand: Coping with the impact of standards change. In *Global business: Concepts, methodologies, tools and applications* (pp. 105–120). Hershey, PA: IGI Global. doi:10.4018/978-1-60960-587-2.ch108

Egyedi, T. M., & Koppenhol, A. (2013). The standards war between ODF and OOXML: Does competition between overlapping ISO standards lead to innovation? In K. Jakobs (Ed.), *Innovations in organizational IT specification and standards development* (pp. 79–90). Hershey, PA: IGI Global. doi:10.4018/978-1-4666-2160-2.ch004

Egyedi, T. M., & Muto, S. (2012). Standards for ICT: A green strategy in a grey sector. *International Journal of IT Standards and Standardization Research*, 10(1), 34–47. doi:10.4018/jitsr.2012010103

El Kharbili, M., & Pulvermueller, E. (2012). Semantic policies for modeling regulatory process compliance. In S. Smolnik, F. Teuteberg, & O. Thomas (Eds.), *Semantic technologies for business and information systems engineering: Concepts and applications* (pp. 311–336). Hershey, PA: IGI Global. doi:10.4018/978-1-60960-126-3.ch016

El Kharbili, M., & Pulvermueller, E. (2013). Semantic policies for modeling regulatory process compliance. In *IT policy and ethics: Concepts, methodologies, tools, and applications* (pp. 218–243). Hershey, PA: IGI Global. doi:10.4018/978-1-4666-2919-6.ch011

Ervin, K. (2014). Legal and ethical considerations in the implementation of electronic health records. In J. Krueger (Ed.), *Cases on electronic records and resource management implementation in diverse environments* (pp. 193–210). Hershey, PA: IGI Global. doi:10.4018/978-1-4666-4466-3.ch012

Escayola, J., Trigo, J., Martínez, I., Martínez-Espronceda, M., Aragüés, A., Sancho, D., & García, J. et al. (2012). Overview of the ISO/ieee11073 family of standards and their applications to health monitoring. In W. Chen, S. Oetomo, & L. Feijs (Eds.), *Neonatal monitoring technologies: Design for integrated solutions* (pp. 148–173). Hershey, PA: IGI Global. doi:10.4018/978-1-4666-0975-4.ch007

Escayola, J., Trigo, J., Martínez, I., Martínez-Espronceda, M., Aragüés, A., Sancho, D., . . . García, J. (2013). Overview of the ISO/IEEE11073 family of standards and their applications to health monitoring. In User-driven healthcare: Concepts, methodologies, tools, and applications (pp. 357-381). Hershey, PA: IGI Global. doi:10.4018/978-1-4666-2770-3.ch018

Espada, J. P., Martínez, O. S., García-Bustelo, B. C., Lovelle, J. M., & Ordóñez de Pablos, P. (2011). Standardization of virtual objects. In M. Lytras, P. Ordóñez de Pablos, & E. Damiani (Eds.), *Semantic web personalization and context awareness: Management of personal identities and social networking* (pp. 7–21). Hershey, PA: IGI Global. doi:10.4018/978-1-61520-921-7.ch002

Falkner, N. J. (2011). Security technologies and policies in organisations. In M. Quigley (Ed.), *ICT ethics and security in the 21st century: New developments and applications* (pp. 196–213). Hershey, PA: IGI Global. doi:10.4018/978-1-60960-573-5.ch010

Ferrer-Roca, O. (2011). Standards in telemedicine. In A. Moumtzoglou & A. Kastania (Eds.), *E-health systems quality and reliability: Models and standards* (pp. 220–243). Hershey, PA: IGI Global. doi:10.4018/978-1-61692-843-8.ch017

Ferullo, D. L., & Soules, A. (2012). Managing copyright in a digital world. *International Journal of Digital Library Systems*, *3*(4), 1–25. doi:10.4018/ijdls.2012100101

Fichtner, J. R., & Simpson, L. A. (2011). Legal issues facing companies with products in a digital format. In T. Strader (Ed.), *Digital product management, technology and practice: Interdisciplinary perspectives* (pp. 32–52). Hershey, PA: IGI Global. doi:10.4018/978-1-61692-877-3.ch003

Fichtner, J. R., & Simpson, L. A. (2013). Legal issues facing companies with products in a digital format. In *Digital rights management: Concepts, methodologies, tools, and applications* (pp. 1334–1354). Hershey, PA: IGI Global. doi:10.4018/978-1-4666-2136-7.ch066

Folmer, E. (2012). BOMOS: Management and development model for open standards. In E. Kajan, F. Dorloff, & I. Bedini (Eds.), *Handbook of research on e-business standards and protocols: Documents, data and advanced web technologies* (pp. 102–128). Hershey, PA: IGI Global. doi:10.4018/978-1-4666-0146-8.ch006

Fomin, V. V. (2012). Standards as hybrids: An essay on tensions and juxtapositions in contemporary standardization. *International Journal of IT Standards and Standardization Research*, *10*(2), 59–68. doi:10.4018/jitsr.2012070105

Fomin, V. V., & Matinmikko, M. (2014). The role of standards in the development of new informational infrastructure. In M. Khosrow-Pour (Ed.), *Systems and software development, modeling, and analysis: New perspectives and methodologies* (pp. 149–160). Hershey, PA: IGI Global. doi:10.4018/978-1-4666-6098-4.ch006

Fomin, V. V., Medeisis, A., & Vitkute-Adžgauskiene, D. (2012). Pre-standardization of cognitive radio systems. *International Journal of IT Standards and Standardization Research*, *10*(1), 1–16. doi:10.4018/jitsr.2012010101

Francia, G., & Hutchinson, F. S. (2012). Regulatory and policy compliance with regard to identity theft prevention, detection, and response. In T. Chou (Ed.), *Information assurance and security technologies for risk assessment and threat management: Advances* (pp. 292–322). Hershey, PA: IGI Global. doi:10.4018/978-1-61350-507-6.ch012

Francia, G. A., & Hutchinson, F. S. (2014). Regulatory and policy compliance with regard to identity theft prevention, detection, and response. In *Crisis management: Concepts, methodologies, tools and applications* (pp. 280–310). Hershey, PA: IGI Global. doi:10.4018/978-1-4666-4707-7.ch012

Fulkerson, D. M. (2012). Copyright. In D. Fulkerson (Ed.), *Remote access technologies for library collections: Tools for library users and managers* (pp. 33–48). Hershey, PA: IGI Global. doi:10.4018/978-1-4666-0234-2.ch003

Galinski, C., & Beckmann, H. (2014). Concepts for enhancing content quality and eaccessibility: In general and in the field of eprocurement. In *Assistive technologies: Concepts, methodologies, tools, and applications* (pp. 180–197). Hershey, PA: IGI Global. doi:10.4018/978-1-4666-4422-9.ch010

Related References

Gaur, R. (2013). Facilitating access to Indian cultural heritage: Copyright, permission rights and ownership issues vis-à-vis IGNCA collections. In *Digital rights management: Concepts, methodologies, tools, and applications* (pp. 817–833). Hershey, PA: IGI Global. doi:10.4018/978-1-4666-2136-7.ch038

Geiger, C. (2011). Copyright and digital libraries: Securing access to information in the digital age. In I. Iglezakis, T. Synodinou, & S. Kapidakis (Eds.), *E-publishing and digital libraries: Legal and organizational issues* (pp. 257–272). Hershey, PA: IGI Global. doi:10.4018/978-1-60960-031-0.ch013

Geiger, C. (2013). Copyright and digital libraries: Securing access to information in the digital age. In *Digital rights management: Concepts, methodologies, tools, and applications* (pp. 99–114). Hershey, PA: IGI Global. doi:10.4018/978-1-4666-2136-7.ch007

Gencer, M. (2012). The evolution of IETF standards and their production. *International Journal of IT Standards and Standardization Research*, *10*(1), 17–33. doi:10.4018/jitsr.2012010102

Gillam, L., & Vartapetiance, A. (2014). Gambling with laws and ethics in cyberspace. In R. Luppicini (Ed.), *Evolving issues surrounding technoethics and society in the digital age* (pp. 149–170). Hershey, PA: IGI Global. doi:10.4018/978-1-4666-6122-6.ch010

Grandinetti, L., Pisacane, O., & Sheikhalishahi, M. (2014). Standardization. In *Pervasive cloud computing technologies: Future outlooks and interdisciplinary perspectives* (pp. 75–96). Hershey, PA: IGI Global. doi:10.4018/978-1-4666-4683-4.ch004

Grant, S., & Young, R. (2013). Concepts and standardization in areas relating to competence. In K. Jakobs (Ed.), *Innovations in organizational IT specification and standards development* (pp. 264–280). Hershey, PA: IGI Global. doi:10.4018/978-1-4666-2160-2.ch016

Grassetti, M., & Brookby, S. (2013). Using the iPad to develop preservice teachers' understanding of the common core state standards for mathematical practice. In D. Polly (Ed.), *Common core mathematics standards and implementing digital technologies* (pp. 370–386). Hershey, PA: IGI Global. doi:10.4018/978-1-4666-4086-3.ch025

Gray, P. J. (2012). CDIO Standards and quality assurance: From application to accreditation. *International Journal of Quality Assurance in Engineering and Technology Education*, *2*(2), 1–8. doi:10.4018/ijqaete.2012040101

Graz, J., & Hauert, C. (2011). The INTERNORM project: Bridging two worlds of expert- and lay-knowledge in standardization. *International Journal of IT Standards and Standardization Research*, *9*(1), 52–62. doi:10.4018/jitsr.2011010103

Graz, J., & Hauert, C. (2013). The INTERNORM project: Bridging two worlds of expert- and lay-knowledge in standardization. In K. Jakobs (Ed.), *Innovations in organizational IT specification and standards development* (pp. 154–164). Hershey, PA: IGI Global. doi:10.4018/978-1-4666-2160-2.ch009

Grobler, M. (2012). The need for digital evidence standardisation. *International Journal of Digital Crime and Forensics*, *4*(2), 1–12. doi:10.4018/jdcf.2012040101

Grobler, M. (2013). The need for digital evidence standardisation. In C. Li (Ed.), *Emerging digital forensics applications for crime detection, prevention, and security* (pp. 234–245). Hershey, PA: IGI Global. doi:10.4018/978-1-4666-4006-1.ch016

Guest, C. L., & Guest, J. M. (2011). Legal issues in the use of technology in higher education: Copyright and privacy in the academy. In D. Surry, R. Gray Jr, & J. Stefurak (Eds.), *Technology integration in higher education: Social and organizational aspects* (pp. 72–85). Hershey, PA: IGI Global. doi:10.4018/978-1-60960-147-8.ch006

Gupta, A., Gantz, D. A., Sreecharana, D., & Kreyling, J. (2012). The interplay of offshoring of professional services, law, intellectual property, and international organizations. *International Journal of Strategic Information Technology and Applications*, *3*(2), 47–71. doi:10.4018/jsita.2012040104

Hai-Jew, S. (2011). Staying legal and ethical in global e-learning course and training developments: An exploration. In V. Wang (Ed.), *Encyclopedia of information communication technologies and adult education integration* (pp. 958–970). Hershey, PA: IGI Global. doi:10.4018/978-1-61692-906-0.ch058

Halder, D., & Jaishankar, K. (2012). Cyber space regulations for protecting women in UK. In *Cyber crime and the victimization of women: Laws, rights and regulations* (pp. 95–104). Hershey, PA: IGI Global. doi:10.4018/978-1-60960-830-9.ch007

Han, M., & Cho, C. (2013). XML in library cataloging workflows: Working with diverse sources and metadata standards. In J. Tramullas & P. Garrido (Eds.), *Library automation and OPAC 2.0: Information access and services in the 2.0 landscape* (pp. 59–72). Hershey, PA: IGI Global. doi:10.4018/978-1-4666-1912-8.ch003

Hanseth, O., & Nielsen, P. (2013). Infrastructural innovation: Flexibility, generativity and the mobile internet. *International Journal of IT Standards and Standardization Research*, *11*(1), 27–45. doi:10.4018/jitsr.2013010102

Hartong, M., & Wijesekera, D. (2012). U.S. regulatory requirements for positive train control systems. In F. Flammini (Ed.), *Railway safety, reliability, and security: Technologies and systems engineering* (pp. 1–21). Hershey, PA: IGI Global. doi:10.4018/978-1-4666-1643-1.ch001

Hasan, H. (2011). Formal and emergent standards in KM. In D. Schwartz & D. Te'eni (Eds.), *Encyclopedia of knowledge management* (2nd ed.; pp. 331–342). Hershey, PA: IGI Global. doi:10.4018/978-1-59904-931-1.ch032

Hatzimihail, N. (2011). Copyright infringement of digital libraries and private international law: Jurisdiction issues. In I. Iglezakis, T. Synodinou, & S. Kapidakis (Eds.), *E-publishing and digital libraries: Legal and organizational issues* (pp. 447–460). Hershey, PA: IGI Global. doi:10.4018/978-1-60960-031-0.ch021

Hauert, C. (2013). Where are you? Consumers' associations in standardization: A case study on Switzerland. In K. Jakobs (Ed.), *Innovations in organizational IT specification and standards development* (pp. 139–153). Hershey, PA: IGI Global. doi:10.4018/978-1-4666-2160-2.ch008

Hawks, V. D., & Ekstrom, J. J. (2011). Balancing policies, principles, and philosophy in information assurance. In M. Dark (Ed.), *Information assurance and security ethics in complex systems: Interdisciplinary perspectives* (pp. 32–54). Hershey, PA: IGI Global. doi:10.4018/978-1-61692-245-0.ch003

Henningsson, S. (2012). International e-customs standardization from the perspective of a global company. *International Journal of IT Standards and Standardization Research, 10*(2), 45–58. doi:10.4018/jitsr.2012070104

Hensberry, K. K., Paul, A. J., Moore, E. B., Podolefsky, N. S., & Perkins, K. K. (2013). PhET interactive simulations: New tools to achieve common core mathematics standards. In D. Polly (Ed.), *Common core mathematics standards and implementing digital technologies* (pp. 147–167). Hershey, PA: IGI Global. doi:10.4018/978-1-4666-4086-3.ch010

Heravi, B. R., & Lycett, M. (2012). Semantically enriched e-business standards development: The case of ebXML business process specification schema. In E. Kajan, F. Dorloff, & I. Bedini (Eds.), *Handbook of research on e-business standards and protocols: Documents, data and advanced web technologies* (pp. 655–675). Hershey, PA: IGI Global. doi:10.4018/978-1-4666-0146-8.ch030

Higuera, J., & Polo, J. (2012). Interoperability in wireless sensor networks based on IEEE 1451 standard. In N. Zaman, K. Ragab, & A. Abdullah (Eds.), *Wireless sensor networks and energy efficiency: Protocols, routing and management* (pp. 47–69). Hershey, PA: IGI Global. doi:10.4018/978-1-4666-0101-7.ch004

Hill, D. S. (2012). An examination of standardized product identification and business benefit. In E. Kajan, F. Dorloff, & I. Bedini (Eds.), *Handbook of research on e-business standards and protocols: Documents, data and advanced web technologies* (pp. 387–411). Hershey, PA: IGI Global. doi:10.4018/978-1-4666-0146-8.ch018

Hill, D. S. (2013). An examination of standardized product identification and business benefit. In *Supply chain management: Concepts, methodologies, tools, and applications* (pp. 171–195). Hershey, PA: IGI Global. doi:10.4018/978-1-4666-2625-6.ch011

Holloway, K. (2012). Fair use, copyright, and academic integrity in an online academic environment. In V. Wang (Ed.), *Encyclopedia of e-leadership, counseling and training* (pp. 298–309). Hershey, PA: IGI Global. doi:10.4018/978-1-61350-068-2.ch022

Hoops, D. S. (2011). Legal issues in the virtual world and e-commerce. In B. Ciaramitaro (Ed.), *Virtual worlds and e-commerce: Technologies and applications for building customer relationships* (pp. 186–204). Hershey, PA: IGI Global. doi:10.4018/978-1-61692-808-7.ch010

Hoops, D. S. (2012). Lost in cyberspace: Navigating the legal issues of e-commerce. *Journal of Electronic Commerce in Organizations*, *10*(1), 33–51. doi:10.4018/jeco.2012010103

Hopkinson, A. (2012). Establishing the digital library: Don't ignore the library standards and don't forget the training needed. In A. Tella & A. Issa (Eds.), *Library and information science in developing countries: Contemporary issues* (pp. 195–204). Hershey, PA: IGI Global. doi:10.4018/978-1-61350-335-5.ch014

Hua, G. B. (2013). The construction industry and standardization of information. In *Implementing IT business strategy in the construction industry* (pp. 47–66). Hershey, PA: IGI Global. doi:10.4018/978-1-4666-4185-3.ch003

Huang, C., & Lin, H. (2011). Patent infringement risk analysis using rough set theory. In Q. Zhang, R. Segall, & M. Cao (Eds.), *Visual analytics and interactive technologies: Data, text and web mining applications* (pp. 123–150). Hershey, PA: IGI Global. doi:10.4018/978-1-60960-102-7.ch008

Huang, C., Tseng, T. B., & Lin, H. (2013). Patent infringement risk analysis using rough set theory. In *Digital rights management: Concepts, methodologies, tools, and applications* (pp. 1225–1251). Hershey, PA: IGI Global. doi:10.4018/978-1-4666-2136-7.ch060

Iyamu, T. (2013). The impact of organisational politics on the implementation of IT strategy: South African case in context. In J. Abdelnour-Nocera (Ed.), *Knowledge and technological development effects on organizational and social structures* (pp. 167–193). Hershey, PA: IGI Global. doi:10.4018/978-1-4666-2151-0.ch011

Jacinto, K., Neto, F. M., Leite, C. R., & Jacinto, K. (2014). Accessibility in u-learning: Standards, legislation, and future visions. In F. Neto (Ed.), *Technology platform innovations and forthcoming trends in ubiquitous learning* (pp. 215–236). Hershey, PA: IGI Global. doi:10.4018/978-1-4666-4542-4.ch012

Jakobs, K., Wagner, T., & Reimers, K. (2011). Standardising the internet of things: What the experts think. *International Journal of IT Standards and Standardization Research*, *9*(1), 63–67. doi:10.4018/jitsr.2011010104

Juzoji, H. (2012). Legal bases for medical supervision via mobile telecommunications in Japan. *International Journal of E-Health and Medical Communications*, *3*(1), 33–45. doi:10.4018/jehmc.2012010103

Kallinikou, D., Papadopoulos, M., Kaponi, A., & Strakantouna, V. (2011). Intellectual property issues for digital libraries at the intersection of law, technology, and the public interest. In I. Iglezakis, T. Synodinou, & S. Kapidakis (Eds.), *E-publishing and digital libraries: Legal and organizational issues* (pp. 294–341). Hershey, PA: IGI Global. doi:10.4018/978-1-60960-031-0.ch015

Kallinikou, D., Papadopoulos, M., Kaponi, A., & Strakantouna, V. (2013). Intellectual property issues for digital libraries at the intersection of law, technology, and the public interest. In *Digital rights management: Concepts, methodologies, tools, and applications* (pp. 1043–1090). Hershey, PA: IGI Global. doi:10.4018/978-1-4666-2136-7.ch052

Kaupins, G. (2012). Laws associated with mobile computing in the cloud. *International Journal of Wireless Networks and Broadband Technologies*, *2*(3), 1–9. doi:10.4018/ijwnbt.2012070101

Kaur, P., & Singh, H. (2013). Component certification process and standards. In H. Singh & K. Kaur (Eds.), *Designing, engineering, and analyzing reliable and efficient software* (pp. 22–39). Hershey, PA: IGI Global. doi:10.4018/978-1-4666-2958-5.ch002

Kayem, A. V. (2013). Security in service oriented architectures: Standards and challenges. In *Digital rights management: Concepts, methodologies, tools, and applications* (pp. 50–73). Hershey, PA: IGI Global. doi:10.4018/978-1-4666-2136-7.ch004

Kemp, M. L., Robb, S., & Deans, P. C. (2013). The legal implications of cloud computing. In A. Bento & A. Aggarwal (Eds.), *Cloud computing service and deployment models: Layers and management* (pp. 257–272). Hershey, PA: IGI Global. doi:10.4018/978-1-4666-2187-9.ch014

Khansa, L., & Liginlal, D. (2012). Regulatory influence and the imperative of innovation in identity and access management. *Information Resources Management Journal, 25*(3), 78–97. doi:10.4018/irmj.2012070104

Kim, E. (2012). Government policies to promote production and consumption of renewable electricity in the US. In M. Tortora (Ed.), *Sustainable systems and energy management at the regional level: Comparative approaches* (pp. 1–18). Hershey, PA: IGI Global. doi:10.4018/978-1-61350-344-7.ch001

Kinsell, C. (2014). Technology and disability laws, regulations, and rights. In B. DaCosta & S. Seok (Eds.), *Assistive technology research, practice, and theory* (pp. 75–87). Hershey, PA: IGI Global. doi:10.4018/978-1-4666-5015-2.ch006

Kitsiou, S. (2010). Overview and analysis of electronic health record standards. In J. Rodrigues (Ed.), *Health information systems: Concepts, methodologies, tools, and applications* (pp. 374–392). Hershey, PA: IGI Global. doi:10.4018/978-1-60566-988-5.ch025

Kloss, J. H., & Schickel, P. (2011). X3D: A secure ISO standard for virtual worlds. In A. Rea (Ed.), *Security in virtual worlds, 3D webs, and immersive environments: Models for development, interaction, and management* (pp. 208–220). Hershey, PA: IGI Global. doi:10.4018/978-1-61520-891-3.ch010

Kotsonis, E., & Eliakis, S. (2011). Information security standards for health information systems: The implementer's approach. In A. Chryssanthou, I. Apostolakis, & I. Varlamis (Eds.), *Certification and security in health-related web applications: Concepts and solutions* (pp. 113–145). Hershey, PA: IGI Global. doi:10.4018/978-1-61692-895-7.ch006

Kotsonis, E., & Eliakis, S. (2013). Information security standards for health information systems: The implementer's approach. In *User-driven healthcare: Concepts, methodologies, tools, and applications* (pp. 225–257). Hershey, PA: IGI Global. doi:10.4018/978-1-4666-2770-3.ch013

Koumaras, H., & Kourtis, M. (2013). A survey on video coding principles and standards. In R. Farrugia & C. Debono (Eds.), *Multimedia networking and coding* (pp. 1–27). Hershey, PA: IGI Global. doi:10.4018/978-1-4666-2660-7.ch001

Krupinski, E. A., Antoniotti, N., & Burdick, A. (2011). Standards and guidelines development in the american telemedicine association. In A. Moumtzoglou & A. Kastania (Eds.), *E-health systems quality and reliability: Models and standards* (pp. 244–252). Hershey, PA: IGI Global. doi:10.4018/978-1-61692-843-8.ch018

Kuanpoth, J. (2011). Biotechnological patents and morality: A critical view from a developing country. In S. Hongladarom (Ed.), *Genomics and bioethics: Interdisciplinary perspectives, technologies and advancements* (pp. 141–151). Hershey, PA: IGI Global. doi:10.4018/978-1-61692-883-4.ch010

Kuanpoth, J. (2013). Biotechnological patents and morality: A critical view from a developing country. In *Digital rights management: Concepts, methodologies, tools, and applications* (pp. 1417–1427). Hershey, PA: IGI Global. doi:10.4018/978-1-4666-2136-7.ch071

Kulmala, R., & Kettunen, J. (2012). Intellectual property protection and process modeling in small knowledge intensive enterprises. In *Organizational learning and knowledge: Concepts, methodologies, tools and applications* (pp. 2963–2980). Hershey, PA: IGI Global. doi:10.4018/978-1-60960-783-8.ch809

Kulmala, R., & Kettunen, J. (2013). Intellectual property protection in small knowledge intensive enterprises. *International Journal of Cyber Warfare & Terrorism*, *3*(1), 29–45. doi:10.4018/ijcwt.2013010103

Küster, M. W. (2012). Standards for achieving interoperability of egovernment in Europe. In E. Kajan, F. Dorloff, & I. Bedini (Eds.), *Handbook of research on e-business standards and protocols: Documents, data and advanced web technologies* (pp. 249–268). Hershey, PA: IGI Global. doi:10.4018/978-1-4666-0146-8.ch012

Kyobe, M. (2011). Factors influencing SME compliance with government regulation on use of IT: The case of South Africa. In F. Tan (Ed.), *International enterprises and global information technologies: Advancing management practices* (pp. 85–116). Hershey, PA: IGI Global. doi:10.4018/978-1-60960-605-3.ch005

Lam, J. C., & Hills, P. (2011). Promoting technological environmental innovations: What is the role of environmental regulation? In Z. Luo (Ed.), *Green finance and sustainability: Environmentally-aware business models and technologies* (pp. 56–73). Hershey, PA: IGI Global. doi:10.4018/978-1-60960-531-5.ch003

Lam, J. C., & Hills, P. (2013). Promoting technological environmental innovations: The role of environmental regulation. In Z. Luo (Ed.), *Technological solutions for modern logistics and supply chain management* (pp. 230–247). Hershey, PA: IGI Global. doi:10.4018/978-1-4666-2773-4.ch015

Laporte, C., & Vargas, E. P. (2012). The development of international standards to facilitate process improvements for very small entities. In S. Fauzi, M. Nasir, N. Ramli, & S. Sahibuddin (Eds.), *Software process improvement and management: Approaches and tools for practical development* (pp. 34–61). Hershey, PA: IGI Global. doi:10.4018/978-1-61350-141-2.ch003

Laporte, C., & Vargas, E. P. (2014). The development of international standards to facilitate process improvements for very small entities. In *Software design and development: Concepts, methodologies, tools, and applications* (pp. 1335–1361). Hershey, PA: IGI Global. doi:10.4018/978-1-4666-4301-7.ch065

Lautman, R., & Curran, K. (2013). The problems of jurisdiction on the internet. In K. Curran (Ed.), *Pervasive and ubiquitous technology innovations for ambient intelligence environments* (pp. 164–170). Hershey, PA: IGI Global. doi:10.4018/978-1-4666-2041-4.ch016

Layne-Farrar, A. (2011). Innovative or indefensible? An empirical assessment of patenting within standard setting. *International Journal of IT Standards and Standardization Research*, *9*(2), 1–18. doi:10.4018/jitsr.2011070101

Layne-Farrar, A. (2013). Innovative or indefensible? An empirical assessment of patenting within standard setting. In K. Jakobs (Ed.), *Innovations in organizational IT specification and standards development* (pp. 1–18). Hershey, PA: IGI Global. doi:10.4018/978-1-4666-2160-2.ch001

Layne-Farrar, A., & Padilla, A. J. (2011). Assessing the link between standards and patents. *International Journal of IT Standards and Standardization Research*, *9*(2), 19–49. doi:10.4018/jitsr.2011070102

Layne-Farrar, A., & Padilla, A. J. (2013). Assessing the link between standards and patents. In K. Jakobs (Ed.), *Innovations in organizational IT specification and standards development* (pp. 19–51). Hershey, PA: IGI Global. doi:10.4018/978-1-4666-2160-2.ch002

Lee, H., & Huh, J. C. (2012). Korea's strategies for ICT standards internationalisation: A comparison with China's. *International Journal of IT Standards and Standardization Research*, *10*(2), 1–13. doi:10.4018/jitsr.2012070101

Li, Y., & Wei, C. (2011). Digital image authentication: A review. *International Journal of Digital Library Systems*, *2*(2), 55–78. doi:10.4018/jdls.2011040104

Li, Y., Xiao, X., Feng, X., & Yan, H. (2012). Adaptation and localization: Metadata research and development for Chinese digital resources. *International Journal of Digital Library Systems*, *3*(1), 1–21. doi:10.4018/jdls.2012010101

Lim, W., & Kim, D. (2013). Do technologies support the implementation of the common core state standards in mathematics of high school probability and statistics? In D. Polly (Ed.), *Common core mathematics standards and implementing digital technologies* (pp. 168–183). Hershey, PA: IGI Global. doi:10.4018/978-1-4666-4086-3.ch011

Linton, J., & Stegall, D. (2013). Common core standards for mathematical practice and TPACK: An integrated approach to instruction. In D. Polly (Ed.), *Common core mathematics standards and implementing digital technologies* (pp. 234–249). Hershey, PA: IGI Global. doi:10.4018/978-1-4666-4086-3.ch016

Liotta, A., & Liotta, A. (2011). Privacy in pervasive systems: Legal framework and regulatory challenges. In A. Malatras (Ed.), *Pervasive computing and communications design and deployment: Technologies, trends and applications* (pp. 263–277). Hershey, PA: IGI Global. doi:10.4018/978-1-60960-611-4.ch012

Lissoni, F. (2013). Academic patenting in Europe: Recent research and new perspectives. In I. Yetkiner, M. Pamukcu, & E. Erdil (Eds.), *Industrial dynamics, innovation policy, and economic growth through technological advancements* (pp. 75–91). Hershey, PA: IGI Global. doi:10.4018/978-1-4666-1978-4.ch005

Litaay, T., Prananingrum, D. H., & Krisanto, Y. A. (2011). Indonesian legal perspectives on biotechnology and intellectual property rights. In S. Hongladarom (Ed.), *Genomics and bioethics: Interdisciplinary perspectives, technologies and advancements* (pp. 171–183). Hershey, PA: IGI Global. doi:10.4018/978-1-61692-883-4.ch012

Litaay, T., Prananingrum, D. H., & Krisanto, Y. A. (2013). Indonesian legal perspectives on biotechnology and intellectual property rights. In *Digital rights management: Concepts, methodologies, tools, and applications* (pp. 834–845). Hershey, PA: IGI Global. doi:10.4018/978-1-4666-2136-7.ch039

Losavio, M., Pastukhov, P., & Polyakova, S. (2014). Regulatory aspects of cloud computing in business environments. In S. Srinivasan (Ed.), *Security, trust, and regulatory aspects of cloud computing in business environments* (pp. 156–169). Hershey, PA: IGI Global. doi:10.4018/978-1-4666-5788-5.ch009

Lu, B., Tsou, B. K., Jiang, T., Zhu, J., & Kwong, O. Y. (2011). Mining parallel knowledge from comparable patents. In W. Wong, W. Liu, & M. Bennamoun (Eds.), *Ontology learning and knowledge discovery using the web: Challenges and recent advances* (pp. 247–271). Hershey, PA: IGI Global. doi:10.4018/978-1-60960-625-1.ch013

Lucas-Schloetter, A. (2011). Digital libraries and copyright issues: Digitization of contents and the economic rights of the authors. In I. Iglezakis, T. Synodinou, & S. Kapidakis (Eds.), *E-publishing and digital libraries: Legal and organizational issues* (pp. 159–179). Hershey, PA: IGI Global. doi:10.4018/978-1-60960-031-0.ch009

Lyytinen, K., Keil, T., & Fomin, V. (2010). A framework to build process theories of anticipatory information and communication technology (ICT) standardizing. In K. Jakobs (Ed.), *New applications in IT standards: Developments and progress* (pp. 147–186). Hershey, PA: IGI Global. doi:10.4018/978-1-60566-946-5.ch008

Macedo, M., & Isaías, P. (2013). Standards related to interoperability in EHR & HS. In M. Sicilia & P. Balazote (Eds.), *Interoperability in healthcare information systems: Standards, management, and technology* (pp. 19–44). Hershey, PA: IGI Global. doi:10.4018/978-1-4666-3000-0.ch002

Madden, P. (2011). Greater accountability, less red tape: The Australian standard business reporting experience. *International Journal of E-Business Research, 7*(2), 1–10. doi:10.4018/jebr.2011040101

Maravilhas, S. (2014). Quality improves the value of patent information to promote innovation. In G. Jamil, A. Malheiro, & F. Ribeiro (Eds.), *Rethinking the conceptual base for new practical applications in information value and quality* (pp. 61–82). Hershey, PA: IGI Global. doi:10.4018/978-1-4666-4562-2.ch004

Marshall, S. (2011). E-learning standards: Beyond technical standards to guides for professional practice. In F. Lazarinis, S. Green, & E. Pearson (Eds.), *Handbook of research on e-learning standards and interoperability: Frameworks and issues* (pp. 170–192). Hershey, PA: IGI Global. doi:10.4018/978-1-61692-789-9.ch008

Martino, L., & Bertino, E. (2012). Security for web services: Standards and research issues. In L. Jie-Zhang (Ed.), *Innovations, standards and practices of web services: Emerging research topics* (pp. 336–362). Hershey, PA: IGI Global. doi:10.4018/978-1-61350-104-7.ch015

McCarthy, V., & Hulsart, R. (2012). Management education for integrity: Raising ethical standards in online management classes. In C. Wankel & A. Stachowicz-Stanusch (Eds.), *Handbook of research on teaching ethics in business and management education* (pp. 413–425). Hershey, PA: IGI Global. doi:10.4018/978-1-61350-510-6.ch024

McGrath, T. (2012). The reality of using standards for electronic business document formats. In E. Kajan, F. Dorloff, & I. Bedini (Eds.), *Handbook of research on e-business standards and protocols: Documents, data and advanced web technologies* (pp. 21–32). Hershey, PA: IGI Global. doi:10.4018/978-1-4666-0146-8.ch002

Medlin, B. D., & Chen, C. C. (2012). A global perspective of laws and regulations dealing with information security and privacy. In *Cyber crime: Concepts, methodologies, tools and applications* (pp. 1349–1363). Hershey, PA: IGI Global. doi:10.4018/978-1-61350-323-2.ch609

Mehrfard, H., & Hamou-Lhadj, A. (2011). The impact of regulatory compliance on agile software processes with a focus on the FDA guidelines for medical device software. *International Journal of Information System Modeling and Design, 2*(2), 67–81. doi:10.4018/jismd.2011040104

Mehrfard, H., & Hamou-Lhadj, A. (2013). The impact of regulatory compliance on agile software processes with a focus on the FDA guidelines for medical device software. In J. Krogstie (Ed.), *Frameworks for developing efficient information systems: Models, theory, and practice* (pp. 298–314). Hershey, PA: IGI Global. doi:10.4018/978-1-4666-4161-7.ch013

Mendoza, R. A., & Ravichandran, T. (2011). An exploratory analysis of the relationship between organizational and institutional factors shaping the assimilation of vertical standards. *International Journal of IT Standards and Standardization Research, 9*(1), 24–51. doi:10.4018/jitsr.2011010102

Mendoza, R. A., & Ravichandran, T. (2012). An empirical evaluation of the assimilation of industry-specific data standards using firm-level and community-level constructs. In M. Tavana (Ed.), *Enterprise information systems and advancing business solutions: Emerging models* (pp. 287–312). Hershey, PA: IGI Global. doi:10.4018/978-1-4666-1761-2.ch017

Mendoza, R. A., & Ravichandran, T. (2012). Drivers of organizational participation in XML-based industry standardization efforts. In M. Tavana (Ed.), *Enterprise information systems and advancing business solutions: Emerging models* (pp. 268–286). Hershey, PA: IGI Global. doi:10.4018/978-1-4666-1761-2.ch016

Mendoza, R. A., & Ravichandran, T. (2013). An exploratory analysis of the relationship between organizational and institutional factors shaping the assimilation of vertical standards. In K. Jakobs (Ed.), *Innovations in organizational IT specification and standards development* (pp. 193–221). Hershey, PA: IGI Global. doi:10.4018/978-1-4666-2160-2.ch012

Mense, E. G., Fulwiler, J. H., Richardson, M. D., & Lane, K. E. (2011). Standardization, hybridization, or individualization: Marketing IT to a diverse clientele. In U. Demiray & S. Sever (Eds.), *Marketing online education programs: Frameworks for promotion and communication* (pp. 291–299). Hershey, PA: IGI Global. doi:10.4018/978-1-60960-074-7.ch019

Metaxa, E., Sarigiannidis, M., & Folinas, D. (2012). Legal issues of the French law on creation and internet (Hadopi 1 and 2). *International Journal of Technoethics*, *3*(3), 21–36. doi:10.4018/jte.2012070102

Meyer, N. (2012). Standardization as governance without government: A critical reassessment of the digital video broadcasting project's success story. *International Journal of IT Standards and Standardization Research*, *10*(2), 14–28. doi:10.4018/jitsr.2012070102

Miguel da Silva, F., Neto, F. M., Burlamaqui, A. M., Pinto, J. P., Fernandes, C. E., & Castro de Souza, R. (2014). T-SCORM: An extension of the SCORM standard to support the project of educational contents for t-learning. In F. Neto (Ed.), *Technology platform innovations and forthcoming trends in ubiquitous learning* (pp. 94–119). Hershey, PA: IGI Global. doi:10.4018/978-1-4666-4542-4.ch006

Moon, A. (2014). Copyright and licensing essentials for librarians and copyright owners in the digital age. In N. Patra, B. Kumar, & A. Pani (Eds.), *Progressive trends in electronic resource management in libraries* (pp. 106–117). Hershey, PA: IGI Global. doi:10.4018/978-1-4666-4761-9.ch006

Moralis, A., Pouli, V., Grammatikou, M., Kalogeras, D., & Maglaris, V. (2012). Security standards and issues for grid computing. In *Grid and cloud computing: Concepts, methodologies, tools and applications* (pp. 1656–1671). Hershey, PA: IGI Global. doi:10.4018/978-1-4666-0879-5.ch708

Moreno, L., Iglesias, A., Calvo, R., Delgado, S., & Zaragoza, L. (2012). Disability standards and guidelines for learning management systems: Evaluating accessibility. In R. Babo & A. Azevedo (Eds.), *Higher education institutions and learning management systems: Adoption and standardization* (pp. 199–218). Hershey, PA: IGI Global. doi:10.4018/978-1-60960-884-2.ch010

Moro, N. (2013). Digital rights management and corporate hegemony: Avenues for reform. In H. Rahman & I. Ramos (Eds.), *Ethical data mining applications for socio-economic development* (pp. 281–299). Hershey, PA: IGI Global. doi:10.4018/978-1-4666-4078-8.ch013

Mula, D., & Lobina, M. L. (2012). Legal protection of the web page. In H. Sasaki (Ed.), *Information technology for intellectual property protection: Interdisciplinary advancements* (pp. 213–236). Hershey, PA: IGI Global. doi:10.4018/978-1-61350-135-1.ch008

Mula, D., & Lobina, M. L. (2013). Legal protection of the web page. In *Digital rights management: Concepts, methodologies, tools, and applications* (pp. 1–18). Hershey, PA: IGI Global. doi:10.4018/978-1-4666-2136-7.ch001

Mulcahy, D. (2011). Performativity in practice: An actor-network account of professional teaching standards. *International Journal of Actor-Network Theory and Technological Innovation, 3*(2), 1–16. doi:10.4018/jantti.2011040101

Mulcahy, D. (2013). Performativity in practice: An actor-network account of professional teaching standards. In A. Tatnall (Ed.), *Social and professional applications of actor-network theory for technology development* (pp. 1–16). Hershey, PA: IGI Global. doi:10.4018/978-1-4666-2166-4.ch001

Mustaffa, M. T. (2012). Multi-standard multi-band reconfigurable LNA. In A. Marzuki, A. Rahim, & M. Loulou (Eds.), *Advances in monolithic microwave integrated circuits for wireless systems: Modeling and design technologies* (pp. 1–23). Hershey, PA: IGI Global. doi:10.4018/978-1-60566-886-4.ch001

Nabi, S. I., Al-Ghmlas, G. S., & Alghathbar, K. (2012). Enterprise information security policies, standards, and procedures: A survey of available standards and guidelines. In M. Gupta, J. Walp, & R. Sharman (Eds.), *Strategic and practical approaches for information security governance: Technologies and applied solutions* (pp. 67–89). Hershey, PA: IGI Global. doi:10.4018/978-1-4666-0197-0.ch005

Nabi, S. I., Al-Ghmlas, G. S., & Alghathbar, K. (2014). Enterprise information security policies, standards, and procedures: A survey of available standards and guidelines. In *Crisis management: Concepts, methodologies, tools and applications* (pp. 750–773). Hershey, PA: IGI Global. doi:10.4018/978-1-4666-4707-7.ch036

Naixiao, Z., & Chunhua, H. (2012). Research on open innovation in China: Focus on intellectual property rights and their operation in Chinese enterprises. *International Journal of Asian Business and Information Management, 3*(1), 65–71. doi:10.4018/jabim.2012010106

Naixiao, Z., & Chunhua, H. (2013). Research on open innovation in China: Focus on intellectual property rights and their operation in Chinese enterprises. In *Digital rights management: Concepts, methodologies, tools, and applications* (pp. 714–720). Hershey, PA: IGI Global. doi:10.4018/978-1-4666-2136-7.ch031

Ndjetcheu, L. (2013). Social responsibility and legal financial communication in African companies in the south of the Sahara: Glance from the OHADA accounting law viewpoint. *International Journal of Innovation in the Digital Economy, 4*(4), 1–17. doi:10.4018/ijide.2013100101

Ng, W. L. (2013). Improving long-term financial risk forecasts using high-frequency data and scaling laws. In B. Alexandrova-Kabadjova, S. Martinez-Jaramillo, A. Garcia-Almanza, & E. Tsang (Eds.), *Simulation in computational finance and economics: Tools and emerging applications* (pp. 255–278). Hershey, PA: IGI Global. doi:10.4018/978-1-4666-2011-7.ch013

Noury, N., Bourquard, K., Bergognon, D., & Schroeder, J. (2013). Regulations initiatives in France for the interoperability of communicating medical devices. *International Journal of E-Health and Medical Communications*, 4(2), 50–64. doi:10.4018/jehmc.2013040104

Null, E. (2013). Legal and political barriers to municipal networks in the United States. In A. Abdelaal (Ed.), *Social and economic effects of community wireless networks and infrastructures* (pp. 27–56). Hershey, PA: IGI Global. doi:10.4018/978-1-4666-2997-4.ch003

O'Connor, R. V., & Laporte, C. Y. (2014). An innovative approach to the development of an international software process lifecycle standard for very small entities. *International Journal of Information Technologies and Systems Approach*, 7(1), 1–22. doi:10.4018/ijitsa.2014010101

Onat, I., & Miri, A. (2013). RFID standards. In A. Miri (Ed.), *Advanced security and privacy for RFID technologies* (pp. 14–22). Hershey, PA: IGI Global. doi:10.4018/978-1-4666-3685-9.ch002

Orton, I., Alva, A., & Endicott-Popovsky, B. (2013). Legal process and requirements for cloud forensic investigations. In K. Ruan (Ed.), *Cybercrime and cloud forensics: Applications for investigation processes* (pp. 186–229). Hershey, PA: IGI Global. doi:10.4018/978-1-4666-2662-1.ch008

Ortt, J. R., & Egyedi, T. M. (2014). The effect of pre-existing standards and regulations on the development and diffusion of radically new innovations. *International Journal of IT Standards and Standardization Research*, 12(1), 17–37. doi:10.4018/ijitsr.2014010102

Ozturk, Y., & Sharma, J. (2011). mVITAL: A standards compliant vital sign monitor. In C. Röcker, & M. Ziefle (Eds.), Smart healthcare applications and services: Developments and practices (pp. 174-196). Hershey, PA: IGI Global. doi:10.4018/978-1-60960-180-5.ch008

Ozturk, Y., & Sharma, J. (2013). mVITAL: A standards compliant vital sign monitor. In IT policy and ethics: Concepts, methodologies, tools, and applications (pp. 515-538). Hershey, PA: IGI Global. doi:10.4018/978-1-4666-2919-6.ch024

Parsons, T. D. (2011). Affect-sensitive virtual standardized patient interface system. In D. Surry, R. Gray Jr, & J. Stefurak (Eds.), *Technology integration in higher education: Social and organizational aspects* (pp. 201–221). Hershey, PA: IGI Global. doi:10.4018/978-1-60960-147-8.ch015

Parveen, S., & Pater, C. (2012). Utilizing innovative video chat technology to meet national standards: A Case study on a STARTALK Hindi language program. *International Journal of Virtual and Personal Learning Environments*, *3*(3), 1–20. doi:10.4018/jvple.2012070101

Pawlowski, J. M., & Kozlov, D. (2013). Analysis and validation of learning technology models, standards and specifications: The reference model analysis grid (RMAG). In K. Jakobs (Ed.), *Innovations in organizational IT specification and standards development* (pp. 223–240). Hershey, PA: IGI Global. doi:10.4018/978-1-4666-2160-2.ch013

Pina, P. (2011). The private copy issue: Piracy, copyright and consumers' rights. In T. Strader (Ed.), *Digital product management, technology and practice: Interdisciplinary perspectives* (pp. 193–205). Hershey, PA: IGI Global. doi:10.4018/978-1-61692-877-3.ch011

Pina, P. (2013). Between Scylla and Charybdis: The balance between copyright, digital rights management and freedom of expression. In Digital rights management: Concepts, methodologies, tools, and applications (pp. 1355-1367). Hershey, PA: IGI Global. doi:10.4018/978-1-4666-2136-7.ch067

Pina, P. (2013). Computer games and intellectual property law: Derivative works, copyright and copyleft. In *Digital rights management: Concepts, methodologies, tools, and applications* (pp. 777–788). Hershey, PA: IGI Global. doi:10.4018/978-1-4666-2136-7.ch035

Pina, P. (2013). The private copy issue: Piracy, copyright and consumers' rights. In *Digital rights management: Concepts, methodologies, tools, and applications* (pp. 1546–1558). Hershey, PA: IGI Global. doi:10.4018/978-1-4666-2136-7.ch078

Piotrowski, M. (2011). QTI: A failed e-learning standard? In F. Lazarinis, S. Green, & E. Pearson (Eds.), *Handbook of research on e-learning standards and interoperability: Frameworks and issues* (pp. 59–82). Hershey, PA: IGI Global. doi:10.4018/978-1-61692-789-9.ch004

Ponte, D., & Camussone, P. F. (2013). Neither heroes nor chaos: The victory of VHS against Betamax. *International Journal of Actor-Network Theory and Technological Innovation*, *5*(1), 40–54. doi:10.4018/jantti.2013010103

Pradhan, A. (2011). Pivotal role of the ISO 14001 standard in the carbon economy. *International Journal of Green Computing, 2*(1), 38–46. doi:10.4018/jgc.2011010104

Pradhan, A. (2011). Standards and legislation for the carbon economy. In B. Unhelkar (Ed.), *Handbook of research on green ICT: Technology, business and social perspectives* (pp. 592–606). Hershey, PA: IGI Global. doi:10.4018/978-1-61692-834-6.ch043

Pradhan, A. (2013). Pivotal role of the ISO 14001 standard in the carbon economy. In K. Ganesh & S. Anbuudayasankar (Eds.), *International and interdisciplinary studies in green computing* (pp. 38–46). Hershey, PA: IGI Global. doi:10.4018/978-1-4666-2646-1.ch004

Prentzas, J., & Hatzilygeroudis, I. (2011). Techniques, technologies and patents related to intelligent educational systems. In G. Magoulas (Ed.), *E-infrastructures and technologies for lifelong learning: Next generation environments* (pp. 1–28). Hershey, PA: IGI Global. doi:10.4018/978-1-61520-983-5.ch001

Ramos, I., & Fernandes, J. (2011). Web-based intellectual property marketplace: A survey of current practices. *International Journal of Information Communication Technologies and Human Development, 3*(3), 58–68. doi:10.4018/jicthd.2011070105

Ramos, I., & Fernandes, J. (2013). Web-based intellectual property marketplace: A survey of current practices. In S. Chhabra (Ed.), *ICT influences on human development, interaction, and collaboration* (pp. 203–213). Hershey, PA: IGI Global. doi:10.4018/978-1-4666-1957-9.ch012

Rashmi, R. (2011). Biopharma drugs innovation in India and foreign investment and technology transfer in the changed patent regime. In P. Ordóñez de Pablos, W. Lee, & J. Zhao (Eds.), *Regional innovation systems and sustainable development: Emerging technologies* (pp. 210–225). Hershey, PA: IGI Global. doi:10.4018/978-1-61692-846-9.ch016

Rashmi, R. (2011). Optimal policy for biopharmaceutical drugs innovation and access in India. In P. Ordóñez de Pablos, W. Lee, & J. Zhao (Eds.), *Regional innovation systems and sustainable development: Emerging technologies* (pp. 74–114). Hershey, PA: IGI Global. doi:10.4018/978-1-61692-846-9.ch007

Rashmi, R. (2013). Biopharma drugs innovation in India and foreign investment and technology transfer in the changed patent regime. In *Digital rights management: Concepts, methodologies, tools, and applications* (pp. 846–859). Hershey, PA: IGI Global. doi:10.4018/978-1-4666-2136-7.ch040

Reed, C. N. (2011). The open geospatial consortium and web services standards. In P. Zhao & L. Di (Eds.), *Geospatial web services: Advances in information interoperability* (pp. 1–16). Hershey, PA: IGI Global. doi:10.4018/978-1-60960-192-8.ch001

Rejas-Muslera, R., Davara, E., Abran, A., & Buglione, L. (2013). Intellectual property systems in software. *International Journal of Cyber Warfare & Terrorism*, *3*(1), 1–14. doi:10.4018/ijcwt.2013010101

Rejas-Muslera, R. J., García-Tejedor, A. J., & Rodriguez, O. P. (2011). Open educational resources in e-learning: standards and environment. In F. Lazarinis, S. Green, & E. Pearson (Eds.), *Handbook of research on e-learning standards and interoperability: Frameworks and issues* (pp. 346–359). Hershey, PA: IGI Global. doi:10.4018/978-1-61692-789-9.ch017

Ries, N. M. (2011). Legal issues in health information and electronic health records. In *Clinical technologies: Concepts, methodologies, tools and applications* (pp. 1948–1961). Hershey, PA: IGI Global. doi:10.4018/978-1-60960-561-2.ch708

Riillo, C. A. (2013). Profiles and motivations of standardization players. *International Journal of IT Standards and Standardization Research*, *11*(2), 17–33. doi:10.4018/jitsr.2013070102

Rodriguez, E., & Lolas, F. (2011). Social issues related to gene patenting in Latin America: A bioethical reflection. In S. Hongladarom (Ed.), *Genomics and bioethics: Interdisciplinary perspectives, technologies and advancements* (pp. 152–170). Hershey, PA: IGI Global. doi:10.4018/978-1-61692-883-4.ch011

Rutherford, M. (2013). Implementing common core state standards using digital curriculum. In D. Polly (Ed.), *Common core mathematics standards and implementing digital technologies* (pp. 38–44). Hershey, PA: IGI Global. doi:10.4018/978-1-4666-4086-3.ch003

Rutherford, M. (2014). Implementing common core state standards using digital curriculum. In *K-12 education: Concepts, methodologies, tools, and applications* (pp. 383–389). Hershey, PA: IGI Global. doi:10.4018/978-1-4666-4502-8.ch022

Ryan, G., & Shinnick, E. (2011). Knowledge and intellectual property rights: An economics perspective. In D. Schwartz & D. Te'eni (Eds.), *Encyclopedia of knowledge management* (2nd ed.; pp. 489–496). Hershey, PA: IGI Global. doi:10.4018/978-1-59904-931-1.ch047

Ryoo, J., & Choi, Y. (2011). A taxonomy of green information and communication protocols and standards. In B. Unhelkar (Ed.), *Handbook of research on green ICT: Technology, business and social perspectives* (pp. 364–376). Hershey, PA: IGI Global. doi:10.4018/978-1-61692-834-6.ch026

Saeed, K., Ziegler, G., & Yaqoob, M. K. (2013). Management practices in exploration and production industry. In S. Saeed, M. Khan, & R. Ahmad (Eds.), *Business strategies and approaches for effective engineering management* (pp. 151–187). Hershey, PA: IGI Global. doi:10.4018/978-1-4666-3658-3.ch010

Saiki, T. (2014). Intellectual property in mergers & acquisitions. In J. Wang (Ed.), *Encyclopedia of business analytics and optimization* (pp. 1275–1283). Hershey, PA: IGI Global. doi:10.4018/978-1-4666-5202-6.ch117

Santos, O., & Boticario, J. (2011). A general framework for inclusive lifelong learning in higher education institutions with adaptive web-based services that support standards. In G. Magoulas (Ed.), *E-infrastructures and technologies for lifelong learning: Next generation environments* (pp. 29–58). Hershey, PA: IGI Global. doi:10.4018/978-1-61520-983-5.ch002

Santos, O., Boticario, J., Raffenne, E., Granado, J., Rodriguez-Ascaso, A., & Gutierrez y Restrepo, E. (2011). A standard-based framework to support personalisation, adaptation, and interoperability in inclusive learning scenarios. In F. Lazarinis, S. Green, & E. Pearson (Eds.), *Handbook of research on e-learning standards and interoperability: Frameworks and issues* (pp. 126–169). Hershey, PA: IGI Global. doi:10.4018/978-1-61692-789-9.ch007

Sarabdeen, J. (2012). Legal issues in e-healthcare systems. In M. Watfa (Ed.), *E-healthcare systems and wireless communications: Current and future challenges* (pp. 23–48). Hershey, PA: IGI Global. doi:10.4018/978-1-61350-123-8.ch002

Scheg, A. G. (2014). Common standards for online education found in accrediting organizations. In *Reforming teacher education for online pedagogy development* (pp. 50–76). Hershey, PA: IGI Global. doi:10.4018/978-1-4666-5055-8.ch003

Sclater, N. (2012). Legal and contractual issues of cloud computing for educational institutions. In L. Chao (Ed.), *Cloud computing for teaching and learning: Strategies for design and implementation* (pp. 186–199). Hershey, PA: IGI Global. doi:10.4018/978-1-4666-0957-0.ch013

Selwyn, L., & Eldridge, V. (2013). Governance and organizational structures. In *Public law librarianship: Objectives, challenges, and solutions* (pp. 41–71). Hershey, PA: IGI Global. doi:10.4018/978-1-4666-2184-8.ch003

Seo, D. (2012). The significance of government's role in technology standardization: Two cases in the wireless communications industry. In C. Reddick (Ed.), *Cases on public information management and e-government adoption* (pp. 219–231). Hershey, PA: IGI Global. doi:10.4018/978-1-4666-0981-5.ch009

Seo, D. (2013). Analysis of various structures of standards setting organizations (SSOs) that impact tension among members. *International Journal of IT Standards and Standardization Research, 11*(2), 46–60. doi:10.4018/jitsr.2013070104

Seo, D. (2013). Background of standards strategy. In *Evolution and standardization of mobile communications technology* (pp. 1–17). Hershey, PA: IGI Global. doi:10.4018/978-1-4666-4074-0.ch001

Seo, D. (2013). Developing a theoretical model. In *Evolution and standardization of mobile communications technology* (pp. 18–42). Hershey, PA: IGI Global. doi:10.4018/978-1-4666-4074-0.ch002

Seo, D. (2013). The 1G (first generation) mobile communications technology standards. In *Evolution and standardization of mobile communications technology* (pp. 54–75). Hershey, PA: IGI Global. doi:10.4018/978-1-4666-4074-0.ch005

Seo, D. (2013). The 2G (second generation) mobile communications technology standards. In *Evolution and standardization of mobile communications technology* (pp. 76–114). Hershey, PA: IGI Global. doi:10.4018/978-1-4666-4074-0.ch006

Seo, D. (2013). The 3G (third generation) of mobile communications technology standards. In *Evolution and standardization of mobile communications technology* (pp. 115–161). Hershey, PA: IGI Global. doi:10.4018/978-1-4666-4074-0.ch007

Seo, D. (2013). The significance of government's role in technology standardization: Two cases in the wireless communications industry. In K. Jakobs (Ed.), *Innovations in organizational IT specification and standards development* (pp. 183–192). Hershey, PA: IGI Global. doi:10.4018/978-1-4666-2160-2.ch011

Seo, D., & Koek, J. W. (2012). Are Asian countries ready to lead a global ICT standardization? *International Journal of IT Standards and Standardization Research, 10*(2), 29–44. doi:10.4018/jitsr.2012070103

Sharp, R. J., Ewald, J. A., & Kenward, R. (2013). Central information flows and decision-making requirements. In J. Papathanasiou, B. Manos, S. Arampatzis, & R. Kenward (Eds.), *Transactional environmental support system design: Global solutions* (pp. 7–32). Hershey, PA: IGI Global. doi:10.4018/978-1-4666-2824-3.ch002

Shen, X., Graham, I., Stewart, J., & Williams, R. (2013). Standards development as hybridization. *International Journal of IT Standards and Standardization Research, 11*(2), 34–45. doi:10.4018/jitsr.2013070103

Sherman, M. (2013). Using technology to engage students with the standards for mathematical practice: The case of DGS. In D. Polly (Ed.), *Common core mathematics standards and implementing digital technologies* (pp. 78–101). Hershey, PA: IGI Global. doi:10.4018/978-1-4666-4086-3.ch006

Singh, J., & Kumar, V. (2013). Compliance and regulatory standards for cloud computing. In R. Khurana & R. Aggarwal (Eds.), *Interdisciplinary perspectives on business convergence, computing, and legality* (pp. 54–64). Hershey, PA: IGI Global. doi:10.4018/978-1-4666-4209-6.ch006

Singh, S., & Paliwal, M. (2014). Exploring a sense of intellectual property valuation for Indian SMEs. *International Journal of Asian Business and Information Management, 5*(1), 15–36. doi:10.4018/ijabim.2014010102

Singh, S., & Siddiqui, T. J. (2013). Robust image data hiding technique for copyright protection. *International Journal of Information Security and Privacy, 7*(2), 44–56. doi:10.4018/jisp.2013040103

Spies, M., & Tabet, S. (2012). Emerging standards and protocols for governance, risk, and compliance management. In E. Kajan, F. Dorloff, & I. Bedini (Eds.), *Handbook of research on e-business standards and protocols: Documents, data and advanced web technologies* (pp. 768–790). Hershey, PA: IGI Global. doi:10.4018/978-1-4666-0146-8.ch035

Spinello, R. A., & Tavani, H. T. (2008). Intellectual property rights: From theory to practical implementation. In H. Sasaki (Ed.), *Intellectual property protection for multimedia information technology* (pp. 25–69). Hershey, PA: IGI Global. doi:10.4018/978-1-59904-762-1.ch002

Spyrou, S., Bamidis, P., & Maglaveras, N. (2010). Health information standards: Towards integrated health information networks. In J. Rodrigues (Ed.), *Health information systems: Concepts, methodologies, tools, and applications* (pp. 2145–2159). Hershey, PA: IGI Global. doi:10.4018/978-1-60566-988-5.ch136

Stanfill, D. (2012). Standards-based educational technology professional development. In V. Wang (Ed.), *Encyclopedia of e-leadership, counseling and training* (pp. 819–834). Hershey, PA: IGI Global. doi:10.4018/978-1-61350-068-2.ch060

Steen, H. U. (2011). The battle within: An analysis of internal fragmentation in networked technologies based on a comparison of the DVB-H and T-DMB mobile digital multimedia broadcasting standards. *International Journal of IT Standards and Standardization Research, 9*(2), 50–71. doi:10.4018/jitsr.2011070103

Steen, H. U. (2013). The battle within: An analysis of internal fragmentation in networked technologies based on a comparison of the DVB-H and T-DMB mobile digital multimedia broadcasting standards. In K. Jakobs (Ed.), *Innovations in organizational IT specification and standards development* (pp. 91–114). Hershey, PA: IGI Global. doi:10.4018/978-1-4666-2160-2.ch005

Stoll, M., & Breu, R. (2012). Information security governance and standard based management systems. In M. Gupta, J. Walp, & R. Sharman (Eds.), *Strategic and practical approaches for information security governance: Technologies and applied solutions* (pp. 261–282). Hershey, PA: IGI Global. doi:10.4018/978-1-4666-0197-0.ch015

Suzuki, O. (2013). Search efforts, selective appropriation, and the usefulness of new knowledge: Evidence from a comparison across U.S. and non-U.S. patent applicants. *International Journal of Knowledge Management, 9*(1), 42-59. doi:10.4018/jkm.2013010103

Tajima, M. (2012). The role of technology standardization in RFID adoption: The pharmaceutical context. *International Journal of IT Standards and Standardization Research, 10*(1), 48–67. doi:10.4018/jitsr.2012010104

Talevi, A., Castro, E. A., & Bruno-Blanch, L. E. (2012). Virtual screening: An emergent, key methodology for drug development in an emergent continent: A bridge towards patentability. In E. Castro & A. Haghi (Eds.), *Advanced methods and applications in chemoinformatics: Research progress and new applications* (pp. 229–245). Hershey, PA: IGI Global. doi:10.4018/978-1-60960-860-6.ch011

Tauber, A. (2012). Requirements and properties of qualified electronic delivery systems in egovernment: An Austrian experience. In S. Sharma (Ed.), *E-adoption and technologies for empowering developing countries: Global advances* (pp. 115–128). Hershey, PA: IGI Global. doi:10.4018/978-1-4666-0041-6.ch009

Telesko, R., & Nikles, S. (2012). Semantic-enabled compliance management. In S. Smolnik, F. Teuteberg, & O. Thomas (Eds.), *Semantic technologies for business and information systems engineering: Concepts and applications* (pp. 292–310). Hershey, PA: IGI Global. doi:10.4018/978-1-60960-126-3.ch015

Tella, A., & Afolabi, A. K. (2013). Internet policy issues and digital libraries' management of intellectual property. In S. Thanuskodi (Ed.), *Challenges of academic library management in developing countries* (pp. 272–284). Hershey, PA: IGI Global. doi:10.4018/978-1-4666-4070-2.ch019

Tiwari, S. C., Gupta, M., Khan, M. A., & Ansari, A. Q. (2013). Intellectual property rights in semi-conductor industries: An Indian perspective. In S. Saeed, M. Khan, & R. Ahmad (Eds.), *Business strategies and approaches for effective engineering management* (pp. 97–110). Hershey, PA: IGI Global. doi:10.4018/978-1-4666-3658-3.ch006

Truyen, F., & Buekens, F. (2013). Professional ICT knowledge, epistemic standards, and social epistemology. In T. Takševa (Ed.), *Social software and the evolution of user expertise: Future trends in knowledge creation and dissemination* (pp. 274–294). Hershey, PA: IGI Global. doi:10.4018/978-1-4666-2178-7.ch016

Tummons, J. (2011). Deconstructing professionalism: An actor-network critique of professional standards for teachers in the UK lifelong learning sector. *International Journal of Actor-Network Theory and Technological Innovation, 3*(4), 22–31. doi:10.4018/jantti.2011100103

Tummons, J. (2013). Deconstructing professionalism: An actor-network critique of professional standards for teachers in the UK lifelong learning sector. In A. Tatnall (Ed.), *Social and professional applications of actor-network theory for technology development* (pp. 78–87). Hershey, PA: IGI Global. doi:10.4018/978-1-4666-2166-4.ch007

Tuohey, W. G. (2014). Lessons from practices and standards in safety-critical and regulated sectors. In I. Ghani, W. Kadir, & M. Ahmad (Eds.), *Handbook of research on emerging advancements and technologies in software engineering* (pp. 369–391). Hershey, PA: IGI Global. doi:10.4018/978-1-4666-6026-7.ch016

Tzoulia, E. (2013). Legal issues to be considered before setting in force consumer-centric marketing strategies within the European Union. In H. Kaufmann & M. Panni (Eds.), *Customer-centric marketing strategies: Tools for building organizational performance* (pp. 36–56). Hershey, PA: IGI Global. doi:10.4018/978-1-4666-2524-2.ch003

Unland, R. (2012). Interoperability support for e-business applications through standards, services, and multi-agent systems. In E. Kajan, F. Dorloff, & I. Bedini (Eds.), *Handbook of research on e-business standards and protocols: Documents, data and advanced web technologies* (pp. 129–153). Hershey, PA: IGI Global. doi:10.4018/978-1-4666-0146-8.ch007

Uslar, M., Grüning, F., & Rohjans, S. (2013). A use case for ontology evolution and interoperability: The IEC utility standards reference framework 62357. In M. Khosrow-Pour (Ed.), *Cases on performance measurement and productivity improvement: Technology integration and maturity* (pp. 387–415). Hershey, PA: IGI Global. doi:10.4018/978-1-4666-2618-8.ch018

van de Kaa, G. (2013). Responsible innovation and standardization: A new research approach? *International Journal of IT Standards and Standardization Research*, *11*(2), 61–65. doi:10.4018/jitsr.2013070105

van de Kaa, G., Blind, K., & de Vries, H. J. (2013). The challenge of establishing a recognized interdisciplinary journal: A citation analysis of the international journal of IT standards and standardization research. *International Journal of IT Standards and Standardization Research*, *11*(2), 1–16. doi:10.4018/jitsr.2013070101

Venkataraman, H., Ciubotaru, B., & Muntean, G. (2012). System design perspective: WiMAX standards and IEEE 802.16j based multihop WiMAX. In G. Cornetta, D. Santos, & J. Vazquez (Eds.), *Wireless radio-frequency standards and system design: Advanced techniques* (pp. 287–309). Hershey, PA: IGI Global. doi:10.4018/978-1-4666-0083-6.ch012

Vishwakarma, P., & Mukherjee, B. (2014). Knowing protection of intellectual contents in digital era. In N. Patra, B. Kumar, & A. Pani (Eds.), *Progressive trends in electronic resource management in libraries* (pp. 147–165). Hershey, PA: IGI Global. doi:10.4018/978-1-4666-4761-9.ch008

Wasilko, P. J. (2011). Law, architecture, gameplay, and marketing. In M. Cruz-Cunha, V. Varvalho, & P. Tavares (Eds.), *Business, technological, and social dimensions of computer games: Multidisciplinary developments* (pp. 476–493). Hershey, PA: IGI Global. doi:10.4018/978-1-60960-567-4.ch029

Wasilko, P. J. (2012). Law, architecture, gameplay, and marketing. In *Computer engineering: concepts, methodologies, tools and applications* (pp. 1660–1677). Hershey, PA: IGI Global. doi:10.4018/978-1-61350-456-7.ch703

Wasilko, P. J. (2014). Beyond compliance: Understanding the legal aspects of information system administration. In I. Portela & F. Almeida (Eds.), *Organizational, legal, and technological dimensions of information system administration* (pp. 57–75). Hershey, PA: IGI Global. doi:10.4018/978-1-4666-4526-4.ch004

White, G. L., Mediavilla, F. A., & Shah, J. R. (2011). Information privacy: Implementation and perception of laws and corporate policies by CEOs and managers. *International Journal of Information Security and Privacy*, *5*(1), 50–66. doi:10.4018/jisp.2011010104

White, G. L., Mediavilla, F. A., & Shah, J. R. (2013). Information privacy: Implementation and perception of laws and corporate policies by CEOs and managers. In H. Nemati (Ed.), *Privacy solutions and security frameworks in information protection* (pp. 52–69). Hershey, PA: IGI Global. doi:10.4018/978-1-4666-2050-6.ch004

Whyte, K. P., List, M., Stone, J. V., Grooms, D., Gasteyer, S., Thompson, P. B., & Bouri, H. et al. (2014). Uberveillance, standards, and anticipation: A case study on nanobiosensors in U.S. cattle. In M. Michael & K. Michael (Eds.), *Uberveillance and the social implications of microchip implants: Emerging technologies* (pp. 260–279). Hershey, PA: IGI Global. doi:10.4018/978-1-4666-4582-0.ch012

Wilkes, W., Reusch, P. J., & Moreno, L. E. (2012). Flexible classification standards for product data exchange. In E. Kajan, F. Dorloff, & I. Bedini (Eds.), *Handbook of research on e-business standards and protocols: Documents, data and advanced web technologies* (pp. 448–466). Hershey, PA: IGI Global. doi:10.4018/978-1-4666-0146-8.ch021

Wittkower, D. E. (2011). Against strong copyright in e-business. In *Global business: Concepts, methodologies, tools and applications* (pp. 2157–2176). Hershey, PA: IGI Global. doi:10.4018/978-1-60960-587-2.ch720

Wright, D. (2012). Evolution of standards for smart grid communications. *International Journal of Interdisciplinary Telecommunications and Networking*, *4*(1), 47–55. doi:10.4018/jitn.2012010103

Wurster, S. (2013). Development of a specification for data interchange between information systems in public hazard prevention: Dimensions of success and related activities identified by case study research. *International Journal of IT Standards and Standardization Research*, *11*(1), 46–66. doi:10.4018/jitsr.2013010103

Wyburn, M. (2011). Copyright and ethical issues in emerging models for the digital media reporting of sports news in Australia. In M. Quigley (Ed.), *ICT ethics and security in the 21st century: New developments and applications* (pp. 66–85). Hershey, PA: IGI Global. doi:10.4018/978-1-60960-573-5.ch004

Wyburn, M. (2013). Copyright and ethical issues in emerging models for the digital media reporting of sports news in Australia. In *Digital rights management: Concepts, methodologies, tools, and applications* (pp. 290–309). Hershey, PA: IGI Global. doi:10.4018/978-1-4666-2136-7.ch014

Xiaohui, T., Yaohui, Z., & Yi, Z. (2012). The management system of enterprises' intellectual property rights: A case study from China. *International Journal of Asian Business and Information Management*, *3*(1), 50–64. doi:10.4018/jabim.2012010105

Xiaohui, T., Yaohui, Z., & Yi, Z. (2013). The management system of enterprises' intellectual property rights: A case study from China. In *Digital rights management: Concepts, methodologies, tools, and applications* (pp. 1092–1106). Hershey, PA: IGI Global. doi:10.4018/978-1-4666-2136-7.ch053

Xuan, X., & Xiaowei, Z. (2012). The dilemma and resolution: The patentability of traditional Chinese medicine. *International Journal of Asian Business and Information Management, 3*(3), 1–8. doi:10.4018/jabim.2012070101

Yang, C., & Lu, Z. (2011). A blind image watermarking scheme utilizing BTC bitplanes. *International Journal of Digital Crime and Forensics, 3*(4), 42–53. doi:10.4018/jdcf.2011100104

Yastrebenetsky, M., & Gromov, G. (2014). International standard bases and safety classification. In M. Yastrebenetsky & V. Kharchenko (Eds.), *Nuclear power plant instrumentation and control systems for safety and security* (pp. 31–60). Hershey, PA: IGI Global. doi:10.4018/978-1-4666-5133-3.ch002

Zouag, N., & Kadiri, M. (2014). Intellectual property rights, innovation, and knowledge economy in Arab countries. In A. Driouchi (Ed.), *Knowledge-based economic policy development in the Arab world* (pp. 245–272). Hershey, PA: IGI Global. doi:10.4018/978-1-4666-5210-1.ch010

Compilation of References

A4AI. (2017). *2017 Affordability Report*. Retrieved from: http://1e8q3q16vyc81g8l3h3md6q5f 5e.wpengine.netdna-cdn.com/wp-content/uploads/2017/02/A4AI-2017-Affordability-Report.pdf

Achimugu, P., Oluwagbemi, O., Oluwaranti, A., & Afolabi, B. (2009). Adoption of information and communication technologies in developing countries: An impact analysis. *Journal of Information Technology Impact, 9*(1), 37–46.

Adams C. (2017). *Global disaster monitoring and learning methodology*. (Forthcoming)

Adams, C., & Fitch, T. (2006). Social Inclusion and the Shifting Role of Technology: Is Age the New Gender in Mobile Access? In *Social Inclusion: Societal and Organizational Implications for Information Systems* (pp. 203-215). Springer.

Adams, C., & Hallsworth, A. (2015a). Virtual Non-productive value (NoPV) creation as a cause of economic instability. *AHE Conference*, Southampton, UK.

Adams, C., & Hallsworth, A. (2015b). Systemic problems in global finance: Non-productive value (NoPV) creation and storing rapidly increasing levels of value. *4th Global Conference on Economic Geography*, 19-23.

Adams, C., & Mouatt, S. (2010a). The rise of complementary currencies and corporafinance: E-commerce driven competition in the financial sector. *Journal of Internet Banking and Commerce, 15*(1), 1–13.

Adams, C., & Mouatt, S. (2010b). Evolution of Electronic and Mobile Business and Services: Government support for E/M-payment systems. *International Journal of Electronic Services and Mobile Applications, 2*(2), 43–54.

Ahmad, A., & Shiratuddin, N. (2010). *Business Intelligence for Sustainable Competitive Advantage: Field Study of Telecommunications Industry*. Paper presented at the Annual International Academic Conference on Business Intelligence and Data Warehousing, Singapore. doi:10.5176/978-981-08-6308-1_38

Ahmad, S., Haamid, A. L., Qazi, Z. A., Zhou, Z., Benson, T., & Qazi, A. I. (2016). A view from the other side: understanding mobile phone characteristics in the developing world. *Proceedings of the 16th ACM Internet Measurement Conference (IMC)*. doi:10.1145/2987443.2987470

Airtel to Support Free Health Hotline in Malawi. (2015, Nov 5). Retrieved from: http://www. villagereach.org/news-press/7387-2/

Alasow, Jumnongruk, Niyamangkoon, & Surin. (2010). *Notice of Retraction People attitude towards telecenter utilization in Roi Et Province of Thailand.* Paper presented at the International Conference on Education and Management Technology (ICEMT).

Al-Busaidy, M. (2011). *Evaluating the institutional factors affecting egovernment implementation.* Brunel University.

Al-Husban, M., & Adams, C. (2016). Sustainable Refugee Migration: A Rethink towards a Positive Capability Approach. *Sustainability*, (8): 451.

AlKhatib, H. (2013). *E-government systems success and user acceptance in developing countries: The role of perceived support quality.* Brunel University. Retrieved from http://dspace.brunel. ac.uk/handle/2438/7471

Alkire, S., & Deneulin, S. (2008). Introducing the Human Development and Capability Approach. In S. Deneulin (Eds.), *Development and Freedom: An Introduction to the Human Development and Capability Approach, Earthscan.* Retrieved from www.ophi.org.uk

Alkire, S. (2010). Development 'a misconceived theory can kill. In C. Morris (Ed.), *Amartya Sen: Contemporary Philosophy in Focus.* New York: Cambridge University Press.

Alsaeed, A., & Adams, C. (2015). E-Service adoption in developing countries with instability status: The case of e-government in Syria. In *Proceedings of the European Conference on e-Government, ECEG* (pp. 393–402). Portsmouth, UK: Academic Press.

Alsaeed, A., Adams, C., & Boakes, R. (2014). The need for policies to overcome egov implementation challenges. *International Journal of Electronic Government Research, 10*(3), 66–79. doi:10.4018/ijegr.2014070105

Alshehri, M., Drew, S., & Alfarraj, O. (2012). A comprehensive analysis of e-government services adoption in Saudi Arabia: Obstacles and challenges. *International Journal of Advanced Computer Science and Applications, 3*(2), 1–6. Retrieved from papers3://publication/uuid/A1CEA70F-B951-4D95-9F49-566F06677E09

Alsmadi, I. (2011). Security challenges for expanding e- governments services. *International Journal of Advanced Science and Technology, 37*, 47–61.

Andrade, A. D., & Urquart, C. (2010). The affordances of actor network theory in ICT for development research. *Information Technology & People, 23*(4), 352–374. RetrievedSeptember42016. doi:10.1108/09593841011087806

Ardichvili, A., Maurer, M., Li, W., Wentling, T., & Stuedemann, R. (2006). Cultural influences on knowledge sharing through online communities of practice. *Journal of Knowledge Management, 10*(1), 94–107. doi:10.1108/13673270610650139

Ariyabandu, R. (2009). *Role of Telecentres as Knowledge Networks: Successes and Challenges.* Bangkok: ESCAP.

Attwood, H., & Braathen, E. (2010). *Telecentres and poor communities in South Africa: What have we learnt?* Paper presented at the panel "Comparative Experiences of Chronic Poverty and access to Information and Communication Technologies (ICT)", Manchester, UK.

Attwood, H., Diga, K., Braathen, E., & May, J. (2013). Telecentre functionality in South Africa: Re-enabling the community ICT access environment. *The Journal of Community Informatics, 9*(4).

Avgerou, C. (2009). Discourses on innovation and development in information systems in developing countries research. In E Byrne B Nicholson & F Salem (Eds.), *Assessing the Contribution of ICT to Development Goals*. Dubai, UAE: Dubai School of Government. Retrieved on 1 May, 2014, from http:// www.ifip.dsg.ae

Avgerou, C. (2010). Discourses on ICT and development. *Information Technologies and International, 6*(3), 1-18.

Avgerou, C. (2001). The Significance of Context in Information Systems and Organisational Change. *Information Systems Journal, 11*(1), 43–63. doi:10.1046/j.1365-2575.2001.00095.x

Avgerou, C. (2008). Information systems in developing countries: A critical research review. *Journal of Information Technology, 23*(3), 133–146. doi:10.1057/palgrave.jit.2000136

Avgerou, C. (2010). Discourses on ICT and development. *Information Technologies and International Development, 6*(3), 1–18.

Avgerou, C., & Walsham, G. (2000). IT in developing countries. In C. Avgerou & G. Walsham (Eds.), *Information Technology in Context*. Aldershot, UK: Ashgate.

Ayanso, D. I., & Lertwachara, K. (2015). An analytical approach to exploring the link between ICT development and affordability. *Government Information Quarterly, 32*(4), 389–398. doi:10.1016/j.giq.2015.09.009

Azab, N., Kamel, S., & Dafoulas, G. (2009). A suggested framework for assessing electronic government readiness in Egypt. *eJournal of eGov, 7*(1), 11–28.

Bailey, A. N., & Ojelanki. (2010). Community mediation and violence prevention through telecentre usage: ICTs mediating the 'Border Line'. *Proceedings of SIG GlobDev Third Annual Workshop*.

Bailey, A. (2009). Issues affecting the social sustainability of telecentres in developing contexts: A field study of sixteen telecentres in Jamaica. *The Electronic Journal on Information Systems in Developing Countries, 36*(4), 1–18.

Bailur, S. (2007). Using Stakeholder Theory to Analyze Telecenter Projects. *Information Technologies and International Development, 3*(3), 61–80.

Baloh, P. (2007). Role of Fit in Knowledge Management Systems: Tentative Proposition of the KMS Design. *Journal of Organizational and End User Computing, 19*(4), 22–41. doi:10.4018/joeuc.2007100102

Barja, G., & Gigler, B.-S. (n.d.). *The Concept of Information Poverty and How to Measure it in the Latin American Context*. Retrieved from: http://citeseerx.ist.psu.edu/viewdoc/download?doi=10.1.1.571.5933&rep=rep1&type=pdf

Baron, L. F., & Gomez, R. (2012). Social network analysis of public access computing: Relationships as a critical benefit of libraries, telecenters and cybercafés in developing countries. *Proceedings of the 2012 iConference*. doi:10.1145/2132176.2132225

Baron, L. F., & Gomez, R. (2013). Relationships and Connectedness: Weak Ties that Help Social Inclusion Through Public Access Computing. *Information Technology for Development*, *19*(4), 271–294. doi:10.1080/02681102.2012.755896

Barrantes, R. (2007). Analysis of ICT Demand: What is Digital Poverty and How to Measure It? In H. Galperin & J. Mariscal (Eds.), Digital poverty: Latin American and Caribbean perspectives (pp. 29-53). Ottawa: IDRC.

Barrett, C. B. (2001). Does food aid stabilize food availability? *Economic Development and Cultural Change*, *49*(2), 335–349. doi:10.1086/452505

Barron, P., Pillay, Y., Fernandes, A., Sebidi, J., & Allen, R. (2016). The MomConnect mHealth initiative in South Africa: Early impact on the supply side of MCH services. *Journal of Public Health Policy*, *37*(S2), 201–212. doi:10.1057/s41271-016-0015-2 PMID:27899795

Barzilai-Nahon, K. (2006). Gaps and bits: Conceptualizing measurements for digital. *The Information Society*, *22*(5), 269–278. doi:10.1080/01972240600903953

Bayo, Gomez, & Ricardo. (2012). *Better Learning Opportunities through Public Access Computing*. Paper presented at the the Prato CIRN Community Informatics Conference, Prato Italy.

Bednar & Welch. (2017). *The innovation-diffusion cycle: Time for a sociotechnical agenda*. Twenty-Fifth European Conference on Information Systems (ECIS), Guimarães, Portugal.

Benjamin, P. (2001). *Telecentres and Universal Capability (PhD)*. Aalborg, Denmark: Aalborg University.

Benjamin, P. (2009). Does 'Telecentre' mean the centre is far away? Telecentre development in South Africa. *The Southern African Journal of Information and Communication*, *1*, 32–50.

Bhagat, R., Kedia, B., Harveston, P., & Triandis, H. (2002). Cultural variations in the cross-border transfer of organizational knowledge: An integrative framework. *Academy of Management Review*, *2*, 204–221.

Bhandari, P. (2015). *Connected Women: Grameen Foundation Case Study on Bringing "Mobile Midwife" to Nigeria*. Retrieved March 2015, from http://www.gsma.com/mobilefordevelopment/wp-content/uploads/2015/06/Connected-Women-Grameen-Case-Study-final.pdf

Bjerga, A. (2013). Obama Wants More Food Aid to Be Locally Sourced. *Bloomberg*. Available from http://www.bloomberg.com/bw/articles/2013-04-25/obama-wants-more-food-aid-to-be-locally-sourced

Boonperm, J. (2013). *Telecentres: helping to develop a knowledge-based society that can be self-sufficient. Community ICT Learning Centre.* Chiang Mai: ITU.

Bornman, E. (2016). Information society and digital divide in South Africa: Results of longitudinal surveys. *Information Communication and Society*, *19*(2), 2016. doi:10.1080/1369 118X.2015.1065285

Brett, E. A. (2009). *Reconstructing development theory.* Palgrave Macmillan. doi:10.1007/978-1-137-05768-6

Britz, J. J. (2007). *A critical analysis of information poverty from a social justice perspective* (Unpublished D.Phil thesis). University of Pretoria.

BTA. (2012). *Guidelines for sharing of passive communications infrastructure.* Retrieved From:www.researchictafrica.net/.../Draft_Guidelines_for_Passive_Communication_Infrastrure

Butler, R. (1991). *Designing Organizations.* New York: Routledge.

Calabrese, M. (2006). *Examples of Consumer Benefits from TV 'White Spaces' Legislation.* Retrieved September 10, 2017, from https://www.newamerica.org/oti/policy-papers/examples-of-consumer-benefits-from-tv-white-spaces-legislation/

Careerride. (2016). *Free basics- pros and cons.* Available on http://www.careerride.com/view/free-basics-pros-and-cons-26314.aspx

Carew, D. (2015). *Zero-rating: Kick-starting Internet ecosystems in developing countries.* Policy Memo. Progressive Policy Institute. Retrieved from: http://www.progressivepolicy.org/wpcontent/uploads/2015/03/2015.03-Carew_ZeroRating_Kick- Starting-Internet-Ecosystems-inDeveloping-Countries.pdf

Carew, D. (2015). *Zero-rating: kick-starting Internet ecosystems in developing countries.* Policy Memo.

Carter, M., & Grover, V. (2015). Me, My Self, and I(T): Conceptualizing information technology identity and its implications. *Management Information Systems Quarterly*, *39*(4), 931–957. doi:10.25300/MISQ/2015/39.4.9

Carter, M., Grover, V., & Thatcher, J. B. (2012). Mobile devices and the self: developing the concept of mobile phone identity. In I. Lee (Ed.), *Strategy, adoption, and competitive advantage of mobile services in the global economy* (pp. 150–164). Hershey, PA: IGI Global.

Castells, M., Fernanadez-Ardevol, M., Qiu, J., & Sey, A. (2007). *Mobile communication and society: A global perspective.* Cambridge, MA: MIT Press.

Chair, C., Futter, A., Gillwald, A., Koranteng, K., Odufwa, F. & Walubengo. J. (2016). *Much Ado About Nothing? Zero-Rating in the African Context.* Department for International Development.

Chatfiel, A. T., & Alhujran, O. (2009). A cross-country comparative analysis of e-government service delivery among Arab countries. *Information Technology for Development*, *15*(3), 151–170. doi:10.1002/itdj.20124

Cheang, S. L., & Jeong-Dong. (2010). *Evaluation telecenter performance in social sustainability context: A Cambodia case study.* Paper presented at the 6th International Conference on Advanced Information Management and Service (IMS).

Cheuk, , Azuriaty, Lo, & May-Chiun. (2012). Community Attitudes towards the Telecentre in Bario, Borneo Malaysia: 14 Years on. *International Journal of Innovation, Management and Technology, 3*(6), 682–687.

Chimuka, T. (2001). Ethics Among the Shona. *Zambezia, 28*(1).

Choudrie, J., & Dwivedi, Y. (2006). Investigating factors influencing adoption of broadband in the household. *Journal of Computer Information Systems, 46*(4), 25–34.

Coleman, J. S. (1988). Social capital in the creation of human capital. *American Journal of Sociology, 94,* S95–S120. doi:10.1086/228943

Colle, R. D. (2005). Memo to telecenter planners. *The Electronic Journal on Information Systems in Developing Countries, 21*(1), 1–13.

Coutts, A., & Fouad, F.M. (2013). Response to Syria's health crisis – poor and uncoordinated. *The Lancet, 381*(9885), 2242-2243.

Crespo, R. (2008). *On Sen and Aristotle.* Working paper series IAE Business School – Austral University CONICET. Retrieved www.iae.edu.ar/pi/.../Working%20Papers/DTIAE%2003_2008.pdf

Creswell, J. W. (1998). *Qualitative inquiry and research design. Choosing among five traditions.* Thousand Oaks, CA: Sage.

Curry, R. J. Jr, & Sura, K. (2007). Human resource development (HRD) theory and Thailand's sufficiency economy concept and Its "OTOP" Program. *Journal of Third World Studies, 24*(2), 85–94.

Dada, D. (2006). The Failure of e-Government in Developing Countries. *The Electronic Journal on Information Systems in Developing Countries, 26*(1), 1–10.

Dada, D. (2006). The failure of e-government in developing countries: A literature review. *The Electronic Journal on Information Systems in Developing Countries, 26*(7), 1–10.

Darkwa, O. K. (2016, July). *The role of tv white space technology.* Retrieved from The Ghananian Times: http://www.ghanaiantimes.com.gh/role-of-tv-white-space-technology/

De Herdr, T., & Deneulin, S. (Eds.). (2007). Special Issue: Freedoms as Relational Experiences. *Journal of Human Development, 8,* 2.

De Silva, H., & Zainudeen, A. (2017). *Teleuse on a shoestring: Poverty reduction through telecom access at the 'Bottom of the Pyramid'.* Retrieved from http://www.lirneasia.net/wp-content/uploads/2007/04/lirneasia_teleuse_cepa_-mar07_v 30.pdf

Dean-Swarray, M., Moyo, M. & Stork, C. (2013). ICT access and usage among informal businesses in Africa. *Info*, *15*(5), 52-68.

Deichmann, J. I., Eshghi, A., Haughton, D., Masnghetti, M., Sayek, S., & Topi, H. (2006). Exploring breakpoints and interaction effects among predictors of the international digital divide. *Journal of Global Information Technology Management*, *9*(4), 47–71. doi:10.1080/109 7198X.2006.10856432

Deloitte. (2012). *What is the impact of mobile telephony on economic growth? A Report for the GSM Association.* Retrieved from https://www.gsma.com/publicpolicy/wp-content/ uploads/2012/11/gsma-deloitte-impact-mobile-telephony-economic-growth.pdf

Devereux, S. (2001). Sen's entitlement approach: Critiques and counter critiques. *The Journal of Development Studies*, *29*, 245–263.

Dicken, P. (2007). *Global shift: Mapping the changing contours of the world economy.* London: Sage.

Dominique Noguet, M. G. (2011, November 15). Advances in opportunistic radio technologies for TVWS. *EURASIP Journal on Wireless Communications and Networking*, *170*, 1–12.

Donner, J., & Toyama, K. (2009). Persistent themes in ICT4D research: priorities for inter methodological. In *57th Session of the International Statistical Institute* (pp. 1–8). Durban: International Statistical Institute.

Donner, J. (2007). Customer acquisition among small and informal businesses in urban India: Comparing face-to-face mediated channels. *The Electronic Journal on Information Systems in Developing Countries*, *32*. Retrieved from www.ejisdc.org/Ojs2/index.php/ejisdc/article/view/464

Donner, J. (2008). Research approaches to mobile use in the developing world: A review of the literature. *The Information Society*, *24*(3), 140–159. doi:10.1080/01972240802019970

Duffy, N. (2012b). Learning for disaster resilience. Earth: Fire and Rain - Australian & New Zealand Disaster and Emergency Management Conference, Brisbane, Australia.

Duffy, N. (2012a). Using social media to build community disaster resilience. *Australian Journal of Emergency Management*, *27*(1).

Dusek, V. (2007). *Philosophy of Technology: An introduction.* Oxford, UK: Blackwell.

Dutta, S., Geiger, T., & Lanvin, B. (Eds.). (2015). *The global information and technology report 2015: ICTs for inclusive growth. Insight report.* World Economic Forum. Retrieved from: http://www3.weforum.org/docs/WEF_Global_IT_Report_2015.pdf

Dynamic Spectrum Alliance. (2015). *Worldwide Commercial Deployments, Pilots, and Trials.* BristolUnited Kingdom: Dynamic Spectrum Alliance.

Eisenach, J. (2015). *The Economics of Zero Rating.* NERA Economic Consulting. Retrieved March 2015, from http://www.nera.com/content/dam/nera/publications/2015/Economic sofZeroRating.pdf

Eisenhardt, K. M., & Graebner, M. E. (2007). Theory Building from Cases: Opportunities and Challenges. *Academy of Management Journal, 50*(1), 25–32. doi:10.5465/AMJ.2007.24160888

Ellison, N. B., Steinfield, C., & Lampe, C. (2007). The benefits of Facebook 'friends:' social capital and college students' use of online social network sites. *Journal of Computer-Mediated Communication, 12*(4), 1143–1168. doi:10.1111/j.1083-6101.2007.00367.x

Elsheikh, Y. M. a. (2011). *A model for the adoption and implementation of web-based government services and applications. a study based on grounded theory validated by structural equation modelling analysis in a Jordanian context.* Retrieved from http://hdl.handle.net/10454/5378

European Commission. (2001). *European governance: A white paper.* Retrieved from http://ec.europa.eu/transparency/regdoc/rep/1/2001/EN/1-2001-428-EN-F1-1.Pdf

Eyring, M., Johnson, M. W., & Nair, H. (2011, January). New business models in emerging markets. *Harvard Business Review.* Retrieved from https://hbr.org/2011/01/new-business-models-in-emerging-markets

Ferguson, N. (2011). *Civilization: The West and the Rest.* London: Allen Lane.

Fowler, J. (2017). *Don't forget refugees and migrants when tackling risk.* Discussion paper, UNISDR. Retrieved from https://www.unisdr.org/archive/52560

FTC. (2009). *FTC Staff Report: February 2009 Self-Regulatory principles For online behavioral advertising.* Available at: https://www.ftc.gov/sites/default/files/documents/reports/federal-trade-commission-staff-report-self-regulatory-principles-online-behavioral-advertising/p085400behavadreport.pdf

Futter, A., & Gillwald, A. (2015). *Zero-rated internet services: What is to be done?* Broadband 4 Africa, Policy Paper 1, 2015. Retrieved Sept 2015, from http://www.researchictafrica.net/docs/Facebook%20zerorating%20Final_Web.pdf

Gable, G. G. (1994). Integrating case study and survey research methods: An example in information systems. *European Journal of Information Systems, 3*(2), 112–126. doi:10.1057/ejis.1994.12

Gant, J. (2008). Electronic government for developing countries. International Communication Union, 2(52).

Garcia, J. M., & Kelly, T. (2016). *The economic and Policy Implications of Infrastructure Sharing and Mutualisation in Africa. World development report. Background Paper.* Academic Press.

Gebhart, G. (2016). Zero-rating in emerging mobile markets: free Basics and Wikipedia Zero in Ghana. *Proceedings of ICTD'16.* doi:10.1145/2909609.2909663

Giddens, A. (1984). *The Constitution of Society.* Cambridge, UK: Polity Press.

Gillwald, A. (2017). *Beyond access: addressing digital inequality in Africa.* Centre for International Governance Innovation and Chatham House. Retrieved from: https://www.cigionline.org/sites/default/files/documents/GCIG%20no.48_0.pdf

Gillwald, A., Chair, C., Futter, A., Koranteng, K., Odufuwa, F., & Wa lubengo, J. (2016). *Much ado about nothing? Zero-rating in the African context.* Retrieved from: https://www. researchictafrica.net/publications/Other_publications/2016_RIA_Zero-Rating_Policy_Paper_-_ Much_ado_about_nothing.pdf

Gilwald, A. (2017). *Beyond access. Addressing digital inequality in Africa.* Paper Series: NO. 48 — March 2017. Retrieved from: https://www.cigionline.org/sites/default/files/documents/ GCIG%20no.48_0.pdf

Gilwald, A., Chair, C., Futter, A., Koroteng, K., Odufuwa, F., & Walubengo, J. (2016). *Much ado about nothing? Zero-rating in the African context.* Academic Press.

Glaser, B. G. (1992). *Basics of grounded theory analysis.* Sociology Press.

Gold, L. (2005). Are the Millennium development goals addressing the underlying causes of injustice? Understanding the risks of the MDGs. *Developmental Review*, 23–42. Retrieved from http://www.trocaire.org/resources/tdr-article/are-millennium-development-goals-addressing-underlying-causes-injustice

Gomez, R. B.-P., & Fernando, L. (2011). Does public access computing really contribute to community development? Lessons from libraries, telecenters and cybercafés in Colombia. *The Electronic Journal on Information Systems in Developing Countries*, 49, 1–11.

Gomez, R. P., & Dosono, B. (2012). Public access computing in South Africa: Old lessons and new challenges. *The Electronic Journal on Information Systems in Developing Countries*, 52(1), 1–16.

Gomez, R., & Pather, S. (2012). ICT evaluation: Are we asking the right questions? *The Electronic Journal on Information Systems in Developing Countries*, 50(1), 1–14.

Government of Tamil Nadu. State Planning Commission. (2012). *Approach Paper for Twelfth Five Year Plan (2012 - 17).* Retrieved from http://www.spc.tn.gov.in/fiveyearplans/approachnew.pdf

GSM Association. (2012). *Universal access: How mobile can bring communications to all.* GSM Association Universal Access Report. Retrieved from https://www.gsma.com/ publicpolicy/wp-content/uploads/2012/03/universalaccessfullreport.pdf

GSM Association. (2015). *The mobile economy Sub-Saharan Africa 2015.* Retrieved from https:// www.gsma.com/mobileeconomy/archive/GSMA_ME_SubSaharanAfrica_2015.pdf

GSMA. (2013). *Arab states mobile observatory 2013.* Retrieved from https://www.gsma.com/ publicpolicy/wp-content/uploads/2012/03/GSMA_MobileObservatory_ArabStates2013. pdf

GSMA. (2014a). *Maternal messaging mHealth programmes. Empowering and enabling decision makers to include mHealth services into their budgets.* Retrieved 2014 from http:// www.gsma. com/mobilefordevelopment/wp-content/uploads/2014/12/GSMA-mHealth- Programme-high-resolution.pdf

GSMA. (2014b). *Understanding the needs and wants of pregnant women and mothers.* Retrieved from http://www.gsma.com/mobile fordevelopment/wp-content/uploads/2014/07/Consumer-Research-Report.pdf?_s m_au_=ijVWr264Nr0mRQQq.

Guardian. (2015). *South-east Asia migrant crisis: numbers are now 'alarming', talks told.* Retrieved from http://www.theguardian.com/world/2015/may/29/south-east-asia-migrant-crisis-numbers-are-now-alarming-talks-told

Guildford, M. (2014). To the next billion: Mobile Network Operators and the content distribution value chain. *Innovations, 9*(3-4), 21–31. doi:10.1162/inov_a_00213

Gurumurthy, A., & Chami, N. (2016). Internet governance as 'ideology in practice' – India's' Free Basics' controversy. *Internet Policy Review, 5*(3). doi:10.14763/2016.3.431

Habermas, J. (1984). The Theory of Communicative Action.: Vol. 1. *Reason and Rationalization of Society.* Boston, MA: Beacon Press.

Hall, M. (2103). *The Syrian crisis in Jordan. Middle East Research and Information Project.* Academic Press.

Hansson, L., Wrangmo, A., & Søilen, K. S. (2013). Optimal ways for companies to use Facebook as a marketing channel. *Journal of Information, Communication and Ethics in Society, 11*(2), 112–126. doi:10.1108/JICES-12-2012-0024

Harris, R. W. (2007). *Telecentre evaluation in the Malaysian context.* Paper presented at the the the 5th International Conference on IT in Asia, Kuching, Sarawak, Malaysia.

Harvey, D. (2005). *A Brief History of Neoliberalism.* Oxford, UK: Oxford University Press.

Harvey, D. (2014). *Seventeen Contradictions and the End of Capitalism.* London: Profile Books.

Hassan, S., Yusof, Y., Seman, M. A. A., & Sheik, W. R. (2010). *Impact Analysis on Utilization of Telecenter: The Case of Telecentre in Baling.* Academic Press.

Hatsu, S., Mabeifam, U. M., & Paitoo, P. C. (2016). *Infrastructure sharing among Ghana's mobile telecommunication networks*: Benefits and challenges. *American Journal of Networks and Communications, 5*(2), 35–45. doi:10.11648/j.ajnc.20160502.14

Hayes, N., & Westrup, C. (2012). Context and the processes of ICT for development. *Information and Organization, 22*(1), 23–36. doi:10.1016/j.infoandorg.2011.10.001

Heeks, R. (2002). Failure, Success and Improvisation of Information Systems Projects in Developing Countries. *Development Informatics. Working Paper Series.* Manchester: Institute for Development Policy and Management, University of Manchester. Retrieved on 3 April 2011, from http://unpan1.un.org/intradoc/groups/public/documents/NISPAcee/UNPAN015601.pdf _wp42.htm

Heeks, R. (2002). *iGovernment: Working Paper Series* (No. 13). eGovernment in Africa: Promise and Practice. Manchester, UK: University of Manchester, Precinct Centre. Retrieved from http://idpm.man.ac.uk/wp/igov/index.htm

Heeks, R. (2003). *Most e-Government for Development Projects Fail: How can Risks be Reduced?* iGovernment Working Paper Series, Paper no. 14. Retrieved from http://unpan1.un.org/intradoc/groups/public/documents/NISPAcee/UNPAN015488.pdf

Heeks, R. (2009). *The ICT4D 2.0 Manifesto: Where Next for ICTs and International Development?* Retrieved on 3 April 2011, from http://www.sed.manchester.ac.uk/idpm/research/publications/wp/di/di_wp42.htm

Heeks, R., & Bailur, S. (2007). Analyzing e-government research: Perspectives, philosophies, theories, methods, and practice. *Government Information Quarterly*, *24*(2), 243–265. doi:10.1016/j.giq.2006.06.005

Helbig, N., Ramón Gil-García, J., & Ferro, E. (2009). Understanding the complexity of electronic government: Implications from the digital divide literature. *Government Information Quarterly*, *26*(1), 89–97. doi:10.1016/j.giq.2008.05.004

Hellström, J., & Tröften, P. (2010). *The innovative use of mobile applications in East Africa.* Stockholm, Sweden: Swedish International Development Cooperation Agency (SIDA).

Hempel, J. (2015, September). Facebook renames its controversial Internet.org app. *Wired.* Retrieved from http://www.wired.com

Hofstede, G. (2001). *Culture's Consequences: Comparing Values, Behaviors, Institutions and Organizations Across Nations.* Thousand Oaks, CA: Sage.

Hubbard, B. (2013, July). Momentum Shifts in Syria, bolstering Assad's position. *The New York Times.*

Hudson, H. E. (2001). Telecentre evaluation: Issues and strategies. In C. L. D. Walker (Ed.), Telecentres: Case studies and key issues (pp. 169-181). Vancouver: The Commonwealth of Learning.

Human Network International. (2015). *Human Network International & its services* [PowerPoint slides]. Retrieved from http://www.slideshare.net/SandraGubler1/human-network-international-its-services

Hunt, P. (2001). True stories: Telecentres in Latin America and the Caribbean. *The Electronic Journal on Information Systems in Developing Countries*, *4*(5), 1–17.

Independent, Z. (2010). *Econet threatened with closure.* Retrieved from: https://www.theindependent.co.zw/2010/06/17/econet-threatened-with-closure/

Information Business Publications. (2013). *Syria energy policy, low and regulations handbook.* Washington, DC: Author.

Information Management Unit. (2016). *DYNAMO:Syria dynamic monitoring report.* Gaziantep: Assistance Coordination Unit.

Intaratat, K. (2008). Telecentres in Thailand: The Way Thus Far. *Telecentre Magazine.* http://www.telecentremagazine.net/articles/article-details.asp?

International Telecommunication Union. (2009). *eGovernment implementation toolkit: A framework for e-government readiness and action priorities.* Author.

International Telecommunication Union. (2014). *Measuring the information society report.* International Telecommunication Union. Retrieved from: https://www.itu.int/en/ITUD/Statistics/Documents/publications/mis2014/MIS2014_without_Annex_4.pdf

Internet.org. (2015). *Where we've launched - internet.org.* Available on https://info.internet.org/en/story/where-weve-launched/

Ishmael, J., Bury, S., Pezaros, D., & Race, N. (2008). Deploying Rural Community Wireless Mesh Networks. *IEEE Internet Computing, 12*(4), 22–29. doi:10.1109/MIC.2008.76

ITU. (2003). *World telecommunication development report 2003 Access Indicators for the Information Society Executive summary.* Retrieved from: https://www.itu.int/ITU-D/ict/publications/wtdr_03/material/WTDR2003Sum_e.pdf

ITU. (2016). *Key ICT indicators for developed and developing countries and the world (totals and penetration rates).* Retrieved From: http://www.itu.int/en/ITU-D/Statistics/Pages/stat/default.aspx

ITU. (2017). *Connecting the Unconnected Working together to achieve Connect 2020 Agenda Targets.* A background paper to the special session of the Broadband Commission and the World Economic Forum at Davos Annual Meeting 2017. Accessed 21 August 2017, http://broadbandcommission.org/Documents/ITU_discussion-paper_Davos2017.pdf

ITU. (2017a, September 13). *Connect 2020 Agenda.* Retrieved from Connect 2020 Agenda: http://www.itu.int/en/connect2020/Pages/default.aspx

ITU. (2017b). *Status of the transition to Digital Terrestrial Television Broadcasting: Summary.* Retrieved from http://www.itu.int/en/ITU-D/Spectrum-Broadcasting/Pages/DSO/Summary.aspx

Jacobs, S. H., (2006). Information access for development: A case study at a rural community centre in South Africa. *Issues in Informing Science and Information Technology, 3,* 295–306. doi:10.28945/892

Jait, A. (2012). *Government e-services delivery requires citizens a wareness :the case of brunei darussalam.* Loughborough University.

Jansen, B. J., Zhang, M., Sobel, K., & Chowdury, A. (2009). Twitter power: Tweets as electronic word of mouth. *Journal of the American Society for Information Science and Technology, 60*(11), 2169–2188.

Jasek-Rysdal, K. (2001). Applying Sen's capability framework to neighborhoods: Using local asset maps to deepen our understanding of well being. *Review of Social Economy, 59*(3), 313–329. doi:10.1080/00346760110053923

Jekassi, I., & Enders, A. (2005). *Strategies for e-business.* Hallow, UK: FT Prenticehall.

Jensen, M. (2013). The role of TV White Spaces and dynamic spectrum in helping to improve internet access in Africa and other developing regions. In E. A. M. Zennaro (Ed.), TV White Space: A pragmatic approach (pp. 83-89). ICTP-The Abdus Salam International Centre for Theoretical Physics.

Johnson, K. (2016). *Facebook Messenger now has 11,000 chatbots for you to try.* Retrieved from http://venturebeat.com/2016/06/30/facebook-messenger-now-has-11000-chatbots-for-you-to-try/

Johnson. (n.d.). *Evaluation of a single radio rural mesh network in South Africa.* Retrieved from: http://www.fmfi.org.za/wiki/images/3/3e/Peebles_mesh_ictd_india.pdf

Jones, M., & Alony, I. (2007). The cultural impact of information systems –through the eyes of hofstede – A critical journey. *Issues in Informing Science and Information Technology, 4*, 407-419. Retrieved January 14 2012 from http://proceedings.informingscience. org/InSITE2007/IISITv4p407-419Jone365.pdf

Jones, M., & Alony, I. (2007). The Cultural Impact of Information Systems –Through the Eyes of Hofstede – A Critical Journey. *Issues in Informing Science and Information Technology, 4*, 407–419. doi:10.28945/960

Kalpic, B., & Bernus, P. (2006). Business process modeling through the knowledge management perspective. *Journal of Knowledge Management, 10*(3), 40–56. doi:10.1108/13673270610670849

Kalyanamitra, W. (2012, January). ICT telecentre: new model of social development for rural communities in Thailand. *Graduated Volunteer Institute Journal.*

Kalyani, P. (2016). Studying the impact and awareness of free basics and net neutrality in reference to Internet usage in contemporary scenario. *Journal of Management Engineering and Information Technology, 3*(1), 1–15.

Kant, I. (1956). *Critique of practical reason* (L. W. Beck, Trans.). Indianapolis, IN: Bobbs-Merrill. (Original work published 1788)

Karanasios, S. (2013, May). Framing ICT4D Research Using Activity Theory. *Proceedings of the 12th International Conference on Social Implications of Computers in Developing Countries,* 318-333.

Karanasios, S. (2014). Framing ICT4D research using activity theory: A match between the ICT4D field and theory? *Information Technologies and International Development, 10*(2), 1–17.

Keenan-Alspector, J. (2016). *What is free about Free Basics?* Boulder, CO: University of Colorado.

Kemp, S. (2016). *Digital in 2016. We are Social.* Retrieved 1 December, 2016, from http://www.slideshare.net/wearesocialsg/digital-in-2016

Khan, G. F., Moon, J., Rhee, C., & Rho, J. J. (2010). E-government skills identification and development : Toward a staged-based user-centric approach for developing countries. *Asia Pacific Journal of Information Systems, 20*(1), 1–31.

Kitiyadisai, K. (2000). The implementation of IT in reengineering the Thai Revenue Department. *Information Flows, Local Improvisations and Work Practices, Proceedings of the IFIP WG9.4 Conference 2000.*

Klein, H., & Myers, M. (1999). A Set of Principals for Conducting and Evaluating Interpretive Field Studies in Information Systems. *Management Information Systems Quarterly, 23*(1), 67–94. doi:10.2307/249410

Knieps, G. & Zenhäusern, P. (2007). The fallacies of network neutrality regulation. *Diskussionsbeiträge // Institut für Verkehrswissenschaft und Regionalpolitik, 115*.

Kondra, A. Z., & Hurst, D. C. (2009). Institutional processes of organizational culture. *Culture and Organization, 15*(1), 39–58. doi:10.1080/14759550802709541

KPMG. (2011). *Passive Infrastructure Sharing in Telecommunications*. Retrieved from: https://www.kpmg.com/BE/en/IssuesAndInsights/ArticlesPublications/Documents/Passive-Infrastructure-Sharing-in-Telecommunications.pdf

Kumar, R. (2004). eChoupals: A study on the financial sustainability of village internet centers in rural Madhya Pradesh. *Information Technologies and International Development, 2*(1), pp-45. doi:10.1162/1544752043971161

Kurokawa, K., Tembo, F., & te Velde, D. (2010). *Challenges for the OVOP Movement in Sub-Saharan Africa – Insights from Malawi, Japan and Thailand.* JICA-RI working paper 18 of 2010. Nepal: JICA.

LaFrance, A. (2016, February 11). Facebook and the new colonialism. *Atlantic*. Retrieved from http://www.theatlantic.com/technology/archive/2016/02/facebook-and-the-new-colonialism/462393/

Lashgarara, , Mirdamadi, & Mehdi. (2012). Effective factors on the villagers use of rural telecentres (case study of Hamadan province, Iran). *African Journal of Agricultural Research, 7*(13), 2034–2041.

Latour, B. (2007). *Re-assembling the social: An introduction to Actor-Network-Theory*. Oxford, UK: Oxford University Press.

Leerapong, A., & Mardjo, A. (2013). Applying Diffusion of Innovation in Online Purchase Intention through Social Network: A Focus Group Study of Facebook in Thailand. *Information Management and Business Review, 5*(3), 144–154.

Lele, A. (2016). *Facebook's Free Basics: A digital apartheid – Analysis*. Available at http://www.eurasiareview.com/08012016-facebooks-free-basics-a-digital-apartheid-analysis/

Lemaire, J. (2011). *Scaling Up Mobile Health: Elements for the Successful Scale Up of mHealth in Developing Countries.* Retrieved from https://www.k4health.org/sites/default/files/ADA_mHealth%20White% 20Paper.Pdf

Lemaire, J. (2013). *Developing mHealth Partnerships for Scale.* Advanced Development for Africa. Retrieved from http://www.adaorganization.net/uploads/2/3/7/1/23713723/developing_mhealth_partnerships_for_scale_printer_friendly_low.pdf

Lerner, D. (1958). *The Passing of Traditional Society: Modernizing the Middle East.* New York: Free Press.

Lethbridge, T. C., Sim, S. E., & Singer, J. (2005). Studying software engineers: Data collection techniques for software field studies. *Empirical Software Engineering, 10*(3), 311–341. doi:10.1007/s10664-005-1290-x

Li, Y.-M., Lee, Y.-L. & Lien, N-J. (2012). Online social advertising via influential endorsers. *International Journal of Electronic Commerce, 16*(3), 119–153.

Lu, M.-T. (2001). Digital divide in developing countries. *Journal of Global Information Technology Management, 4*(3), 1–4. doi:10.1080/1097198x.2001.10856304

Madura Microfinance. (2016, November 23). *Numerical literacy in microentrepreneurs*. Retrieved from http://maduramicrofinance.co.in/insights/2016/11/23/data-spotlight-numerical-literacy-in-microentrepreneurs/

Mahendra, R. (2013). *"Commons" in the Telecoms Sector: Competition Policy Challenges in a Small Economy*. Working Paper Series No. 03/13. Retrieved From: http://www.fnu.ac.fj/new/images/CBHTS/Working_Paper/2013/wps_03_13_commons.pdf

Malhotra, A., Kanesathasan, A., & Patel, P. (2012). *Connectivity: How mobile phones, computers and the internet can catalyze women's entrepreneurship. India: A case study*. International Center for Research on Women. Retrieved from https://www.icrw.org/wp-content/uploads/2016/10/Connectivity-how-mobile-phones-computers-and-the-internet-can-catalyze-womens-entrepreneurship.pdf

Mangone, E. R., Agarwal, S., L'Engle, K., Lasway, C., Zan, T., van Beijma, H., & Karam, R. et al. (2016). Sustainable Cost Models for mHealth at Scale: Modeling Program Data from m4RH Tanzania. *PLoS One, 11*(1), e0148011. doi:10.1371/journal.pone.0148011 PMID:26824747

Manyika, J., Chui, M., Bughin, J., Dobbs, R., Bisson, P., & Marrs, A. (2013). *Disruptive technologies: Advances that will transform life, business, and the global economy*. McKinsey Global Institute. Retrieved from https://www.mckinsey.com/business-functions/digital-mckinsey/our-insights/disruptive-technologies

Marlien Herselman, K. B. (2002). Analysing the role of ICT in bridging the digital divide amongst learners. *South African Journal of Education, 22*(4), 270–274.

Matunhu, J. (2011). A critique of modernization and dependency theories in Africa: Critical assessment. *African Journal of History and Culture, 3*(5), 65–72.

Mazantsana, S. (n.d.). *Zenzileni networks Makhosi Ltd, Youtube video*. Retrieved from: https://www.youtube.com/watch?v=YxTPSWMX26M

McConnell, S. R. D., Doehler, M., & Wong, W. (2001). *Telecentres Around the World: Issues to be considered and lessons learned*. Retrieved from http://portal.unesco.org/ci/en/file_download.php/053c2bb713f94903fc72a2a910a4e495Telecentres+around+the+world.pdf

McNamara, K. S. (2003). *Information and Communication Technologies, Poverty and Development: Learning from Experience Information for Development Program*. A Background Paper for the infoDev Annual Symposium, Geneva, Switzerland. Retrieved from www.infodev.org

Meddie, M. (2006). Rethinking telecentre sustainability: How to implement a social enterprise approach-Lessons from India and Africa. *Journal of Community Informatics, 2*(3), 45–57.

Meddour. (n.d.). *On the Role of Infrastructure sharing for Mobile Network Operators in Emerging Markets.* Retrieved from: https://arxiv.org/ftp/arxiv/papers/1211/1211.7113.pdf

Microsoft. (2016, December 30). Retrieved from http://research.microsoft.com/en-us/projects/spectrum/pilots.aspx

Mills, D. (2014). *Aussies diplomat's incredible photos of the crisis in Syria ... and how he gave up a cosy office to make a difference.* Retrieved from http://www.dailymail.co.uk/news/article-2675841/Australian-worker-heading-relief-effort-worst-humanitarian-crisis-history-bringing-Syrian-refugee-crisis-control.html

Ministry of Communications and Information Technology, Government of India. (2008). *Impact assessment of e-governance projects.* National e-Governance Plan, Department of Information Technology, Ministry of Communications and Information Technology & Indian Institute of Management, Ahmedabad. Retrieved from http://www.iimahd.ernet.in/egov/documents/impact-assessment-of-egovernance-projects.pdf

Miniwatts Marketing Group. (2017, June 30). *World Internet Users and 2017 Population Stats.* Retrieved September 13, 2017, from World Internet Users and 2017 Population Stats: www.internetworldstats.com/stats1.htm

Min, S.-J. (2010). From the digital divide to the democratic divide: Internet skills, political interest, and the second-level digital divide in political internet use. *Journal of Information Technology & Politics, 7*(1), 22–35. doi:10.1080/19331680903109402

Mishra, S. M., Hwang, J., Filippini, D., Du, T., Moazzami, R., & Subramanian, L. (2005) Economic Analysis of Networking Technologies for Rural Developing Regions. *Workshop on Internet and Network Economics.* doi:10.1007/11600930_19

Mobile Phone and Smartphone Users in India 2014-19. (2015). Retrieved from https://apsalar.com/wp-content/uploads/2016/03/India-Mobile-Users.jpg

Moore, A. S., & Stilgoe, J. (2009). Experts and anecdotes the role of "anecdotal evidence"in public scientific controversies. *Science, Technology & Human Values, 34*(5), 654–677. doi:10.1177/0162243908329382

Morawczynski, O. (2009). Exploring the Usage and Impact of Transformational M-Banking: The Case of M-PESA in Kenya. *Journal of Eastern African Studies: The Journal of the British Institute in Eastern Africa, 3*(3). doi:10.1080/17531050903273768

Mossberger, K. T., & Caroline,, J., & Hamilton, A. (2012). Broadband Adoption| Measuring Digital Citizenship: Mobile Access and Broadband. *International Journal of Communication, 6,* 37.

Mouatt, S., & Adams, C. (Eds.). (2010). *Corporate and Social Transformation of Money and Banking: Breaking the Serfdom.* Basingstoke, UK: Palgrave-Macmillan.

Mutula, S. M. (2002). Internet Connectivity and Services in Kenya: Current Developments. *The Electronic Library*, *20*(6), 466–472. doi:10.1108/02640470210453949

Myers, M., & And Tan, F. (2002). Beyond Models of National Culture in Information Systems Research. *Journal of Global Information Management*, *10*(2), 24–32. doi:10.4018/jgim.2002010103

Naik, G. (2011). Designing a sustainable business model for e-governance embedded rural telecentres (EGERT) in India. *IIMB Management Review*, *23*(2), 110–121. doi:10.1016/j.iimb.2011.04.001

Naik, G., Joshi, S., & Basavaraj, K. (2012). Fostering inclusive growth through e-governance embedded rural telecenters (EGERT) in India. *Government Information Quarterly*, *29*, S82–S89. doi:10.1016/j.giq.2011.08.009

Namisiko, P., Sakwa, M., & Waweru, M. (2015). Effects of Network Infrastructure sharing Challenges on Open Information Communication Technology Infrastructure Sharing among Mobile Service Providers in Kenya. *I.J. Information Engineering and Electronic Business*, *3*(3), 11–19. doi:10.5815/ijieeb.2015.03.02

National policy on urban street vendors: Report & recommendations. (2006). Retrieved from http://nceuis.nic.in/Street Vendors policy.pdf

Natsuda, K., Igusa, K., Gush, K., Wiboonpongse, A., Cheamuangpan, A., Shinghkharat, S., & Thoburn, J. (2011). *One village, one Product – Rural Development Strategy in Asia. The Case of OTOP in Thailand.* Retrieved 22 August, 2014, from http://www.apu.ac.jp/

NDP 2030. (n.d.). *Our future – make it work, National Development Plan 2030.* Pretoria: The Presidency.

Neuman, W. (2006). *Social research methods:qualitative and quantitative approaches* (6th ed.). Boston, MA: Allyn and Bacon.

Nhundu, N. (2015). *Is Infrastructure Sharing a game changer in Zimbabwe.* Academic Press.

Noknoi, C., Boripunt, W., & Lungtae, S. (2012). Key Success Factors for Obtaining a One Tambon One Product Food Five-Star Rating in Phatthalung and Songkhla Provinces. *European Journal of Economics, Finance and Administrative Sciences*, *48*, 96–103.

Nyabola, N. (2016). *Facebook's Free Basics Is An African Dictator's Dream.* Retrieved from http://foreignpolicy.com/2016/10/27/facebooks-plan-to-wire-africa-is-a-dictators-dream-come-true-free-basics-internet/

OECD. (2003). *ICT and Economic Growth: Evidence from OECD countries, industries and firms.* OECD Publications Service. Retrieved from http://www.cla.org.pt/docs/OCDE_TIC.PDF

OECD. (2005). *Good practice paper on ICTs for economic growth and poverty reduction.* Retrieved from https://www.itu.int/net/wsis/docs2/pc3/contributions/co1.pdf

OECD. (2006). Internet neutrality: a policy overview. OECD Working Party on Telecommunication and Information Services Policies, OECD Report, DSTI/ICCP/TISP(2006)4/FINAL.

Ogonek, N., Gorbacheva, E., Räckers, M., Becker, J., Krimmer, R., Broucker, B., & Crompvoets, J. (2016). Towards efficient egovernment: identifying important competencies for egovernment in european public administrations. Electronic Government and Electronic Participation. *Proceedings of IFIP EGOV 2016 and ePart 2016, 23*, 155–162. doi:<ALIGNMENT.qj></ALIGNMENT>10.3233/978-1-61499-670-5-155

Ohuruogu, V., Fernan Flores, P., & Foh, K. (2015). *GSMA: Mobile for Development: Catalysing mHealth Services for Scale and Sustainability in Nigeria*. Retrieved May 2015, from http://www.gsma.com/mobilefordevelopment/wp-content/uploads/2015/05/GSMA-Nigeria-Business-Framework-web.pdf

Ojo, T. (2005). Wiring sub-Saharan Africa for development. *International Journal of Education and Development using Information and Communication Technology, 1*(3), 94-107.

Olwan, M., & Shiyab, A. (2012). *Forced migration of Syrians to Jordan: An exploratory study. Migration Policy Centre (MPC)*. Badia Fiesolna, San Domenico Di Fiesole.

Onishi, T., & Tsuna, Y. (2010). Introduction and Expansion of Infrastructure Sharing among Japanese MNO, Will Infrastructure Sharing be the key to cost cuts in a saturated market. Mizuho Industry Focus, 91.

Opawoye, I., Faruk, N., Bello, O. W., & Ayeni, A. A. (2015). Recent trends on TV White space deployments in Africa. *Nigerian Journal of Technology, 34*(3), 556–563. doi:10.4314/njt.v34i3.19

Ornelas, I. (2016). *Legal Framework for Infrastructure Sharing in Ghana*. Retrieved From: https://www.google.co.zw/?gws_rd=cr&ei=KGHrV--tCIXXa_rUm_AO#q=LEGAL+FRAMEWORK+FOR+INFRASTRUCTURE+SHARING+IN+GHANA%2C+pdf

Oxoby, R. (2009). Understanding Social Inclusion, Social Cohesion, and Social Capital. *International Journal of Social Economics, 36*(12), 1133–1152. doi:10.1108/03068290910996963

Pallas, C., Anderson, Q., & And Sidel, M. (2017). Defining the Scope of Aid Reduction and Its Challenges for Civil Society Organizations: Laying the Foundation for New Theory. *Voluntas*, 1–25.

Palmer, A., & Koenig-Lewis, N. (2009). An experimental, social network-based approach to direct marketing. *Direct Marketing: An International Journal, 3*(3), 162–176. doi:10.1108/17505930910985116

Pancham, J. (2016). *Determining and Developing Appropriate Methods for Requirements Verification and Modelling of Telecentre Operational Monitoring in a Developing Country* (Unpublished Master's Thesis). Durban University of Technology, Durban, South Africa.

Pancham, J., & Millham, R. (2015). Design phase consistency: A tool for reverse engineering of uml activity diagrams to their original scenarios in the specification phase. In Computational Science and Its Applications-ICCSA 2015 (pp. 655-670). Heidelberg, Germany: Springer.

Pancham, J., Millham, R., & Singh, P. (2013). *A validated model for operational monitoring of telecentres' activities in a developing country.* Paper presented at the Public and private access to ICTs in developing regions, 7th International Development Informatics Association Conference, Bangkok, Thailand.

Park, S. J., & Lejano, R. P. (2013). ICT4D Partnership: A Review and Reframing. IFIP Working Group 9.4: 12th International Conference on Social Implications of Computers in Developing Countries. Mona, Jamaica: University of the West-Indies.

Parkinson, S. (2005). *Telecentres, Access and Development.* Bourton-on-Dunsmore: ITDG.

Parkinson, S. (2005). *Telecentres, access and development: experience and lessons from Uganda and South Africa.* Warwickshire, UK: IDRC.

Pather, S. G. (2010). *Public Access ICT: A South-South comparative analysis of libraries, telecentres and cybercafés in South Africa and Brazil.* Paper presented at the AMCIS, Lima Peru.

Pettigrew, A. M. (1985). Contextualist research and the study of organisational change processes. In E. Mumford, R. Hirschheim, G. Fitzgerald, & A. T. Wood-Harper (Eds.), *Research Methods in Information Systems* (pp. 53–78). Amsterdam: North -Holland.

Philbeck, I. (2017). *Connecting the unconnected, working together to archive Connect 2010 Agenda targets.* Davos: ITU.

Poiani, T. H., Rocha, R. S., Degrossi, L. C., & Albuquerque, J. P. (2016) *Potential of Collaborative Mapping for Disaster Relief: A Case Study of OpenStreetMap in the Nepal Earthquake 2015. Hawaii International Conference on System Sciences (HICSS)*, Kauai, HI. doi:10.1109/HICSS.2016.31

POTRAZ. (2016). *Post and telecommunications Communications Regulatory Authority of Zimbabwe. Post and telecommunications sector report.* First Quarter of 2016.

Praekelt Foundation and Praekelt PBC. (2015). *Tune Me – project showcase.* Retrieved from https://www.praekelt.org/projects/

Praekeltfoundationblog. (2015, November 16). *Praekelt Foundation Incubator for Free Basics.* Retrieved October 19, 2017, from http://blog.praekeltfoundation.org/post/133335778822/praekelt-foundation-incubator-for-free-basics

Prahalad, C. K., & Hammond, A. (2002). What works: Serving the poor, profitably. World Resources Institute.

Proenza, F. J. (Ed.). (2015). *Public Access ICT across Cultures.* Cambridge, MA: MIT Press.

Progressive Policy Institute. (2015). Retrieved from: http://www.progressivepolicy.org/wpcontent/uploads/2015/03/2015.03-Carew_Zero-Rating_Kick- Starting-Internet-Ecosystems-in-Developing-Countries.pdf

Putnam, P. D. (2000). *Bowling alone:tThe collapse and revival of American community.* New York: Simon and Schuster. doi:10.1145/358916.361990

Qiu, J. L. (2008). Working-class ICTs, migrants, and empowerment in South China. *Asian Journal of Communication*, *18*(4), 333–347. doi:10.1080/01292980802344232

Qureshi, S. (2006). Collaboration for knowledge networking in development. *Information Technology for Development*, *12*(2), 87–89. doi:10.1002/itdj.20039

Qureshi, S. (2015). Are we making a better world with information and communication technology for development (ICT4D) research? Findings from the field and theory building. *Information Technology for Development*, *21*(4), 511–522. doi:10.1080/02681102.2015.1080428

Radnitzky, G. (1973). *Contemporary schools of metascience*. Chicago: Humanities Press / Henry Regnery Company.

Rahmat, R., Ahmad, A., Razak, R., Din, R., & Abas, A. (2013). Sustainability model for rural telecenter using business intelligence technique. *International Journal of Social Human Science and Engineering*, *7*(12), 1356–1361.

Rajapakse, J. (2012). *Impact of telecentres on Sri Lankan society*. Paper presented at the the 2012 8th International Conference on Computing and Networking Technology (ICCNT), Gyeongju, South Korea.

Ramlah, H., Norshidah, M., Abdul-Rahman, A., Murni, M., & Umar, A. (2010). G2C adoption of e-government in malaysia: Trust, perceived risk and political self-efficacy. *International Journal of Electronic Government Research*, *6*(3), 57–72. doi:10.4018/jegr.2010070105

Ramos, I., Adams, C., & Desouza, K. C. (2015). Economic Resilience and Crowdsourcing Platforms. *Resilience and Information Systems (RIS) workshop, Pre – 23rd European Conference on Information Systems*.

Rao, S. S. (2008). Social development in Indian rural communities: Adoption of Telecentres. *International Journal of Information Management*, *28*(6), 474–482. doi:10.1016/j.ijinfomgt.2008.01.001

Razak, N. A., Hassan, Z., & Din, R. (2010). *Bridging the Digital Divide: An Analysis of the Training Program at Malaysian Telecenters*. Academic Press.

Rey-Moreno, C. (2013). *Alternatives for Affordable Communications in rural South Africa Innovative regulatory responses to increase affordable rural access*. Retrieved from: http://www.r2k.org.za/wp-content/uploads/Policy-brief-Cost-to-Communicate_13092016_FOR-SUBMISSION.pdf

Rey-Moreno, C. (2017). *Report on Understanding Community Networks in Africa*. Keynote Presentation at 2nd Summit on Community Networks in Africa Agenda, 2nd Summit on CN's in Africa, Nairobi, Kenya. Retrieved from: https://www.youtube.com/watch?v=uX4TDHWVClo&feature=youtu.be&list=PLi2ljTGe63GIB_WMlbKsz8Rym95uvqbR_

Rey-Moreno, C., Blignaut, R., Tucker, W.D. &May, J. (2016). An in-depth study of the ICT ecosystem in a South African rural community: Unveiling expenditure and communication patterns. *Information Technology for Development*, *22*(S1), 101-120. DOI: 10.1080/02681102.2016.1155145

Rey-Moreno, C., Sabiescu, A. G., Siya, M. J., & Tucker, W. D. (2015). Local Ownership, Exercise of Ownership and Moving from Passive to Active Entitlement: A practice-led inquiry on a rural community network. *The Journal of Community Informatics, 11*(2).

Rey-Moreno, C., Tucker, W. D., Cull, D., & Blom, R. (2015). Making a community network legal within the South African regulatory framework. *Proceedings of the 7th international conference on information and communication technologies and development*, 57. doi:10.1145/2737856.2737867

Rhodes, J. (2003). Can E-commerce enable marketing in an African rural women's community based development organisation? *Informing Science, 6*, 157–172. doi:10.28945/523

Riley, B. (2016) What it means to have a trade deal that puts America first. *The Daily Signal.* Retrieved from http://dailysignal.com/2016/07/15/what-it-means-to-have-a-trade-deal-that-puts-america-first/

Roberts, S. P. (2015). Connecting Africa using the TV white spaces: from research to real world deployments. *The 21st IEEE International Workshop on Local and Metropolitan Area Networks, 21*, 1-6.

Robeynes, I. (2003). The Capability Approach in Practice. *Journal of Political Philosophy, 14*(3), 351–376. doi:10.1111/j.1467-9760.2006.00263.x

Robeynes, I. (2008). Sen's capability approach and feminist concerns. In F. Comim, M. Qizilbash, & S. Alkire (Eds.), *The Capability Approach: Concepts, Measures and Applications.* Cambridge, UK: Cambridge University Press. doi:10.1017/CBO9780511492587.004

Rodríguez, A., Fernández-Medina, E., Trujillo, J., & Piattini, M. (2011). Secure business process model specification through a UML 2.0 activity diagram profile. *Decision Support Systems, 51*(3), 446–465. doi:10.1016/j.dss.2011.01.018

Sahay, S. (2016). Are we building a better world with ICTs? Empirically examining this question in the domain of public health in India. *Information Technology for Development, 22*(1), 168–176. doi:10.1080/02681102.2014.933522

Samarajiva, R., & Zainudeen, A. (Eds.). (2008). *ICT Infrastructure in emerging Asia: policy and regulatory roadblocks.* Los Angeles, CA: Sage.

Sambuli, N. (2016). Challenges and opportunities for advancing Internet access in developing countries while upholding net neutrality. *Journal of Cyber Policy, 1*(1), 61–74. doi:10.1080/23 738871.2016.1165715

Saunders, M., Lewis, P., & Thornhill, A. (2002). Research methods for business students. Prentice Hall.

Schlinke, J., & Crain, S. (2013, March). Social media from an integrated marketing and compliance perspective. *Journal of Financial Service Professionals*, 85-92.

Schonfeld, E. (2009). Twitter finds growth abroad with 58.4 million global visitors in September. *TechCrunch*. Retrieved 23 August, 2014, from: http://techcrunch.com/2009/10/26/twitterfinds-growth-abroad-with-58-4-million-global-visitors-in-september

Schrage, M. (1990). *Shared minds: The new technologies of collaboration*. New York: Random House.

Sciadas, G. (2005). *From the digital divide to digital opportunities: Measuring infostates for development*. Montreal: ORBICOM International Secretariat.

Scott, R. W. (2001). *Institutions and organizations*. Thousand Oaks, CA: Sage Publications.

Scott, R. W. (2004). Institutional theory. In G. Ritzer (Ed.), *Encyclopedia of Social Theory* (pp. 408–414). Thousand Oaks, CA: SAGE Publications Inc.

Scott, R. W. (2008). Approaching adulthood: The maturing of institutional theory. *Theory and Society*, *37*(1), 427–442. doi:10.1007/s11186-008-9067-z

Selwyn, B. (2014). *The global development crisis*. Cambridge, UK: Polity Press.

Seman, , & Haji, , Khairudin, Iadah, Mat, Zulkhairi Md, & Yasin. (2013). Community Characteristics for Self-Funding and Self-Sustainable Telecenter. *Global Journal on Technology*, *3*, 1666–1671.

Sen, R., Ahmad, S., Phokeer, A., Farooq, Z.A., Qazi, I.A., Choffness, D., & Gummadi, K.P. (2017). *Inside the walled garden: deconstructing Facebook's Free Basics program*. Academic Press.

Sen, A. (1999). *Development as freedom*. OU Press.

Sen, A. K. (1985). Well-being, agency, and freedom: The Dewey Lectures 1984. *The Journal of Philosophy*, *82*(4), 169–221.

Sen, A. K. (1999). *Development as Freedom*. Oxford, UK: Oxford University Press.

Sengupta, K. (2012). *Syria's sectarian war goes international as foreign fighters and arms pour into country*. The Independent.

Sen, R., Pirzada, H. A., Farooq, A., Sengupta, S., Choffness, D., & Gummade, K. P. (2016). On the free bridge across the digital divide: assessing the quality of Facebook's Free Basics Service. *Proceedings of the IMC*. doi:10.1145/2987443.2987485

Seo, D. B., & Bernsen, M. (2016). Comparing attitudes toward e-government of non-users versus users in a rural and urban municipality. *Government Information Quarterly*, *33*(2), 270–282. doi:10.1016/j.giq.2016.02.002

Sethi, N., & Sethi, V. (2008). *E-government Imple-mentation: A Case Study of Dubai e-Government*. Singapore: In Nanyang Technological University.

Sey, A. F. (2009). *Literature review on the impact of public access to information and communication technologies*. Retrieved from 2009: http://library.globalimpactstudy.org/sites/default/files/docs/CIS-WorkingPaperNo6.pdf

Shangaza. (2015). *Free Data Bundles with Safaricom Airtel & Mt.* Retrieved from: http://shangaza. net/blogs/1/73/free-data-bundles-with-safaricom-airtel-mtn

Sheth, J. N., Mittal, B., & Newman, B. I. (1999). *Consumer behavior and beyond.* Harcourt Brace.

Siya, M. R. (n.d.). *Zenzileni networks Makhosi Ltd, Youtube video.* Retrieved from: https://www. youtube.com/watch?v=YxTPSWMX26M

Smith, M., Spence, R., & Rashid, A. T. (2011). Mobile Phones and Expanding Human Capabilities. *Information Technologies and International Development, 7*(3), 77–88.

Songco, J. A. (2002). *Do Rural Infrastructure Investments Benefit the Poor? Evaluating Linkages: A Global View, A Focus on Vietnam.* Washington, DC: World Bank.

Sopazi, P. N. A. (2008). Evaluation of a Telecentre Using Stakeholder Analysis and Critical Systems Heuristics: A South African Case Study. *Scientific Inquiry, 9*(1), 19–28.

Spence, R., & Smith, M. (2009). *Harvard Forum II: Information and Communication Technologies, Human Development, Growth and Poverty Reduction: A Background Paper.* Ottawa: IDRC.

Stanton, E. A. (2007). *The human development index: A history.* Working Paper Series Number 127. Retrieved From: http://scholarworks.umass.edu/cgi/viewcontent.cgi?article=1101&context=peri_workingpapers

Stewart, F. (2005). Group Capabilities. *Journal of Human Development, 6*(2), 2. doi:10.1080/14649880500120517

Stoilov, T., & Stoilova, K. (2006). *Automation in business processes.* Paper presented at the International Conference Systems for Automation of Engineering and research-SAER.

Stopford, J., & Strange, S. (1991). Rival states, rival firms: Competition for world market shares. Cambridge University Press.

Strachan, P., Wanous, M., & Mofleh, S. (2008). Developing countries and ICT initiatives: Lessons learnt from Jordan's experience. *The Electronic Journal on Information Systems in Developing Countries, 34*(5), 1–17.

Strange, S. (1996). *The Retreat of the State: The Diffusion of Power in the World Economy.* Cambridge University Press. doi:10.1017/CBO9780511559143

Strange, S. (1998). *Mad Money.* Manchester University Press. doi:10.3998/mpub.10897

Sturchio, J. L. (2013, Jan. 10). The Evolving Role of the Private Sector in Global Health. *Huffington Post.* Retrieved from http://www.huffingtonpost.com/jeffrey-l-sturchio/the-evolving-role-health_b_2432823.html

Sumbwanyambe, M., Nel, A., & Clarke, W. (2011, May). Challenges and proposed solutions towards telecentre sustainability: a Southern Africa case study. In *IST-Africa Conference Proceedings* (pp. 1-8). IEEE.

Sweisi, N. A. A. O. (2010). *E-government services: An exploration of the main factors that contribute to successful implementation in Libya.* University of Portsmouth.

Takavarasha, S., Jr. (2017). *The impact of affordable access on ICT4D initiatives in Africa.* Key note address at The 3rd ICT Summit on ICT for Digital Entrepreneurship and Industrial Revolution Institute of Finance Management, Dar Es Salaam, Tanzania.

Takavarasha, J., & Makumbe, J. (2012). The effect of politics on ICT4D: A case of econet wireless's struggle for a license in Zimbabwe. *International Journal of E-Politics, 3*(3), 40–60. doi:10.4018/jep.2012070103

Takavarasha, S., Bednar, P., & Adams, C. (2011). Using mixed methods for addressing researcher's safety in a conflict area: An innovative use of mixed methods research in Zimbabwe. *International Journal of Mixed Methods in Applied Business and Policy, 1*(1).

Tata Teleservices Limited. (2015). *Mobile-owning households in Madhya Pradesh enjoy a 63 percent economic prosperity premium compared to those without a mobile.* Retrieved from https://www.tatateleservices.com/Downloads/NewsRoom/ttsl/The-Mobile-Multiplier-Study-Madhya-Pradesh-Press-Release.pdf

Telecentre Foundation. (2016). *Digital Empowerment, Entrepreneurship, and Innovation.* Retrieved 1 February, 2016, from www.telecentre.org

Telecom Regulatory Authority of India. (2016). *Highlights of Telecom Subscription Data as on 31ˢᵗ March, 2016* (Press Release No. 34/2016). Retrieved from http://www.trai.gov.in/sites/default/files/Press_Release_34_25may_2016_5_25-05-2016.pdf

Telecommunication Regulatory Authority, Sultanate of Oman. (2012). *TRA Position paper on Telecentres.* Retrieved from https://www.tra.gov.om/pdf/563_trapositionpaperontelecetnersen.pdf

Teo, H. H., Wei, K. K., & Benbasat, I. (2003). Predicting intention to adopt interorganizational linkages: An institutional perspective. *Management Information Systems Quarterly, 27*(1), 19–49.

Thailand National Statistical Office. (2013). *Information and Communication Technology Survey in Household.* Retrieved May 3, 2015, from http://web.nso.go.th/en/survey/ict/ict_house13.htm

The World Bank. (2013). *World Development Indicators 2013 released.* Retrieved 18 May, 2015, from http://www.worldbank.org/en/news/press-release/2013/04/18/world-development-indicators-2013-released

Thompson, L. C. (2010). *Refugee Workers in the Indochina Exodus, 1975-1982.* Jefferson, NC: McFarland & Co.

Townsend, L. S., Sathiaseelan, A., Fairhurst, G., & Wallace, C. (2013). Enhanced broadband access as a solution to the social and economic problems of the rural digital divide. *Local Economy, 28*(6), 580–595. doi:10.1177/0269094213496974

Transtec, S. A. (2015). *Independent programme evaluation (IPE) of UNHCR's Response to the refugee influx in Lebanon and Jordan.* Retrieved from www.transtec.be

Tuncer Baykas, M. K. (2012). Developing a standard for TV white space coexistence: Technical challenges and solution approaches. *IEEE Wireless Communications*, *19*(1), 10–22. doi:10.1109/MWC.2012.6155872

Turoff, M. (2002). Past and future emergency response information systems. *Communications of the ACM*, *45*(4), 29–32. doi:10.1145/505248.505265

Tushar Banerjee. (2014, February 12). *Five unusual ways in which Indians use mobile phones.* Retrieved from http://www.bbc.com/news/world-asia-india-26028381

UN. (2006). *International migration and development: Report of the Secretary General.* United Nations.

UN. (2014). *2014 revision of the World Urbanization Prospects.* Available from http://www.un.org/en/development/desa/publications/2014-revision-world-urbanization-prospects.html

UN/ISDR. (2004). *Living with Risk: A global review of disaster reduction initiatives.* Author.

UN/ISDR. (2014). *Sendai Framework for Disaster Risk Reduction 2015-2030.* Retrieved from http://www.unisdr.org/we/coordinate/sendai-framework

UNDP. (2015). *Transforming our world: the 2030 Agenda for Sustainable Development.* Retrieved from: https://sustainabledevelopment.un.org/content/documents/21252030%20Agenda%20for%20Sustainable%20Development%20web.pdf

UNDP. (2016). *Human development for everyone.* Retrieved from: http://hdr.undp.org/sites/default/files/2016_human_development_report.pdf

UNHCR Syria. (2015). *Protecting and supporting the displaced in syria: unhcr syria end of year report 2015.* Damascus, Syria: Author.

UNHCR, & Accenture. (2016). *Connecting refugee: how internet and mobile connectivity can improve refugee well-being and transform humanitarian action/united nations high commissioner for refugees.* London, UK: UNHCR's Division of Information Systems and Telecommunications (DIST) & Accenture Development Partnerships (ADP).

UNHCR. (2013). *Syria regional response plan January to June 2013. Field information coordination support section.* Retrieved from http:/data.unhcr.org/syrianrefugees

UNHCR. (2014). *2014 Syria regional response plan: Strategic overview.* Retrieved from http://reliefweb.int/sites/reliefweb.int/files/resources/Syria-rrp6-full-report.pdf

UNICEF. (2015). *Humanitarian response plan 2016 - Syrian Arab Republic.* Office for the Coordination of Humanitarian Affairs. Retrieved from www.humanitarianresponse.info/en/operations/syria

Unicef. (n.d.). *Millennium Development Goals.* Retrieved 17 November 2014, from http://www.unicef.org/mdg/index_aboutthegoals.htm

United Nations Development Programme (UNDP). (2015). *Human Development Report 2015: Work for human development.* Retrieved from http://hdr.undp.org/sites/default/files /2015_human_development_report.pdf

United Nations Development Programme. (2012). *Mobile technologies and empowerment: enhancing human development through participation and innovation.* Retrieved from http://www.undp.org/content/dam/undp/library/DemocraticGovernance/AccesstoInformationandE-governance/MobileTechnologiesandEmpowerment_EN.pdf

United Nations. (2000). *Resolution 55/2 of General Assembly. United Nations Millennium Declaration.* New York: UN.

United Nations. (2010). *Information Economy Report. ICTs, Enterprises, and Poverty Alleviation.* New York: UN.

United Nations. (2010). *United Nations eGov development database: overview - United Nation eGov Database.* Retrieved from http://unpan3.un.org/egovkb/egovernment_overview/ereadiness.htm

United Nations. (2012a). *E-government survey 2012: E-Government for the People.* New York: Department of Economic and Social Affairs Division for Public Administration and Development Management. Retrieved from https://publicadministration.un.org/egovkb/Portals/egovkb/Documents/un/2012-Survey/Complete-Survey.pdf

United Nations. (2012b). *Implementation of general assembly resolution 66/253 b on the situation in the Syrian Arab republic report* (Vol. 46820). Author.

United Nations. (2014). *E-government survey 2014: e-government for the future we want.* New York: Department of Economic and Social Affairs Division for Public Administration and Development Management. Retrieved from https://publicadministration.un.org/egovkb/Portals/egovkb/Documents/un/2014-Survey/E-Gov_Complete_Survey-2014.pdf

United Nations. (2015). *Information Economy Report. Unlocking the potential of e-commerce for developing countries.* New York: UN.

United Nations. (2016). *Progress towards the Sustainable Development Goals.* United Nations Economic and Social Council. Retrieved from https://http://www.un.org/ga/search/view_doc.asp?symbol=E/2016/75&Lang=E

Urquhart, C. (2007). The evolving nature of grounded theory method: The case of information systems discipline. In A. Bryant & K. Charmaz (Eds.), The Sage handbook of grounded theory (pp. 311-331). London: Sage.

Urquhart, C., Lehman, H., & Myers, M. (2010). Putting the 'theory' back into grounded theory: Guidelines for grounded theory studies in information systems. *Information Systems Journal*, *20*(4), 357–381. doi:10.1111/j.1365-2575.2009.00328.x

USAASA. (2011). *USAASA Business plan 2011 - 2012.* South Africa Retrieved from http://www.usaasa.org.za/export/sites/usaasa/resource-centre/download-centre/downloads/USAASA_Business_Plan_2011-2012.pdf

USAFID. (2004*). Celebrating 'Food for Peace' 1954-2004. U.S. Agency for International Development report 2004*. Author.

USAID. (2015). *Gender and extreme poverty Getting to Zero: A USAID discussion series.* Retrieved from: https://www.usaid.gov/sites/default/files/documents/1870/Gender_Extreme_Poverty_Discussion_Paper.pdf

Van der Vyver, A. G., & Marais, M. (2013). Evaluating Users' Perceptions of the Digital Doorway: A Narrative Analysis. *Information Technology for Development.* doi:10.1080/02681102.2013.841629

Van Dijk, J. A. (2005). *The deepening divide: Inequality in the information society.* Sage Publications.

Veeraraghavan, R., Singh, G., Toyama, K., & Menon, D. (2006). *Kiosk usage measurement using a software logging tool.* Paper presented at the Information and Communication Technologies and Development. doi:10.1109/ICTD.2006.301870

Velamuri, S. R. (2003). *Resisting political corruption: Econet Wireless Zimbabwe* (Research Case Study). Retrieved May 18, 2011, from http://ssrn. com/abstract=1009452

Vodafone Group. (2009). *India: The impact of mobile phones.* Retrieved from http://www.icrier.org/pdf/public_policy19jan09.pdf

Walsham, G., & Sahay, S. (2005). *Research on IS in developing countries: Current landscape and future prospects.* Retrieved from http://www.ifi.uio.no/forskning/grupper/is/wp/022005.pdf

Walsham, G. (2001). *Making a World of Difference: IT in a Global Context.* Chichester, UK: Wiley.

Walsham, G. (2002). Cross-Cultural Software Production and Use: A Structurational Analysis. *Management Information Systems Quarterly, 26*(4), 359–380. doi:10.2307/4132313

Walsham, G. (2012). Are we making a better world with ICTs? Reflections on a future agenda for the IS field. *Journal of Information Technology, 27*(2), 87–93. doi:10.1057/jit.2012.4

Walubengo, J., & Takavarasha, S. Jr. (2017). The Challenges of Using Zero-Rating (Free Basics) for Addressing the Affordability of ICT Access in Developing Countries. *International Journal of ICT Research in Africa and the Middle East, 6*(2), 47–61. doi:10.4018/IJICTRAME.2017070104

Warshauer, M. (2003). *Technology and social inclusion: Rethinking the digital divide.* Cambridge, MA: The MIT Press.

Waters, R. D., Burnett, E., Lamm, A., & Lucas, J. (2009). Stakeholder engagement and social networking sites: How nonprofit organizations are using Facebook. *Public Relations Review, 35*(2), 102–106. doi:10.1016/j.pubrev.2009.01.006

Waverman, L., Meschi, M., & Fuss, M. (2005). *The Impact of Telecoms on Economic Growth in Developing markets.* Retrieved from https://www.gsma.com/publicpolicy/wp-content/uploads/2012/11/gsma-deloitte-impact-mobile-telephony-economic-growth.pdf

Web Foundation. (2016). *Digging into Data on the Gender Digital Divide*. Retrieved from: https://webfoundation.org/2016/10/digging-into-data-on-the-gender-digital-divide/

West, D. M. (2015). Digital divide: Improving Internet access in the developing world through affordable services and diverse content. Washington, DC: Center for Technology Innovation, Brookings Institution.

Whyte, A. (2000). *Assessing community telecentres: Guidelines for researchers*. Ottawa: International Development Research Centre. Retrieved 12 December, 2013, from http://www.telecentre-europe.org/

Whyte, A. V. (2000). *Assessing community telecentres: Guidelines for researchers*. IDRC.

Wikipedia. (2004). *Countries affected by the 2004 Indian Ocean Earthquake*. Available from https://en.wikipedia.org/wiki/Countries_affected_by_the_2004_Indian_Ocean_earthquake_and_tsunami

Wikipedia. (2017a). *IEEE 802.22*. Retrieved from https://en.wikipedia.org/wiki/IEEE_802.22

Wikipedia. (2017b). *TV White Space Database*. Retrieved from https://en.wikipedia.org/wiki/TV_White_Space_Database

Wiles. (1992). *The political economy of communism*. Blackwell.

Willems, W. (2016). *Beyond Free Basics: Facebook, data bundles and Zambia's social media internet*. African Elections, Featured, International Affairs, Media, September 2017.

World Bank Group. (2016). *World Development Report 2016: Digital dividends*. Washington, DC: The World Bank. Retrieved from http://documents.worldbank.org/curated/en/896971468194972881/pdf/102725-PUB-Replacement-PUBLIC.pdf

World Bank. (2011). *E-government*. Retrieved from http://web.worldbank.org/wbsite/external/topics/extinformationandcommu nicationandtechnologies/extegovernment/0,menupk:702592~pagepk:1490 18~pipk:149093~thesitepk:702586,00.html

World Bank. (2016). *Migration and Remittances Factbook 2016*. Retrieved from www.worldbank.org

World Bank. (2016). *World Development Report 2016: Digital Dividends*. Washington, DC: World Bank. Retrieved from http://documents.worldbank.org/curated/en/896971468194972881/pdf/102725-PUB-Replacement-PUBLIC.pdf

World Bank. (2016). *World development report 2016: Digital dividends*. Washington, DC: World Bank. Retrieved from: http://documents.worldbank.org/curated/en/896971468194972881/pdf/102725-PUB-Replacement-PUBLIC.pdf

World Development Report. (2016). *Digital Dividends*. Washington, DC: World Bank Group.

World Health Organization. (2014). *WHO Global Health Expenditure Atlas, September 2014*. Geneva, Switzerland: Department of Health Systems Financing. Retrieved from http://www.who.int/health-accounts/atlas2014.pdf

World Health Organization. (2017). *World Bank Country and Lending Groups.* World Health Organization. Retrieved from https://datahelpdesk.worldbank.org/knowledgebase/articles/906519-world-bank-country-and-lending-groups

Xiaodong, L. (2007). A review of SOA. *Computer Applications and Software, 24*(10), 122–124.

Yin, M., Gomez, R., & Carter, M. (2017). Facebook's 'free basics' and implications for development: IT dentify and social capital. *Proceedings of the 50th Hawaii International Conference on System Sciences.*

Yin, R. K. (1994). *Case Study Research, Design and Methods* (2nd ed.). Newbury Park, CA: Sage.

Yu, L. (2010). How poor informationally are the information poor? Evidence from an empirical study of daily and regular information practices of individuals. *Journal of Documentation, 66*(6), 906-933. <ALIGNMENT.qj></ALIGNMENT>10.1108/00220411011087869

Yunus, M. (2008). *A Poverty Free World—When?How?* Romanes Lecture at Oxford University. Retrieved from http://www.muhammadyunus.org/index.php/news-media/speeches/212-a-poverty-free-world-when-how

Yu, P. K. (2002). Bridging the digital devide: Equality in the information age. *Cardozo Arts & Entertainmnet, 20*(1), 1–52.

Zheng, Y., & Stahl, B. C. (2011). Technology, capabilities and critical perspectives: What can critical theory contribute to Sen's capability approach? *Ethics and Information Technology, 13*(2), 69–80. doi:10.1007/s10676-011-9264-8

Zhi, J., & Zhenhua, Y. (2009). The local e-government practice in china: a survey of the G2C practice of "Changxing county". In *International Conference on information Management, Innovation Management and Industrial Engineering* (pp. 548 – 551). Academic Press.

ZIMVAC & FEWSNET. (2010). *Zimbabwe Livelihoods Zone Profiles.* Accessed 14 May from: http://pdf.usaid.gov/pdf_docs/PNADG540.pdf

Zschau, J., & Küppers, A. N. (2002). *Early Warning Systems for Disaster Mitigation.* Berlin: Springer.

About the Contributors

Sam Takavarasha Jr. is a research fellow at University of Fort Hare South Africa. He is a University of Portsmouth UK graduate and he acquired his Ph.D. in Information Systems specializing in ICT4D at the University of Zimbabwe. Sam is the author of many peer-reviewed academic papers and he has conducted three national consultancy projects, two of which as the principal investigator. His editorial experience includes being a co-guest editor of an IS journal special issue, track chair of the general of ECIS 2017, track chair of the ICT4D track of the ECIS 2018, advisory board member of two book projects and a technical committee member of the e-leadership conference. Sam's research interests include ICT4D, e-Remittances, e-Politics, e-Commerce in the Developing World, Mixed Methods Research, and Health Informatics. His teaching interests include e-Commerce, Project Management for Information Systems and Research methods.

Carl Adams had over a decade of professional experience before going into academia. His research interests explore the impact of the digital economy and include ICT4D, e/m-commerce/government, mobile IS, social media, e-money, and impact of technology on society. He has over 130 peer-reviewed publications.

* * *

Abraheem Alsaeed is a doctoral candidate at the University of Portsmouth, his research focuses on the study of factors affecting the successful adoption of electronic services during geopolitical instabilities and the role of technology in supporting displaced people. Prior to his doctoral studies Abraheem lectured IT and Computer Science (Mainly Web Design and Programming) to undergraduate students at the following universities: The International University for Science and Technology(IUST), Arab International University(AIU) and Syrian Virtual University (SVU), and Teacher assistant at the University of Portsmouth. He carried out varieties of duties including designing, preparing, developing and teaching materials. Moreover, assessing student coursework; setting and marking examinations; supervising students' research activities; carrying out administrative tasks related to the department and participating in staff training activities.

Indira Ananth is a Professor at Loyola Institute of Business Administration (LIBA), Chennai in the dual areas of economics and management science. She teaches macroeconomics, managerial economics, international economics and game theory. Her research interest is in development economics. She has earlier worked as a policy and action researcher in the areas of local governance and technology diffusion.

Rich Boakes is a senior lecturer at the University of Portsmouth from August 2009 – Present. Course Leader for BSc (Hons) Web Technologies and Coordinator and lecturer of taught -units at all undergraduate levels. -PhD supervision. -Masters project supervision. some comments from a student: "Rich is more than a lecturer. He has an answer for nearly every question both course-related and otherwise, is extremely knowledgeable in vast amounts of technologies and languages, and has the amazing ability to explain himself and portray his teachings well to every type of student." Rich worked for IBM, Netscape, and as an independent contractor on various projects for many companies including larger projects for Orange, Vodafone and BT before his academic career. His long-term aim is to help earth-based life forms escape the planet before the heat death of our sun.

Liezel Cilliers is a senior lecturer and Head of Department of Information Systems at the University of Fort Hare, South Africa. She has written several peer-reviewed articles on research interest that include health informatics, ICT4D, Social media, and crowdsourcing. Her teaching interest includes Project Management, Databases, and Research Methodology.

Benard Mapako is a lecturer at University of Zimbabwe Computer Science department, he holds an MSc Computer Science and a BSc Honors Computer Science from the University of Zimbabwe where he teaches computer networks, security, and mathematics in computer science. His research interests are in Network Security and Graph theory. His ongoing doctoral research is on risk analysis of attack graphs. During the last eight years as a computer science lecturer, Bernard has conducted several consultancy research projects in both Information Systems and Computing.

Richard Millham is a faculty member of the Durban University of Technology, Department of Information Technology. After working in industry for fifteen years, he joined academe where he has worked at several universities in different countries. His research interests include software evolution, aspects of big data, aspects of cloud computing with m-interactions, and computer security. He is a Chartered Engineer (UK) and Senior Member of IEEE.

314

Michael Munyaradzi obtained the bachelor of Science Honors degree in Physics in 1991 and M.Sc. in Applied Physics in 1995, both from the University of Zimbabwe. He is studying towards a PhD in Computer Science at the University of Zimbabwe where he has been teaching embedded systems and Computer networks at since 2008. He has research interests in automated irrigation control, embedded systems and internet of things.

Benny M. Nyambo is a senior lecturer in Computer science at the University of Zimbabwe since. His research interests include performance modeling of communication networks and in embedded systems. He obtained his Ph.D. in Computer Science at the Hasselt University, Belgium. He also has a bachelor of Science Honours degree in Physics and M.Sc. in Applied Physics from the University of Zimbabwe.

Jay Pancham is a senior lecturer in the Department of Information Technology at the Durban University of Technology with a specialization in project management and software engineering. Prior to joining academia, he spent 12 years in the telecommunications and ICT industry. Mr Jay Pancham holds a MICT (DUT) and is currently studying for Ph.D. in the area of optimization of Real-Time Localization Systems (RTLS) for assets and patients.

Debbie Rogers is the Managing Director of Praekelt.org, a non-profit that uses mobile technology to improve the health and wellbeing of people around the world. Prior to that, her role entailed being the lead Strategist and Head of the Health Portfolio for the organisation. Her work at Praekelt has exposed her to both the commercial dimension of the mobile industry and the ways that mobile solutions might be applied to development problems. Her service design work includes leading the development of the digital strategy for one of the largest TELCOs in South Africa and designing and managing the implementation of South Africa's national maternal mHealth programme, MomConnect.

Taurai Rupere is an IS researcher and senior lecturer in Computer Science at the University of Zimbabwe. His research interest is multimedia e-learning, Human and Computer Interaction and Cloud Computing. He has done a number of consultancy research projects for industry and peer-reviewed publications. Of late he is more interested in how computers can support human empowerment and reduce poverty. He is aspiring to develop an ICT usage and adoption framework that can fit the developing country perspective.

Ambika Samarthya-Howard is a video producer, writer, and communications specialist. Her work focuses on social issues, specifically gender, public health, and child rights. She received her MFA in Film at Columbia University, producing her thesis film in Bollywood as a Fulbright scholar. As a video producer, she has done documentary projects in Japan, Mumbai, and Liberia, and worked with the BBC Media Action in Nigeria. She currently lives in New York and is the Head of Communications at Praekelt.org.

Abraham Gert van der Vyver has got multiple degrees in law, marketing, communications, and information systems. He obtained his Ph.D. in political communication in 1998 from the University of South Africa. His research interests include development informatics and the social media.

Ngonidzashe Zanamwe is a computer science lecturer at the University of Zimbabwe. He has published in various journals in the area of Ecommerce and Egovernance. He has been involved in various consultancy research in the area of customer satisfaction in industry and government. Ngonidzashe has an MSc Computer Science, MBA, and Bachelor in Business Studies and Computer Science all from the University of Zimbabwe. His ongoing Ph.D research combines health informatics, knowledge modeling and algorithm optimization. Zanamwe is an avid software developer who has undertaken various projects both in the private sector and government.

Index

W

Wi-Fi 13, 47-48, 52, 59-60, 62, 202
wireless communication 48

Z

Zambia 33, 42, 222
Zenzeleni 1, 4, 7, 12-13, 16-18, 20-21
zero-rating 30, 32-33, 42, 195, 197, 200,
    202-204

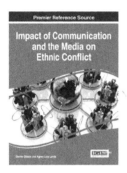

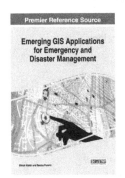

Printed in the United States
By Bookmasters